INTERROGATING HISTORY

Essays for Hermann Kulke

INTERROGATING HISTORY

Essays for Hermann Kulke

Edited by

MARTIN BRANDTNER

SHISHIR KUMAR PANDA

MANOHAR
2006

First published 2006

ISBN 81-7304-679-4

Published by
Ajay Kumar Jain for
Manohar Publishers & Distributors
4753/23 Ansari Road, Daryaganj
New Delhi 110 002

Printed at
Lordson Publishers Pvt Ltd
Delhi 110 007

Distributed in South Asia by
FOUNDATION BOOKS
4381/4, Ansari Road
Daryaganj, New Delhi 110 002
and its branches at Mumbai, Hyderabad,
Bangalore, Chennai, Kolkata

Contents

Preface

'Siddham!' One would like to exclaim with the authors of early Indian inscriptions after finishing this task of putting together 19 papers authored by scholars from different parts of the world to celebrate the 65th birthday of Hermann Kulke. It was a difficult task, as not only were the contributors scattered round the world, but also that the editors were living more than 8,000 km apart from each other, with communication even in this age of emails not always being easy. Therefore, the book comes out a little bit behind schedule, but we're, nevertheless, glad to be able to present it to Hermann Kulke and the public.

It is, in our view, a very lively mix of contributions being, in one way or the other, connected with topics to which our *guruji* has devoted his own research. It reflects his wide range of interests stretching from ancient to modern Indian and Southeast Asian history, from historiography to highly specialized studies in the formation of regional or ethnic identities. It also bears witness to another important aspect in the life and work of Hermann Kulke: his interdisciplinary approach to Indian and Southeast Asian history and culture. Subjects like Indology, archaeology, epigraphy, anthropology, and art history form as much a part of his research as several historical disciplines and approaches. And, although officially retired now, he does not show any signs of being tired of his work. May he be able to pursue it in many fields in the years to come!

Our sincere thanks go to all the contributors for their cooperation and patience. Two of them, Biswamoy Pati and Bhairabi Prasad Sahu deserve special mention for their help. Biswamoy Pati often acted as a hub of communication between the editors themselves and the publishers as a 'man on the spot'. Without him, it would have taken considerably longer for this book to see the light of day. We also particularly thank Ramesh Jain and the Manohar editorial team for all their assistance and understanding.

MARTIN BRANDTNER
SHISHIR KUMAR PANDA

PART I

Ways of Questioning: Historians and Historiography

CHAPTER 1

Hermann Kulke's Contribution to the Study of Indian History and Culture

MARTIN BRANDTNER and SHISHIR KUMAR PANDA

'The best we get from history is the enthusiasm it creates' says Goethe in *Wilhelm Meister's Wanderings*. The life and work of Hermann Kulke, which most aptly can be described by the intranslatable German term 'Gesamtkunstwerk', serve as a perfect illustration of this dictum. Both of us, who have an association with him lasting for a quarter of a century now, were, already as his students at the South Asia Institute at Heidelberg University, infected by this enthusiasm and continue to be so as his fellow scholars. And, of course, we have been much influenced by him in the topics we work on, the questions we ask, and the methods we apply. In the following pages we'll try to do justice to some facets of the work of our *guruji*, concentrating mainly on his contributions on Indian history and on Orissa in particular.

Kulke's area of study is not confined to proper history but he has dealt with Indology, epigraphy, historiography and some major contemporary socio-religious problems that India is facing today. His list of publications[1] covers many aspects of the history of India, Sri Lanka and Southeast Asia. Such a vast field of historical research could perhaps be handled with competence because of an early schooling in history, Indology and political science at the University of Freiburg. Besides Sanskrit and epigraphy, Kulke has studied the Khmer language at Yale and the School of Oriental and African Studies. Also, he has a working knowledge of Oriya and Bhasa Indonesia. His works are mainly based on extensive field studies in South and Southeast Asia.

During his studies at Freiburg under the guidance of U. Schneider, Kulke took a trip to Sri Lanka and India. Travelling extensively in south India, infatuated by the temples, their rituals and ceremonies, he visited the Madurai temple where the priests did not allow him entry. This was a turning point in the life of Hermann Kulke. He vowed then to work on the Hindu temple. After painstaking research and several visits to the University of Madras and the temple city of Chidambaram, in 1967 he submitted his Ph.D. dissertation[2] on the *Cidambaramāhātmya* and the historical background of the rise of a south Indian temple city. In this study Kulke dealt with the traditional history of Chidambaram and with the transformation of a local to a regional sacred centre. He demonstrated how the *Cidambara-māhātmya*, composed in the twelfth century, provides insights into the subsequent evolution of the cult and the process of Sanskritization.

It was probably his early studies on the Chidambaram temple that motivated Kulke to undertake another project, on the cult of Jagannātha and the temple city of Puri, a virgin field of research. As a founder member of the German Orissa Research Project, he visited Orissa in 1969 for a pilot study to prepare the project. The project was sanctioned by the German Research Council and started in September 1970 as a part of the South Asia Interdisciplinary Regional Research Programme of Heidelberg University with a group of young German and Indian scholars from such diverse fields as history, Indology, economics, political science, anthropology, sociology, and geography. The outcome was the monumental *The Cult of Jagannath and the Regional Tradition of Orissa*,[3] 1978. Contributing six of the papers, Kulke was one of the editors along with A. Eschmann and G. C. Tripathi. It is the first major work on the regional culture of Orissa based on an interdisciplinary approach, highlighting the origin, development and organization of a regional tradition. A major achievement was the development of a methodology to relate the archaeological and textual evidence with the living traditions of the tribal people, so that subjects were handled from diverse points of view.

Kulke's essays dealt with the political aspects of the Jagannātha cult and its relation to the Gajapati kingdom and kingship. He has convincingly shown that the proper understanding of the institution of Jagannātha cannot be understood without reference to the political history of Orissa and the association of Gajapati kingship with the cult, the social structure, and the beliefs and traditions. His analysis of the role of the temples in the formation and consolidation of medieval kingship through royal patronage, the mechanism of legitimation of a hierarchical Hindu royal power in the tribal areas and establishing its superiority, has opened a new area of research in Indian history.

In 1975, Kulke submitted his D.Litt. thesis on the Jagannātha cult and the Gajapati kingdom to the University of Heidelberg and it was published in 1979.[4] In this work, he gives a total new interpretation to the history of Orissa. His treatment of the subject is from an all-India perspective, even with parallels drawn from medieval South-east Asia, a field on which he had contributed substantially in the meantime.[5] His medieval kingdom is not limited to the medieval period. Beginning with early state formation in Orissa, he continues to the period of the feudatory chiefs and beyond. In the broad historical context of state formation and the legitimation of royal authority in medieval India, this work analyses the development of Gajapati kingship, its ideology, and its relations with the Jagannātha cult up to the nineteenth century.

Kulke was one of the first to discuss the applicability of the 'Indian Feudalism' model to Orissan history. According to this theory[6] Indian feudalism originated with the increasing number of land grants to brahmanas, religious institutions and officials (with fiscal rights and immunities from taxation, from the inspections of royal officers, and from police interference). By this a class of landed intermediaries were created, land and people were separated from the daily activities of royal governments. Land grants led to fragmentation and decentralization. But Kulke interprets land grants as a means of integration, not decentralization. In his opinion:

> The early land grants to Brahmins and religious institutions, i.e. monasteries and temples, were thus part of a systematic royal policy which did not lead to the weakening of the central authority, but, on the contrary, aimed at its strengthening by ritual means.[7]

This was a major challenge to the theory of 'Indian Feudalism' which he disproved by drawing examples from Orissan historical development. He has shown that Orissa's political development, characterized by the gradual integration of an increasing number of scattered nuclear areas, came under the control of single dynasties. Political developments under the Śailodbhavas, the Bhaumakaras, the Somavaṃśīs, the Later Gaṅgas and the Suryavaṃśa Gajapatis, who had successively ruled over an increasing area, is characterized by a process of gradual integration.

This work is based on epigraphic sources, traditional accounts, legends, Persian sources and British accounts. Kulke has almost exhausted all the sources of Orissan history, including the Muslim sources and British archival materials collected from the India Office Library, London. We have been greatly benefited from his bibliography because many works/sources on Orissan history cited therein were not known to the scholars of Orissan history before.

Kulke's familiarity with medieval European history and a wide range of history writing led him to use the interdisciplinary approach to understand social formations. As a follower of Max Weber, he used materials from ethnology and anthropology for historical interpretation. His anthropological insights are one of his chief contributions to the students of early Orissan society. In an article entitled, 'Kshatriyaization and Social Change: a Study in Orissa Setting',[8] Kulke has gone beyond the concepts of 'Sanskritization' of M. N. Srinivas and 'Rajputization' of Surjit Sinha to analyse the transformation of tribes into castes. He used 'Kṣatriyaization' to explain this process by implementing Max Weber's classic, *The Religion of India*[9] for understanding Hinduization. His emphasis was on legitimation as the main motivation for the incorporation of tribal chiefs into the Hindu fold. In 'Early State Formation and Royal Legitimation in Tribal Areas of Eastern India',[10] he looks at the process from both the Hindu and the tribal perspective.

During his Visiting Professorship to the Department of History, Utkal University (1978-9), Kulke worked on a comprehensive and classified bibliography of Orissa[11] in collaboration with the department. This is the first complete bibliography of Orissan studies including history, epigraphy, archaeology, economies, politics, geography, anthropology, sociology and literature. Further, along with German colleagues he has also published a bibliographical guide[12] to Indian history from the ancient times to the present.

When the study of the structural models of early medieval kingdoms of the post-Gupta period was a burning topic of discussion among scholars, Kulke contributed 'Fragmentation and Segmentation versus Integration? Reflections on the concept of Indian Feudalism and the Segmentary State in Indian History',[13] where he advanced a new model, that of 'concentric integration'. This added to the existing three models, such as the unitary model (a centralized kingdom with a strong central bureaucracy), Indian Feudalism (decentralized feudal states) and the segmentary state model (emphasizing continuity between the tribal stateless form and the unitary state). The concentric integration model suggests three stages in a continuous process of integration which leads to the foundation of trans-local (or sub-regional) early kingdoms and culminates in the establishment of the imperial regional states. It describes the characteristic feature of the early medieval kingdom as a state which attained the status of a regional imperial state by growing from a nuclear area to incorporation of its fringes and finally also the neighbouring core areas.

Kulke evaluated the applicability of Burton Stein's segmentary state model to early medieval Orissa. He holds that

> for the South Indian Cōḷa empire, with its strong and autochthonous local 'segments' as represented in the *nāḍus* based on ethnic and lineage affiliation and on one thousand years' documented history, the conception of a segmentary state sounds fascinating and is much more convincing than any other conception offered so far.[14]

Kulke accepts Stein's theory in general but raises several questions. He, for example, questions the concept of ritual sovereignty. Stein argues that the royal orders which were sent to the segments through royal officers and which are inscribed in the inscriptions are 'not evidence of political control but of ritual sovereignty'.[15] Kulke on the other hand interprets them as 'documents of a systematic ritual policy which was as much a part of a general "power policy" as, for instance, economic or military policies'.[16]

Kulke's new 'integrative' model raised serious discussions in the scholarly world and opened a new approach to the structure of early medieval kingdoms. Now it is an established model often quoted and discussed. Recognizing its merit he was invited to edit a volume on *The State in India 1000-1700*.[17] In his paper 'The Early and the Imperial Kingdom: A Processural Model of Integrative State Formation in Early Medieval India'[18] Kulke extended his integrative model, to a 'processural model of state formation':

> The conceptual model of integrative state formation which emerges from an

analysis of the dynamics of these interdependent socio-economic, political and cultural processes is a model which may be called processural. It stresses diachronic development and change rather than synchronic structures and their static nature. For analytical purposes, however, it operates with the heuristical tool of three successive stages of state formation.[19]

Kulke, with D. Rothermund, wrote a history of India in German in 1982. It gives a survey of Indian history[20] from antiquity to the present day. It serves as a standard textbook for students at European universities. A great departure from the traditional historical writings on India, this emphasizes the structural patterns of Indian history rather than the chronology of events. It explains the major political, economic, social and cultural forces which have shaped the history of South Asia. The popularity of this book led to American and British editions in English in 1986. In 1990/1998, the second and third revised editions of this work came out. The Indian edition came out in 1991. It was also translated into Italian (1991) and recently into Turkish (2001).

During the years 1983-6, Kulke took on another project on the Sources of Orissan Studies, jointly sponsored by the German Research Council and Indian Council of Historical Research. In this project he worked with the vast treasure of research materials collected by the former Orissa Research Project. These include the traditional accounts of Orissa, such as various versions of the *Mādaḷā Pāñji* and the *Chāmu Ciṭāus* (royal letters). The study of such sources are one of the most intricate problems of Orissan history. The first outcome was the edition and translation with historical notes, of the *Kaṭakarājavaṃśavalī*[21] with G. C. Tripathi and a series of articles on the *Mādaḷā Pāñji* and the *Chāmu Ciṭāus.*[22] The *Kaṭakarājavaṃśavalī* is a Sanskrit work of the early nineteenth century, compiled from the older records of the Jagannātha temple. The text describes the political history of Orissa from the beginning of the Kali era. It is a traditional history of Orissa as visualized by the priests of the Jagannātha temple, with significant historical facts bearing on the temple faithfully recorded. The text forms part of the corpus of literature broadly categorized as *Mādaḷā Pāñji*. This manuscript has been collected from the India Office Library, London and originally formed a part of Col. Mackenzie's collection.

In 'The Chronicles and the Temple Records of the *Mādaḷā Pāñji* of Puri: a Reassessment of the Evidence',[23] he deals with the historicity of the *Mādaḷā Pāñji* and also its validity for the reconstruction of Orissa's holy tradition of Jagannātha. He analyses different versions of the *Mādaḷā Pāñji* maintained by the Deula Karaṇa and Taḍhāu Karaṇa of the temple and the Puri palace. He has discussed certain features of these versions of the text: the *Kaliyuga*, the system of symbolic numbers, the increasing number of Kesari kings, the Oriya *aṅka* system, etc. Although the compilation of the Puri chronicle began around 1600, soon after the re-establishment of the Jagannātha cult, it was only after 1820, during Company rule, that it marked the culmination of traditional as well as modern historical writing in Orissa. In 1822, A. Stirling published an 'Account, Geographical, Statistical and Historical of Orissa Proper, or Cuttack',[24] on the basis of the *vaṃśavalīs* or traditional accounts of Orissa. Kulke thinks Stirling's interest in the history of Orissa had a deep impact on the contemporary brahman chroniclers of Puri.

> This impact seems to have led to a stronger awareness of their historical tradition and, at least in the case of the author of the Sanskrit Vaṃśavalīs, to an attempt to systematize this tradition. This systematization, however, was still done according to indigenous and brahmanical standards and norms, and was based solely on local material. It was thus neither 'fabricated' under direct British influence (as were certainly later attempts of historical writings of Feudatory states of Orissa) nor was it influenced by European ideas of history.[25]

Discussing the meaning of '*Mādaḷā Pāñji*', Kulke distinguishes between the *Mādaḷā Pāñji* as a whole corpus of the Puri temple records and the *Mādaḷā Pāñji* only as chronicles or *vaṃśavalīs*. He agrees with R. P. Chanda and K. C. Panigrahi that the rubric included a vast archive of material, and that temple records and chronicles formed only a part of it.

To date scholars have worked only on the chronicle (*vaṃśavalīs*) part of the *Mādaḷā Pāñji* and other records are a neglected field of research. Thus Kulke continued research on the untouched aspect of temple records. In 1970, the Orissa Research Project purchased a collection of about 15,000 palm-leaves from the Deula Karaṇa of Puri. They were in a poor state of preservation. After some were copied by professional copyists, they were returned to the Orissa

State Museum and at present are preserved there. This is a lasting contribution from German scholars to the heritage of Orissa.

The records that formed a part of the *Mādaḷā Pāñji* contained a vast rage of subjects, e.g. accounts of daily donations to the temple, land property and other allied properties of the temple and *maṭhas* of Puri, investiture of priests and *mahants*, ritual regulations and *Chāmu Ciṭāus*, etc. These records date from the seventeenth century to the early twentieth century and were maintained by the ancestors of the Deula Karaṇa.

Kulke worked on the royal letters to study the diplomatic relationships of the Khurda kingdom with the feudatory chiefs through the cult of Jagannātha. So far, early 150 such letters have been identified. In 'Kṣetra and Kṣatra: The Cult of Jagannātha of Puri and the "Royal Letters" (*Chāmu Ciṭāus*) of the Rājās of Khurda',[26] he has shown the political ritual relationship of the Khurda kings with the feudatories and the independent kings beyond Orissa. The Gajapati kings utilized the cult of Jagannātha as a political weapon to overcome internal and external dangers and to gain the support of certain feudatories. At times of crisis, they tried to win the loyality of the feudatory kings by sharing the ritual position with them. The feudatory kings, as well as rulers from different parts of India who came to worship Jagannātha were given special privileges and honours according to their status. Kulke continues his intensive study on the *Chāmu Ciṭāus* and plans to publish a critical edition with English translation.

Kings and Cults: State Formation and Legitimation in India and Southeast Asia,[27] published in 1993, is a collection of sixteen papers. These focus on state formation and royal policy in medieval India and Southeast Asia. Broadly, in this work, Kulke attempts to show the close and interdependent relationship between Kṣetra and Kṣatra, the sacred and temporal domains of power. Of these sixteen papers, ten deal with the medieval Orissan kingdom and the Jagannātha cult. He has drawn an excellent example of Puri Jagannātha's relationship with tribal cults. Another major theme is historiography, i.e. the *Mādaḷā Pāñji* tradition and its relationship with legitimation of royal authority in the process of state formation. Two papers deal with south Indian history, on the *Cidambaramāhātmya* and the foundation of the institution of the Śaṅkarācārya of Sringeri. In the papers on Southeast Asia Kulke developed an 'evolutionary model' of medieval state formation. In this regard, he has drawn close parallels with his Orissan experiences on subjects like legitimation and divinity of kingship.

In the broader perspective of Indian history, Kulke has written papers on a variety of themes such as India's 'Axial Age',[28] the date of Buddha,[29] the Rājasūya ceremony,[30] fundamentalism in South Asia,[31] the destruction of the Babri Masjid in Ayodhya,[32] maritime history,[33] Hinduism,[34] and Max Weber.[35] He has also contributed a number of articles on Orissa at international conferences. He has co-edited a number of volumes on themes such as urbanization,[36] regionalism and regional traditions.[37]

In particular Kulke has brought the study of Orissan history and culture, a neglected field of research, to the international forum. He has also inspired a number of young research scholars in Germany to take up Indian/Orissan history, continuing in Germany the *guru-śiṣyaparampara* that he inherited from Schneider.

In June 1997, together with his colleague B. Schnepel, Kulke organized an international seminar, 'Jagannath Revisited: Studying Society, Religion and State in Orissa', where he invited members of the former Orissa Research Project as well as some young scholars. A programme for a future research project was devised. Entitled, 'Various Identities: Socio-Cultural Profiles of Orissa in Historical and Regional Perspectives'. It received sanction from the German Research Council and has started operating since April 1999. This is the largest project on India in the humanities ever funded by the German Research Council. Unlike the former Orissa Research Project, in which the study was concentrated to the coastal areas and the Jagannātha cult, this project aims to shift its focus to the so-called peripheral areas of Orissa. So we can expect more insights concerning the tribal and interior regions.

This project, which will continue until 2005, makes one thing very clear: he may have retired in 2003 from the chair of Asian History he held at Kiel University since 1988, but his work continues as before. His enthusiasm, 'the best we get from history', has not been curbed, and it does not seem likely that this will happen in the near future. May Jagannātha protect him and allow him to enjoy his studies and to inspire his colleagues for many years to come.

NOTES

1. See the Hermann Kulke Bibliography at the end of this volume.
2. *Cidambaramāhātmya: Eine Untersuchung der religionsgeschichtlichen und historischen Hintergründe fur die Entstehung der Tradition einer südindischen Tempelstadt*, Wiesbaden, 1970.
3. A. Eschmann, H. Kulke and G. C. Tripathi (eds.), *The Cult of Jagannātha and the Regional Tradition of Orissa*, New Delhi, 1978.
4. *Jagannātha-Kult und Gajapati-Königtum: Ein Beitrag zur Geschichte religiöser Legitima.ion hinduistischer Herrschaft*, Wiesbaden, 1979.
5. 'Der Devarāja-Kult: Legitimation und Herrscherapotheose im Angkor-Reich', *Saeculum*, 25, 1974, pp. 24-55; 'The Devarāja Cult: a Reassessment of the Evidence', *Proceedings, 7th IAHA Conference*, Bangkok, 1979, pp. 1371-84; *The Devarāja Cult*, transl. from German by I. W. Mabbett and notes on the translation of Khmer terms by J. M. Jacob, Ithaca, N.Y., 1978.
6. For details see D. D. Kosambi, *An Introduction to the Study of Indian History*, Bombay, 1956; R. S. Sharma, *Indian Feudalism: 300-1200*, Calcutta, 1965; B. N. S. Yadav, *Some Aspects of Society in Northern India in the 12th century A.D.*, Allahabad, 1956; D. N. Jha, 'Early Indian Feudalism: A Historigraphical Critique', Presidential Address, Ancient Indian Section, Indian Historical Congress, XL Session, Waltair, 1979; *idem* (ed.), *Feudal Social Formation in Early India*, Delhi, 1987.
7. *Jagannāth-Kult und Gajapati-Königtum, op. cit.*, p. 224.
8. S. Devadas Pillai, (ed.), *Aspects of Changing India, in Honour of Prof. G. S. Ghurye.* Bombay, 1976, pp. 398-409.
9. Max Weber, *The Religion of India: Sociology of Hinduisms and Buddhism*, transl. by H. Gerth and D. Martindale, Glencoe, 1958.
10. R. R. Moser, Mohan K. Gautam (eds.), *Aspects of Tribal Life in South Asia. Strategy and Survival*, Bern, 1977, pp. 29-37.
11. *Orissa: A Comprehensive and Classified Bibliography*, by Hermann Kulke in collaboration with G. N. Dash, M. N. Dash and K. S. Behera, Cuttack, 1981.
12. H. Kulke, H. J. Leue, J. Lütt, D. Rothermund, *Indische Geschichte vom Altertum bis zur Gegenwart: Literaturbericht über neuere Veröffentlichungen* (*Historische Zeitschrift*, Special Volume 10), München, 1982.
13. *Studies in History*, IV, 1982, pp. 237-63.
14. *Ibid.*, pp. 248-9.
15. B. Stein, 'Integration of the Agrarian System of South India', in R. E. Frykenberg (ed.), *Land Contol and Social Structure in Indian History*, Madison, 1969, pp. 175-2:6.
16. 'Fragmentation and segmentation . . .' (ref. 13), p. 254.
17. H. Kulke (ed.), *The State in India 1000-1700*, New Delhi, 1995.

18. *Ibid.*, pp. 233-62.
19. *Ibid.*, p. 234.
20. H. Kulke, D. Rothermund, *Geschichte Indiens*, Stuttgart, 1982.
21. G. C. Tripathi, H. Kulke (ed. and transl.), *Kaṭakarājavaṃsāvaliḥ: A Traditional History of Orissa*, Allahabad, 1986.
22. 'The Chronicles and the Temple Records of the Mādaḷā Pāñji of Puri: a Reassessment of the Evidence', *Indian Archives*, 36, 1987, pp. 1-24; 'Kṣatra and Kṣetra: The Cult of Jagannātha of Puri and the "Royal Letters" (*Chāmu Ciṭāu*) of the Rājās of Khurda', in H.T. Bakker (ed.), *The Sacred Centre as the Focus of Political Interest* (Groningen Oriental Studies, Vol. VI), Groningen, 1992, pp. 131-42.
23. *Ibid.*
24. A Stirling, 'An Account, Geographical, Statistical and Historical of Orissa Proper or Cuttack', *Asiatic Researches*, 15, 1822, pp. 163-338.
25. 'The Chronicles and the Temple Records . . .', (ref. 22), p. 10.
26. *Op. cit.* (ref. 22).
27. *Kings and Cults: State Formation and Legitimation in India and Southeast Asia*, New Delhi, 1993.
28. 'The Historical Background of India's Axial Age', in S. N. Eisenstadt (ed.), *The Origins and Diversity of Axial Civilizations*, New York, 1986, pp. 374-92.
29. 'Some Considerations on the Significance of Buddha's Date for the History of North India', in H. Bechert (ed.), *When did the Buddha live? The Controversy on the Dating of the Historical Buddha*, Delhi, 1995, pp. 161-7.
30. 'The Rājasūya—a Paradigm of Early State Formation in India?', in A.W. van den Hoek, D. H. A. Kolff and M. S. Oort (eds.), *Ritual, State and History in South Asia: Essays in Honour of J. C. Heesterman*, Leiden, 1992, pp. 188-98.
31. "Ethnisch-nationalistische Konflikte and Fundamentalismus in Südasien", in *Bericht der 7. Sitzung des Gesprächkreises 'Kultur und Entwicklung', 12.11.1993*, Sankt Augustin, 1994, pp. 19-28.
32. 'Der militante Hindunationalismus und die Zerstörung der Babri-Moschee in Ayodhya', in D. Lange (ed.), *Religionen-Fundamentalismus-Politik*, Frankfurt, 1996, pp. 177-208.
33. 'Die Geschichte markitimer Beziehungen im Indischen Ozean. Einführung in das Thema', in S. Conermann (ed.), *Der Indische Ozean*, Hamburg, 1998, pp. 1-8; 'Rivalry and Competition in the Bay of Bengal: A View from the Eleventh Century and its Bearing on Indian Ocean Studies', in Om Prakash and Denys Lombard (eds.), *Commerce and Culture in the Bay of Bengal, 1500-1800*, New Delhi, 1999, pp. 17-36.
34. G.-D. Sontheimer, H. Kulke (eds.), *Hinduism Reconsidered*, New Delhi, 1989, 2nd rev. and enlarged edn., New Delhi, 1997.

35. 'Max Weber's Contribution to the Study of "Hinduization", in India and "Indianization" in Southeast Asia', in D. Kantowsky (ed.), *Recent Research on Max Weber's Studies of Hinduism*, München, 1986, pp. 97-116.
36. H. Kulke, Hans C. Rieger, L. Lutze (eds.), *Städte in Südasien: Geschichte, Gesellschaft, Gestalt*, Wiesbaden, 1982.
37. H. Kulke, D. Rothermund (eds.), *Regionale Tradition in Südasien*, Stuttgart, 1985. G. C. Tripathi, H. Kulke (eds.), *Religion and Society in Eastern India: Anncharlott Eschmann Memorial Lectures 1978-87*, New Delhi, 1994; H. Kulke, B. Schnepel (eds.), *Jagannath Revisited: Studying Society, Religion and the State of Orissa*, New Delhi, 2001; G. Berkemer, T. Frasch, H. Kulke, J. Lütt (eds.), *Explorations in South Asian History: Essays in Honour of Dietmar Rothermund*, New Delhi, 2001.

CHAPTER 2

Archaeology of Orissa: A Historiographic Study

KISHOR K. BASA

In reviewing the history of the archaeology of a region, it is important to endeavour for what is known as 'historicising the context'. Archaeologists are what Randall McGuire calls 'socially situated scholars',[1] and hence an archaeologist is as much a producer of knowledge as a creation of his time. It is in this context that Peter Gathercole wrote:

> The recognition as well as interpretation of archaeological evidence will always be biased and incomplete. There can be no archaeologically achieved final truths or wholly objective interpretation. But to recognise such limitation is not to reduce the subject to a set of mere perceptual constructs. Archaeology is a societal activity that embodies both the residues of its past and its changing attitudes towards the past. We call the residues evidence and attitudes interpretation. The continuing dialogue between the two enables archaeology always open to new questions, at the same time to reveal new knowledge.[2]

It is also important to point out the importance of the history of archaeology, as Glyn Daniel has said, it requires study 'because without a historical perspective we can at the present day forget, at our peril, or even repeat past error'.[3]

In India archaeology, like anthropology, developed in a colonial context[4] but there were some references to places or sites of antiquarian importance during the pre-colonial period. Hence the present paper is divided into two parts. A brief history of archaeology in Orissa is followed by an overview of some issues of historiographic importance.

HISTORY OF ORISSAN ARCHAEOLOGY

The theme has already drawn the attention of scholars.[5] Here it is divided into three phases – precolonial (upto 1825), colonial (1825-1947) and post-colonial (1947- till date).

ARCHAEOLOGY DURING THE PRECOLONIAL PERIOD

In this section, brief mention will be made of references to places of antiquarian importance in Orissa upto 1825. References to various places, ports and Buddhist sites are known from the western Classical writers like Ptolemy and the Chinese pilgrim Hieun Tsang during the early historic period. There are also reports of some places during the precolonial period both in the indigenous and foreign accounts. It is important to spell out the reasons for accepting the year 1825 as the terminal point of the precolonial and the beginning of the colonial period as far as writing of history of Orissan archaeology is concerned. There are two reasons. First, although Orissa was conquered by the British in 1803 from the Marathas, the consolidation of the British rule was not possible until the 1820s. Secondly, the first distinct work with a bearing on Orissan archaeology was published in 1825 by Andrew Stirling.

During the precolonial period, there are two kinds of reporting about places and sites of antiquarian importance. First, some authors actually had visited the places and made observations. Second, some others observed the places from a distance or even wrote without visiting them. As regards the former, Mahmud Amir Wali, a Persian traveller of the seventeenth century was in Orissa during 1626 and 1627 and wrote about the height of the Konarak temple in an allegorical manner. The famous Sun temple of Konarak and the Jagannath temple of Puri were important landmarks for the European sailors of the time, the former being known as the Black Pagoda and the latter, the White Pagoda. For example, the Diaries of Streynsham Master contained a statement for 23 December 1676, 'Wee sailed in sight of the Black Pagoda and the White Pagoda'.[6] Abul Fazl, who did not visit Orissa, wrote in his *Ain-i-Akbari* (late sixteenth century) that there were 139 masonry forts in Orissa.[7] Rennell in his *Memoir of a Map of Hindoostan* (1793) referred to the Black Pagoda and White Pagoda as well as to the diamond mines of western Orissa,

Thomas Bowrey described the activities in the Jagannath temple, Puri, and in about 1815 Mackenzie made sketches of the Bhubaneswar temples and of Konarak. But the best account perhaps was that of Motte who, under instruction from Lord Clive to investigate the diamonds of western Orissa, came from Calcutta to coastal Orissa during the 1760s and then went to Sambalpur (western Orissa) by following the riverine tract of the Mahanadi, the biggest river in Orissa. Motte found the Barabati Fort at Cuttack similar to the Windsor castle and also reported on the traditional boats and the means of exchange between western and coastal Orissa. He also made mention of the places and people and in some cases of the antiquarian remains. Thus until the first quarter of the nineteenth century, archaeology in Orissa is characterized by antiquarianism. It was mostly confined to the sacred living monuments and very rarely, as in the case of Rennell and Motte, to forts or diamond mining in western Orissa.

Archaeology during the Colonial Period (1825-1947)

In this section, a broad overview would be made for the period between 1825 – the year of publication of Stirling's account – and 1947.

(a) The Contribution of Stirling

Stirling[8] wrote a general account of the political, economic and social aspects of coastal Orissa, but also treated some important aspects of Orissan archaeology, particularly Puri, Konarak, Bhubaneswar and Jajpur. According to Chakrabarti, this is a singularly important paper because of its introduction of the study of Orissan temple style and antiquities in Indian archaeology.[9] The temples of Bhubaneswar, particularly the Lingaraj temple, became the pivotal point of his analysis. 'The great Pagoda of the Lingaraj . . . lifts its singular form, eminently conspicuous, both for size, loftiness and the superior style of its architecture. . . . About the centre, the tower . . . rises majestically to a height of one hundred and eighty feet – (the summit is) shaped somewhat like a turban, which forms so distinguishing a feature in the temple architecture of Orissa'.[10] As a contrast, Stirling considered the Jagannath temple at Puri as 'the mirror of all wickedness and idolatry'.[11] As regards Konarak, 'the Black Pagoda, even in its imperfect and dilapidated condition presents a highly curious and beautiful specimen of ancient Hindu temple architecture'.[12] Stirling's account had three significant aspects: (i) his emphasis on concentration of religious antiquities around four places of pilgrimage, the Hara Khetr, the Visnu or Purushottama Khetr, Arka or Padma Khetr and the Vijayi or Parvati Khetr; (ii) an illustration of an inscription at Udayagiri, near Bhubaneswar and (iii) an account of civil constructions such as bridges (including illustrations), forts and revetments.

(b) Epigraphy

Although Charles Wilkins laid the foundation of epigraphy in India, it was James Prinsep whose genius and labour helped archaeology to free itself from its antiquarian and literary affiliation. Cunningham described this change as one from the era of 'closet' or scholastic archaeology to that of 'field archaeologists' and 'travelling antiquarians'. As for Orissan epigraphy, there were two major contributions of Prinsep, the decipherment of the Hathigumpha inscription at Udayagiri, and of the Asokan inscription at Dhauli. Prinsep, considered the Hathigumpha inscription 'the most curious (antiquity) that has yet been disclosed to us'.[13] However, he is remembered most for deciphering the Asokan inscriptions. In 1838, he compared the Girnar and Dhauli inscriptions and discovered that the greater part of the Dhauli inscription was identical with the inscription at Girnar, except for the first and the last paragraphs.[14]

Subsequently another Asokan inscription was discovered at Jaugada, a photograph of which was taken by Captain Harington in 1859. This is one of the earliest uses of photography for archaeological documentation in Orissa. The Hathigumpha and Asokan inscriptions engaged the attention of many scholars including Cunningham, Bhagwan Lal Indraji, Fleet, R. D. Banerji, K. P. Jayaswal, B. M. Barua, V. Smith, Hultzsch and D. C. Sircar. More and more inscriptions were reported from various parts of Orissa during the colonial period which helped in writing dynastic histories of Orissa.

The main features of the epigraphic studies in Orissa during the colonial period are the following: (i) To begin with, history of Orissa was text dominated. For example, in Stirling's account of Orissan history, there was reliance on the *Madala Panji*, a chronicle of the Puri temple. Subsequently, epigraphy played an important role. The names of Fleet and Man Mohan Chakrabarti deserve mention for their emphasis on epigraphy for reconstructing Orissa's past. (ii) Through inscriptions dynastic histories were brought to light. (iii) Inscriptions also helped in the reconstruction of the historical geography of Orissa. However, the main limitation of such epigraphic and literary studies was that there was hardly any emphasis on social and economic history.

(c) Sculpture and Architecture

Although Kittoe[15] referred to the ruins and pillars of Jajpur and Dhauli, it was James Fergusson who provided a historical approach to the study of Orissan temple architecture. According to him, there were two methods of studying architecture, scientifically as individual monuments and historically with a focus on style and interaction.[16] He pointed out that in a country like India, the chisels of her sculptors are immeasurably more to be trusted than the pens of her authors. For him, the Udayagiri caves were Buddhist. An important authority on art history in nineteenth century, he came out with clear terms about the typical features of Orissan temples – *vimana* or *bardeula*, *jagamohana*, *natamandir* and *bhogamandapa*. He not only studied the art historic value of temples of coastal Orissa, but also postulated their chronology.[17]

Hunter's[18] *Orissa* had great dependence on the *Madalapanji*. Like Fergusson, Hunter also considered the caves of Udayagiri as Buddhist but he considered them in three phases – ascetic (single cell), ceremonial (commodious chambers), and fashionable (the two-storeyed Queen's place). He also referred to the remains of Lalitgiri, Jajpur and Konarak. As regards religion, he referred to the prevalence of Buddhism, Saivism and Sun worship in different periods.

It was Rajendra Lal Mitra who was the first Indian to work on the archaeology of Orissa in a comprehensive manner. He published two volumes of *Antiquities of Orissa*.[19] He had two objectives – firstly to secure an accurate description, illustrated by plans, measurements, drawings or photographs, and by copies of inscriptions, with their histories and secondly, to throw light on the social history of Orissa as known from such antiquities. The first volume contained general observations on the nature and character of objects, while the second had detailed descriptions of objects. Like Fergusson, he also stated that the typical features of Orissan temples were *vimana*, *jagamohana*, *natamandir* and *bhogamandapa*. He mentioned the use of iron beams at Puri and Konarak, remarking, however, that the iron in Konarak was of superior quality and was perfectly forged. He pointed out that although there was no monumental Asokan pillar in Orissa the pillars at Puri and Jajpur were near to it. Mitra also stated that the canons of the *Silpasastra* provided the foundation of Oriya art; the *Silpasastra* dwelt on forms, proportions and features of gods, but said nothing about ordinary human beings. In Orissan temples, Mitra stated, human beings are light and natural, while for gods, the principles of the *Silpasastra* were generally but not very strictly adhered to. As regards the alleged obscenity of Orissan art, Mitra argued that they represent a desire to typify religious ideas, and not to cater to the decadence of the artists or their employers. Mitra also touched on the social conditions of temple builders – dress, ornament, furniture, domestic utensils, etc., though nothing was known about food. As to religious history, the earliest art was Buddhist, followed by Saiva and Vaisnava. However, hardly anything was known about political history from art history.

While Stirling, Fergusson and Mitra confined their studies to coastal Orissa, it was Beglar – who was asked by Cunningham to survey Orissa – who covered also the western, southern and northern parts. Beglar[20] reported the antiquities of Khiching (northern Orissa), the fortified settlement of Jaugada (southern Orissa) and the Chausath Yogini temple at Ranipur Jharial (western Orissa), among other things.

It was at the behest of the Mayurbhanj Maharaja Sri Ram Chandra Bhanj Deo that Nagendra Nath Vasu[21] made an archaeological survey of Mayurbhanj. He discussed the architectural and sculptural remains and also provided the Sanskrit texts of the copper plates of some Bhanja kings. The sculptures included the pantheon of Jaina, Buddhist, and Brahmanical religions. Unfortunately his second volume could not be published because of the death of his patron.

M. M. Ganguly[22] regarded the Udayagiri cave sculptures as eminently Buddhist. He also mentioned that the rules of proportions as described in the *Manasara* were strictly followed in the Udayagiri columns. He spoke of different classes of Orissan temples according to the plan, such as *ekaratha*, *triratha*, *pancharatha*, *saptaratha*. However, he did not see any *nabaratha*. According to him, Orissan temples could be divided into two groups based on the nature of tower over the cube, curvilinear (*rekha deul*) and pyramidal (*pida deul*).

R. P. Chanda[23] emphasized a 'local school' at Khiching in Mayurbhanj from where there was evidence of Buddhist and Jaina sculptures. Chanda further stated that the peculiar scroll decorations and the careful finish of the lower half of the figures reveal the emergence of a local school of sculpture.

R. D. Banerji[24] regarded the Udayagiri caves as Jaina, but found difficulty in knowing how Orissan architecture developed during the eight centuries between the Khandagiri-Udayagiri of Jaina caves and the earliest medieval temples. On the basis of an inscription in the *mukhamandapa* of the Amritesvara temple at Holal, South India, Banerji talked of the Kalinga style as a distinct style of architecture, besides the Nagara, Dravida and Vesara styles. He chalked out of three phases of what he called medieval Orissan temples. The earliest type had three regular features – the *vimana, jagamohana* and *sikhara* – in complete form. The Parasuramesvara was the earliest, and the Muktesvara and the Gandharadi belonged to the second group. There was also the use of Naga pillars. The second group included the tantric temples at Boudh (central Orissa), and the temple of Chandrasekhar at Khiching (northern Orissa). The main features of the group were the want of a *mandapa* or *jagamohana* and the sudden curvature of the *sikhara* inwards near the top. The third group included the temples of Lingaraja and Anantavasudeva, whose features were the *vimana*, *jagamohana*, *natamandir* and *bhogamandapa*. An important aspect of Banerji's writing was his emphasis on subregional traditions at Khiching and Boudh. Moreover, he laid stress on the *sikhara* in the Kalinga style of architecture. As far as Orissan sculpture was concerned, he found a definite mixture of north and south, in particular the combination of the figure work of the north and the design of the south. Banerji's two volumes were significant for more than one reason. He was the first to include prehistory in his study on Orissan history. Banerji used numismatic sources for the first time to reconstruct Orissan history, and is the first scholar to emphasize the

Kalingan style of architecture as a distinct school on epigraphic grounds. He also mentioned for the first time the appropriation of the Jagannath cult by the Eastern Gangas for the legitimation of their political authority.

Although Mitra and Ganguly had talked of the *Silpasastra* and other texts as providing general guidelines for Orissan architecture, not much emphasis was laid on the living traditions and the textual references. In this regard Nirmal Bose's[25] *Canons of Orissan Architecture* is significant since he studied seven manuscripts that include the *Silpasastra* and the *Bhubanapradipa*. Certain general matters regarding the selection of the building sites and the classification of soils are common to both treatises. Therefore both were used for the first part of his book. The second part dealt with the architecture of temples based on five recensions of the *Bhubanapradipa*.

Stella Kramrisch[26] spoke of the walls of Orissan temples as being either plain as a whole or carved as a whole. During the colonial period, some British civil servants also wrote on antiquities. For example, John Beams wrote about the Buddhist remains at Kopari,[27] while Chandrasekhar Banurji wrote on the Buddhist remains of Lalitgiri[28] and Jajpur[29] and a mosque at Assiagiri.

(d) Secular Remains

As for forts Kittoe and Beglar mentioned Barabati and John Beams[30] drew attention to the Raibania Fort (along with a sketch). Moreover, Kittoe and Beglar also talked about a few bridges, mostly of the medieval period.

(e) Numismatics

It was Beglar who reported Roman coins from Bamanghati in Mayurbhanj district. Moreover, Puri-Kushana coins were recovered for the first time in the Ganjam district in 1858.[31] Subsequently, they were found in Puri (1893), Balasore (1912) and Mayurbhanj districts (1923). P. Acharya argued that the uninscribed Puri-Kushana coins belonged to the third or fourth centuries AD. Moreover, Hultzsch also referred to the Ganga *fanams*.

(f) Prehistory

It was the geologist Valentine Ball who initiated prehistoric studies in Orissa by reporting four palaeolithic artefacts from Angul, Talcher, Dhenkanal and Bursapalli.[32] Half a century later, Paramananda Acharya 1923-4 drew attention to the ground stone tools from his native village of Baidyapur in Mayurbhanj. As has been mentioned earlier, R. D. Banerji incorporated a chapter on prehistory in his study on Orissan history. A preliminary survey in Mayurbhanj by Worman and P. Acharya during the 1930s resulted in the discovery of the well-known palaeolithic site of Kuliana, which was subsequently excavated by Calcutta University.[33] This is the first excavation of a palaeolithic site in India and here a palaeolithic assemblage was studied in the context of geostratigraphic background.

ORISSAN ARCHAEOLOGY DURING THE POST-COLONIAL PERIOD

Since this aspect has been emphasized in greater detail elsewhere[34], only a brief outline would be made here. Moreover, some of the issues will also be discussed in the next section.

(a) Prehistory and Protohistory

Although prehistoric surveys by the Calcutta University continued during the 1950s in Mayurbhanj, it was G. C. Mohapatra[35] – after V. Ball – who showed that palaeolithic sites are to be found in a much larger region of Orissa, beyond the district of Mayurbhanj. Moreover, he argued about the succession of stone age cultures in Orissa. Especially he talked of the middle palaeolithic as a distinct phase in Orissa. While Mohapatra's work was based on his survey in central and northern Orissa, Tripathy[36] brought to light stone age sites of various ages in south-western Orissa. During the 1980s scholars made intensive surveys in smaller areas, which yielded rich evidence of stone age sites belonging to different culture sequences. Thus Nanda[37] worked in the upper Indravati basin (primarily upper palaeolithic and mesolithic sites), Singh[38] in erstwhile Dhenkanal district (primarily palaeolithic and mesolithic sites), Ota[39] in Phulbani district (primarily mesolithic sites), Mohanty[40] in Keonjhar district (primarily mesolithic sites) and Behera[41] in Sundargarh district (primarily neolithic sites). Palaeolithic cultures are also reported from Pallahara[42] in the Brahmani valley and from Kuchinda[43] and Burla[44] in the upper Mahanadi valley. Evidence of the mesolithic culture is also reported in the coastal district of Jajpur.[45] Dash[46] made an extensive survey of neolithic artifacts in Orissa as regards their distribution, typology, technology and raw materials.

Studies on prehistoric rock art have emerged as an important area of research.[47] The sites are mostly concentrated in western Orissa and some such sites are traced back to the mesolithic period.

However, it is the Mayurbhanj district which has received the most attention,[48] although some attempts have been made to review the prehistory at a pan-Orissan level.[49] Thapar's excavations at Kuchai,[50] near Baripada yielded neolithic artefacts together with a coarse grit tempered red ware and an orange-brown ware. Survey and a trial trench around Pallahara yielded the manufacturing evidence for neolithic artefacts as well as the recovery of coarse red ware.[51] An important trend has been the survey and excavation of chalcolithic sites in various parts of Orissa[52] such as Golabai[53] and Gopalpur[54] in coastal Orissa, Sankerjang[55] and Bhejidihi[56] in Angul district, Khameswaripali[57] in Subarnapur district, Kurmigudi[58] in Sambalpur district and Kuanr[59] in Keonjhar district. The importance of Sankerjang lies in its knapped and ground stone axes and adzes, copper bangles, as well as human skeletal remains (the dental ones in particular); moreover, it has yielded the first radiocarbon date (2590±60 BP) (KN 3755) for Orissa for the chalcolithic period. The most spectacular recovery are the bar celts. While Yule and Rath argued that the bar celts from Sankerjang were the earliest musical instruments in India, showing similarity to lithophones in Vietnam, Dash pointed out that they bear thrashing marks and hence might have been used in pounding or corn-crunching, or as mallets or even as nut crackers.

Another important site was Golabai excavated by B. K. Sinha of the Archaeological Survey who divided the culture sequence into three phases – Period I neolithic, Period IIA osteo-chalcolithic and Period IIB ferro-chalcolithic. While Period I yielded neolithic artefacts, the chalcolithic levels were associated with a large number of stone tools, implements of bone and copper, terracotta and faience. Pottery was both handmade and wheelmade. From Khameswaripali painted pottery was recovered for the first time from an excavated site in Orissa.

An important issue is the problem of the iron age in Orissa although it is well known for its iron ore. Sites with iron artefacts have been reported from various places such as Kharligarh, Gudavella in Bolangir and Viratgarh in Mayurbhanj district as well as from the early historic sites of Sisupalgarh (Period IIA) and Jaugada (Period I and II). The recovery of one iron artefact from Period IIB from Golabai provides a clue to the emergence of iron at least in the first half of the first millennium BC. In his survey of western Orissa, Brandtner[60] found a megalithic burial site around Khariar, not yet excavated. An iron artefact has been also reported at Period III at Khameswaripali. Two points need to be mentioned regarding the recent work done by the Department of Anthropology, Utkal University with regard to the iron age. Firstly, survey and trial trench at Malikhoja and Biraka in the Kerjang area of Angul district has resulted in the recovery of iron artefacts along with red, black-and-red, black-polished and grey ware. Thus, although Sankerjang had been earlier emphasized for its neolithic-chalcolithic remains, its importance for the iron age is opening a new arena. Secondly, a survey by Basanta K. Mohanta[61] in the iron ore rich area of Badampahar in the Mayurbhanj district has resulted in the recovery of not only the iron smelting furnaces, but also the rare recovery of charcoal making furnaces (most probably belonging to early twentieth century). Although it is difficult at this stage to determine whether some sites of this area could belong to the iron age, there is no denying the fact that the evidence of pre-industrial iron technology has definite implications for technology in the iron age.

(b) Historical Archaeology

Unlike in the Ganga valley, an important limitation of historical archaeology in Orissa is the limited scale of excavations. The problem is all the more compounded since detailed reports are not available. The most well known site is Sisupalgarh[62] – an early historic site on a square plan with two gates on each side and spanning a period from around the mid first millennium BC to about the fourth century AD. Pottery includes knobbed and rouletted wares. Another important site is Jaugada[63] in the Rushikulya valley with an Asokan inscription which was excavated by Debala Mitra, the final report of which is not yet published. Some other excavated sites[64] include the early historic and early medieval sites of Asurgarh[65] and Manamunda[66] (in western Orissa), Manikapatana,[67] Lalitagiri,[68] Ratnagiri,[69] Udayagiri[70] (in coastal Orissa), and the medieval sites of Barabati[71] in Cuttack and the port site of Khalkattapatana,[72] near Konarak. Langudi Hill[73] in Dharmasala area of Jajpur district is an interesting early historic Buddhist site where excavations have been undertaken by the Institute of Maritime and South-East Asian Studies, Bhubaneswar. It is claimed that two rare statues of the Mauryan King Asoka with an inscription have been excavated there.[74]

Apart from these excavated sites, interesting trends have emerged on the basis of survey of early historic urban centres in various parts of Orissa. Brandtner[75] explored archaeological sites around Bhubaneswar and discussed the ceramic and art historic remains. Monica Smith[76] has shown that Sisupalgarh was a fully-occupied urban zone rather than just a ceremonial or administrative centre. Most of the materials recovered indicated a very local level of production while traded items appeared to be limited. There were few production indicators implying that the walled area was principally a habitation zone. Smith considered the presence of local resources as a key factor of urban success at Sisupalgarh. In their survey in Kalahandi district of western Orissa, Pradeep Mohanty and Baba Mishra[77] have emphasized the role of gemstones in the urbanization process since western Orissa is rich in various semi-precious stones. Jitu Mishra[78] considered the ecological background, the role of trade and the ideological impetus of Buddhism in the urbanization at Radhanagar. He also discussed the early historic remains of Chilika Lake from an ecological perspective.[79] On the basis of survey in the middle Mahanadi valley in central Orissa, Balaram Tripathy[80] has shown that the early historic sites in the study region comprise a few large settlements (centres) and several small habitations (satellites). The latter are concentrated mostly around the large settlements. Manamunda-Asurgarh is one such centre which is located at a strategic point of confluence of the rivers Tel and the Mahanadi. Tripathy also discussed the archaeological evidence of culture contact between coastal and western Orissa. Thus a differentiated picture of the urbanization process is gradually emerging for early historic Orissa.

Research on maritime archaeology[81] is an important aspect of historical archaeology in Orissa. Such studies include identification of port sites,[82] items of trade and trade routes[83] within and outside India,[84] especially South-East Asia,[85] ethnography of boat making,[86] etc. On the basis of place names and correlating them with archaeological survey and finds an attempt has been made recently to reconstruct the maritime history of Kalinga in ancient time.[87]

(c) Art History

There has been a number of interesting works on the art history of Orissa. Here mention will be made of the well known ones. These are basically of two types. The first involves some kind of panoramic survey while the second is associated with in-depth studies of single temples. Regarding the former, the most prolific and in-depth studies are the three volumes by Donaldson[88] on the temple art of Orissa. Some other important works include those by Panigrahi,[89] Dehejia,[90] Das,[91] Behera and Donaldson.[92] There has also been a trend to emphasize a single monument. Thus, Behera's[93] masterly work on Konarak in two volumes and Walter Smith's[94] *Mukteswar* are good examples of it. Moreover, the study on *pattachitra* by J. P. Das,[95] the method of construction of Konarak temple on the basis of some texts[96] and the *Illustration of the Ramayana* by Williams[97] add to the diversity of art history in Orissa.

(d) Epigraphy

There are basically two approaches to the study of Orissan epigraphy during the post-colonial period. The first involves the editing of inscriptions.[98] The other involves the use of epigraphy for reconstructing socio-economic and cultural history apart from dynastic history. Such studies include the examination of land grants by R. S. Sharma (1965) in his Appendix of *Indian Feudalism*, nature of authority and patronage in early historic Orissa,[99] aspects of rural settlement and land grant economy and nature of relationship between kings, brahmanas and temples in Orissa primarily in the early medieval period.[100]

(e) Numismatics

The most important work is by S. Tripathy,[101] who has made a comprehensive study of different coins and currency systems in the early historic and medieval periods. Three points should be made regarding coins of foreign origin found in Orissa. Firstly, Chinese coins have been found at the medieval port site of Khalkattapatna near Konarak, and a Sri Lankan coin at the port site of Manikapatana. Roman coins have been reported from Kotpad and Gumada stated to be in Andhra Pradesh[102] but in fact located in southern Orissa. Moreover, recently some imperial Kushana coins have been reported from Jakara, near Digapahandi in southern Orissa by S. K. Panda of Berhampur University. Punch marked coins were reported from Ghumal near Jamda in Mayurbhanj district by our team from Utkal University. Some of these coins are to be subjected to archaeo-metallurgical analysis, which has not been adequately emphasized in the numismatic study of Orissa.

II

HISTORIOGRAPHY

Some issues that have generated interesting debates during colonial and post-colonial periods will be discussed in this section. We shall first put these debates in perspective.

The travellers' accounts of the pre-colonial period are characterized by antiquarian interest. Sometimes the travellers treated Orissan antiquities as, to use Partha Mitter's phrase, 'much maligned monsters' whose meaning they could not fathom. For example, Plaisted in the *Journal of Calcutta* (1758) stated that in Orissa 'they worship an idol Gopalsami. . . . Around his temple are the figures of men and women in the most obscene postures as also on his palanquin.'

The formation of the Asiatic Society of Bengal in 1784 led to the unravelling of the rich cultural heritage of India by the Europeans.[103] This paved the way for what Raymond Schwab calls 'the Oriental Renaissance':[104] 'whereas the classical Renaissance immured European man within the confines of a self-sufficient Greco-Latin terrain, this later Renaissance deposited the whole world before him'.[105] The second Renaissance, in the words of Edward Said, 'combined India and the Middle Ages and thereby displaced the centuries of Augustus and Louis XIV. The job of displacement was apportioned to the great capitals: Calcutta provided, London distributed, Paris filtered and generalised'.[106] In the process the image of the Orient in the west passed from 'primitive to actual, that is, from disruptive invigoration to condescending veneration'.[107] The 'discovery' of the 'sublime' aspect of the cultural heritage of the Orient led to the construction of what Asher and Metcalf call 'canons of Orientalism'[108] which was a product of British colonialism and which gained its authority with the unflagging search for knowledge of the colonial territory. This canon was based on the assumption that India possessed a great civilization in antiquity and had a 'golden age', but subsequently had stagnated and its artistic work declined as the 'pristine purities' of its early Vedic and Buddhist faith had become contaminated by the idolatry of medieval Hindus.[109] Moreover, the canon was based on the separation of Indian and European on the premise that the former was inferior as well as on the primacy of religion and race as the markers of identity of the former.[110] In the case of Orissa, the role played by Prinsep, Kittoe, Fergusson, Cunningham, Beglar, Beams and other Europeans led to the addition and refinement of information and conceptualization regarding the Orissan cultural heritage, as antiquarian dilettantes gave way to systematic analysis. However, as Tartakov points out, 'the entire British Indological experience – no matter how careful – carried within it the need to demonstrate the failure of the civilisation it was dedicated to explaining'.[111]

The late nineteenth century and the turn of twentieth witnessed the first serious challenge to the pre-eminence of the Orientalist canon from the 'modernist sensibility and, with it the waning belief in Europe's invariable superiority' and from the rise of Indian nationalism.[112] Nationalist Indian historians argued that they did not require the 'civilizing mission' of the colonial rule with its 'virtues' of democracy and science, since India was a great civilization much older than the British. India had in fact 'colonized' South-East Asia many centuries ago. In terms of art history and archaeology they emphasized that most of the important aspects of the Indian cultural heritage were not a result of borrowing from the Greco-Roman world. Guha-Thakurta[113] argued that the claim for an Indian 'national' art was made by insisting that India possessed a 'spiritual essence' that had shaped its art since antiquity. She states, however, that European orientalist knowledge of India determined the main thrust of nationalist, anti-colonial art. The claim that India was somehow uniquely 'spiritual' was accepted by Europeans since it involved no challenge to their pretension to superiority in the contemporary world of politics and authority.[114] Thus nationalist art and archaeology remained suffused with the assumption of Orientalism. The description of antiquities as 'ruins' had a disempowering effect.[115] In the case of Orissa, R. L. Mitra studied the *Antiquities of Orissa* in terms of the growth of cultural heritage at a regional level emphasizing their indigenous nature. Moreover, M. M. Ganguly interpreted the construction of the Udayagiri column in terms of the proportions laid out in *Manasara*; and Nirmal Bose highlighted the *Silpasastra* and *Bhubanapradipa* as important guides for Orissan architects.

For the post-colonial period, Asher and Metcalf speak of three different strategies by which, they said, Indian people have come to terms with their 'inherited colonial landscape'. The first is the construction of an artificial past embodying a nostalgia for 'the world we have lost'; the second is a process of appropriation and assimilation (most visibly represented in post-1947 New Delhi); and the third is a wholesale repudiation of the colonial past on the part of a newly grown elite committed to a modernized India. In the post-colonial cultural scene of Orissa, there has been a resurgence of the Odisi dance, now accepted as a classical form. Dance and cultural festivals organized at Konarak and Puri attract, among other things, tourism. From the standpoint of architecture, the construction of the new capital at Bhubaneswar has been regarded as a combination of tradition and modernity. With this general background, let us now analyse some specific issues in Orissan archaeology during the colonial and post-colonial periods.

Archaeology and Politics

The much publicised issue of the Ramjanmabhumi-Babri Masjid presents the impression that the politicization of archaeology in India is a late twentieth century phenomenon. However, it has been argued that the practice of archaeology during the colonial period had also political implications[116] and that the nature of relationship between archaeology and politics has undergone changes since then.[117] A good example of politicization during the colonial period is the debate between James Fergusson and R. L. Mitra on the issue of the earliest stone architecture in India. Fergusson had argued that since there was no evidence prior to the Asokan pillar in its developed form, the Indians learnt the art of the earliest stone architecture from the Greeks. Mitra argued that there was no proof whatever to show that the Indo-Aryans did not know stone architecture and none, likewise, of their having learnt the art from the Greeks. As to the origin of stone architecture he said, 'it appears perfectly self evolved, self contained and independent of all extraneous admixture'.[118] Elaborating the point subsequently, M. M. Ganguly stated that Burgess conceded that before Alexander's invasion Indians knew the use of stone for bridges, foundations, etc. This would have led them to use it as a building material. Ganguly further mentioned that the Greek columns were invariably cylindrical where as the Indo-Aryan type might be circular, square, pentagonal, hexagonal, octagonal or even sixteen-sided. There are different technical terms to be found in the *Manasara*.[119] Incidentally, the recently excavated Harappan site of Dholavira has shown the use of stone pillars in a much earlier period. In a different vein, Ganguly stated that the 'ulterior object in discovering gradual growth, or the process of evolution in the caves at Udayagiri is to place the elaborately carved ones at a comparatively recent period, and to prove conveniently that they are the products of extraneous influence, and that stone architecture proper was introduced by the Greeks'.[120]

Fergusson was so annoyed with Mitra that he wrote a small book in 1884 *Archaeology in India with Special Reference to the Works of Babu Rajendralal Mitra*.[121] The major limitation of Mitra regarding Orissan antiquities according to Fergusson was that there was 'no attempt to arrange the temples in any order, either chronologically or even as to form'.[122] Mitra, according to Fergusson, had 'no knowledge of architectural draftsmanship, surveying or plan drawing even to a limited degree'.[123] Reacting to Mitra's criticism, Fergusson stated, 'at the time I attached very little importance to the suggestion (that the Indians had taken a hint from the stone-using Greeks) and am inclined to attach still less to it now'.[124]

. . . one of the great charms of the study of Indian architecture is that we find a completely developed style of wooden architecture such as we have nowhere else, and can trace its conversion into lithic forms, till at last we lose all traces of its wooden origin. Though changing the material, as I said long ago, it remained throughout 'a purely indigenous art, without any trace of Egyptian or classical art', 'nor can it be affirmed that it borrowed anything directly from Babylonia or Assyria'. As I have already mentioned, there is nowhere in architectural history any example where we can find a style so thoroughly local and original and where we can trace every step from the earliest 'incunabula' to its decay and final absorption into other styles. Nor do I know any style that was so little influenced or so little interfered with any foreign architectural influence.[125]

Accusing Mitra of distorting his view, Fergusson stated, 'his (Mitra's) patriotic soul was fired with uncontrolled indignation at the bare idea of his countrymen having taken a hint from foreigners, or borrowed a single idea from such a people as the Greeks'.[126] Significantly, he made a link:

The real interest, however, of the volume – if any – will probably be found to reside, not in the analysis of archaeological works of Babu Rajendralal Mitra, but, in these days of discussion on Ilbert Bills, in the question as to whether the natives of India are to be treated as equal to Europeans in all respects. Under present circumstances it can not fail to interest many to dissect the writings of one of the most important members of the native community, that we may lay bare and understand his motives and mode of action, and thus ascertain how far Europeans were justified in refusing to submit to the jurisdiction of natives in criminal actions[127]. . . it is easy to understand why Europeans resident in the country, and knowing the character of the people among whom they are living, should have shrunk instinctively, with purely patriotic motives, from the fatuity of the Ilbert Bill. It may, however, be useful to those who reside at a distance, and who have no local experience, to have it explained to him by a striking living example, wherein the strength and weakness of the cause resides, and for that purpose I do not know any example that can be more appropriate than that of Babu Rajendralal Mitra. If, after reading the following pages, any European feels that he would like to be subjected to his jurisdiction, in criminal cases, he must have a courage possessed by few; or if he thinks he could depend on his knowledge, or impartiality to do him justice, as he could on one of his own countrymen, he must be strangely constituted in mind, body and estate.[128]

There can be no better example of colonial arrogance. Sometime

Fergusson's language was patronising or even condescending: 'Left to themselves, the natives of India possess many virtues and many noble qualities which render them worthy of the esteem and admiration of all who have had familiar intercourse with them; but these have rarely, if ever, been enhanced or improved by contact with European civilisation. . .'.[129] Moreover, 'so little do we understand the nature of the people we have undertaken to govern, that we petted and pampered the Sepoys till they thought they were our equals, and that we were afraid of them. . . . The present sentimental attempt to place "Young Bengal" on an equality with ourselves, may not have so prompt and decisive an answer, but it must lead to one more fatal to our moral influence and probably more disastrous to the good government of the country'.[130]

A reading of Fergusson shows that his appreciation of Indian architecture in antiquity is masked by his condescending and arrogant attitude. A small stir on the part of R. L. Mitra resulted in the oozing of colonial arrogance when condescension about contemporary colonial India got the better of an appreciation of its 'sublime' architectural heritage. This dichotomy remains a hallmark of Oriental scholarship in colonial India.[131]

Dream of Domination: Colonized as Colonizer

From the historiographic point of view, it is indeed interesting to note that R. L. Mitra represents a good example of a 'colonized' individual behaving as a 'colonizer'. This becomes all the more apparent when one compares the diametrically opposite attitude he nourished towards Orissan antiquities, on the one hand and the contemporary language, on the other. Mitra considered that Orissa represented a pristinely traditional Indian civilization cordoned off by mountains and the Bay of Bengal and hence subjected to 'restricted Muslim onslaught'. The ancient monuments of Orissa were thereby 'more authentic than many other parts of India'. At the same time Mitra had the 'Bengali contempt for contemporary Oriya culture and language'.[132] Between 1860 and 1880 there was an intense debate as to whether Oriya was a separate language or not. While Bengalis like Kantichandra Bhattacharya and R. L. Mitra argued that it was not a separate language (the latter even considering Bengali, Oriya and

Assamese actual as one language) and that Oriya language should be abolished from the school curricula, some other enlightened Bengalis like Gourisankar Ray (editor of the *Utkala Dipika*) and R. L. Banerjea, as well as British civil servant John Beams supported the cause of Oriya language and literature. There was a debate between Natabara Samantaray and Gaganendranath Dash – two reputed historians of Oriya language and literature in post-colonial Orissa – over the role of R. L. Mitra.[133] Samantaray tried to exonerate Mitra by stating that the latter (a) did not have any adequate knowledge of the heritage of Oriya literature; (b) laid emphasis on higher education rather than mass education; and (c) desired a pan-Indian unity. On the other hand Dash, citing a number of instances, argued that there was less likelihood of R. L. Mitra being ignorant of the richness of Oriya language and literature. Dash emphasized instead that Mitra was an important text book writer in Bengali and hence his disparaging remarks about Oriya language might have been in no small measure due to his potential benefit as a Bengali text book writer in the event of the introduction of Bengali as a medium of instruction in Orissan schools.

The Appropriation of Jagannath for Political Legitimation

Although the study of the Jagannath cult in Orissan cultural history has been emphasized mostly in the post-colonial period,[134] it is interesting to note that it was R. D. Banerji, writing during the colonial period, who for the first time argued that the Eastern Gangas in medieval times had made active propaganda about Jagannath Puri so that they could be more acceptable as rulers. Thus Banerji pointed out that Puri was originally a local holy place, a shrine of Orissan aboriginals where worship was taken over by the Eastern Gangas. He also stated that the sanctity of Puri is due entirely to very active propaganda which seemed to have begun with the conquest of northern Orissa by the Eastern Gangas.[135] In this context, the shifting of the *Arunastambha* from Konarak to Puri and its erection in front of the Puri Jagannath temple by the Marathas in the eighteenth century – it still stands there now – may in my opinion have been due at least partly to the Maratha desire to show their power over Orissa after they defeated the Orissan king. Because of the importance of the deity Jagannath in Orissan culture, the Marathas might have thought that people visiting the Jagannath temple at Puri would not fail to notice the *Arunastambha* and to be reminded of the Maratha dominance of Orissa.

The use of Jagannath and his temple for political ends has not ceased in the post-colonial period.[136] For example, in the recent past, J. B. Pattnaik, a former Chief Minister, was fond of presenting himself as an humble devotee of Jagannath; the late Biju Pattanaik, another former Chief Minister, had claimed a special relationship with *Kalia* (Jagannath in popular parlance) and found in him a staunch ally for the regeneration of Kalinga. The BJP-VHP-RSS combine on the other hand has sought to counter this by laying particular emphasis on the identity of Jagannath as a Hindu deity so that in their scheme of things Oriya nationalist aspirations may be superseded by a communalist, essentially anti-Muslim, interpretation of Orissa's past.[137] Thus there has emerged a struggle for the monopoly of cultural symbols. In its attempt to stem the tide of aggressive Hindutva, the Biju Pattanaik-led government (1990-5) had even sought to articulate Oriya nationalism by sponsoring the *Bali Yatra* – the voyage to Indonesia – as part of a programme to revive the memories of the glorious maritime tradition of Orissa. The then government's decision to write to the Centre for an annual grant to the Gajapati King of Orissa might be regarded, Nayak and Mishra think, as an attempt to prevent the BJP from hijacking this symbol of Oriya identity.

Archaeology in the Vernacular

The most neglected issue in the history of Indian archaeology is, in my opinion, the study of archaeological writing in the regional languages during the colonial period – this when no other country dominated by a single colonial power had history (or archaeology) written in so many languages. Such vernacular writings took different forms – (i) the translation of important English history books (ii) the writing of Indian history and (iii) regional histories in various languages. Broadly, they seem to have countered colonial historiography and asserted regional identities. In the case of Orissa one has to analyse the works of Pyarimohan Acharya, Krupasindhu Mishra, Jagabandhu Singh, and Sitanath Ray in this perspective.

The Emergence of Complex Society

The reconstruction of the emergence of complex society in a region is an important avenue of archaeological research. In the case of Orissa, one may say that palaeolithic subsistence in Orissa was characterized by hunting and gathering, with the band level of socio-political organization. The cultures of foragers such as the Kharia, Birhor, and Ujjia-Sabara in Mayurbhanj district,[138] and the Malhars around Tikarpada on the middle Mahanadi valley, may hold an important clue to the understanding of the subsistence modes of the old stone age. Although agriculture might have developed during the neolithic period, the chalcolithic period would have consolidated the process of village farming communities. The evidence of human teeth from Sankerjang showing the consumption of food rich in carbohydrates could imply heavy dependence on agriculture by the chalcolithic population. The animal remains from Gopalpur represent two domestic animals (cattle and buffalo) and four wild species (nilgai, chital, wild pig, and rhinoceros).[139] The Orissan chalcolithic is also associated with specialization in arts and crafts. Different kinds of potteries meant the existence of potters. The repertoire of a wide range of bone artefacts at Golabai implied a skilled group of bone tool makers. Copper bangles, rings, fishhooks, etc., meant the existence of coppersmiths. The recovery of various kinds of beads would imply either evidence of local bead making or evidence of trade with other localities. Since copper is available in Mayurbhanj and on the Chhotanagpur plateau, there must have been an exchange network between the copper source areas of Mayurbhanj and Chhotanagpur and settlements in central and coastal Orissa. All these factors imply an emerging complexity in the social and political organization of protohistoric Orissa; the institution of the chiefdom might have emerged as a mechanism for effective maintenance and management of such social complexity. However, there is scanty archaeological evidence for chiefdoms in proto-historic Orissa. At Golabai, out of the thirteen circular huts with postholes and hearths, the biggest hut might be regarded as belonging to the chief. Since copper artefacts are limited in number, their occurrence in the gravegoods from Golabai and Sankerjang may be interpreted as belonging to the chief or members of his family. In the absence of adequate data on the iron age of Orissa, it may suffice to infer that the trends of the chalcolithic period might have continued in the iron age.

The emergence of urbanization and the state may be regarded as an extension of the processes of the earlier period. The early historic fortified settlements at Sisupalgarh, Jaugada, Radhanagar, Asurgarh, and Viratgarh near Khiching speak not only of expansion of the size of the settlements, but also of the emergence of urbanism, with its concomitant features. While Sisupalgarh, Jaugada and Radhanagar are in the coastal area, Asurgarh and Viratgarh are in the upland plains. The first three sites had the advantages of a location in the fertile soil of the alluvial zone, with its riverine network and easy access to other coastal areas such as the Coramandel coast, as well as Sri Lanka and South-East Asia. The typological similarity in iron assemblages of Kharligarh-Gudavella and Manmunda (western Orissa) with that of Sisupalgarh and Jaugada, besides, implies contact between western and coastal Orissa. Thus the coastal urban centres were connected to central and western Orissa basically through the Mahanadi and the Rushikulya and northern Orissa (Mayurbhanj and Keonjhar) over a land route. Apart from being associated with an agricultural base, an important aspect of the upland urban centres was their association with the mineral resources. Western Orissa is rich in semi-precious stones and hence urbanization in western Orissa, including at Asurgarh, has to be understood in terms of the role of these as also forest products. So also, urbanization in northern Orissa near Khiching has to be correlated with the rich iron ore deposits of Mayurbhanj and Keonjhar along with forest resources. The recovery of punch-marked coins and Knobbed Ware at various sites of Orissa, and occupational specialization in crafts as indicated by the pottery, beads, metal artefacts, coins, etc. imply that a suitable social milieu was created for trade and exchange. The recovery of Rouletted Ware in various sites of Orissa and on the Coramandel coast would mean that Orissa was participating in the Bay of Bengal trade network. Palur, Manikapatana and Tamralipti were important ports for voyages to Sri Lanka and South-East Asia. Thus society and economy in early historic Orissa were becoming more and more complex. Reviewing the settlement history, U. Mishra[140] stated that whereas upto the first century AD the main concentration of settlements was in Puri-Ganjam and further south in Srikakulam district, with Bhubaneswar as the nucleus area, thereafter there was an expansion of settlement to the north into the coastal districts of Cuttack and Balasore.

It may not be out of place to mention here briefly three early historic sites – Ghumal in Mayurbhanj, Telkoi in Keonjhar and Korkora in Cuttack district – discovered by our group. All three are rural sites. However, because of their strategic location they were playing an important role in trade or showed an interrelationship between the urban and rural sectors. The latter dimension has not been adequately emphasized in Orissan archaeology. The locational advantage of Ghumal, where punch-marked coins of the imperial or universal type have been found, seems obvious. It is situated on the bank of the river Kharkai which flows through the iron ore area of Sulaipat. Second, two important tributaries of the Kharkai – the Kanu flowing beside Badampahar iron ore area and the Kandria coming from Gorumahisani iron ore area – merge with the Kharkai upstream, not very far from Ghumal. Third, a number of traditional iron smelting sites have been discovered in this region. Ghumal is thus located in a strategic place for the collection and trade of the iron and iron ore of Mayurbhanj and other forest products from the interior of the Similipal hills. The river Kharkai is a major tributary of the river Subarnarekha which is one of the major rivers of Chhotanagpur. The role of iron from the Chhotanagpur region as an important factor in the rise and growth of the Magadhan Empire has been emphasized by historians. The recovery of yet another hoard of imperial punch-marked coins from Ghumal is a pointer to an active trade network between the iron ore rich zone of Mayurbhanj on the one hand, and that of Magadha on the other.

As regards Telkoi, this early historic site is located on the bank of the river Samakoi, a tributary of the Brahmani. It has yielded iron slags, iron artefacts, red ware, etc. It is important that Telkoi lies on the southern fringe of the iron rich zone of Keonjhar district, northern Orissa. Although iron artefacts have been found at early historic sites of coastal Orissa, this is one of the few early historic sites within the iron ore rich zone of Orissa discovered to date. Another site reported from Keonjhar is Sitabhinji,[141] dating to about the fourth-sixth centuries on epigraphic grounds. Korkora, lying on the right bank of the river Debi in the Mahanadi delta, is situated between two important fortified urban settlements – Sisupalgarh and Radhanagar. It has yielded red ware, bricks, terracotta ear ornaments, pendants, etc. These are comparable with the late period of Sisupalgarh.

The issue of early state formation may now be discussed. An important problem is the definition of state. According to Service, the state is characterized by the existence of civil law and formal government that are 'institutionalized, enacted, official' and which 'employ, threaten, or imply the actual use of force'; hence Service visualized force and the power of authority as the essential ingredients of the state.[142] For Fried, social stratification is fundamental to the concept of state; this is based on differential access to basic productive necessities.[143] Fried also made an important distinction between pristine and secondary states.[144] According to him, pristine states emerged from indigenous stimuli, usually with no more advanced models present, while secondary states had the model of already existing states and had their origins because of the pressures from such pristine states. Claessen and Skalnik define the early state as a centralised socio-political organization for the regulation of social relations in a complex, stratified society divided into at least two basic strata, or emergent social classes, viz., the rulers and the ruled.[145] They also speak of three types of early state – the inchoate, typical and the transitional – on the basis of development of trade and markets, mode of succession to important functions, the evidence of the extent of private ownership of land, method of remuneration of functionaries and the degree of development of judicial and taxation system. Thus the origins of the state may be traced to various factors – population pressure, geographical location and circumscription, long distance trade, technological change, control over irrigation network, social stratification, conflict, war and conquest, defence against aggression.[146]

The issue of urbanization and early state formation in India has received much attention of scholars.[147] For example, Romila Thapar[148] did not accept ancient empires as uniform and highly centralized political structures. Rather she suggested that the nature of early empires could be understood best in terms of the relation between the 'metropolitan state' and the peripheral territories. Following Thapar, Seneviratne[149] argued that the process from chiefdom to state formation in Kalinga resulted when autochthonous forces combined with the consequences resulting from a period of political subordination to the metropolitan state of the Mauryas. This process rapidly accomplished the task of transforming the 'rank' society of the pre-state chiefdom into a 'stratified' class society, with the consolidation of the ruling classes and their gaining direct access to the surplus product and its distribution. The accumulation of power of pre-state social elites during the period of metropolitan state hegemony resulted in the legitimation of their political status.

Sahu[150] has pointed out that early Kalinga has been loosely woven into Seneviratne's account, his major thrust being Andhra. Emphasizing the dynamics of the internal transformation of tribal society in ancient Orissa, Sahu begins his discussion with the Kalinga war (261 BC), in the absence, in his opinion, of the existence of a well-defined neolithic or chalcolithic culture. For Kalinga under the Mauryan rule, little is known about the administrative structure. However, the excavation of early historic sites, especially Sisupalgarh, showed the emergence of urbanization, specialization of arts and crafts, and the partial monetization of the economy during the later centuries BC. It is with Kharavela that the institution of kingship emerged during the first century BC along with social stratification. During this time southern and western Orissa was at best at the level of chiefdoms or in a state of proto-state formation. The next stage in Orissa, about from AD 350 to 600, witnessed the emergence of private ownership in land, the subordination of the peasantry, and the rise of a number of dynasties or petty kingdoms in different pockets of Orissa, each dynasty bestowing land grants on brahmanas and religious establishments. Moreover, the association of the state with religion in Orissa may be traced back to Kharavela, but in the post-350 period this association became intense and widespread. In order to gain legitimacy for their political authority, the ruling dynasties made use of autochthonous tribal deities and other religions.

Kulke[151] discussed the issue of state formation at a sub-regional level for the period roughly between AD 500 and 1000. He used Burton Stein's concept of 'nuclear areas' which were politically fundamentally independent, economically autonomous units and socially and culturally centres of Hindu civilization. These 'nuclear areas' in Orissa, Kulke argued, were centres of the integration of tribal elements rather than their 'sustained displacement', as Burton Stein showed in the case of south India. Thence the early Hindu kingdom in Orissa at a sub-regional level has been deeply influenced by tribal culture. Thus, the emergence of a regional kingdom and the incorporation of different geographical units were achieved by a policy of cult appropriation, the construction of temples, and the expansion of brahmanical settlements. Kulke also stated that in Orissa, the riverine tracts constituted important nuclear areas of sub-regional power in the early phase of state formation; in the later period some of these areas became the bases of regional kingdoms.[152]

On the basis of a thorough study of Orissan inscriptions, Upinder Singh[153] argued that the period AD 300 to 1147 was one of intensive state formation and political development, in which royal grants played an important integrative role. Singh further argued that it was the gift of land to the brahmanas, not the royally-endowed temple establishment, that was a major basis of royal legitimation and political integration. As regards the rise of the earliest indigenous kingdoms of Orissa, she considered this to be the consequence of internal developments on the political, economic and social fronts, as well as the impetus of several phases of rule under metropolitan states – the Maurya, Kushana, and Gupta. According to Singh, while there is evidence of secondary state formation in Orissa in the early centuries of the Christian era (the kingdoms of Kharavela and Maharaja Gana), state formation in the post-fourth century period was more intense and sustained. On the basis of the available epigraphic evidence it is difficult, Singh felt, to reconstruct the details of the processes of internal change which made possible the transition to statehood and the political integration of kingdoms. However, epigraphic evidence suggests that royal grants to brahmanas, which were an important component of royal policy throughout the period from AD 300 to 1147, played a major role. Singh argued that the emergence and stabilization of state structure was a complex process based on a variety of factors operating at different levels that could be broadly characterized as cultural.

From an anthropological standpoint, Mahapatra[154] showed the interrelation between gods, kings and the caste system in Orissa, and argued that the state deity and his cult were used for political purposes to achieve the subjugation and integration of vassal princedoms in an empire.

For state formation in medieval and early modern Orissa Berkemer[155] has used the model of the 'little kingdom'. The 'little kings' were, in Berkemer's terminology, rulers who, while accepting the domination of another ruler, in their turn dominated other rulers. Berkemer investigated not only the historical development of the system, but also the methods by which legitimization was obtained as well as the ways in which forces drawing their strength from the system interacted with forces bound to a more centralized authority.

Raymond Allchin[156] has discussed the issue of urbanization and state formation in early historic South Asia as a whole. According to him, although it is tempting to adopt such terms as 'primary' and 'secondary' to distinguish between the first cities and those which followed, these have been used with widely divergent meanings and without much precision. Moreover, they do not adequately convey the important differences in the way cities came into being. Hence he avoided the terms pristine/primary and secondary and discussed three models, indigenous or independent development, city colonization as a factor, and imperial or political expansion as a factor. Referring to 'a most exciting kind' of urbanization in Sisupalgarh, Allchin pointed out that it is a product of the pre-Mauryan Gangetic colonization, since the pre-Mauryan presence is known from the Udayagiri inscription of Kharavela referring to a water channel in the city, constructed by a Nanda king. Allchin also opined that Sisupalgarh appears to be a pre-Mauryan foundation. During the Mauryan period, it must have become a provincial city and later the capital of the Chedi king, Kharavela.

Allchin's scheme is interesting, but at one point he is not sure whether the reference to the construction of a water channel by a Nanda *raja* should be regarded 'as a case of pre-Mauryan Magadhan imperial expansion, or as a part of colonizing episode originating in the Gangetic Valley'.[157] Moreover, his stress on the colonizing factor appears to emphasize external forces over indigenous development. But it is important to note that while discussing the model, Allchin says, 'It is obviously relevant to consider whether a city arose wholly, or partly, as a result of colonial activity, and whether it involved taking over an existing process of indigenous development, at whatever point it had reached'.[158]

An overview of the cultural processes of the Orissan protohistoric period would imply that urbanization was not wholly because of colonial activity. The expansion of the resource base, in terms of agriculture and metals, with the implication of trade and exchange between the metal source zone and protohistoric settlements, does provide a good context for the emergence of cities. In this scenario, contact with the extraneous forces might have served as a crystallizing factor.

The early historic Kalinga and its capital city as which Sisupalgarh is identified are dealt with in a recent book by Martin Brandtner. He shows how the reputation of the country and its inhabitants in Indian and European classical literature and in inscriptions improves continuously from early despised barbarians in the far east of India to noble Aryans at the end of the period examined, and he sees Sisupalgarh as a kind of indicator for that development. According to his view, already its early foundation, long before the coming of the Nandas or Mauryas, precludes an external stimulus for the beginnings of urban development – although the town-planning and the layout of the defences are obviously influenced by the *Kautilya Arthashastra*. The growing economic prosperity of Kalinga, based on its natural resources and on its internal and external trade, became visible both in its early historic urban settlements, some of them, like Sisupalgarh, elaborately fortified, as well as in the inclusion of the former *mlecchas* into the Aryan fold.[159]

GLOBALIZATION AND ORISSAN ARCHAEOLOGY IN THE PRESENT CENTURY

Whether one likes it or not, the inexorable forces of the market have already made deep inroads in India, and it is vital to discuss the possible consequences for theory and practice of archaeology in Orissa. Some scholars assume that globalization in the economy would result in the increasing homogenization of cultures, so that it will be easy to sell the products of the multinational corporations. Others propose that global capitalism lives and thrives on difference, and hence the future will see more of reconstruction of cultural difference. In the field of cultural studies, there might be increasing concern for cultural identity. In this scenario the politicians are put in a paradoxical situation. On the one hand they welcome, irrespective of parties (with the exception of a few), globalization in the hope of potential multinational investment; on the other hand, they know that mere talk of globalization will not win them votes in the face of the loss of jobs in various sectors. Therefore they sometimes fall back on the cultural heritage for political mileage. Hence, it might be more than a mere coincidence that Orissa is not only the first state in India to go for privatization of the electricity sector, but also the first to set up a University of Culture where archaeology is being taught. Moreover, the setting up of a new Department of Ancient Indian History, Culture and Archaeology at Utkal University, the opening of a new gallery of martial arts in the State Museum, Biju Pattanaik's 'intimate relationship with Kalia (Jagannatha)' as well his celebration of the Bali Yatra on a grand scale and J. B. Pattnaik's declaration of the Year of Kharavela, just before he stepped down as Chief Minister of Orissa in 1999, are not isolated events. It will be reductionist if one would say that the cultural responses of globalization would be same everywhere in the Third World. But they constitute a vital point of departure for culture studies in the Third World.

ACKNOWLEDGEMENTS

I convey my sincere thanks to Himanshu Mohapatra and N. James for various help in the preparation of this paper.

NOTES

1. R. McGuire, 1992, *A Marxist Archaeology*, San Diego, p. 251.
2. P. Gathercole, 1990, 'Introduction', in P. Gathercole and D. Lowenthal (eds.), *The Politics of the Past*, London, pp. 3-4.
3. G. Daniel (ed.), 1981, *Towards a History of Archaeology*, London, p. 10.
4. D. K. Chakrabrati, 1988, *A History of Indian Archaeology from the Beginning to 1947*, New Delhi.
5. P. Acharya, 1969, *Odisara Pratnatattva o Anyanya Prabandha* (in Oriya); K. K. Basa, 1994, *Problems and Perspectives in Archaeology of Orissa*, Occasional Paper 4, DSA Dept. of Anthropology, Utkal Univ.; *id*., 2000, 'History of Archaeology in Orissa', in K. K. Basa and P. Mohanty (eds.), *Archaeology of Orissa*, Vol. 1, Delhi, pp. 16-61.
6. S. Digby and J. C. Harle, 1985, 'When did the Sun Temple fall down?', *South Asian Studies* 1, p. 1.
7. H. S. Jarrett and H. N. Sarkar, 1949, *Ain-i-Akbari of Abul Fazl-i-Allami*, Vol. II, Calcutta, p. 138.

8. A. Stirling, 1825, 'An account, geographical, statistical and historical of Orissa proper or Cuttack', *Asiatic Researches* 15, pp. 163-338.
9. Chakrabarti, 1988, *op. cit.*, p. 26.
10. Stirling, 1825, *op. cit.,* p. 308.
11. *Ibid.*, p. 315.
12. *Ibid.*, p. 326.
13. J. Prinsep, 1837, 'Note on Inscriptions of Udayagiri and Khandagiri in Cuttack, in the lat Character', *Journal of the Asiatic Society of Bengal* 6, p. 1084.
14. 1838, 'Examination of the Separate Edicts of the Aswastama Inscription at Dhauli in Cuttack', *ibid.* 7, pp. 434-56.
15. M. Kittoe, 1838, 'Ruins and pillars at Jajpur', *ibid.* 7, pp. 53-6.
16. J. Fergusson, 1893, *A History of Architecture of All Countries* (3rd edn.), London.
17. *Id.*, 1876, *History of Indian and Eastern Architecture* (2 vols.), London. While the first edition of this work (as well as *id.*, 1884. *Archaeology in India, With Especial Reference to the Works of Babu Rajendralala Mitra*, London, particularly pp. 60-75 contains a rather strange and with regards to most of the monuments outdated account of their chronology based on irrational ideas about the 'evolution' of Indian architecture (see also below), the second, posthumous, edition (London, 1910) was revised by J. Burgess and is closer to present days views.
18. W. W. Hunter, 1872, *Orissa,* Vol. 1, London.
19. R. L. Mitra, *Antiquities of Orissa,* Vol. 1 (1875), Vol. 2 (1880), Calcutta.
20. J. D. Beglar, 1882, *Report of Tours in the Southeastern Provinces in 1874-75 and 1875-76*, Archaeological Survey of India Report, Vol. 13.
21. N. N. Vasu, 1911, *Archaeological Survey of Mayurbhanja*, Mayurbhanja State.
22. M. M. Ganguly, 1912, *Orissa and Her Remains*: *Ancient and Medieval*, Calcutta.
23. R. P. Chanda, 1929, *Bhanja Dynasty of Mayurbhanj and Their Ancient Capital Khiching*, Mayurbhanj Archeological Dept.
24. R. D. Banerji, *History of Orissa,* Vol. 1 (1930), Vol. 2 (1931), Calcutta.
25. Nirmal K. Bose, 1932, *Canons of Orissan Architecture*, Calcutta.
26. Stella Kramrisch, 1947, 'The walls of Orissan temples', *Journal of the Indian Society of Oriental Art* 15 (Part 1), pp. 178-96.
27. John Beams, 1871, 'The ruins at Kopari, Balasore district,' *Journal of the Asiatic Society of Bengal,* 1871, Part I (3), pp. 247-50.
28. C. S. Banurji, 1870, 'Notes on the antiquities of the Nalti, the Assia, and the Mahabinayaka hills of Cuttack', *Journal of the Asiatic Society of Bengal* 39 (Part I), pp. 158-71.
29. *Id.*, 1871, 'An account of the antiquities of Jajpur in Orissa', *Journal of the Asiatic Society of Bengal* 40, pp. 151-9.

30. John Beams, 1872, 'The jungle forts of northern Orissa', *Indian Antiquary* 1, pp. 33-6, 74-6.
31. For numismatic studies in Orissa, see S. Tripathy, 1986, *Early and Medieval Coins and Currency System of Orissa*, Calcutta.
32. V. Ball, 1876, 'On stone implements found in the tributary states of Orissa', *Proceedings of the Asiatic Society of Bengal*, 1876, pp. 120-1; 1880, *Jungle Life in India*, London.
33. N. K. Bose and D. Sen, 1948, *Excavation in Mayurbhanj*, Calcutta.
34. K. K. Basa and P. Mohanty (eds.), 2000, *Archaeology of Orissa* (2 vols.), Delhi.
35. G. C. Mohapatra, 1962, *Stone Age Cultures of Orissa*, Pune.
36. K. C. Tripathy, 1980, *Lithic Industries in India: A Study of South Western Orissa*, New Delhi.
37. S. C. Nanda, 2000, 'The Upper Palaeolithic and Mesolithic Cultures of the Indravati Valley, South Orissa', in Basa and Mohanty (eds.), *op. cit.*, pp. 153-72.
38. P. K. Singh, 2000, 'Stone Age Cultures of Central Orissa', in Basa and Mohanty (eds.), *op. cit.*, pp. 102-13
39. S. B. Ota, 1986, 'Mesolithic culture of Phulbani district (Orissa) with special reference to the heavy tool component', *Bulletin of the Deccan College* 45, pp. 47-56.
40. P. Mohanty, 1993, 'Mesolithic hunter gatherers of Keonjhar, Orissa', *Asian Perspectives* 32 (1), pp. 87-104.
41. P. Behera, 2000, 'Neolithic culture complex of Bonaigarh, Orissa' in Basa and Mohanty (eds.), *op. cit.*, pp. 222-63.
42. R. Ray, 'Some observations on the prehistoric sites in the vicinity of Pallahara township', in N. K. Behura and K. C. Tripathy (eds.), *Frontiers of Biocultural Anthropology*, Bhubaneswar.
43. S. N. Ratha and D. K. Bhattacharya, 1988, 'Lower Palaeolithic from Kuchinda (Orissa)', *Man and Environment* 12, pp. 23-8.
44. H. C. Sharma, 1994, 'Palaeolithic finds from Burla', *Man and Environment* 19, pp. 285-90; P. K. Behera, P. Panda and N. Thakur, 1996, 'Techno-typological analysis of lithic artefacts from the Dari-Dungri Acheulian site, Sambalpur district, Orissa', *Man and Environment* 21 (2), pp. 15-26; K. K. Basa and B. K. Mohanta, 1999, 'Stone age cultures around Burla, western Orissa', *Orissa Historical Research Journal* XLIII (Nos. 1-4), pp. 13-26.
45. K. K. Basa and D. Sahoo, 2000, 'Mesolithic culture around Duburi-Tamka region in Orissa', *Man in India* 80 (1-2), pp. 121-40; D. Sahoo, 2000, 'Prehistory of Darpankhas (District Jajpur), Coastal Orissa', in Basa and Mohanty (eds.), *op. cit.*, pp. 173-200.
46. R. N. Dash, 1987, 'Neoliths of Orissa', unpublished Ph.D. thesis, Utkal Univ.; 'The Neolithic Culture of Orissa: A Typo-Technological Analysis' in Basa and Mohanty (eds.), *op. cit.*, pp. 201-21.

47. P. K. Behera, 1991-2, 'Prehistoric rock art pertaining to fertility cult and other subjects of Orissa', *Pragdhara* 2, pp. 7-17; S. Pradhan, 2000, 'Rock Art of Orissa', in Basa and Mohanty (eds.), *op. cit.*, pp. 635-50; 2002, *Rock Art of Orissa*, Delhi.
48. G. C. Mohapatra, 1962, *op. cit.*; *Indian Archaeology: A Review, 1961-62*, p. 36; A. K. Ghosh and A. N. Basu, 1969, An appraisal on the Palaeolithic industries of Mayurbhanj in the light of recent discovery', *Science and Culture* 39, pp. 476-9; A. K. Ghosh, 1970, 'An analysis of Mayurbhanj palaeolithic industry', *Journal of the Indian Anthropological Society* 5, pp. 233-48; K. K. Basa, 1984, 'Palaeohistory of Mayurbhanj: A Review', unpublished M.A. dissertation, Anthropology Deptt., Utkal University; D. K. Chakrabarti and R. K. Chattopadhyay, 1988, 'A note on the lithic industries of Mayurbhanj and Keonjhar, Orissa', *Man and Environment* 12, pp. 203-8; S. Chakrabarti, 1990, 'The stone age prehistory of Khiching, Orissa', *Man and Environment* 15, pp. 13-21; S. K. Mishra, 1987-8, 'Stone age antiquities of Jashipur, Orissa: a resurvey', *Man in Society* 3, pp. 81-8; P. Mohanty, K. K. Basa and B. Tripathy, 1997, 'Stone age cultures of Mayurbhanj District, Orissa', *Man in India* 77 (2), pp. 159-77; P. K. Mishra, 1998, *Archaeology of Mayurbhanj*, New Delhi; D. Sahoo, B. K. Mohanta and T. K. Das, 1998-9, 'Mesolithic culture of Gambharia, northern Orissa', *Man in Society* 12, pp. 74-82; S. Chakrabarti, 2000, 'Recent Advances in Prehistory of Mayurbhanj', in Basa and Mohanty (eds.), *op. cit.*, pp. 77-101; A. Datta, 2000, 'The context and definition of upper Palaeolithic industries in Panchpir, Orissa, India', *Proceedings of the Prehistoric Society* 66, pp. 47-59; B. K. Mohanta, 2000, 'Archaeology of Bamanghaty, Mayurbhanj, Orissa', *The Orissa Historical Research Journal*, Vol. XLV, pp. 87-99.
49. K. C. Tripathy, 1973, 'South Orissan prehistory – the first record of stone age tools', *Asian Perspectives* 4, pp. 47-59; B. P. Sahu, 1979, 'Prehistoric and Early Historic Archaeology of Orissa', unpublished M. Phil dissertation, Delhi University; R. N. Dash, 1984, 'Pre-and-Proto-history of Orissa', in H. Mahtab (ed.), *Glimpses of Orissan Art and Culture*, Bhubaneswar, pp. 284-304; P. Mohanty, 1992, 'Stone age research in Orissa: an overview', *Man in India* 72 (2), pp. 207-32; K. K. Basa, 1994, *op. cit.*
50. *Indian Archaeology: A Review, 1961-62*, p. 36.
51. K. K. Basa, T. K. Das and B. K. Mohanta, 2000, 'Neolithic Culture of Pallahara, Central Orissa', in Basa and Mohanty (eds.), *op. cit.*, pp. 264-84.
52. K. K. Basa, 1999, 'Neolithic and post-Neolithic Cultures of Orissa: An Overview', in S. Pradhan (ed.), *Orissa History, Culture and Archaeology*, Delhi, pp. 9-31; S. Pradhan, 2002, 'Recent Excavations at Chalcolithic sites in Orissa', in G. Sengupta and S. Panja (eds.), *Archaeology of Eastern India: New Perspectives*, Kolkata, pp. 515-26.

53. B. K. Sinha, 2000, 'Golabai: A Protohistoric Site on the Coast of Orissa', in Basa and Mohanty (eds.), *op. cit.*, pp. 322-55.
54. S. K. Kar, K. K. Basa and P. P. Joglekar, 1998, 'Archaeological remains of Gopalpur', *Man and Environment* 23 (1), pp. 107-14; S. K. Kar, 2000, 'Gopalpur: A Neolithic-Chalcolithic Site in Coastal Orissa', in Basa and Mohanty (eds.), *op. cit.*, pp. 368-91.
55. R. N. Dash, 1986, 'Sankerjang: a chalcolithic site in Orissa', *The Orissa Historical Research Journal* 32, pp. 99-125; P. Yule and B. K. Rath, 2000, 'Sankarjang – A Metals Period Burial Site in the Dhenkanal Uplands of Orissa, in Basa and Mohanty (ed.) *op. cit.*, pp. 285-321.
56. S. Pradhan, 2002, *op. cit.*, p. 525.
57. *Ibid.*, pp. 523-4; P. Behera, 2002, 'Khameswaripali: A Protohistoric Site in the Middle Mahanadi Valley, Orissa: Results of First Season's (1996-97) Excavation', in Sengupta and Panja (eds.), *op. cit.*, pp. 493-520.
58. S. Pradhan, 2002, *op. cit.*; p. 526.
59. R. Ray, A. K. Kundu and N. Bhattacharya, 2000, 'Chalcolithic Remains from a site near Kanjipani, Orissa', in Basa and Mohanty (eds.), *op. cit.*, pp. 356-67.
60. M. Brandtner, 1994, 'Archaeology of Western Orissa: Finds from Nehena', in A. Parpola and P. Koskikallio (eds.), *South Asian Archaeology 1993*, Helsinki, pp. 101-14.
61. B. K. Mohanta, 2002-3, 'Neolithic and Post-Neolithic Cultures of Northern Orissa', Ph.D. thesis submitted to Utkal University for examination.
62. B. B. Lal, 1949, 'Sisupalgarh 1948: an early historic fort in eastern India', *Ancient India* 5, pp. 62-105; for a historical interpretation and a revision of the chronology originally proposed by the excavator (*c.* 300 BC to AD 350) see M. Brandtner, 2001a, *Kalinga und seine Hauptstadt in frühgeschichtlicher Zeit Bedeutungswandel einer geographischen und ethnischen Bezeichnung*, Hamburg, pp. 328-406.
63. *Indian Archaeology: A Review, 1956-57*, pp. 30-1.
64. For a general outline on excavated sites in Orissa, see K. K. Basa, 1997, 'Archaeological Heritage', in P. K. Mishra and J. Samal (eds.), *Comprehensive History and Culture of Orissa,* Vol. 1, Part 1, New Delhi, pp. 18-45; P. Mohanty and B. Mishra, 1998, 'Recent archaeological researches in Orissa with special reference to the early historic phase', *Man in India* 78 (3-4), pp. 205-21.
65. R. P. Mohapatra, 1986, *Archaeology in Orissa (Sites and Monuments)*, Delhi, pp. 234-6.
66. C.R. Mishra and S. Pradhan, 1990, *Manamunda Excavation 1990: A Preliminary Report*, Sambalpur University.
67. D. Pradhan, P. Mohanty and J. Mishra, 2000, 'Manikapatana: An Ancient and Medieval Port on the Coast of Orissa', in Basa and Mohanty (eds.), *op. cit.*, pp. 473-94; J. Mishra, n.d., *Manikapatana, an early and medieval harbour complex on the coast of Orissa: a reconsideration.*

68. G. C. Chauley, 2000, 'Excavated Remains at Lalitagiri, a Buddhist site in Orissa', in Basa and Mohanty (eds.), *op. cit.*, pp. 441-55; J. Patnaik, 2000, 'Ceramics of Lalitagiri: a study' in Basa and Mohanty (eds.), pp. 456-72.
69. D. Mitra, *Ratnagiri (1958-61),* Vol. 1 (1981), Vol. 2 (1983), Delhi.
70. The site is being excavated by the Excavation Branch IV, ASI, Bhubaneswar. Also see J. S. Nigam in Basa and Mohanty (eds.), *op. cit.*, pp. 495-506.
71. B. K. Sinha, 1990, 'Excavations at Barabati Fort, Cuttack, Orissa 1989-91', in K. S. Behera *et al.* (eds.), *Cuttack One Thousand Years*, Vol. 1, Cuttack, pp. 59-67; K. V. Rao, 2000, 'Excavation at Barabati Fort, Cuttack', in Basa and Mohanty (eds.), *op. cit.*, pp. 663-80.
72. *Indian Archaeology: A Review, 1984-85*, p. 59; B. K. Sinha, 1992, 'Khalkattapatna', in B. U. Nayak and N. C. Ghosh (eds.), *New Trends in Indian Art and Archaeology*, Delhi, pp. 423-8; L. N. Rout and S. K. Pattanayak, 1993, 'Trade in medieval Orissa: a study on Khalkattapatna port', *The Journal of Historical and Social Analysis*, V (10), pp. 27-32.
73. H. C. Prusti and P. Mohanty, 1995, 'Langudi: a unique rock-cut Buddhist site in Orissa', *Deccan College Bulletin* 53, pp. 325-7; J. Mishra, P. Mohanty and H. Prusty, 1995, 'Langudi: an early historical Buddhist site in coastal Orissa', *Studies in History and Culture* 3 (2), pp. 11-17; R. N. Dash, 2000, 'Buddhist Art and Architecture in the Langudi hills (After the first phase of excavation)', in A. C. Pradhan *et al.* (eds.), *History, Culture and Economy (Professor K. S. Behera Felicitation Volume)*, Bhubaneswar, pp. 33-46; J. Mishra, n.d., *Monks, peasants and monasteries: Light on early Buddhist Sites of Kaima-Langudi region in Orissa.*
74. D. R. Pradhan, 2001, 'Two rare statues of Asoka discovered at Langudi Hill, Orissa, India', *CIAA News Letter*, Issue 13, SOAS, London.
75. M. Brandtner, 1988-89, 'Archaeological exploration around Bhubaneswar', *Manav* 3, pp. 231-50.
76. M. L. Smith, 2002, 'Systematic Survey at the Early Historic Urban Site of Sisupalgarh', in Sengupta and Panja (eds.), *op. cit.*, pp. 109-23.
77. P. Mohanty and B. Mishra, 2002, 'Archaeology of Kalahandi District, Orissa', in Sengupta and Panja (eds.), *op. cit.*, pp. 465-86.
78. J. Mishra, 2000, 'Radhanagar: Early Historic Buddhism, Urban Structure and Trade', in Basa and Mohanty (eds.), *op. cit.*, pp. 507-50.
79. J. Mishra, 2002, 'Early Historic Archaeology of Chilika Lake, Orissa: An Ecological Perspective', in Sengupta and Panja (eds.), *op. cit.*, pp. 163-88.
80. B. Tripathy, 2000, 'Archaeology of Boudh, Central Orissa', in Basa and Mohanty (eds.), *op. cit.*, pp. 392-417; 2001-02, 'Archaeology of Boudh District, Orissa with Special Reference to the Early Historic Settlement Pattern', unpublished Ph.D. thesis, Deccan College, Pune.
81. K. K. Basa and K. S. Behera, 2000, 'Maritime Archaeology of Orissa', in Basa and Mohanty (eds.), *op. cit.*, pp. 566-600.

82. A. K. Pattanaik, 2000, 'Ports of ancient Orissa', in Basa and Mohanty (eds.), *op. cit.*, pp. 601-12.
83. S. K. Panda, 2000, 'Early Trade and Trade Routes in Orissa: A Reassessment of Numismatic and Archaeological Evidence', in Basa and Mohanty (eds.), *op. cit.*, pp. 551-65.
84. B. P. Sahu, 1996, 'Situating Early Historical Trade in Orissa', in K. M. Shrimali (ed.), *Indian Archaeology Since Independence*, Delhi, pp. 96-109.
85. K. K. Basa, 1997, 'Cultural Relations between Orissa and Southeast Asia: An Archaeological Perspective', in P. K. Mishra and J. Samal (eds.), *op. cit.*, Vol. 1, Part II, pp. 730-41.
86. U. Mishra, 2000, 'An Ethnographic Study of Fishermen and Their Boats: Its Importance in the Maritime Archaeology of Ancient Orissa', in Basa and Mohanty (eds.), *op. cit.*, pp. 613-34.
87. A. P. Patnaik, 2003, *The Early Voyagers of the East: The Rise in Maritime Trade of the Kalingas in Ancient India* (2 vols.), Delhi.
88. T. E. Donaldson, *Hindu Temple Art of Orissa*, Vol. I (1985), Vol. II (1986), Vol. III (1987), Leiden.
89. K. C. Panigrahi, 1961, *Archaeological Remains of Bhubaneswar*, Bombay, etc.
90. V. Dehejia, 1979, *Early Stone Temples of Orissa*, New Delhi.
91. D. R. Das, 1982, *Temples of Orissa: The Study of a Sub-Style*, Delhi.
92. K. S. Behera and T. E. Donaldson, 1998, *Sculpture Masterpieces from Orissa: Style and Iconography*, New Delhi.
93. K. S. Behera, 1996, *Konarak: The Heritage of Mankind* (2 vols.), New Delhi.
94. W. Smith, 1994, *The Mukteswara Temple in Bhubaneswar*, Delhi.
95. J. P. Das, 1982, *Puri Paintings*, New Delhi.
96. A. Boner, S. Rath Sarma and R. P. Das, 1972, *New Light on the Sun Temple of Konarka: Four Unpublished Manuscripts Relating to Construction, History and Ritual of This Temple*, Varanasi; for a different view, see K. S. Behera, 1976, 'Review of New Light . . .', *South Asia* (no. 6), pp. 127-9.
97. J. Williams, 1996, *The Two-Headed Deer: Illustration of the Ramayana in Orissa*, Berkeley.
98. S. N. Rajaguru, *Inscriptions of Orissa,* Vol. I (1958), Vol. II (1960), Vol. III (1961-2), Vol. IV (1966), Vol. V (1975); S. Tripathy, 1974, *Inscriptions of Orissa*, Vol. VI.
99. B. P. Sahu, 2000, 'Authority and Patronage in Early Orissa', in Basa and Mohanty (eds.), *op. cit.*, pp. 431-40.
100. U. Singh, 1993, *Kings, Brahmanas and Temples in Orissa: An Epigraphic Study*, Delhi.
101. S. Tripathy, 1986, *op. cit.*

102. P. Turner, 1989, *Roman Coins from India*, London, pp. 54, 61.
103. O. P. Kejariwal, 1988, *The Asiatic Society of Bengal and the Discovery of India's Past 1784-1838*, Delhi.
104. R. Schwab, 1984, *The Oriental Renaissance: Europe's Rediscovery of India and the East, 1680-1880*, New York.
105. E. Said, 1984, 'Foreword', in R. Schwab, op. cit., p. viii.
106. *Ibid.*, p. ix.
107. *Ibid.*, p. x-xi.
108. C. B. Asher and T. R. Metcalf (eds.), 1994, *Perception of South Asia's Visual Past,* Delhi, p. 1.
109. *Ibid.*, p. 2.
110. See also D. K. Chakrabarti, 1997, *Colonial Indology*, Delhi.
111. G. M. Tartakov, 1994, 'Changing Views of India's Art History', in Asher and Metcalf (eds.), *op. cit.,* p. 17.
112. Asher and Metcalf, 1994, *op. cit.,* p. 3.
113. T. Guha-Thakurta, 1992, *The Making of a New 'Indian' Art*, Cambridge.
114. Asher and Metcalf, *op. cit.*, p. 4.
115. *Ibid.*, p. 10.
116. D. K. Chakrabarti, 1997, *Colonial Indology*; M. Brandtner, 1999, 'Koloniale Archãologie: Monopolisierte Vergangenheitsdeutung und Herrschaftslegitimation in Britisch-Indien', in S. Conermann (ed.), *Mythen, Geschichte(n), Identitäten: Der Kampf um die Vergangenheit*, Hamburg, pp. 303-66.
117. K. K. Basa, 1992-3, 'Archaeology and politics in India: A Preliminary Statement', *Man in Society* 7, pp. 29-40; K. K. Basa, 1998, 'Indian Writings on Early History and Archaeology of Southeast Asia: A Historiographical Analysis', *Journal of the Royal Asiatic Society*, Third Series 8, Part 3, pp. 395-410.
118. Mitra, 1875, *op. cit.*, p. 20.
119. Ganguly, 1912, *op. cit.*, Chapter IV.
120. *Ibid.*, p. 63.
121. J. Fergusson, 1884, *op. cit.*
122. *Ibid.*, p. 5.
123. *Ibid.*, p. 6.
124. *Ibid.*, p. 9.
125. *Ibid.*, p. 9.
126. *Ibid.*, pp. 9-10.
127. *Ibid.*, p. vi.
128. *Ibid.*, p. vii.
129. *Ibid.*, p. vi.
130. *Ibid.*, p. vii.
131. An attempt at solving this contradiction can be detected in Fergusson's view of the evolution of Indian architecture which, according to him, can

be, in general, interperted as a story of constant decline. Like many of his contemporaries, Fergusson held the 'racial deterioration' of the Aryans due to intermixture with the 'natives' responsible for this and other developments; see M. Brandtner, 1999, *op. cit.*, pp. 339-53.

132. T. Guha-Thakurta, 1992, *op. cit.*, p. 120.
133. For an outline on this debate, see Gaganendranath Dash, 1986, *'Odiya bhasa surakshya andolana – eka drustipata'* (in Oriya), *Mulyayana* 22, pp. 1-19.
134. H. Kulke, A. Eschmann and G. C. Tripathi, 1978, *The Cult of Jagannath and Regional Tradition of Orissa*, Delhi.
135. Banerji, 1931, *op. cit.*, pp. 370-1.
136. J. Nayak and D. Mishra, 1994, 'Homeless deities and temple politics in Orissa', *New Quest*, July 1994, pp. 227-9.
137. *Ibid.*
138. J. Dash, 1998, *Human Ecology of Foragers: A Study of the Kharia (Savara), Ujia (Savara) and Birhor in Similipal Hills*, New Delhi.
139. Kar et al., 1998, *op. cit.*
140. U. K. Mishra, 1997, 'Seafaring in the Context of the Material Culture of Early Historical Orissa (3rd C.B.C. – 4th-5th C.A.D.) – An Ethnohistorical Approach', unpublished M.Phil. thesis, Jawaharlal Nehru University.
141. T. N. Ramachandran, 1951, 'Find of a tempera painting in Sitabhinji, District Keonjhar, Orissa', *Artibus Asiae* 14, pp. 5-25.
142. E. Service, 1978, 'Classical and Modern Theories of the Origin of Government', in R. Cohen and E.R. Service (eds.), *Origins of the State: The Archaeology of Political Evolution*, Philadelphia, pp. 21-34.
143. M. H. Fried, 1978, 'The State, the Chicken and the Egg: or What Came First', in Cohen and Service (eds.), *op. cit.*, pp. 35-47.
144. *Idem.*, 1967, *Evolution of Political Society: An Essay in Political Anthropology*, New York.
145. H. J. M. Claessen and P. Skalnik, 1978, 'The early state: models and reality', in Claessen and Skalnik (eds.), *The Early State*, The Hague, pp. 637-650.
146. U. Singh, 1993, *Kings, Brahmanas and Temples in Orissa: An Epigraphic Study,* Delhi; also see R. Cohen, 1978, 'State origins: a reappraisal', in Claessen and Skalnik (eds.), *op. cit.*, pp. 31-75; E. Service, 1978, 'Classical and modern theories of the origins of government', in Cohen and Service (eds.), *op. cit.*, pp. 21-34.
147. F. R. Allchin, 1989, 'City and state formation in early historic South Asia', *South Asian Studies* 5, pp. 1-16; 1990, 'Patterns of city formation in early historic South Asia', *South Asian Studies* 6, pp. 163-73; R.S. Sharma, 1983, *Material Culture and Social Formation in Ancient India*, Delhi; 1985, 'Stages in state formation in ancient India', *Social Science Probing,* 2 (1), pp. 1-19; R. Thapar, 1984, *From Lineage to State*, Delhi; for a

review of various models for the pre-modern period, see H. Kulke (ed.), 1995, *The State in India, 1000-1700,* Delhi.

148. R. Thapar, 1981, 'The state as empire', in H.J.M. Claessen and P. Skalnik (eds.), *The Study of the State*, The Hague, pp. 409-26.

149. S. Seneviratne, 1981, 'Kalinga and Andhra: the process of secondary state formation in early India', *ibid.,* pp. 317-38.

150. B. P. Sahu, 1987, 'Ancient Orissa: the dynamics of internal transformation of the tribal society', in K. M. Shrimali (ed.), *Essays in Indian Art, Religion and Society*, Delhi, pp. 169-80.

151. H. Kulke, 1977, 'Early state formation and royal legitimation in late ancient Orissa', in M. N. Das (ed.), *Sidelights on the History and Culture of Orissa*, Cuttack, pp. 104-13.

152. *Idem.,* 1978, 'Royal temple policy and the structure of medieval Hindu Kingdoms' in H. Kulke *et al., op. cit.*, pp. 126-7.

153. U. Singh, 1993, *op. cit.*

154. L. K. Mahapatra, 1976, 'Gods, kings and the caste system in India', in A. Bharati (ed.), *The Realm of the Extra-Human Agents and Audiences*, Paris, pp. 7-26.

155. George Berkemer, 1993, *Little Kingdoms in Kalinga: Ideologie, Legitimation and Politik regionaler Eliten* (in German), Beiträge zur Südasienforschung 156, Stuttgart; for a review, see Rahul Peter Das, 1997, 'Little kingdoms and big theories of history', *Journal of the American Oriental Society* 117 (1), pp. 127-34.

156. F. R. Allchin, 1989, *op. cit.*; 1990, *op. cit.*, also see F. R. Allchin, 1995, *The Archaeology of Early Historical South Asia*, Cambridge.

157. *Idem*, 1990, *op. cit.*, p.169.

158. *Ibid.*, p. 164.

159. M. Brandtner, 2001a, *op. cit.*, see also *id.*, 2001b, 'Representations of Kalinga: The Changing Image and Geography of a Historical Region', in H. Kulke and B. Schnepel (eds.), *Jagannath Revisited: Studying Society, Religion and the State in Orissa*, New Delhi, pp. 179-210.

CHAPTER 3

Ways of Seeing: History and Historiography of the State in Early India

BHAIRABI PRASAD SAHU

The study of the state has gained momentum in recent years and much has been written over the past twenty-five years about the state in early India, which has influenced our understanding of social formations and the general pattern of early Indian history. An issue of *Studies in History* (1982), a Presidential Address to the Ancient India section of the Indian History Congress (1983), a volume in OUP's *Themes in Indian History* series (1995) and more recently a collection of essays on *State and Society in Pre-modern South India* (2002), are devoted to the state in early India. One has witnessed in this period a remarkable increase in the number of detailed empirical studies within more or less sound theoretical frameworks, with different historico-cultural regions as their focus.[1] These writings have partly been produced in India and have partly emerged from western universities. But then one may ask why this enhanced interest in the state? In one way or another it is related to the shift from dynastic history towards an understanding of structures and processes, or to the realization that an integrated study of the state provides an entry point to contemporary society and economy.

Admittedly, the state does not exist in isolation, but in a situation of interaction with the other domains and change. Let me elaborate. Sedentary agriculture, social differentiation and surplus, among others, are factors which help in the emergence of the state, but once it arises it has the potential to bring about changes in these very spheres. The role of land grants by the state (from the Gupta period onwards) in agrarian expansion and economic transformation are well known. Similarly, such grants to members of artisan communities like weavers or potters in lieu of their services to a ritual centre could bring about differentiation within such communities. If land grants ensured better economic status, the continued association with a ritual centre enhanced the social position of a group in the long term. The state not only organises diversity and integrates people with different socio-economic and ritual functions, it also splits up communities.[2] Studies of the state do not just concentrate on the issues of how power is shared, distributed or organized, but also tell us something about the socio-economic competence of individuals or groups and their relationship to the access to or denial of state power, in the general background of the emergence of new social categories (men of substance) and the eclipse of others from time to time.

There are two ways of approaching the subject. One is a constitutional perspective focusing on the definition of the state, derived from texts such as the *Arthashastra* or the *Kural*, but that perhaps is a lazy and unexciting way of going about it. The other is to locate states in the past in terms of how they functioned in relation to specific societies and economic situations and, flowing from that, to profile political processes (including legitimation) that had a bearing on their nature and character. The second approach, with a set of questions touching upon issues of state formation, social foundations, state typologies, the extent of organized political intrusion, and the authority of the state in time and space is surely a more interesting and intellectually rewarding exercise. This shift in the terrain of discussion is of more recent origin. The question then would be, how did we reach here—what has been the trajectory of studies on the state in early India?

That brings us to the historiography of ancient Indian polities, an area which over the past two centuries has witnessed the making and unmaking (if not the total disappearance) of about half a dozen approaches: the imperialist, nationalist, conventional, Marxist, idealist, and processual or what Hermann Kulke terms processural.[3] Before proceeding further one may make two brief, and fairly obvious, observations. The first is that these labels are somewhat arbitrary categories of convenience and most historians may not be too happy to be slotted as such. Second, no historiography is homogeneous: each comprises a wide range of positions in matters of details.[4] Within the nationalist approach, for example, R. G. Bhandarkar, K. P. Jayaswal and R. C. Majumdar represent different strands, and in ignoring these differences one will be doing injustice to their individual contributions. Similarly, to paper over the differences in method within the dominant historiography is to simplify and not problematize the issues. Moreover, notwithstanding the differences between the numerous approaches, there are discernible continuities running through some, if not all, of them.

In its early stages this area of study was afflicted by two sets of totalizing and, deriving from it, hegemonic assertions: the imperialist and nationalist perspectives. Colonial Indology marked the beginning of modern writings on ancient India. From James Mill to Vincent Smith, administrator-scholars wrote on a wide spectrum of issues, but did not give any specific attention to polity. Reflections on it were subsumed under generalities or woven into general discussions on India. In brief, early India was seen to represent a congeries of polities, a conglomeration of peoples (with nothing more than force holding them together) and unchanging despotic monarchies dominating a political map characterized by atomism. We are further told that there was no rule of law, no administered states, popular involvement (not to speak of participation) was absent, moments of larger political unity were rare and civilization prospered only under foreign rule. The situation was compounded by religion permeating all aspects of life. 'The village community' remained impervious to the shifts and turns in the political fortunes of kings and dynasties and persisted throughout, preserving its harmonic character.[5] Continued manifestation of the core formulations, though their lineage extends to Mill, can be seen even in V. Smith's *Early History of India* (1904). His efforts at writing objective history were dented by the occasional Eurocentric bias, discernible in his treatment of Alexander's campaigns, India in the post-Alexander phase and India after Harsha. The emphasis on 'the bewildering annals of Indian petty states' and what ensues in the wake of the withdrawal of a supreme authority was perhaps meant to defend the British against charges of despotism at the turn of the century and to turn the idea of Oriental Despotism on its head,[6] making a virtue out of it in the background of this perceived continuous political anarchy; in the process Smith was providing a justification for British rule in India.

The damning indictment of ancient Indian political ideas and institutions need to be situated in the wider context of the shift from

'Indomania' to 'Indophobia', a development not entirely unrelated to the politics and compulsions of the imperial enterprise. It is said that 'Indophobia' was not born, it was made.[7] That explains why the underlying ideological assumption in colonial Indology was the superiority of the European, including British, cultural heritage and conversely the inferiority of the Indian inheritance.

Nationalist historiography in one fashion or the other was a response to such Imperialist claims, bordering on insistence. Thus, it is the rebuttal aspect of these writings that strikes one's attention. However, in doing so the 'oppositionists' transformed some of the governing hypotheses and formulations to stereotypes. With the progress of the National Movement, ancient India was called upon to prove the existence of democracy, representative institutions, local self-government, republics and constitutional monarchy (with in-built checks and balances), among a host of other claims. The *abhishekha*, for example, is said to have symbolized the subordination of power to *dharma* and civil society. While K. P. Jayaswal in his by now famous *Hindu Polity* (1918), argued for most of it in the manner of a brilliant defence counsel, Radha Kumud Mookerji urged the recognition of *The Fundamental Unity of India* from the earliest times onwards. In his perception India as known in the twentieth century existed in the ancient past. The construction of the idea of a Golden Age and private ownership of land constituted an inversion of Oriental Depotism. The discovery of the *Arthashastra* was a shot in the arm. Armed with it, early India could be credited with a long tradition of political philosophy, large unified political enterprises, a welfare state, and so on.[8] The nationalists recovered and revived dynasties such as the Guptas, Vakatakas and Nagas, and bestowed them with undue honour and glory. They emphasized the great constitutional progress made in early India, which was comparable to the best anywhere, including contemporary England.

The nationalists questioned individual items, but not the basic theoretical presuppositions, of the imperialists. Despite all their protests, their approach was rooted in that framework which had set the terms of discussion. There was continuity in the major premises, though they were suitably modified. Thus, we are faced with two kinds of national historiographies, the imperialist and the nationalist viewed from the Indian perspective, trying to prove the presence or absence of a set of political ideas, practices, and institutions in India's past. History was placed at the service of politics, and both were making significant use of the past for opposite purposes. The polemics highlight the role of ideology in historical constructions. They also make the point that unless new questions are asked or there is a shift in the ground of discussion, historiography does not move ahead.

The writings of the 1940s and 1950s, especially those of K. A. N. Sastri and A. S. Altekar, may be characterized with the advantage of hindsight as traditional or conventional. They were marked by a meticulous concern for accuracy and obsessive avoidance of systemic generalization and evaluation. They usually presented a descriptive account of government and administration at various levels, under numerous dynasties. Administrative details, it was assumed, represented the nature and structure of the state and, flowing from it, they went on to create the picture of centralized, unitarian imperial states with numerous and powerful bureaucracies.[9] In this construction, which equated dynastic and administrative history with the study of the state and largely took its existence for granted, there were a plethora of empires, but little concern for the problem of the origin of states, types of states, and change. Politics was perceived to be an independent, autonomous domain, abstracted from society. Their engagement with discourses on empire was a carry over from the past. In their enthusiasm to reconcile centralization at the top with the autonomy of the village republics at the bottom they failed to see the inherent theoretical inconsistency in the argument. However, one may quickly add that in this apparent conceptual ambiguity was embedded an interesting possibility for future historians, who argued for 'autonomous spaces' within the ambit of the state;[10] with significant implications for understanding the structure of the state, to which we shall return below.

People write histories not in an intellectual vaccum, but in situations they inherit and encounter. Thus writing history is a dialogic process involving a response to past historiographical traditions and contemporary influences. The problem of reconciling the irreconcilable in the conventionalists' characterization of the state then, can be explained by invoking the shadow of earlier traditions and the debates surrounding the making of the constitution and the nature of the state to be around the time of India's independence. The Indian constitution provides for a quasi-federal system with the balance clearly tilted in favour of the centre. More or less the basic orientation of inscribing the present continued.

The aforesaid forms of writing political history, in the absence of much analysis of ideas, institutions and historical change, from the later part of the 1950s, and particularly since the 1960s, made way (if not entirely abandoned) for new perspectives. The earliest efforts to understand the state in relation to society and economy were made by D. D. Kosambi and R. S. Sharma; both inaugurated the sober, scientific Marxist intervention in the historiography of early Indian polity. They were the first to raise discussions to a level of conceptualization, to which we shall return later.

Meanwhile, there has been a range of writings, incidentally emanating mostly from Western universities, which perhaps for the want of a better term have been classified as 'idealist'. Notwithstanding the differences in the focus of their research interest, treatment of the subject, and style of presentation, what is common to the writings of J. Gonda, Louis Dumont, J. C. Heesterman, Burton Stein and Ronald Inden, among others, is that they are somewhat abstracted from reality and therefore ahistorical. Gonda's[11] treatment of kingship in ancient India mixes up the ideal with the real and in generalizing about the institution, based on sources separated in time (and space), ignores the context or stages in its evolution. Dumont[12] in subscribing to the brahmanical view of the caste system, believes that the king having conceded hierarchical pre-eminence to the brahmana was perpetually under the shadow and influence of the latter. His notion of 'secularized kingship' not only separated the two domains but also actually subordinated the political to the moral or social sphere. Dumont seems to have marginalized kingship and replaced it with the idea of 'theocratic despotism'. Proceeding from the understanding that Indian reality was fraught with contradictions, Heesterman segregates power and authority.[13] The brahmana was endowed with authority because of his association with the transcendental value of renunciation, which was held in esteem by Indian society. Having said that, Heesterman moves on to argue that 'authority having been siphoned off, the state lacked the means to rise above the essential instability of personal relations'.[14] What we are faced with is the picture of a hapless, permanently incapacitated state. It may be of some interest to note that Heesterman extrapolates an atrophied state even from the *Arthashastra*, a text which most historians have used to construct the image of a centralized Mauryan empire.

The problem inherent in these works is perhaps partly related to an unwillingness or refusal to concede the role of ideology in the making of early state societies. It also needs to be recognized that the state has a logic of its own, and though it closely interacts with society, it is not necessarily always determined by it. Early Indian ideologues, as in other ancient societies, mystified reality and the relations of power. By continuously according pre-eminence to the brahmana or kshatriya alternately in text after text, they successfully projected the image of endemic conflictual relations between them. However, neither precedence of the one over the other, nor categorical separation of the two, explains their dynamic relationship or how authority was constituted in ancient India. Competition apart, there was collaboration between them, involving patronage for one and validation for the other. In fact, they constituted the power élite.[15] It was in their mutual interest that the secret was not given away and that reality was camouflaged.

Burton Stein's contributions to early medieval studies cannot be overestimated. Through his emphasis on ritual sovereignty and the *nadus* (in charting the history of the state during Pallava-Chola times) he compelled discussion on the role of the sacred domain and local agrarian bases in understanding the structure of polities. Where he seems to have erred is in his preference for a theoretical framework, the segmentary state, which detached the state from its socio-economic foundations and the absolute distinction he made between political and ritual sovereignty.[16] This analysis was bereft of socio-political substance as well as of the dynamics of change. Ronald Inden[17] too focuses on the symbols of power, courtly culture and ideational aspects, instead of power relations and politics, drawing on perspectives from a text to the exclusion of the wealth of epigraphical material.

In brief, the 'idealists' believe in changeless, unstable, continuously post-tribal political formations in pre-colonial India.[18] Like James Mill they assume that once the transition from tribe to monarchy was over Indian political institutions showed no more change. They wish away the historical transitions in the realms of ideology, state and society. The envisaged arrested political growth is generally explained with reference to in-built cultural impediments or the religious mentality of the Indians – caste, transcendental value of renunciation or atavistic, restricted peasant mentality. The cycle had come full circle, from Oriental Despotism, through 'theocratic despotism' and 'oriental desperatism', it was back to the early formulations.

D. D. Kosambi's and R. S. Sharma's interventions in the later 1950s, raised discussions of early Indian polity 'from variations in narratives to contending formulations'. They posed the state in the wider context of economy and society and bridged the gap between politics and society, instead of the compartmentalized approach of the earlier traditions. Kosambi was not specifically interested in early Indian polity, but he provocatively suggested a possible relationship between the rise of Magadha, the emergence of urban centres and that of the 'heterodox' sects in the middle of the first millennium BC[19] The significance of his well-known formulations, feudalism 'from above' and 'from below', and the envisaged relationship between *bhakti* in the *Gita* and the emergent social formation need no emphasis.[20] Some of his suggested ideas were amended, refined and systematized in later years by Sharma. Sharma's *Aspects of Political Ideas and Institutions in Ancient India* (1959), raised new and controversial questions. Did ancient Indians deserve credit for developing nuanced political ideas, intricately weaving the political, social and the religious? Were ideas and institutions unchanging owing to the continuity of traditions, or do they reflect changes in consonance with change intrinsic to South Asian society, as elsewhere? His evaluation of these issues and delineation of stages in ancient Indian polity (as in the domains of society and economy) were path-breaking.[21] From the Gupta period onwards, Sharma argues, the alienation of state revenues and administrative rights by land grants to brahmanas and officials led to feudal decentralization.[22] The creation of multiple foci of power and *samantas* of various grades (who were held together by grant of privileges, symbolic means, and force), in this perception, were the product of state initiative. In addition, terms denoting different levels in the *samanta* hierarchy, graded land rights, hierarchized structure of management in religious institutions, including non-brahmanical establish-ments, and the visible manifestation of hierarchies in temple art, are seen to represent the feudal order.[23] Both Kosambi and Sharma saw religion and religious ideas as a social force, and as ideology providing legitimacy and coherence to the state. In their concern for a theoretical framework to under-stand early Indian history or in making systematic generalizations, derived from an ideological position, Kosambi and Sharma provided food for thought.

The work of M. G. S. Narayanan, R. N. Nandi and Kesavan Veluthat, among others, can be linked to R. S. Sharma's thesis of the feudalization of the state in early medieval times.[24] While Narayanan charts the history of the Chera kingdom of Makotai in the context of the problems associated with state formation in Kerala and Veluthat focuses on the structure of polity in south India, Nandi, on the basis of evidence from Karnataka and Andhra, addresses issues related to lord-vassal relationship and the hierarchy of *samantas*.

The Political Structure of Early Medieval South India by Veluthat is an excellent work bearing on religious and political symbols and the structure of legitimation, sans the author's preference for a certain model which is ill at ease with the available evidence. The fact that state power was enjoyed by many individuals and corporate bodies at different levels and that there was a great deal of decentralization leads him to argue for south Indian feudalism. However, its genesis remains to be explained. The trajectory of socio-political developments in early Tamilakam does not anticipate or explain it. Haziness surrounds the question of the payment of tribute and transfer of resources by chiefs to their overlords. Similarly, political relationships or the hierarchies of domination and subordination do not emerge with unmistakable clarity. The envisaged three-tiered feudal order comprising the Chola overlord, Chera king and his *nad* chiefs seems to run into rough weather when one realizes that the relationship between the *Perumal* (the Chera-king) and the hereditary, traditional chiefs of the bigger *nads* was more flexible than generally assumed.[25] Again, what Nandi perceives as 'the ceremonial act of vassalization amounting to legitimatization' of ambitious chiefs may equally be seen to represent the incorporation of local chiefs, rising from below. When the state bestowed land grants and honour on a *gavunda*, *heggade* or *pergadde* for their outstanding military service it was, in fact, reinforcing and strengthening their existing competence. As men of substance already associated with revenue administration, they did not entirely derive their authority from such acts of benevolence on the part of the state. It is possible that through these local élites the state was trying to reach out to newer areas and extend its authority.[26] In discussions on political relations, allusions to the lotus feet of the lord in the copper plate inscriptions, presented in different forms and styles, need not be taken seriously, because there is no dearth of evidence to show that overlords were overthrown by their *samantas* at the first opportunity. At best such evidence may be seen as rhetoric contributing and/or conforming to contemporary images of royalty.

Reality was far more complex and problematic than the perceived neat hierarchies, involving relations of protection and loyalty at various levels.[27] The nature of relations between the king and his subordinates at the intermediate and local levels was not static, but dynamic. Great kings in regional or supra-regional formations were not absolute masters because lesser kings and chiefs accepted their own subordinate positions largely owing to political compulsion or having entered into mutually beneficial deals. However, this is not to suggest that there were no moments of larger political unity when states tried to intrude as far as possible and achieve vertical administrative integration. The history of the Cholas between Rajaraja and Kulottunga is a case in point. So were the efforts at administrative reorganization by the later Gangas of Orissa under Vajrahastadeva III (1038-70) and Anantavarman Codagangadeva (1078-1152). Such examples also provide a corrective to tendencies to generalize for long periods. The early and later Chola periods provide different histories of the state, pointing to structural changes over time.[28]

There is lack of evidence to support the development of a feudal political structure from around the middle of the first millennium AD. Not that it makes a difference to the larger argument, but incidentally all the evidence that Nandi cites belong largely to the end of the first or early second millennium. To posit that the inability to centrally administer large territorial states led to the feudalization of the state or suggest that may be the earliest form of state in south India assumed the feudal form[29] amounts to not explaining what needs to be explained. That brings us to the question of what prompted ruling houses to delegate administrative and fiscal rights. The idea of the Kali Age, supposedly representing an ubiquitous crisis, has been adduced to explain the phenomenon of land grants and consequent changes.[30] However, this interpretation has been questioned, and alternatively it is argued that the concept represents the spread of puranic and epic ideas and the importance of brahmanas in the making of dominant ideology, in a situation of the formation and spread of local states. It was not a historical crisis, but a crisis of confidence related to the anxieties of the brahmanas, in the face of unprecedented social and cultural change related to economic growth in the early centuries of the common era, which influenced the formulation of the idea.[31] Land grants are mostly reported from regions outside the Gangetic plains. They were issued by kings and chiefs belonging to the newly emerging local states. The spatio-temporal correspondence between land grants and local state formation clearly brings out the inherent relationship between the two phenomena.[32] It then disturbs the epicentric view of land grants and the unmaking of the state in early medieval India.

Generalizations about the state in the dominant historiography tend to homogenize the variety of human experiences and, in doing so, they do violence to the conceptual category (feudalism in this case) by spreading it thin across the varied regions. The characterization of the Mauryan state as centralized and more or less uniform and the subsequent Kushana and Satavahana states as different not so much in form as in scale is closely related to the understanding that the nature of the post-Gupta states was feudal. Post-Gupta political fragmentation could be explained only in the background of some kind of larger unity or wholesomeness. In perceiving the early historic state as being reflective of a certain techno-economic base, insofar as it is related to the iron-productivity-surplus-complex society paradigm, and the state in early medieval India as the prime-mover, which brought about the gamut of significant changes through its decision to make land grants, the dominant historiography does not help the cause of a coherent theory of state. At the level of a long-distance vision of Indian history the fragmented political world of early medieval India does not cohere with the centralized structure of the Sultanate.

The representation of the state within the dominant historiography began to lose some of its lustre as more and more historians moved towards understanding the structure of states in relation to contemporary political processes, in the background of the shift from simple mechanical explanations to locating historical developments in terms of the interplay of multiple forces. Romila Thapar, B. D. Chattopadhyaya, Hermann Kulke, Y. Subbarayalu and S. Seneviratne, among many others, have documented the way the state structures were varied, flexible, continuously evolving and trying to come to grips with different local and regional situations.[33] An intellectual affinity between these works and those of S. K. Panda, Swapna Bhattacharya, James Heitzman, Cynthia Talbott, Nandini Sinha, the present author, and some of the contributions of Rajan Gurukkal and Kesavan Veluthat is easily discernible.[34] They have addressed concrete specific situations to improve our understanding in terms of the fact that the state is not something of a standard, finished product which, once actualized, would reproduce itself more or less in similar forms across varied spatial contexts. The career of historiographic unease can be traced to Thapar's writings since the late 1960s,[35] and the works of B. Stein, Nicholas Dirks, G. W. Spencer, B. D. Chattopadhyaya and Hermann Kulke in the 1970s.[36]

The processual approach, and within it the integrative model of state formation in early medieval India, emerged formally in the early 1980s, but derived considerably from the intellectual ferment of the 1970s, as well as a different reading of some of the formulations of the dominant historiography and those of Stein.[37] In the early historical context, while Thapar focuses on the origin of the state in north India and the Mauryan state, highlighting the complexities associated with the transition from pre-state to state society as also the different faces of the state in the varied regions, Chattopadhyaya, Seneviratne, Gurukkal, and this author address the trajectory of the evolution of political society in the Deccan, Andhra, Tamilakam, and Orissa respectively. The emergence of state society in these regions was the consequence of considerable internal evolution and interaction with Gangetic northern India in the wake of the Mauryan conquest. The transition derived itself not from administrative integration under the Mauryas, because it did not happen uniformly across regions, but from the network of linkages and internal dynamics of local societies. In arguing for the integrative paradigm, in the early medieval scenario, Chattopadhyaya and Kulke also provide a critique of the other two contending conceptual frameworks: the 'Indian feudalism' model and that of the 'segmentary state'.[38] The process of integrative state formation shows the phased spatial extension (including territorial integration) and structural evolution of states in areas peripheral to or outside the Ganga valley from the mid first millennium AD onwards. The stages in state formation are expressed either in terms of chiefdoms, early kingdoms and imperial kingdoms, or local, sub-regional and regional/supra-regional polities. The relationship between the sacred and temporal domains, the changing forms of ideological intervention by the state and cultural integration through incorporation and transformation of regional traditions are inextricably woven into the discussion. The linkages between the extension of state power and expansion of the agrarian frontier, market, and nodes are continuously treated as simultaneous, interrelated developments.[39] Instead of macro-generalizations the focus is on regional structural changes and within it the sub-regional and local formations get their due. Regional state formation is, thus, situated in the wider context of numerous political processes; and change coming from within local societies as well as from the network of transregional linkages.

There has been some engagement with the intermediate levels of the socio-political order[40] and the issue of legitimation. While the *kutumbins* appear as addressees in the early land-grant charters, the *mahattaras/mahamahattaras, gavundas* and other region-specific rich peasants acquired prominence in the later land transaction documents. These groups seem to have shared the confidence and authority of the state. However, the recognition and incorporation of the newly emerging significant local landed categories into the regional state structures and forms of legitimation, bearing on state-society interface, are areas which warrant greater attention. This is not the place to go into the details of various approaches, including the one under discussion, to the study of legitimation of power in early Indian society, which has attracted the attention of Indian and non-Indian scholars in the last forty years or so. The subject is important and deserves comprehensive treatment. Here it may be said that the significance of the theme has gained acceptance over the last quarter century and some new questions have been posed.[41]

Chattopadhyaya envisages the existence of 'autonomous spaces' in early India, which were organised differently from the 'administered' territories.[42] They comprised physical spaces as well as also alternative centres of authority within the frontiers of the state such as the village community (with its corporate institutions), localities, castes, guilds, etc., bound by and managing their affairs through commonly arrived at decisions, customs, and *dharma*. It is argued that matters of common concern such as local law and order, policing, defence, and so on were looked after by them to the exclusion of the superior, transcendent authority of the state.[43] However, this did not entirely preclude state intervention. There are examples of the state being invoked to resolve local knotty problems and surely as and when necessary, as in the case of the Cholas and the Later Eastern Gangas mentioned above, the state could intrude even without invitation. The concept makes two significant points: first, that such spaces did not exist in isolation but were open to interactions and change; and secondly that any search for homogeneity or a great degree of cohesiveness within the territorial limits of the state will not be rewarding. Apart from the fact that integration was never perfect, it needs mention that the process was not always harmonious; it involved competition and contestation, and, flowing from it, continuous engagement and negotiations.[44] In this perspective the evolution of the state was neither unilinear nor unidimensional, states could and did consolidate and expand, and, similarly, they also suffered shrinkage.

The ways in which the state has been perceived are largely a product of choice and consequence of historiographies rarely questioned on their paradoxes and inconsistencies until recently. In course of the shift from consciously inscribing the present to deciphering the past historians have moved beyond the merely descriptive approach to the subject and developed conceptual tools to sharpen our understanding of institutional structures and society.[45] With the recognition of the possibility of more than one reading of the available source material the understanding of the state, as in other areas, in early India has gained immensely. Similarly, the regional empirical studies focusing on Tamil Nadu, Andhra, Orissa, and Rajasthan, and their related issues, have thrown up new questions and modified some of our cherished notions. Recent perspectives of the state on the face of it constitute an inversion of the dominant historiography, but change of perspective need not always mean change of ideological position. The processual model of socio-political change in early India has, in fact, corrected and refined some of the arguments and assumptions in the 'Indian feudalism' model. The authors of the processual model or integrative paradigm cannot be viewed as opponents of the dominant historiography insofar as their writings are embedded in, and form an extension of, the same social formation approach. It only demonstrates the possibilities and prospects inherent in the approach.

NOTES

1. One may mention the works of Romila Thapar, *From Lineage to State (Social Formations in the Mid-First Millennium B.C. in the Ganga Valley)*, New Delhi, 1984; R. S. Sharma, *The State and Varna Formation in the Mid-Ganga Plains: An Ethnoarchaeological View,* Delhi, 1996; *idem., Aspects of Political Ideas and Institutions in Ancient India,* Delhi, 1991 (3rd edn.); S. K. Panda, *The State and Statecraft in Medieval Orissa under the Later Eastern Gangas (A.D. 1038-1434)*, Calcutta, 1995; H. Kulke, *Kings and Cults: State Formation and Legitimation in India and Southeast Asia,* Delhi, 1993; Nandini Sinha, *State Formation in Rajasthan: Mewar during the Seventh-Fifteenth Centuries*, Delhi, 2002; C. Talbot, *Precolonial India in Practice*, New Delhi, 2000; Kesavan Veluthat, *The Political Structure of Early Medieval South India*, Delhi, 1993; B. Stein, *Peasant State and Society in Medieval South India*, Delhi, 1980 and R. N. Nandi, *State Formation, Agrarian Growth and Social Change in Feudal South India, c. A.D. 600-1200*, Delhi, 2000, which focus either entirely or substantially on the state.

   B. D. Chattopadhyaya, like Kulke, has contributed substantially to this area of study. See *idem, The Making of Early Medieval India*, Delhi, 1994, Chs. 2, 3 and 8 and *Studying Early India: Archaeology, Texts and Historical Issues*, Delhi, 2003, chs. 3, 7 and 8. For some other important contributions during the same period see H. Kulke (ed.), *The State in India, 1000-1700*, Delhi, 1995, and N. Karashima (ed.), *Kingship in Indian History*, Delhi, 1999.
2. See, for example, B. D. Chattopadhyaya, 'Political Processes and the Structure of Polity in Early Medieval India – Problems of Perspective', Presidential Address, Ancient India Section, in *Proceedings of the Indian History Congress* (hereafter *PIHC*), Burdwan session, 1983, pp. 25-63.
3. See Kulke, 'The Early and the Imperial Kingdom : A Processural Model of Integrative State Formation in Early Medieval India', in *idem* (ed.), *The State in India . . ., op. cit.*, pp. 233-62.

4. For a detailed discussion see B. D. Chattopadhyaya, 'Confronting Fundamentalisms: The Possibilities of Early Indian History', in *Studies in History*, 18 (1), 2002, pp. 103-20.
5. For some good discussions see R. S. Sharma, *Aspects of Political Ideas . . .* , *op. cit.*, Ch.1; Ronald Inden, *Imagining India*, Oxford, 1990, Ch. 5; D. K. Chakrabarti, *Colonial Indology: Sociopolitics of the Ancient Indian Past*, New Delhi, 1997, pp. 86-116 and 'Conclusions', and D. Lorenzen, 'Imperialism and the Historiography of Ancient India', in S. N. Mukherjee (ed.), *India: History and Thought*, Calcutta, 1982.
6. See Romila Thapar, 'Interpretations of Ancient Indian History', in *idem*, *Ancient Indian Social History – Some Interpretations*, Delhi, 1987 (rpt.), pp. 1-25.
7. For an excellent analysis of the complexities associated with the competing ideas and shifting dominant positions in Colonial India see T. R. Trautmann, *Aryans and British India*, New Delhi, 1997.
8. Good surveys of the nationalist positions are available in Sharma, *Aspects of Political Ideas . . .* , *op. cit.*, Thapar, supra n. 6 and A. L. Basham, 'Modern Historians of Ancient India', and R. C. Majumdar, 'Nationalist Historians', in C. H. Philips (ed.), *Historians of India, Pakistan and Ceylon*, London, 1967 (rpt.), pp. 260-93 and 416-28.
9. See Kesavan Veluthat, *The Political Structure of Early Medieval South India*, *op. cit.*, Ch. 1.
10. See B. D. Chattopadhyaya, 'Autonomous Spaces and the Authority of the State: The Contradiction and its Resolution in Theory and Practice in Early India', in Bernhard Kölver *et al.* (eds.), *The State, the Law and Administration in Classical India*, München, 1997, pp. 1-14; also in Chattopadhyaya, *Studying Early India . . .* , *op. cit.*, pp. 135-52.
11. J. Gonda, *Ancient Indian Kingship from the Religious Point of View*, Leiden, 1969.
12. L. Dumont, 'Conception of Kingship in Ancient India', in *Contributions to Indian Sociology*, 1966, pp. 48-77.
13. For J. C. Heesterman's views see 'The Conundrum of the King's Authority', 'Power, Priesthood and Authority' and 'Kautilya and the Ancient Indian State', in *idem, The Inner Conflict of Tradition: Essays in Indian Ritual, Kingship and Society*, Delhi, 1985.
14. J. C. Heesterman, 'Power and Authority in Indian Tradition', in R. J. Moore (ed.), *Tradition and Politics in South Asia*, New Delhi, 1979, p. 82.
15. See for details Sibesh Bhattacharya, 'Political Authority and Brahmana-Kshatriya Relationship in Early India – An Aspect of the Power Elite Configuration', in 1984, *The Indian Historical Review* (hereafter *IHR*), X (1-2) pp.1-20.
16. B. Stein, 'The Segmentary State in South Indian History', in Richard G. Fox (ed.), *Realm and Region in Traditional India,* New Delhi, 1977, pp. 3-

51; *idem*, 'The Segmentary State: Interim Reflections', in H. Kulke (ed.), *The State in India . . .*, *op. cit.*, pp. 134-61; for a critique see D. N. Jha, 'Validity of the Brahmana-Peasant Alliance and the Segmentary State in Early Medieval India', in *Social Science Probings*, 1 (2), 1984, pp. 270-96 and R. S. Sharma, 'The Segmentary State and the Indian Experience', in *IHR*, XVI (1-2), 1989-90, pp. 80-108.

17. R. Inden, 'Hierarchies of Kings in Early Medieval India', in T. N. Madan (ed.), *Way of Life: King, Householder, Renouncer, Essays in Honour of Louis Dumont*, Delhi, 1982, pp. 99-127.
18. *Idem*, *Imagining India*, *op. cit.*, Ch. 5; also see B. P. Sahu, 'The State in Early India: An Overview', in *PIHC*, Aligarh Session, 1994, pp. 88-98.
19. See D. D. Kosambi, *An Introduction to the Study of Indian History*, Bombay, 1956, Ch. 6.
20. *Ibid.*, Chs. 9 and 10; *idem*, *The Culture and Civilization of Ancient India in Historical Outline*, London, 1965, pp. 206-9.
21. See R. S. Sharma, *Aspects of Political Ideas . . .*, *op. cit.*, Chs. IV, XII, XIV, XVI, XVII, XXII, and XXIII, for example.
22. See, for example, R. S. Sharma, *Indian Feudalism, c. 300-1200*, Calcutta, 1965, and *idem*, 'How Feudal was Indian Feudalism?', in *Journal of Peasant Studies*, 12 (2-3), 1985, pp.19-43.
23. Sharma, 'The Feudal Mind', in *idem*, *Early Medieval Indian Society – A Study in Feudalization*, Kolkata, 2001, pp. 266-82.
24. M. G. S. Narayanan, 'The Hundred Groups and the Rise of Nayar Militia in Kerala', in *PIHC*, Burdwan Session, 1983, pp. 113-19; 'The Cera Kingdom of Makotai – Factual and Conceptual Problems Related to State Formation in Kerala', Paper presented at the Seminar on State Formation in Precolonial South India, CHS, JNU, New Delhi, March 1989 (forthcoming), and *idem* and Kesavan Veluthat, 'The Bhakti Movement in South India', in S. C. Malik (ed.), *Indian Movements: Some Aspects of Dissent, Protest and Reform*, Simla, 1978, pp. 33-66; Kesavan Veluthat, *The Political Structure . . .*, *op. cit.*, R. N. Nandi, 'Feudalization of the State in Medieval South India', in *Social Science Probings*, 1 (1), 1984, pp. 33-59; also in *idem*, *State Formation, Agrarian Growth . . .*, *supra* n. 1.
25. See M. G. S. Narayanan, 'The Cera Kingdom of Makotai . . .', *supra* n. 24.
26. See, for example, Kesavan Veluthat, 'Landed Magnates as State Agents: The Gavundas under the Hoysalas in Karnataka', in *PIHC*, Gorakhpur session, 1989, pp. 118-23; also in B. P. Sahu (ed.), *Land System and Rural Society in Early India*, Delhi, 1997, pp. 322-8.
27. Nandi himself provides evidence for the complex relations between different grades of chiefs and *samantas*, *supra* n. 24; also B.P. Sahu, 'The State in Early India . . .', *supra* n. 18, pp. 94-5.
28. See, for example, Y. Subbarayalu, 'The Cola State', in *Studies in History*, 4, 1982, p. 304, and J. Heitzman, 'State Formation in South India, 850-

1280', *Indian Economic and Social History Review* (hereafter *IESHR*) 24 (1), 1987, pp. 44-61.

29. See R. N. Nandi, *op. cit.*, Kesavan Veluthat, *The Political Structure . . .*, *op. cit.*, p. 267.
30. See R.S. Sharma, 'The Kali Age: A Period of Social Crisis', in S. N. Mukherjee (ed.), *India: History and Thought*, *op. cit.*, pp. 186-203; also in *idem*, *Early Medieval Indian Society . . .*, *supra* n. 23, pp. 45-76, and B. N. S. Yadava, 'The Accounts of the Kali Age and the Social Transition from Antiquity to the Middle Ages', in *IHR*, V (1-2), 1978-9, pp. 31-63.
31. The initial doubts were raised by B. D. Chattopadhyaya in his 'Political Processes and the Structure of Polity . . .', *op. cit.*, and 'Introduction' to *The Making of Early Medieval India*, *op. cit.*, for a detailed discussion see B. P. Sahu, 'Conception of the Kali Age in Early India: A Regional Perspective', in *Trends in Social Science Research,* 4 (1), 1997, pp. 27-36.
32. See B. D. Chattopadhyaya, 'State and Economy in North India: Fourth Century to Twelfth Century', in Romila Thapar (ed.), *Recent Perspectives of Early Indian History*, Bombay, 1995, pp. 309-46.
33. *Supra* nn. 1-3 and 28; also see Romila Thapar, *The Mauryas Revisited*, Delhi, 1987; S. Seneviratne, 'Kalinga and Andhra: The Process of Secondary State Formation in Early India', in *IHR*, VII (1-2), 1980-81, pp. 54-69; B. D. Chattopadhyaya, 'Transition to the Early Historical Phase in the Deccan: A Note', in B. M. Pande and B. D. Chattopadhyaya (eds.), *Archaeology and History*, Vol. II, Delhi, 1987, pp. 727-32; and H. Kulke, 'Royal Temple Policy and the Structure of Medieval Hindu Kingdoms', in A. Eschmann, H. Kulke and G. C. Tripathi (eds.), *The Cult of Jàgannath and the Regional Tradition of Orissa*, Delhi, 1978, pp. 125-38.
34. *Supra* nn. 1 and 28; also see Kesavan Veluthat, 'Landed Magnates as State Agents . . . ', *op. cit.*, *idem*, 'Into the "Medieval" – and out of it: Early South India in Transition', Presidential Address, Medieval India Section, Bangalore session, *PIHC*, 1997; Rajan Gurukkal, 'Towards the Voice of Dissent: Trajectory of Ideological Transformation in Early South India', in *Social Scientist*, nos. 236-7, 1993, pp. 2-22; B. P. Sahu, 'Conception of the Kali Age in Early India . . .', and *id.*, 'Early State in Orissa: From the Perspective of Changing Forms of Patronage and Legitimation', in B. Pati, B. P. Sahu and T. K. Venkatasubramanian (eds.), *Negotiating India's Past: Essays in Memory of Partha Sarathi Gupta*, Delhi, 2003, pp. 29-51.
35. Thapar has always been focusing on the mutual interaction between numerous historical forces. See her Presidential Address, Ancient India section, *PIHC*, Varanasi session, 1969.
36. For Stein and Kulke *supra* nn. 16 and 33. For some of Kulke's other contributions see A. Eschmann *et al.* (eds.) *The Cult of Jagannath . . .*, *op. cit.*, also see Chattopadhyaya, 'Origin of the Rajputs: The Political, Economic and Social Processes in Early Medieval Rajasthan', in *IHR*, III,

1976, pp. 59-82; N. Dirks, 'Political Authority and Structural Change in South Indian History', in *IESHR*, 13 (2), 1976, pp. 125-57, and G. W. Spencer, 'Religious Networks and Royal Influence in Eleventh century South India, in *Journal of the Economic and Social History of the Orient*, 12, 1969, pp. 42-56, and *idem*, 'The Politics of Plunder: The Cholas in Eleventh Century Ceylon', in *Journal of Asian Studies*, 35 (3), 1976, pp. 405-19.

37. See B. P. Sahu, 'Early Medieval Orissa: Recent Historiographic Trends', *PIHC*, Dharwad session, 1988, p.163; and H. Kulke, 'The Integrative Model of State Formation in Early Medieval India: Some Historiographic Remarks', in M. Kimura and A. Tanabe (eds.), *The State in India: Past and Present* (forthcoming).
38. For example, see Kulke, 'Fragmentation and Segmentation Versus Integration? Reflections on the Concepts of Indian Feudalism and the Segmentary State in Indian History', in *Studies in History*, 4, 1982, pp. 237-63; Chattopadhyaya, 'Political Processes and the Structure of Polity . . .', *op. cit.*, and 'State and Economy in North India . . .', *op. cit.*
39. *Ibid.*, also see Chattopadhyaya, 'Markets and Merchants in Early Medieval Rajasthan', in idem, *The Making of Early Medieval India*, *op. cit.*, pp. 89-119; *idem*, *Aspects of Rural Settlements and Rural Society in Early Medieval India*, Calcutta, 1990, Ch. 3; and B. P. Sahu 'Agrarian Changes and the Peasantry in Early Medieval Orissa (*c.* A.D. 400-1100)', in V. K. Thakur and A. Aounshuman (eds.), *Peasants in Indian History*, Vol. I, Patna, 1996, pp. 283-311.
40. See Kesavan Veluthat, 'Landed Magnates as State Agents . . .', *op. cit.*, Cynthia Talbot, 'Political Intermediaries in Kakatiya Andhra, 1175-1325', in *IESHR*, 31 (3), 1994, pp. 261-89 and Chattopadhyaya, *Aspects of Rural Settlements . . .*, *op. cit.*, Ch. 2.
41. For a recent statement on the issue see B. P. Sahu, 'Legitimation, Ideology and State in Early India', Presidential Address, Ancient India section, *PIHC*, Mysore session, 2003, pp. 44-76.
42. *Supra* n. 10.
43. *Ibid.*, also see Rajan Gurukkal, 'Aspects of Warrior Power in Localised Agriculture: The Case of Pandya Region during the Early Medieval Period', in *PIHC*, Srinagar session, 1986, pp. 192-8, and V. S. Elizabeth, 'Hero-stones in the Rashtrakuta Period : Their Implications for Society and Polity', *PIHC*, Gorakhpur session, 1989, pp. 828-33, and Romila Thapar, 'Death and the Hero', in *idem*, *Cultural Pasts: Essays in Early Indian History*, New Delhi, 2000, especially pp. 690-1.
44. See Chattopadhyaya, *The Making of Early Medieval India*, *op. cit.*, p. 30 and Kulke, *supra* n. 37.
45. For a good discussion of the idea of 'little kingdom', for example, which was a structural constituent of the expansive, incorporative states see

B. Schnepel and G. Berkemer,'History of the Model'; G. Berkemer and Margret Frenz, 'Hermann Kulke: An Appreciation of His Contribution to the Debate', among others, in Georg Berkemer and Margret Frenz (eds.), *Sharing Sovereignty: The Little Kingdom in South Asia,* Berlin, 2003.

CHAPTER 4

The Horse in Indian History

DIETMAR ROTHERMUND

The horse enables the man who masters it to rise above those who remain pedestrians. As a warrior the man on horseback not only gains stature but also speed. The natural habitat of horses are the steppes of Central Asia from which they have migrated with their masters throughout Eurasia and then even overseas. The horse was presumably domesticated in the fourth millennium BC. but its initial spread took a long time. The lack of suitable pastures and of a moderate climate inhibited this spread. Thus the Indus Civilization remained horseless throughout the millennia of its long existence. It was not until invaders from Central Asia arrived in India around 1500 BC that the horse came to India along with them. This pattern of invasion was repeated again and again in subsequent periods.

The fact that the Indus Civilization was a horseless one was of great importance for its social structure and political organization. It obviously did not produce an empire, but it also did not give rise to disconnected city states. Mastering the inundations of the mighty Indus which carried twice as much water as the Nile obviously required planning and this was probably the task of an astronomer-priesthood which also showed its hand in the amazingly uniform system of weights and measures which prevailed throughout the vast, 'civilized' territory. This elite rather than warriors on horseback controlled the society of its day and age. Oligarchy rather than monarchy suited this style of social and political organization. Warrior kings were buried in impressive tombs—even in the steppes of Central Asia. The rich Indus Civilization could have produced magnificient royal monuments—but they are conspicuous by their absence.

The riders who invaded India around 1500 BC in small bands, roaming around as nomads in the northern plains, had a very different lifestyle. They were dominated by a warrior élite which constituted a stratified nobility, making a distinction between royal lineages and a lower nobility which was probably recruited by the kings. The main instrument of warfare was the horse-drawn chariot which had been invented and developed in Western Asia and had even reached Egypt before 1500 BC. It was brought to India in its fully developed form and required highly trained professional warriors, both charioteers and archers, who presumably devoted most of their time to this pursuit.

The archer on a chariot was in a much better position to aim his arrows at an enemy than the man on horseback. Ancient Mesopotamian sculptures of archers on horseback show them mostly shooting at animals at close range. But this style of shooting was not suitable when fighting another archer. In chariot warfare two skills were combined – that of the charioteer who knew how to guide the horses so as to change from rapid speed to a sudden stop and that of the archer who made use of this brief stop to take aim and shoot with precision.

Chariot warfare did not contribute to centralizing power. It could be practised by numerous small states. Typically the test of strength among such states was organized around the *ashvamedha*, the horse-sacrifice. Before being sacrificed the horse was permitted to roam freely. Guards would follow it to see whether anybody dared to stand in its way. Whoever did this showed that he contested the power of him to whom the horse belonged. Such a contest would then lead to chariot warfare which was conducted in a chivalrous way. Only the archer was protected by a kind of armour, the charioteer was naked to the waist, shooting at him would be ruled out in a *dharmayuddha* (righteous war).

Small states based on chariot warfare spread in the Gangetic plains. They were finally eclipsed by the rise of eastern empires whose power was based on the war-elephant which was truly an imperial animal. These empires, from the Nandas and Mauryas to the Guptas, depended on the control of a fertile central region supplemented by a control of farflung trade routes. They left out many areas that were difficult to rule and would have been of little benefit to the empire. When these empires were replaced by the spread of regional kingdoms throughout the subcontinent, the horse once more came into prominence. Intermittently new invaders from Central Asia such as the Sakas and

Kushanas who could depend on ready access to the horses of their homeland had made inroads into India and had introduced a new type of cavalry warfare. The chariot was not revived and remained a purely ceremonial vehicle in later times. The *ashvamedha* also lost its original function and was celebrated as a manifestation of royal power – it had become a 'quotation' that merely reflected its earlier ritual importance.

Medieval Indian kingdoms used both cavalry and contingents of war-elephants as documented in the innumerable lively battle scenes that adorn the friezes of Indian temples. The structure of the medieval Indian regional kingdoms gave rise to a balance of power. A more or less narrowly circumscribed area under direct rule was complemented by a much wider outreach of military intervention, but the latter was usually ephemeral. It could lead to grandiose expeditions termed 'digvijaya' (conquest of all quarters of the earth)—something to be carved in stone to impress future generations. But it rarely led to permanent domination.

The medieval balance of power was rudely disturbed when Islamic invaders from Central Asia stormed into India on their swift horses. Not only did they have an ample supply of horses but also military slaves who were trained from their boyhood to ride and fight. Being slaves they could never give rise to a nobility as the charioteers of old had done. But due to military valour the most daring slaves could usurp the throne. The 'slave sultan' became a common feature of Islamic rule everywhere. The cavalry of the sultans in India was of enormous dimensions, maintained by revenue assignments (*iqta*) to the cavalry commanders. This system soon covered most of the north Indian plains. The new type of cavalry warfare also increased the potential of long-distance military intervention. Southern India was ransacked by the cavalry of the north. The remaining Hindu rulers of the south could only defend themselves by turning their realms into cavalry states as well. They did not have a system of military slavery but they privileged cavalry captains (*nayaks*) who also received revenue assignments.

Procuring good war-horses for the rapidly proliferating cavalry became increasingly a problem. The breeding of horses in India did not succeed, primarily due to the lack of pastures and adequate feeding. The hot climate made horses sick and there were no specialized veterinarians to take care of them. For southern India the access to the horses of Central Asia was almost impossible because of the long distance and covetous rulers in between. Shipping horses from Arabia and the Persian Gulf was the only alternative. Many horses died at sea. Indian rulers were prepared to pay for horses dead or alive so as to insure the horse trade. Persian horse traders rose to great wealth and prominent political positions in India. One of the most famous among them was Mahmud Gawan, minister and general of the Bahmani-Sultan. He conquered southern India from coast to coast for his ruler from 1461 to 1481. After the Portuguese captured Goa in 1511, they participated in the overseas horse trade with great success, emerging as the main suppliers of the Vijayanagar kingdom. Goa had actually been a landing place of the Persian horse traders before the Portuguese captured it.

The high price of imported horses implied that only rich rulers could afford to buy them in sufficient numbers. In this way the war-horse contributed to the centralization of power. At the same time, the maintenance of large cavalry units necessitated a higher revenue – and the man on horseback was an awe-inspiring revenue collector. By about 1400, the cavalry system covered practically the whole of South Asia and this led to a rather uniform pattern of local government. The country was dotted by towns which served triple purposes: cavalry garrisons, market places and district headquarters. The king-pin was the cavalry captain who was also at the head of the local government. Earlier forms of local government were extinguished by cavalry rule which spread everywhere. Most of these towns survived as district headquarters until present times, a few became big cities like Bangalore, founded by Kempe Gowda, a cavalry captain of the Vijayanagar kingdom in the sixteenth century.

The Great Mughals based their military success on the field artillery that they pioneered in India, but for the most part their empire remained a cavalry state. They continued the practices of their predecessors backed up by their enhanced central power. As far as expenditure on warfare and the maintenance of enormous armed forces was concerned, they surpassed their predecessors. After the eclipse of the Mughal empire the successor states continued the same traditions of administration and warfare. Their élite had a cavalry mentality which prevented it from recognising the effectiveness of the European-trained infantry which finally emerged as a deadly threat to cavalry power. Shooting salvo after salvo in a well organized manner, an infantry could mow down a cavalry with merciless precision. With the rise of the infantry the war-horse was marginalized in Indian military history.

But even the British, who based their military success on the infantry, paid some attention to the horse. They succeeded in breeding horses in India. The function of the horse as a symbol of superior authority was respected even by the Indian Civil Service which replaced the earlier élite of cavalry captains. A district officer had to be able to ride through his district. The riding test was one of the greatest hurdles in the civil service examination. It was no use passing the other parts of this exam if one finally fell from the horse. Some famous Indian candidates for the ICS ended their careers prematurely in this way and then turned their attention to nationalist politics.

Although the horse played such a highly visible role in Indian history, it never had a share in the extension of Indian agriculture. In Europe the horse as draught-animal was of invaluable help in ploughing the heavy soil of the marshy plains in the late middle ages. This soil would only yield to a strong iron plough which bullocks could not draw. But whereas bullocks could be easily yoked to the plough, the anatomy of the horse was unsuitable for a yoke. It was only when the padded horse-collar was invented in the late middle ages that the horse could be made to draw the plough. Horse breeding was then aimed at producing sturdy animals for this purpose. True, European knights with their heavy armour had already required sturdy horses and it was only one further step to breed draught-horses. In India cavalry men were rarely protected by heavy armour. In most cases the slave riding the horse in battle was cheaper than his mount. As far as draught-animals were concerned, bullocks and buffalos were all that was needed. The Indian plough remained more or less the same simple wooden tool from the days of the Indus civilization to the present. This was due to the fact that it was best suited for Indian soils which would only lose moisture if ploughed more deeply. Thus the horse was not needed for Indian agriculture and could devote itself to 'noble' pursuits such a warfare and ceremonial appearances. At north Indian weddings the bridegroom must still arrive on horse-back – which often is the first and the last horse ride of his life.

BIBLIOGRAPHY

Digby, Simon, *War-horse and Elephant in the Delhi Sultanate*, Oxford, 1971.

Gommans, Jos J. L., *The Rise of the Indo-Afghan Empire, c.1710-1780*, New Delhi, 1994.

———, *Mughal Warfare*, London, 2002.

Kuhrt, Amélie, *The Ancient Near East, c.3000-330 BC.*, 2 vols., London, 1995.

Moorey, P. R. S., 'The emergence of the light horse-drawn chariot in the Near East', in *World Archaeology*, Vol. 18, No. 2, 1986, pp. 196-215.

PART II

Issues in South and South-East Asian History

CHAPTER 5

Khāravela and the Connected Problems

SNIGDHA TRIPATHY

Since the mid-nineteenth century, a galaxy of scholars has endeavoured to establish the truth about the enigmatic Khāravela, the 'lord of Kaliṅga'. The only source for this king, so far the earliest known ruler of Kaliṅga, is the well-known Hātigumphā inscription on the twin hills of Udayagiri-Khaṇḍagiri in the Orissan capital city of Bhubaneswar. Unfortunately, this inscription is, at present, in an extremely sad state of preservation, and controversies prevail among scholars on the ancestry of Khāravela, the identification of his capital of Kaliṅganagari, the extent of the kingdom of Kaliṅga during his rule, the period of his reign, and so on. Although much has been said about this illustrious king of Kaliṅga since James Prinsep deciphered the Hātigumphā inscription during 1837, and subsequently by scholars like Bhagwanlal Indraji, K. P. Jayaswal, B. M. Barua, and D. C. Sircar,[1] still more remains to be done. The present paper aims at providing a rational basis for further research on Khāravela and connected problems of Orissan history. It also aims at finding a solution for certain major historical problems connected with Khāravela's reign, such as, the location of his capital Kaliṅganagari, the extent of his kingdom of Kaliṅga and above all, the ancestry of this enigmatic king. A rational settlement to these problems will no doubt, pave the way for an easy access to other connected problems arisen out of the historical data provided by the Hātigumphā inscription.

Unfortunately, the majority of letters in the Hātigumphā inscription are now lost. Scholars, in spite of incessant efforts to decipher and interpret the contents, have not yet been successful in establishing, a final reading, Rather, the variant readings of the text have yielded peculiar interpretations and complicated the problem. For this reason, there have arisen confusing views on Khāravela's ancestry. Hence it is imperative to search for other epigraphic and other records that may corroborate the data furnished in the Hātigumphā inscription.

Scholars have not yet been successful in establishing convincingly the ancestry of Khāravela, the royal family to which he belonged. Although there is no paucity of materials yielding corroborative evidence on this point, scholars so far have ignored them and remained rigid on their arguments.

It is now well known that the Hātigumphā inscription contains a succinct account of the career and achievements of Khāravela during the thirteen years of his reign in Kaliṅga. The record throws sufficient light on the ancestry of this 'lord of Kaliṅga', though scholars, basing on the misinterpretation of the words engraved on it and on some fabricated and legendary accounts furnished in the ancient Indian literary texts, still believe, that Khāravela belonged to the ancient Cedi dynasty. There is clear evidence in the first line of the inscription to indicate the ancestry: fortunately, the letters are still quite clear and the scholars are quite unanimous on the reading of the text which is in Prakrit language and runs thus: *Aireṇa mahārājena Mahāmeghavāhanena Cetarāja-vasa-vadhanena pasatha-subha-lakhanena-caturaṁta-luṭhana-guṇa-upitena-Kaliṅgādhipatinā-Siri-Khāravelena.*[2] This is generally regarded to be in *gadya-kāvya* style. The Sanskritized text of this line is as follows: *Āryeṇa mahārājena Mahāmeghavāhanena Cetarāja-vaṁśa-vardhanena praśasta-śubha-lakṣaṇena caturanta-luṇṭhana-guṇ-opetena Kaliṅg-Ādhipatinā Śrī-Khāravelena.*

This text line introduces Khāravela, endows him with some epithets, and states the name of the family to which he belonged in a eulogical manner. He has been endowed with the honorific *aira* (in Sanskrit *ārya*). Previously, the expression *aira* was believed to be the name of the eulogised king, when James Prinsep deciphered the inscription during 1837. But subsequently during 1885, it was discarded as a personal name by Bhagwanlal Indraji who read the name of the king mentioned in the record as Khāravela. It was also often taken by earlier scholars to be the name of Khāravela's family. But this honorific of *aira* or *ārya* has now been noticed especially in the early Prakrit inscriptions of southern India, generally assigned to about the second or third centuries of the Christian era. Thus an inscription from Velpuru in the Sattenapalle taluk of the Guntur district of Andhra Pradesh[3] reveals the name Siri-Mānasada or Siri-Mahāsada[4] prefixed with an epithet of *airasa* (Skt. *āryasya*). He had the matronymic Hāritiputa (Skt. Hāritiputra) like those of the later Sātavāhanas, such as, Vāśiṣṭhiputra Pulumāvi, although previously, scholars were of the opinion that Siri-Mānasada belonged to the *Aira* family. That the Prakrit form of *aira* stands for *ārya* is evidenced in the epigraphic records of the later Sātavāhana kings. In the Nasik cave inscription of Vāśiṣṭhiputra Pulumāvi[5] we find the expression *mahā-airakena* (Skt. *mahāryakena*) applied to the ruling members of the family and their predecessors. The expression is also found with the name of a king named Viśākhamitra prefixed with the honorific *ārya*[6] who ruled over Magadha in about AD 100 in the northern part of India. Kuḍepa-siri, who was presumably the son and successor of Khāravela mentioned in the Manchapuri cave inscription, assigned to the same period as that of the Hātigumphā, has also been endowed with this honorific, *aira*.[7]

Another expression, *mahāmeghavāhana*, inscribed in the first line in the introduction of Khāravela, and also found with the name of Kuḍepa-siri in the above said Manchapuri cave inscription, is sometimes believed to be the name of the grandfather of Khāravela.[8] He is also taken to be the founder of the dynasty to which Khāravela belonged. There is, however, no evidence to support such a speculation. The expression is in the third case-ending in the Hātigumphā inscription where as in the Manchapuri cave inscription it is in the sixth case-eding, both used as an epithet in the introductory portion indicating also the family name for the respective kings. It is, however, to be taken as a family name like that of the Sātavāhana of the Deccan. It is pertinent in the present context to refer to another equally important inscription in four copies, engraved on four different stone pillars at Guntupally in the West Godavari district of Andhra Pradesh.[9] This inscription is significant from various points of view, so far as the history of Khāravela and his time is concerned. This is a record of the time of one Siri-Sada who belonged to the Mahāmeghavāhana family and was the lord of Kaliṅga and Mahiṣaka as stated therein, and this further corroborates the assumption relating to the existence of the Mahāmeghavāhana family not only in Kaliṅga but in Mahiṣaka too during about the 1st century BC. Other significant facts revealed by this record as will be subsequently discussed, have remained so far ignored by the scholarly world. Some scholars, however, find the name of Mahāmeghavāhana a synonym for the god Indra or Mahendra, whose vehicle is the great cloud, and believe that the kings of this dynasty claimed descent from Indra-*kula* or god Indra.[10] This needs further investigation but we may refer to a Sātavāhana inscription discovered in recent years from the Buddhist site at Sannati in the Gulbarga district of Karnataka, wherein we find an expression apparently synonymous with Mahāmeghavāhana.[11] Unfortunately, the said inscription is in a very bad state of preservation and almost half of it is now damaged and lost. It reads the name of Siri-Sātakarṇi, possibly, indicating Vāśiṣṭhiputra Siri-Sātakarṇi of the Sātavāhana dynasty. It enumerates by way of epithets of Siri-Sātakarṇi, his military achievements in the Deccan, his successful expeditions against the Kṣatrapas and others, in this long description, we find the expression of *Abhagavāhanasa*. . . . But the subsequent words are lost. This could be an epithet of Siri-Sātakarṇi as the context would suggest. The word *abhaga* has been interpreted by the editors to mean 'dark cloud', which may be taken as a synonym for *mahā-megha* and thus Abhagavāhana would tend to indicate same as Mahāmeghavāhana. The intended reading of the missing word after Abhagavāhana may indicate that Śrī Sātakarṇi, along with the enemies like the western Kṣatrapas, also annihilated the Abhagavāhanas or the Mahāmeghavāhanas.

Apart from Khāravela and his successor Kuḍepa-siri, we find thus a third king of the Mahāmeghavāhana dynasty of Kaliṅga named Siri-Sada. It is to be noted that while Khāravela and Kuḍepa-siri were endowed with the title of 'lord of Kaliṅga', Siri-Sada assumed the royal title of 'lord of Kaliṅga and Mahiṣaka'.

Before we determine the exact relationship between Khāravela and Siri-Sada of the Guntupally inscription, it is pertinent to discuss another significant epithet of Khāravela in the first line of the Hātigumphā inscription, generally read as *Cetarāja-vaṁśa-vardhanena*. The medial *e* sign in *C* in the original is very much doubtful now. It looks like *Catarāja-vaṁśa-vardhanena*. Whatever may be the reading of this name, either *Ca* or *Ce*, it would also be significant. The epithet tends to mean 'one who extends or increases the family of Cetarāja' or 'Catarāja'. Scholars read previously the word Ceta, but corrected it as Ceti and finally modified it as Cedi, obviously to suit their assumptions and interpreted the epithet as 'one who enhances the glory of the Cedi royal family'.[12] It has now become almost an established fact that Khāravela belonged to the Cedi dynasty.

This belief has been further strengthened by another epithet of Khāravela incised at the end of the Hātigumphā inscription (line 17), which reads, *rājisi-Vasu-kula vinisito* (Skt. *rājarṣi-Vasu-kula-viniśritaḥ*) and the meaning of which is 'one who has hailed from the family of *rājarṣi*-Vasu'. Here the word *rājarṣi* (the saint king) is an epithet of Vasu to whose family Khāravela is stated to have belonged.[13] The arguments of historians on this point appear to be highly conjectural and confusing when they try to identify this *rājarṣi*-Vasu[14] with a Paurava king described in the *Mahābhārata* as Uparicara-Vasu. He is again identified with the Cetiya (Cedi) king named Upacara mentioned in the Buddhist Cetiya-jātaka. Further, another king named Vasu is found in the Jain *Harivaṁśa-Purāṇa* who has been called the son of Abhicandra, the founder of the Cedirāṣṭra at the foot of the Vindhyas.

It is interesting to note that the stories relating to each of these personalities, Vasu, Uparicara-Vasu and Upacara, are different. Yet scholars have made frantic efforts to corroborate the traditions and prove that the king named Uparicara-Vasu or Upacara of the Brahmanic, Buddhist and Jain traditions was the same person and the ancestor of Khāravela of the historical Mahāmeghavāhana dynasty. Further, during recent years, another speculation has arisen out of the misinterpretation of the epithet of *rājarṣi-Vasu.* Some scholars now believe that the dynastic name Mahāmeghavāhana has a synonymous link with *rājarṣi-Vasu-kula,* which according to them is 'same as Vāsava-kula, just like Yadu-kula may be described as Yādava-kula and Raghu-kula as Rāghava-kula and so Vasu-kula would mean descendant of Indra-kula, i.e. Mahāmeghavāhana-kula'.[15] But in their explanation, the epithet of *rājarṣi* with Vasu, the saintly king, has been totally ignored. The expression *rājarṣi* with which the name of Vasu is endowed seems to indicate that he was a historical personage and not a mythical king like Indra or Yadu as has been speculated and may have been a remote ancestor of Khāravela. The practice of showing reverence to predecessors with such expressions as *rājarṣi* is not rare in the inscriptions of the contemporary Sātavāhana and other dynasties of the Deccan. In the Nasik cave inscription of Vāsiṣṭhiputra Pulumāvi, the mother of Gautamīputra Sātakarṇi (or Śrī-Sātakarṇi) named Gautamī-Balaśriyā has been described *rājarṣi-vadhū*.[16] The early Ikṣvāku kings of southern India were hailed in reverence by the Kekayas of Karnataka region of about the fourth-fifth centuries who were matrimonially related, and endowed with the epithet of *rājarṣi,* which has been recorded in one of their inscriptions.[17] Thus *rājarṣi*-Vasu seems to be one of the predecessors of Khāravela, who regarded it a matter of pride that he hailed from the royal family to which this saint king belonged.

In lines 2 and 3 of the Hātigumphā inscription, there is a passage, *tatiye Kaliṅga-rāja-vase-purisa-yuge mahārājābhisecanam pāpunāti* (Skt. *tṛtīye Kaliṅga-rājavaṁśe puruṣa-yuge mahārāj-ābhiṣecanaṁ prāpnoti).* It indicates that Khāravela belonged to the third generation in the royal family of Kaliṅga. But some historians have interpreted the expression *Kaliṅga-rājavaṁśa* as the family of king named Kaliṅgarāja who they say is the grandfather of Khāravela. They have also shown instances of the existence of the name of Kaliṅgarāja in the royal family such as the Kalachuri who is said to be the founder of the Kalachuri family of Tummana (Madhya Pradesh). But this is highly conjectural and confusing, and based on the wrong interpretation of the expression. It is possible to think that *rājarṣi*-Vasu was the grandfather of Khāravela and the founder of the royal family of Mahāmeghavāhana of Kaliṅga.

Now, if we accept the epithet of Khāravela in the first line of the Hātigumphā inscription, *Cetarāja-vaṁśa-vardhanena* in the sense of 'one who extended the family of Cetarāja' (or Catarāja)', it would give us a clue to Khāravela's ancestry. Cetarāja would evidently indicate the name of Khāravela's father, whose family was extended by him. In this context, we may point out here the influence of south Indian pronunciation of Prakrit words in the early Prakrit inscriptions, especially of southern India. According to Prakrit grammar and Sauraṣeṇi Prakrit the pronounciation of *ta* and *tha* usually change to *da* and *dha* respectively. In the Hātigumphā as well as the other Brāhmī inscriptions in the Udayagiri-Khaṇḍagiri caves, for this several examples are found, especially those which are frequently met with in the south Indian Prakrit inscriptions of the early historic period. Thus we notice the pronounciation of *tha* being changed to *dha* in the words like *padhame* for *prathame* (line 3), *radha* for *ratha* (line 4), *Madhuraṁ* for *Mathurām* (line 8), etc. Even *tha* sometimes changed to *ṭha* as is know in the Nanaghat inscription of the Sātavāhana queen Nāyanikā, in which we find *Dakhinapaṭha* for *Dakṣiṇāpatha* (line 2).[18] There is also frequent use of *da* in place of *ta* as in *Sada* for *Sata* or *Sāta*, *Sādavāhana* for *Sātavāhana*, *Sadakaṁni* for *Sātakarṇi* in the Sātavāhana inscriptions as well as in the above mentioned Velpuru and Guntupally inscriptions. Again, *ga* in place of *ka* and *va* in place of *pa* are found written according to Dravidian pronounciation in the word *uvāsaga* for *upāsaka* in line 14 of the Hātigumphā inscription. The Guntupally inscription of Siri-Sada (Śrī-Sāta) has *Mahāmekhavāhana* for *Mahāmeghavāhana* (in line 2 of one of the copies of the record). This is an example of the influence of Paiśācī Prakrit in the pronounciation of *kha* for *gha* in the south Indian Prakrit inscriptions. Further, the exchange of *ca* for *sa* or *śa* or *ṣa* was not altogether unknown in the south Indian records. There are instances of *sa* or *śa* changing to *ca* due mainly under the influence of Dravidian pronounciation in the Prakrit inscriptions of the early centuries of the Christian era. Thus we notice *Cāṁtisiri* for *Śāntiśrī*, *Cāṁtamula* for *Śāntamūla* or *Kṣantamūla* in the Ikṣvāku inscriptions of Nagarjunikonda in Andhra Pradesh.[19]

In the context of change of letters in the Dravidian Prakrit words, D. C. Sircar has rightly observed the change of *ṣa* into *ca* in the name of two kings of the Kadambas of Goa:

> The name Ṣaṣṭha or Ṣaṣṭhadeva has in these cases the Prakrit forms of Caṭṭa. . . . Sten Know for this reason is inclined to take Cāṁtamula as a Prakrit form of Sanskrit Kṣāntamula. It must also be remembered that Tamil, a typical Dravidian language, has no letter in its alphabet corresponding to *śa* of Sanskrit and that Sanskrit *śa* generally represented in Tamil by *ca*, e.g. Sanskrit-*paśu* = Tamil-*pacu*; Sanskrit-*śatru* = Tamil-*catturu*; Sanskrit-*śastraka* = Tamil-cattakam, etc. This is due possibly to the fact that Sanskrit *śa* is represented in Prakrit by sa which again is almost identical in sound with Dravidian *ca*, cf. Kulacarman for Kulaśarman in the Udayendiram grant of Nandivarman of the Pallava dynasty. Sometimes *śa* is represented by *ca* in Prakrit, e.g. Sanskrit *śava* = Pali *cava*. The word Śaka has sometimes been mentioned in Indian literature, e.g. in the *Gārgīsaṁhitā* as *caka*. . . .[20]

Similar peculiarities in the Hātigumphā inscription and other minor Brāhmī records in the Udayagiri-Khaṇḍagiri caves had escaped the the attention of scholars including D. C. Sircar. In the present context,

Cetarāja or *Catarāja* in Khāravela's epithet may have been intended for Sanskrit *Sātarāja* or *Śatarāja*. There is every reason to believe, then that Catarāja or Sātarāja was the father of Khāravela. For this reason the epithet conveys the meaning that Khāravela extended or increased the family of Sātarāja (or Catarāja). So the Cedi dynasty of the ancient literary texts has nothing to do with the Mahāmeghavāhana family of Sātarāja, Khāravela and their successors. We have noticed similar epithets for early Sātavāhana rulers.[21]

Another Prakrit form of *Śāta* or *Śata is* Sada, *the letter* ta *being changed to* da as already noted above. That Catarāja/Satarāja, the father of Khāravela of the Hātigumphā inscription, was the same king as mentioned the Guntupally inscription, endowed with the royal titles of *mahārāja* and the 'lord of Kaliṅga and Mahiṣaka', can now be established with further corroborative evidence gathered from minor Brāhmī inscriptions assigned to the same period as that of the Hātigumphā in the caves of Udayagiri-Khaṇḍagiri hills. Further, as will be known from the discussion below, the writer of all these inscriptions including the big Hātigumphā and the Guntupally records was one and the same person. The record also reveals the southern origin of Khāravela and the writer of his inscription. Unfortunately, though the Hātigumphā inscription of Khāravela has been examined, deciphered and interpreted in various ways from time to time by numerous scholars since its discovery, the other minor Brāhmī records of the same period in the twin hills have not attracted adequate attention. Even though they are short called minor inscriptions, and are recent investigations have shown that these are no less important for the reconstruction of Kaliṅgan history.[22] A detailed study of them has now become necessary.

We begin with three short Prakrit records in the caves now called Sarpagumphā and Haridasgumphā close to the Hātigumphā on the Udayagiri hill. The Sarpagumphā has two inscriptions, while the Haridas cave is engraved with one. Palaeographically, all these records may be assigned to the same period as that of the Hātigumphā, i.e. to the late first century BC. This is corroborated by the internal evidence. The first inscription of the Sarpagumphā, consisting of one line, reads, *Culakamasa koṭhā jeyā ca.*

This has been translated by R. D. Banerji, the editor of the inscription, as 'the unsurpassable chamber of Culakama' (Skt.

Kṣudrakarma). The suggestion of F. W. Thomas, one of the editors of *Epigraphia Indica*, Vol. XIII, to interpret the name Culakama as Cuḍākarman is not tenable as Prakrit Cula is Kṣudra in Sanskrit. As regards the expressions *koṭhā* and *jeyā,* the editor of the inscription at first thought the two words *koṭhā* and *jeyā* were united by a *sandhi*, but later interpreted only *koṭhā* as denoting a chamber; he took *jeyā* to be *ajeya* because of the *sandhi* and interpreted it as 'unconquerable', qualifying *koṭhā*. But he overlooked the conjunction *ca* which follows *koṭhā* and *jeyā*. The latter seems to have a technical meaning denoting a veranda or some other part of a chamber or *koṭhā*. The inscription may thus be interpreted as 'chamber and veranda (or a side-chamber) of Culakama or Cullakarman or Kṣudrakarman'.

The second inscription in the Sarpagumphā consists of two lines of Brāhmī of the same period. The text has been read by R. D. Banerji as 1. *Kaṁmasa Halakhi*, 2. *ṇaya ca pasādo.*

The vowel marks and sign for *anusvāra* are difficult to distinguish as the inscription has been engraved on a very rough surface, but the facsimile shows on the left, at the beginning of the first line, very faintly a letter resembling *la*, not noticed by the editor. So the first word of the first line may have been intended for Culakaṁmasa (Kṣudrakarmasya or Cullakarmasya), indicating the name of the same person who has been mentioned in the first inscription. It has been translated by the editor as the 'temple of Cullakarman and Halakhiṇa'. He has taken the word *pasādo* in the sense of *pāsādo* (prāsādaḥ) or the 'temple'. But in the absence of a medial *ā* sign over the letter *pa*, it should be read as *pasādo* or in Sanskrit *prāsādaḥ* in the sense of 'gift. Interestingly, the same word *pasādo* has been repeated in the third inscription in the Haridās cave as will be shown below. So the inscription indicates a gift made by two persons, Cullakarman and Halakhiṇa. As regards the name of the second person, F. W. Thomas tentatively Sanskritized it as Ślakṣaṇāyāḥ (?) with a question mark.[23] In this context again, there is considerable influence of south Indian pronounciation. The change of *śa* or *sa* into *ha* is frequently met in the Prakrit inscriptions of the early centuries of the Christian era. The epigraphic records of the early Sātavāhanas of the Deccan often exhibit such peculiarities in the names of the members of the dynasty such as Hakusiri Śaktiśrī in Sanskrit.[24]

The name Halakhiṇaya in the sixth case – ending appears to denote a female. Though the medial signs are now obliterated, there is no difficulty to Sanskritize the name as Sulakṣaṇāyā and since her name is mentioned with that of Cullakarman or Kṣudrakarman, she appears to be his wife. Both of them made a gift of the said cave, evidently to some Jaina monks.

We may now refer to the third inscription of Culakama engraved in the Haridas cave in the Udayagiri hill. It is written in one line and incised over one of the entrances to the main chamber of the cave from the veranda. It reads *Culakamasa pasāto koṭhā jeyā ca*. There seems to be a chisel mark just below the letter *ka* in the name of Culakama, which has been read by R. D. Banerji as Culakrama and again he has presumed the word *pasāto* to be *pāsāto* in the sense of a temple, Banerji translated the text as 'the temple and unsurpassable chamber of Cullakarman (or Kṣudrakarman)'. But the correct reading should be *prasādaḥ* in Sanskrit, similar to the case of the first inscription of the Sarpagumphā. The point to be noted here is that, in the present record *pasāto* is written in place of *pasādo* (Skt. *prasādaḥ*), *da* being changed to *ta* but carrying the same meaning. A similar peculiarity of *ta* being changed to *da* noticed in *Mahiṣakādhipadi* for *Mahiṣākadhipati* in one of the versions of the Guntupally inscription of Siri-Sada (or Śrī-Sāta).[25] While Sten Konow and F. W. Thomas[26] suggest that the meaning of *pasādo* or *pasāto* (Skt. *prasādaḥ*) is gift, the editor has interpreted it as *pāsādo* (*prasādaḥ*) in the sense of a temple. The word *pasāto* or *pasādo* cannot be taken as a scribal error (as belived by R. D. Banerji) for *pāsādo* as both the inscriptions of Cullakarman (or Kṣudrakarman) have the same word denoting a gift.

Thus all these three inscriptions indicate that Cullakarman or Kṣudrakarman and his wife Sulakṣaṇā caused the construction of the chambers (caves) and dedicated them in favour of Jaina monks. Further, they also built two chambers along with the verandas for the purpose of their own residence (*koṭhā* and *jeyā*) in the said caves, side by side with the donated caves.

The above discussion on the influence of South Indian pronunciation, change of letters in the Prakrit words found in the Hātigumphā and other minor Brāhmī inscriptions of the twin hills of Udayagiri-Khandagiri shows that all these records were written and engraved by a south Indian scribe who seems to have accompanied Khāravela and his family to the Bhubaneswar region. The engravings also give the impression that the scribe tried to follow the local pronounciation of Prakrit words, though at places he left marks of his own Dravidian peculiarities. The subsequent discussion would furnish more evidences on this assumption.

The interesting fact to be noted is that we find one Culagoma as the writer of the Guntupally inscription of the time of Siri-Sada, the lord of Kaliṅga and Mahiṣaka of the Mahāmeghavāhana dynasty of about the early first century BC. Evidently, there is a striking similarity in the name of Culagoma (Skt. Cullakarman or Kṣudrakarman) with that of Culakama of the Sarpagumphā and Haridās cave inscriptions. Further, the scripts used in all these inscriptions have striking similarity even though scholars assign the Guntupally inscription to a later date than that of the Hātigumphā records.[27]

The writer of this record, Culagoma, seems to have followed the local Dravidian pronounciation of words like Mahāmekhavāhana in place of Mahāmeghavāhana, *Sada* for *Sata* or *Sāta*, and of his own name Culagoma for Culakama (Skt. Cullakarman or Kṣudrakarman). Here *ka* has been changed to *ga* as is noticed in the south Indian pronounciation even in the present day. Scholars, however, have read the named Cula-Goma and Sanskritized it as Kṣudra-Goma.[28] This is not convincing. Culagoma was evidently the same person named Culakama of the Haridās cave and the Sarpagumphā inscriptions who along with his wife accompanied Khāravela and his family to the great Jaina centre in the Udayagiri and Khaṇḍagiri hills, and probably was the writer of all the Brāhmī inscriptions of the period and place in question, including that of the big Hātigumphā inscription of Khāravela. It may be pointed out here that Culagoma or Kṣudrakarman is stated in the Guntupally inscription to be the writer of Siri-Sada of the Mahāmeghavāhana dynasty of Kaliṅga and Mahiṣaka and who was the father-predecessor of Khāravela. This would also indicate that Culagoma served two generations of the said dynasty. It would be better to cite one of the four copies of the record here:

1. *Mahārājasa Kaliṅga-Mahi*
2. *sakādhipadisa Mahāme-*
3. *khavāhanasa Siri-Sada-*
4. *sa lekhakasa Culago-*
5. *masa maṁdapa dānaṁ* [11*][29]

If both names, Culagoma and Culakama, in all these records are taken to be the same, it would be clear that Khāravela and Siri-Sada were closely related to each other, the former being the son of the latter as corroborated by the epithet reading *Catarāja-vaṁśa-vardhanena* in the first line of his inscription.

Yet many believe, on palaeographical considerations, that Siri-Sada (or Śrī-Sāta) of the Guntupally inscription was a later successor of Khāravela. According to them, some of the characters of the Guntupally inscription are very considerably later than those of the Hātigumphā.[30] But it is not always safe to rely upon palaeography, especially of stone inscriptions, in order to determine the date of the same. Differences can be ascribed to the nature of the stones on which the inscriptions (four copies of the same inscription) were copied.

'Sada' or 'Sāta', used as a contraction of typical Sātavāhana names, is frequently met with in the epigraphic records and coins of the Sātavāhana rulers. It is evident from the contemporary records of other royal families, such as the Mahāmeghavāhana, the unknown family of Hāritiputra-Manȧsada of the Velpuru inscription, and the inscribed coins of Mahāsada, Sivamaka-Sada and Asaka-Sada of the Guntur region of Andhra Pradesh,[31] the Cuṭu-Kula-Sātakarṇis of Karnataka region, etc., that these rulers have borne the popular name. It has even been suggested that the rulers of these dynasties may have been born of Sātavāhana princesses.[32]

In his Hātigumphā inscription Khāravela has been endowed with the royal epithets *Kaliṅgādhipati* or the 'lord of Kaliṅga' and *mahārāja*. In the record of his chief queen (*agra-mahiṣī*) he is Kaliṅga-*cakravartin*. Further, his successor, Kuḍepasiri, is also *mahārāja* and *Kalingadhipati* in his own record in the Manchapuri cave. But it should be noted in this context that Siri-Sada, the father and immediate predecessor of Khāravela had borne the title of *Kaliṅga-Mahiṣakādhipati* (lord of Kaliṅga and Mahiṣaka), whereas his successors had control only over Kaliṅga.

Controversy prevails on the identification and location of the country of Mahiṣaka , but it is now generally accepted on the basis of copper plate records of the Kadambas (of about the fifth century) and old coins found in the old Mysore State as well the southern part of the old Hyderabad State, that these areas constituted the ancient Mahiṣaka country.[33] The Hebbata grant of Kadambe king

Viṣṇuvarman I (fifth century) found in Tunkur district in the northern part of old Mysore State (now Karnataka) refers to the *Mahiṣa-viṣaya*[34] evidently forming a part or a district of the Mahiṣaka country. Besides, there is reference to this country and its people in the Puranic literature, as situated in Dakṣiṇāpatha. It is now believed, 'the name of the *Mahiṣa-viṣaya* (cf. Mahiṣaka of the Puranic lists) is evidently the source from which the present Mahisūr (Mysore in English) has derived its name.[35] The ancient Kadambas acquired the kingdom of Kuntala or Karnata from the later Sātavāhana rulers during the fourth or fifth century. In the Puranic literature there are references to different branches of the Sātavāhana dynasty of the Deccan, of which the Cuṭu-kula Sātakarṇis were the rulers of the Kuntala country, with heir capital at Vanavāsi or Vaijayanti. Their epigraphic records are known.[36] In the *Vāyu* and *Matsya Purāṇas*, the Sātavāhanas of Kuntala have been named the Kuntala-Sātakarṇis. During about second and third centuries the Ikṣvākus of Krishna-Guntur region had matrimonial relationships with these Kuntala-Sātakarṇis of Karnataka, as known from some of the Nagarjunikonda inscriptions of the Ikṣvākus.[37]

The country of Kuntala seems to have comprised the southernmost districts of the Bombay Presidency and the northern part of Mysore.[38]

Kaliṅga and Mahiṣaka are mentioned side by side in the list of countries and people of Dakṣiṇāpatha division in the Puranic texts. The *Mārkaṇḍeya*, *Vāyu*, *Brahmāṇḍa*, *Vāmana* and *Matsya Purāṇas* have the verse, *Setuka Muṣikāś=c=aiva Kumārā Vanavāsakā Mahārāṣṭra Mahiṣākaḥ Kaliṅgāś=c=aiva sarvasaḥ.*[39]

It should also be noted that these two countries are not found in the list of countries or people included in the Uttarāpatha division. There is every reason to believe, thus that the kingdom of Kaliṅga was extended in the south-western direction during Siri-Sada's reign and the kingdom of Mahiṣaka was annexed to it. He probably acquired Mahiṣaka from the Kuntala-Sātakarṇis and thus assumed the title of lord of Kaliṅga and Mahiṣaka . It is evident from his title as well as the above verse in the Purāṇas that Kaliṅga had an extensive territory as far as the north-eastern part of Karnataka. But the area comprising Mahiṣaka was lost to Khāravela, possibly soon after the death of Siri-Sada (or Śrī-Sata) and was annexed by the Sātavāhanas into their empire subsequently.

A detailed study of the early inscriptions of different dynasties of the Deccan is indispensable if we are to determine the extent of Khāravela's kingdom. Scholars so far are inclined to believe it comprised northern and southern Orissa and the region upto the river Godāvarī since the time Aśoka. The earliest epigraphic evidence referring to Kaliṅga as a territorial unit has been found in the Rock Edict XIII of Aśoka.[40] Interestingly though, this rock edict has not yet been found in any part of the present Orissa. We have two special Rock Edicts of the Mauryan emperor in place of his 11th, 12th and 13th Edicts, found at Dhauli (Bhubaneswar) and Jaugaḍa (Ganjam district).[41] It is significant that these two special edicts do not refer to Kaliṅga. The Dhauli edict has a reference to Tosali and the royal officers like the *nagara-vyavahārakas* and *mahāmātras* posted here during Mauryan rule. Historians so far are of opinon, due mainly to the location of these two special edicts within the boundary of the present state of Orissa, that Kaliṅga during Mauryan supremacy was divided into two administrative units, the north-eastern with head-quarters at Tosali (the present Dhauli near Bhubaneswar) and the south-western centred on Samāpā near Jaugaḍa in the Ganjam district. Further, scholars believe that Khāravela, the 'lord of Kaliṅga' of the Mahāmeghavāhana dynasty, whose inscription is located in the twin hills of Udayagiri and Khaṇḍagiri, had his capital of Kaliṅganagara (or Kaliṅganagari) at Sisupalgarh near Dhauli at Bhubaneswar.

Tosali was possibly in existence before the advent of the Mauryans and flourished under their supremacy into a city. The Orissan epigraphic records of the subsequent period suggest that since at least the third century BC Tosali was in the process of growing into a wider geographical unit and during Aśoka's time it had become a separate province of the Mauryan empire. These records also furnish evidence of Tosali being a separate kingdom called Ubhaya Tosali, with two divisions, Uttara-Tosali (northern Tosali) and Dakṣiṇa-Tosali (southern Tosali), the river Mahānadī being the dividing line between them. As known from these inscriptions northern Tosali comprised the present coastal districts of south-western Midnapore (West Bengal) or the ancient Daṇḍabhuktimaṇḍala, Balasore, Dhenkanal and Cuttack (undivided) up to the Mahānadī. Southern Tosali extended from the southern bank of that river up to the river Ṛṣikulyā in Ganjam district.

Yet there is no evidence to prove that Dhauli Sisupalgarh was ever the city of Kaliṅganagarī, nor the entire coastal region now comprising districts of Balasore, Cuttack, and Puri ever was known as the kingdom of Kaliṅga as the location of the Aśokan special edicts and the inscription of Khāravela in the Bhubaneswar region have led historians to speculate.

In support of this theory scholars often quote a verse from the *Tīrtha-yātrā* section of the *Vanaparvan* of the *Mahābhārata*: *ete Kaliṅgāh Kaunteya Yātrā Vaitaraṇī nadī.*[42] The *Tīrtha-yātrā* section of the epic, a sort of gazetteer for pilgrims, seems to have been interpolated in a later period, though the location of Kaliṅga indicated therein does not tally with the inscriptions of any period of history. The main objective of this stanza is to present a broad idea to pilgrims about the location of different pilgrim centres situated in different countries. The name of the river Vaitaraṇī and the celebrated centre of Virajākṣetra (the present Jajpur in the Jajpur district) on its bank was so popular in other parts of India that reference to these gave people a general idea about the location of the different kingdoms of orissa, Kaliṅga, Kośala, Utkala, etc. Though scholars are inclined to believe on the basis of the above verse that the river Vaitaraṇī formed the northern border of the ancient Kaliṅga country, our enormous epigraphic records ranging from the earliest historical period have negated this assumption. These records have furnished evidence relating to the existence of Kaliṅga, Kośala, Tosali, and Utkala, as separate geographical units and separate kingdoms.

Arbitrary descriptions of the locations of different countries is very often found in the epics and Purāṇas so that contradictions arise. Sometimes great confusion occurs due to the insufficient geographical knowledge of their authors. There is no evidence to show that a kingdom of greater Kaliṅga was formed in any period of history along with that of the kingdom of Tosali or Ubhaya Tosali. Instead we have epigraphic evidence that Kaliṅga extended into the Deccan during different periods of history. Further, there is no definite evidence to show that the city of Tosali ever assumed the name of Kaliṅganagari nor even during the reign of Khāravela as historians now believe.

The geographic position of different countries or kingdoms as described in the Puranic literature in relation to the geographical position of Kaliṅga is significant. These literary texts generally give an account of the fivefold division of India, dividing the country into Madhyadeśa, Udicya, Prācya, Dakṣiṇāpatha and Aparānta. Kaliṅga was in the Dakṣiṇāpatha division. Sometimes, apart from these fivefold divisions, another division comprising the region and the people around the Vindhya mountain range is added as Vindhyapṛṣṭha. We notice that Utkala, Kośala and Tosala/Tosali are placed in this division in the Purāṇas:

> *Maladāś=ca Kāruṣāś=ca Mekalāś=c=Otkalaiḥ saha*
> *Tosalāḥ Kośalāś=c=aiva Traipurā Vaidiśās=tathā.*[43]

These geographical divisions tend to suggest that Kaliṅga and Tosala were two different countries in ancient times. This would also corroborate the Orissan epigraphic records of different periods. We have references to Tosali from the earliest historical period upto about the twelfth century, and there is no evidence to show that the Tosali region was ever named Kaliṅga. Rather, a portion of northern Kaliṅga comprising the region around Aska-Khallikote-Bhanjanagar near the Ṛṣikulyā, along with a portion of the undivided Puri district around the Chilka lake, then under Dakṣiṇa-Tosali, formed a separate kingdom called Koṅgodamaṇḍala in the seventh century, as will be shown below. So there is no reason to believe that the capital of Kaliṅganagari was situated within the territory of Tosali. During the third century BC the city of Tosala was the chief locality of the land of Tosali/Tosala which formed one of the provinces of the Aśokan empire. Unfortunately, the history of this region after the fall of the Mauryan supremacy, is shrouded in obscurity. There is, however, a reference to Tosali in a Nagarjunikonda inscription[44] of the time of Vīrapuruṣadatta the Ikṣvākus, around the beginning of the third century. During this period the city of Tosali, or the country, was celebrated as an eminent centre of Buddhism. In the said inscription 'Tosali' evidently means a country as it is listed with Kaśmira, Gandhāra, Cīna, Aparānta, Vaṅga, etc. The Buddhist monks of Tosali country used to participate in the discourses held in other centres of Buddhism, especially in southern India..

There are references in inscriptions to the kingdom of Ubhaya Tosali from at least AD 400 or so,[45] the southern part of Dakṣiṇa

Tosali, comprising Buguda-Khallikote-Aska regions of the Ganjam district and the present Gajapati district, formed a part of Kaliṅgarāṣṭra under the control of the Vigraha dynasty. Subsequently, in the beginning of the seventh century, the northern portion of Kaliṅgarāṣṭra and the area around Chilka Lake became part of a new kingdom, Koṅgodamaṇḍala with Banpur on the Chilka Lake (in the undivided Puri district) as headquarters of the Śailodbhava royal family.[46] The Śailodbhavas, at the beginning of their rule, were feudatories under Śaśāṅka of Gauḍa for some time, but later ruled independently until eighth century, when the Bhauma-karas annexed Koṅgodamaṇḍala upto the river Ṛṣikulyā, to the southern Tosali division. The Śailodbhava king Mādhavarāja II at the beginning of his rule is known to have occupied for a short period a portion of the kingdom of Kaliṅga situated to the south-western fringe of Koṅgodamaṇḍala and assumed the prestigious title of the 'lord of Kaliṅga'.[47] Evidently, he managed to seize that area from the Eastern Gaṅgas of Kaliṅganagara who had started their rule from about the close of fifth century and called themselves *Sakala-Kaliṅgādhipati* or 'lord of all Kaliṅga'.[48] This Kaliṅganagara the capital of the Eastern Gangas has now been generally taken to be the same as Mukhalingam near Śrīkakulam, on the confluence of the river Vaṁśadhārā in Andhra Pradesh. The great port of Kaliṅgapattanam is also situated contiguous to it on the same river and still known by the same name.

That the northern boundary of Kaliṅga country was the river Ṛṣikulyā through the ages is corroborated by recent findings of inscriptions of the Māṭharas, the Vāśiṣṭhas and other rulers, assuming the title of *Kaliṅgādhipati* and ruling contemporaneously during the fourth and fifth centuries in the Ganjam district of Orissa up to the Ṛṣikulyā in the north, and the northern coastal Andhra Pradesh upto the river Kṛṣṇā. In one of the copper plate charters of Prabhañjanavarman, son of Śaktivarman of the Māṭhara family, it is stated that his predecessors ruled the country between the Kṛṣṇavenna and the Mahānadī (*Kṛṣṇavennā-Mahānady = antaram sva-prajā-dharmeṇ-ānuśāsinaḥ* . . .).[49] Earlier scholars mistook the Mahānadī in this charter to be the well-known river now called Mahānadī flowing through the Cuttack district in Orissa. This led them to believe that the Māṭharas, the Vāśiṣṭhas and other contemporary lords of Kaliṅga of the period under discussion had extended their kingdom of Kaliṅga upto at least Cuttack district. This belief also strengthened their earlier view relating to the extent of Kaliṅga upto the river Vaitaraṇī based on the stanza in the epic as well as the existence of the Hātigumphā inscription of Khāravela and the Aśokan edict in the northern part of Orissa. But the Mahānandī referred to in the above Māṭhara record, is in fact, a river of the same name (locally called Badnadi), flowing into the Ṛṣikulyā near Aska in the Ganjam district. This river has, since ancient times, been known as the Mahānadī and until recently, it has been mentioned by the same name in the modern Orissan maps. Early European writers[50] called it the Mahānadī. Interestingly enough, there is a mountain pass joining the Bhanjanagar-Aska region near this river with the Phulbani district in the north-western part of Orissa that which is still called the Kaliṅga-*ghāṭi*. This indicates the north-western limit of the ancient Kalinga country.

It is curious that the Vāśiṣṭhas, the Māṭharas and other contemporary lords of Kaliṅga do not refer to the city of Kaliṅganagari in their records. They are so far known to have issued their copper plate charters from other well-known cities, Piṣṭapura, Siṁhapura, Sunagara, and Devapura. Thus the hypothesis that during the fourth and fifth centuries AD the kingdom of Kaliṅga was divided into several small principalities is now corroborated: various lords of Kaliṅga were ruling independently and issuing charters from their headquarters.

In this context, the southern campaign of Samudragupta, the second monarch of the Gupta dynasty of Northern India, as recorded in the Allahabad Pillar Inscription,[51] may throw welcome light. Some of the small kingdoms invaded were then known as Veṅgi, Kaurālaka, Piṣṭapura, Devarāṣṭra, Koṭṭuraka, and Eraṇḍapallaka, and are generally identified as situated between the Kṛṣṇā (in Andhra Pradesh) and the so-called Mahānadī in the Ganjam district. The Allahabad pillar inscription would indicate that different parts of the ancient Kaliṅga region were named differently and ruled by the petty chieftains whose names have also been mentioned in the record. Subsequently, these regions were occupied by the Māṭharas, the Vāśiṣṭhas, and other lords of Kaliṅga as known from their charters issued from Piṣṭapura, Devapura (of Devarāṣṭra), etc. Of the principalities mentioned in the Allahabad inscription, Kauralāka, ruled by Maṇṭarāja during Samudragupta's campaign, has been variantly mentioned in the later epigraphic records of the Deccan as Kaunāla/ Kunāla[52] is now believed to be the same as the present region around the Koleru lake, south of Piṣṭapura. The region around Piṣṭapura in the present East Godāvarī district formed another principality of the ancient Kaliṅga country, ruled by Mahendragiri, believed to have acknowledged the suzerainty of Samudragupta. Later it was occupied by the Māṭharas. Devarāṣṭra, then ruled independently by Kubera and subsequently by the Vāśiṣṭhas of Kaliṅga, was situated in the East Godāvarī district. The region around Guntupally in the West Godāvarī district had already formed an independent kingdom and its ruler was Hastivarman of the Śālaṅkāyana dynasty during Samudragupta's southern campaign. This Śālaṅkāyana king is also known from other records of his family.[53] Besides, there were other small principalities included in ancient Kaliṅga, that were subjugated by Samudragupta like Koṭṭuraka which was situated in the region around Mahendragiri in the present Gajapati district of Orissa, and Eraṇḍapallaka near Viśākhapatnam in Andhra.

At about the beginning of the first century AD the Sātavāhanas had extended their sphere of supremacy by annexing regions of Mahārashtra, northern Karnataka, the region between the Kṛṣṇā and the Godāvarī. The latter comprised the Kaliṅgan territory during the time of the Mahāmeghavāhanas. It is probable that the early Sātavāhanas were responsible for the annihilation of the Mahāmeghavāhanas from the eastern Deccan. In the last part of the second century we notice the Kṛṣṇā-Guntur region coming under the supremacy of the Ikṣvākus, who were previously under the suzerainty of the Sātavāhanas . Besides, there were other royal families who owed allegiance to the Sātavāhanas. The Bṛhatphalāyanas, the Śālaṅkāyanas, the Viṣṇukuṇḍins, and the Pallavas in the eastern Deccan, also declared independence soon after the downfall of the Sātavāhanas. They raised their kingdoms on the ruins of the Sātavāhana territory in the Kṛṣṇa-Guntur region which was previously under the control of Kaliṅga before the advent of the Sātavāhanas. Some of these territories, Veṅgi, Kauralaka, etc., were never recovered by the Kaliṅgan kings in the subsequent period as they were split into small principalities subdued by Samudragupta.

Thus it is essential to study the gradual rise of the small powers of the region and the political conditions of the period in question, in order to know about the extent of the Kaliṅgan territory.

Thus, the southern boundary of Kaliṅga which once touched the northern-most part of Karnataka during the Mahāmeghavāhana rule became very much circumscribed by the time the early Eastern Gaṅgas established their supremacy. The kingdom of Kaliṅga remained confined within the Ṛṣikulyā in the Ganjam district in the north and roughly the Godāvarī in the south until the advent of the imperial line of the same dynasty, which opened a new chapter in the history of Kaliṅga.

The Māṭharas and other contemporary lords of Kaliṅga do not refer to Kaliṅganagari, yet the early Eastern Gaṅgas who succeeded them, made it their political headquarters after consolidating their power. The reason behind the long desertion of the city, cannot, however, be definitely established. It is also irrational to think of two Kaliṅganagaris, one at Sisupalgarh near Bhubaneswar and the other near Mukhalingam on the confluence of the Vaṁśadhārā in Andhra Pradesh. There is every reason to believe that Kaliṅganagari was situated in an area frequented by cyclone and flood. This is indicated by the Hatigumpha inscription of Khāravela and who spent a large amount for repairing the city-walls, *gopuras* and other structures badly damaged by a cyclone. Kaliṅganagari also suffered political unrest in some periods, as evidenced by the rise and fall of various small powers during the later Sātavāhanas, the Ikṣvākus, Samudragupta's southern campaign, as well as during the period of the Māṭharas, the Vāśiṣṭhas and other small ruling families. It was possibly the early Easter Gaṅgas who were responsible for uniting the small states of Kaliṅga and they rebuilt Kaliṅganagari as their capital. In the vicinity was the great port of Kaliṅgapattanam, still known by the same name. So there is every reason to believe that this place was in all probability the same Kaliṅganagari of Khāravela's time.

It will not be out of context to point to another interesting fact furnished by the Hātigumphā inscription of Khāravela. From the second year of his reign, he went out on military expeditions towards the west, paying no heed to Sātakarṇi (presumably Sātakarṇi I); on the course of the Kṛṣṇā he terrorized the army of Ṛṣikanagara. The early Sātavāhanas were then ruling in the north-western Deccan from the river Kṛṣṇā and in the Vidarbha region and to the west of Kaliṅga. Perhaps, then Ṛṣikanagara, the chief city of the country of that name, was on the bank of the Kṛṣṇā in the north-western Deccan. This Ṛṣika country and its people are mentioned in the Purāṇas in the context of the geographical position of Kaliṅga. This country was situated in Dakṣiṇāpatha, close to the Sātavāhana kingdom. Besides, we notice a verse in the *Rāmāyaṇa*[54] wherein the Ṛṣika country is placed along with Vidarbha and Mahiṣaka (*Vidarbhān = Ṛṣikāṁś = c = aiva ramyān-Māhiṣakān = api*). It is clear from the inscription that Khāravela went to the western Deccan on the course of the Kṛṣṇā from his kingdom of Kaliṅga. Interestingly, while Khāravela mobilized his army against Ṛṣikanagara, his inscription is silent about Mahiṣaka , and he did not assume the title of Mahiṣākadhipati as his predecessor, Siri-Sada had done. This may indicate that Mahāmeghavāhana rule was over in Mahiṣaka.

There are still numerous questions to be raised on Khāravela's connection with Tosali; several of his expedition were directed against different kingdoms of both southern and northern India within a short period of thirteen years of his reign. As stated in the Hātigumphā inscription. Khāravela ascended the throne of Kaliṅga when he was twenty-five and he continued to rule for thirteen years. He was then possibly succeeded by his son Kuḍepasiri, whose inscription in the Manchapuri cave shows that he was anointed king of Kaliṅga, and took the titles of *mahārāja* and *Kaliṅgādhipati*, before his visit to the Udayagiri-Khandariri Jain religious centre along with Khāravela and other members of his family. Perhaps Khāravela was no longer on the Kaliṅgan throne. Unfortunately, there is no evidence so far available on Kuḍepasiri's rule in Kaliṅga after Khāravela. Nor can it be said with any certainty that there was Mahāmeghavāhana rule in Kaliṅga after Khāravela. Other questions may be raised. Why was the only extant record of Khāravela incised in the Tosali region? Did Khāravela conquer Tosali? Why, then, is the Hātigumphā record silent about this country? We may find some clues and other connected problems of the history of Khāravela if we undertake a thorough study and a re-appraisal of the early Prakrit inscriptions contemporaneous to the period in question, especially those of the Sātavāhanas which may reveal significant facts on the problems.

The letters of the Hātigumphā record have striking similarity with that of the Nanaghat inscription of Nāyaṇikā,[55] queen of Sātakarṇi I. Similarities have also been observed in the phrasaeology, and language. From the orthographical point of view, the Hātigumphā inscription also has striking resemblance with the early Prakrit record at Nanaghat of the above queen, the Andhra-Sātavāhana inscriptions, and those of the Ikṣvākus. This would suggest that Khāravela was associated with the political activities in the Deccan region. He had nothing to do with northern Orissa nor with the western part of Orissa as believed by previous scholars.

NOTES

1. Studies on Khāravela and the Hātigumphā inscription since its discovery by different scholars have been incorporated by N. K. Sahu in *Khāravela*, Bhubaneswar, 1984; see also, D. C. Sircar, Calcutta, 1942, *Select Inscriptions, Bearing on Indian History & Civilization*, Vol. I, pp. 206 ff. For a different opinion, see also M. Brandtner, *Kaliṅga and seire Hauptstod in fruhgeschichtlicher Zeit*, Hamburg, 2000.
2. D. C. Sircar, *Select Inscriptions,* Vol. I, pp. 2006 ff & plate; though he has read *Ceti*, the medial sign *e* for *ca* is not found in the inscription. Other scholars have taken the word as *Ceta* and corrected later for *Cedi* as stated by Sircar in fn. 1, p. 207 of the same book.
3. *Epigraphia Indica*, Vol. XXXII (1957-8), pp. 82 ff and plate. D. C. Sircar on the basis of this inscription as well as the Hātigumphā record suggested the rule of Aira family was established in the Kṛṣṇa-Guntur region 'as a result of one of Khāravela's expeditions in those areas' (pp. 85-6).
4. *Journal of Epigraphical Society of India* (Mysore), Vol. XIV, (1993), pp. 13 ff; A.M. Shastri informs us that recent archaeological excavations at Vaḍḍamānu 10 km from Amaravati have yielded a good number of lead coins inscribed with the names of Mahāsada, Sivamakasada, and Asakasada, having *sada*-endings. It is generally believed that the Guntur region was occupied by the later Sātavāhanas for the first time during the reign of Vāśiṣthiputra Pulumāvi (second century), as can be inferred from the presence of a record of his reign at Amaravati. According to Shastri, these kings with *sada*-ending names preceded Vāśiṣthiputra Pulumāvi in the area in question. It may be pointed out here that Mānasada or Mahāsada of the Velpuru inscription has been described as Hāritiputra-Mānasada.
5. *EI*, Vol. VIII (1904-5), pp. 65 ff.
6. *EI*, Vol. XXXI, 229 ff; as also see the expression *aira-hathāna* Sanskritized *ārya-saṁghānām* in an Ikṣvāku inscription of about third century AD from Nagarjunikonda Andhra Pradesh, in *EI*, Vol. XX, pp. 16, 19 ff.
7. Sircar, *Select Inscriptions,* Vol. I, p. 214. Sircar suggests that the use of the same word in the case of Kuḍepasiri also would indicate that it is connected with the name of the family, n. 5. Kuḍepasiri has been variantly read by

previous scholars as Vakadepa (Vakradeva?), Kuḍepa and Kadampa (Kandarpaśrī ?).

8. *Journal of Orissan History*, Vol. XV (1996), pp. 28-9.
9. This inscription was originally published by R. Subrahmanyam in The *Guntupally Brāhmī Inscription of Khāravela* (Andhra Pradesh Government Epigraphic Series, No. 3) Hyderabad, 1968. Subsequently, D. C. Sircar published it as 'An Alleged Inscription of Khāravela', in the *Journal of Ancient Indian History*, Vol. III, 1969-70, pp. 35-6; also see, *JESI*, Vol. V (1978), pp. 48 ff.
10. *JOH*, Vol. XV (1996), pp. 28-9.
11. I.K. Sarma and J. Varadaprasada Rao, *Early Brāhmī Inscriptions from Sannati*, Delhi 1993, pp. 65 ff. Portions resembling that of the Dhauli-Jaugada special edicts engraved on a slab, now cut into size to use as a pedestal for the installation of the image of Mahākali were found in the village of Sannati on the river Bhimā. According to them, the Dhauli-Jaugada edicts were issued in place of Rock Edicts, XI, XII, and XIII, whereas at Sannati, among the extant records the XII Edicts is found. It is surmised that there also existed the XI and XIII Edicts at Sannati. The slab containing the Edicts must have been collected from a nearby place. Sannati, stated to be a famous centre of pilgrimage on account of the temple dedicated to Candralamba, was recognized as one of the greatest Buddhist sites in Karnataka since its discovery in 1954. Besides the Aśokan edicts are scores of early Brāhmī inscriptions which include some of the early Sātavāhana rulers, which may shed welcome light on the history of the Mahāmegha-vāhana dynasty of Kaliṅga and Mahiṣaka .
12. D. C. Sircar, *Select Inscription*, Vol. I, p. 207 and note; N.K. Sahu, *Khāravela*, pp. 18 ff.
13. In a recent paper, entitled 'Ancestry of Khāravela-re-examined' in the JOH, Vol. XV (1996), p. 31, J. K. Sahu has opined that *rājarṣi* is an epithet of Khāravela. But it should be noted that the whole expression *rājarṣi-Vasu-kula-viniśritah* has been used as an epithet of Khāravela and *rājarṣi* has been used in honour of Vasu, the hitherto unknown predecessor of Khāravela.
14. D. C. Sircar, *Select Inscriptions*, Vol. I, p. 207, n. 1, and p. 211 n. 4; N. K. Sahu, *Khāravela*, p. 18 ff.
15. *JOH*, Vol. XV (1996), p. 31.
16. *Idem*, *Select Inscriptions*, Vol. I, pp. 198 ff.
17. *Idem*, *The Successors of the Sātavāhanas in the Lower Deccan*, Calcutta, 1939, p. 15.
18. *Idem*, *Select Inscriptions*, Vol. I, pp. 187 ff.
19. *Ibid.*, pp. 229 ff; concerning the Nagarjunikonda Ikṣvāku inscriptions, Sten Konow observed, 'we are faced with a normalised semi-literary Prakrit used by people whose home-tongue was Dravidian and probably Kanarese.

41. *Ibid.*, Vol. I, pp. 97, 115 ff.
42. *Mahābhārata* 3. 114. 4 (critical edn.)
43. Sircar, *Stud. Geog. Anc. & Med. Ind.*, pp. 42-3.
44. Idem, *Select Inscriptions*, Vol. I, pp. 224-7 ff. *EI*, Vol. XX, pp. 22 ff.
45. *EI*, Vol. XLI, (1973), pp. 121-6 ff. S. Tripathy, *Inscriptions of Orissa*, Vol. I, Delhi, 1997, pp. 171-2; there is a reference to Ubhaya Tosali (both the Tosalis) in this stone inscription of Satrubhanja of the Naga family, the lord of Vindhyatavi, discovered in a village called Asanpat in the Keonjhar district of Orissa. Satrubhanja of this record is stated to have travelled extensively in the famous pilgrim centres situated in Ubhaya Tosali along with other countries.
46. For an up to date history of the Sailodbhavas and their inscriptions, see, S. Tripathy, *Ins. Or.*, Vol. I.
47. S. Tripathy, *Ibid.*
48. For the records of the early Eastern Gangas of Kalinga and Svetaka, see, S. N. Rajaguru, *Ins. Or.*, Vol. II (1960), Bhubaneswar.
49. *EI*, Vol. XXX (1953-4), pp. 112-18 ff. S. Tripathy, *Ins. Or.*, Vol. I (1997), pp. 92 ff.
50. T. J. Maltby, *Ganjam District Manual*, Madras, 1918, p. 2.
51. *EI*, Vol. III (1888), pp. 1 ff.
52. *EI*, Vol. VI (1900-1), p. 3 and note. Sircar, *Succ. Sat.*, pp. 115 ff.
53. Sircar, *Ibid.*, pp. 91 ff.
54. *Rāmāyaṇa*, IV. 41. 11; as stated by Sircar, in his *Select Inscriptions*, Vol. I, p. 195 and n. 3, Rsika is sometimes spelt as Asika in Prakrit as is known from the Nasik cave inscription of Vāśiṣṭhīputra Pulumāvi.
55. Sircar, *Select Inscriptions*, Vol. I, pp. 196 ff.

CHAPTER 6

The Date Formula in Early Ceylonese Inscriptions

HARRY FALK

The Buddhist communities of Sri Lanka were in constant contact with their Indian counterparts. The relationship between secular rulers is far less obvious, but it can be ascertained by parallel developments of scripts in both areas. If we compare Indian scripts with those on the island we have to state that the letters and the language used by the Ceylonese Buddhists to record on rocks a donation by a private donor is in several respects remarkably different from the language and script used by the clerks of kings and high officials for their own donation records. The script of the monks is old-fashioned and their language remains clumsy, whereas the script of the kings shows developments akin to those in India.

Here, a single feature of the courtly language is examined, the date formula. This is made possible by the recent publication of the second part of the second volume of Senarat Paranavitana's monumental *Inscriptions of Ceylon* (Paranavitana 2001), adding 18 more cases to the single one known from the first fascicule (Paranavitana 1983).

A date can be expressed as a regnal year – as did Aśoka – or including the month and the day or, alternatively, a regnal year referring back to the beginning of a dynastic era. Both day-date and era have their own history. For Sri Lanka it must be said that an era is still unknown or unwelcome to the authors of the records of the time concerned, i.e. AD 177-361. At around the same time in the third century, the earliest preserved Pali chronicle, the *Dīpavaṃsa* tries to connect the successive regnal years of all kings to the Parinirvāṇa of the Buddha, but the artificial nature of this attempt is all too obvious: the list of regnal years starts with a series of numbers which are never odd and mostly 8 or multiples of 8. Only after Devanampiya Tissa do we get dates which look more trustworthy. Although in our inscriptions no such era has been adopted, the royal donatory texts show a certain development regarding the day-dates. The texts now published allow us to pose the following questions:

- When do Ceylonese kings start to date their records?
- What is the structure of their formula and how do we explain its terminology?
- To what extent is the formula indigenous, to what extent borrowed?
- What is the exact provenance of the borrowed parts?
- How flexible is the formula? Does it react to Indian innovations?

THE START

The first to date his donations was Gajabahu, *c.* AD 177-199, following the time scale as worked out by W. Geiger (1953, II: ix-xv). This is the time of the imperial Kuṣāṇas in northern India; it is the time of the Sātavāhanas in the Deccan and southern India. Whereas the north-west has a long tradition in dating, using eras since around the beginning of the common era, and using day-dates right from that start, the foreign Kṣatrapas of Malwa and Gujarat join in by the second half of the first century with their own era. The Deccan adopts dates in general in the second century, with Gautamīputra Sātakarṇi in his Nasik cave inscription (Sircar 1965: 198,6), using the regnal year, month and day. Yet neither here nor further south was an era used. Thus, a picture emerges of a practice spreading from the north-west to Ceylon. It needed almost two centuries to cover the distance.

THE STRUCTURE OF THE FORMULA

Despite some license, the earliest dates in Sri Lanka follow a remarkably fixed pattern. They go, with optional entries in square brackets:

[father's name] - king's name (genitive) - *catalagita* - number of years (locative) - month's name - *cada – puṇamasa/avamasa* - number - *pakṣadivasa.*

Some of the terms used are not fully comprehensible at first glance and deserve a comment.

catalagita is equivalent to Sanskrit *chattralaṅghita*, this much is certain. Paranavitana translates it as 'raising the umbrella of dominion'. This phrase goes parallel to *chattaṃ ussāpeti*, as it occurs many times in the chronicles (MahV 35, 15, 38, 69; 45, 62, etc.). Since the root *laṅgh* basically expresses the idea of 'leaping over' the semantic change to 'raising' is not apparent. Nonetheless, this meaning is found in modern Sinhala (Geiger 1941: 151, no. 2247), taken up, with other sources, in Turner 1966 (CDIAL 10905), and is connected with the meaning 'to ascend, to mount' of *laṅghayati* in classical Sanskrit court poetry.

The combination *catalagita* does, then, denote 'raised umbrella', or, as a Bahuvrīhi, someone 'having a raised umbrella'. One would expect the reversed order *lagitacata*, but Bahuvrīhis including a past participle rather often come in this order. The two cases of a *catalagitaka* are one of the many cases in epigraphical Ceylonese, where a *ka*-suffix can change a past participle into an agent noun meaning 'one who does what the root behind the ppp implies'. A *lagitaka* could therefore be a 'raiser' of the umbrella. The difference is slight, and the reversal may also be compared to terms like *ambapakka* (*Dīpavaṃsa* 6,6), corresponding to *pakvāmra* in Sanskrit.

Although *catalagita* is part of the standard phrase of the inscriptions, this expression is almost non-existent in the Pali chronicles, where 'exercised power', *rajjam akāresi*, is the usual phrase. Only in one case do we meet with a comparable diction, MahV 37,100:

kumāro jeṭṭhatisso'tha bhātā tassa kaṇiṭṭhako
chattaṃ laṅghesi laṅkāyaṃ dantasippamhi kovido.

'The young Jeṭṭhatissa, the youngest brother of (Sirimeghavaṇṇa), raised the (royal) umbrella in Laṅkā, himself skilled in the art of (elephant-) tooth (-carving).'[1]

The second term which needs discussion is *avanaka*. According to Paranavitana (2001: 327), *avanaka* could be a *tadbhāva* of Skt. *āhvānaka*, changing a cardinal number into an ordinal one. Several cases of *paṭhama-avanaka-vasahi* seem to contradict this explanation, since *paṭhama/prathama* is already an ordinal number. The number of the day is never followed by *avanaka*, although it clearly is another case of ordinality. On the other hand, the only case of a missing *avanaka* is found in § 86, again with *paṭhama*. Paranavitana refers to Eḷu *vanu*, *väni* as direct descendants of Skt. *āhvānaka*, and, in fact, even in present-day Sinhalese *-väni* changes cardinals into ordinals, with *pe-väni* being the last step from an original *prathama-āhvānaka*. Since Paranavitana's explanation holds good we have to state that day numbers obviously are not presented as ordinals.

Next comes the specific month name followed by *cada*, Skt. *candra*. The month-names are not wholly identical with the classical Sanskrit names. On the one hand we find the spring month of *vaiśākha* in several spellings, but other month names found only in Sri Lanka, e.g. *baga* or *majimadina*, are still in use today, different from north-Indian and from Tamil terminology alike. With regard to month-names, Sri Lanka displays an independance, although the similarities are much closer to north-Indian than to Tamil names, showing that a northern scheme was adapted to local conditions.

The day-phrase is similar to the year-phrase: first comes the name of the *pakṣa*, be it *puṇamasa*, i.e. the waxing moon, or *avamasa*, i.e. *āmāvāsya*, the waning moon. Then comes the running number of the day, then *pakṣa*, followed by *divasa*, 'day'. This way we get a day-compound, e.g. *avamasa-tatiya-paka-divasa*, 'on the third *pakṣa* day of the waning moon'. The word -order may be compared to the year compound, e.g. *cata-lagita-catara-avanaka-vasahi*, 'in the fourth year of the raised umbrella'.

In addition, the date can be preceded or closed by the term *puva[ya]* in diverse spellings and cases, all representing *pūrvā[yāṃ]*, 'date', so well known in Kuṣāṇa and other records in Brāhmī script.

The 19 preserved examples occur at the beginning of a text, somewhere in the middle, or, most often, at its end. The spellings given here are those of Paranavitana, or, where-ever the rubbing is legible, my own. Unfortunately, the plates as reproduced are too indistinct in many cases to allow a safer reading. Hyphens separate the parts of a compound, as I understand it.

2a. Dates Beginning a Text

IC II, 1: 100f. § 66, time of Gajabāhu (AD 177-199):

gamani-aba-rajaha vapu puva doḷasevanaka vasa /

'Date is the twelfth year of the time of King Gāmaṇī Abhaya.'

The scribe first wrote *vapu*, then correctly *puva*. This oldest date is still very rudimentary. Paranavitana's treatment of the term (1983: 100) is exhaustive and reliable whereas the derivation from Skt. *parva* in the glossary (2001: 345) may not go back to this author.

§ 105 IC II,2:180, time of Sirināga II (AD 300-302):

tisa-maharajaha puta sirinaka-maharajaha cata-lagitaka-vijaya-(do)-avana(ka-va)sahi-bagu-cada-avamasa-tatiya-paka-divasi

'On the third *pakṣa*-day of the waning moon of the month of Baga, in the second year of the raised umbrella and victory, the great king Sirināga, son of the great king Tissa.'

Month *bagu* relates to Skt. *bhaga*, as a *nakṣatra* synonymous with (*uttara*) *phalgunī*; as a month it coincides with *caitra* in India.

§ 109 II,2:187, time of Goṭhābhaya (AD 309-322):

mekavaṇa-aba-raja-cata-lagita-paḍama-(avana)ka-va(sahi)

'In the first year of the raised umbrella of king Meghavarṇa Abhaya.'

§ 111 II, 2: 191, time uncertain:

. . . ha paḍamaka-avanaka-vasahi

'In the first year of. . . .'

§ 120 II, 2: 210, time uncertain:

(gamani-abaya-rajaha) catara-avanaka-vasa(hi)

'In the fourth year of king Gāmaṇī Abhaya.'

2b. DATE IN THE MIDDLE OF A TEXT

§ 108 II, 2: 185, time of Goṭhābhaya (AD 309-322):

me-vavi-dina-(puva)ya (sirinaka-maha)rajaha puta-raja-mekavaṇa-abaya(ha cata-lagita-tiṇ)i-avanaka-vasahi visaki-cada-pura/// divasa dini

'Donation-date of this very tank: (it was) given on the (?th) day of the waxing moon of month Vaiśākha, in the third year of the raised umbrella of king Meghavarṇa Abhaya, son of the great king Śirināga.'

The reading *pura///* being certain, a reading *puramasa* instead of *puṇamasa* must be expected.

2c. Dates at the End

§ 73 II, 1: 108, time of Mahallakanāga or Bhātiya II (AD 199-205):

me-vavi-dina-puvaya naka-mahara[ja]ha cata-lagita-catara-avanaka-vasahi dini hiri-cadahi do[ḷa]sa-paka-daha dini

'Donation-date of this very tank: (it was) given on the twelfth *pakṣa*-day in month Hiri, given in the fourth year of the raised umbrella of the great king Nāga.'

Paranavitana reads *piri-cadahi* and believes 'there appears to be very little possibility of *piri* being the name of a lunar month' (1983: 108), although the standard word order leaves no other choice. A month-name *hiri* can be linked to Sinhala *hīl*, from Skt. *śītala*, also called *sihil* from Skt. *śiśira*. Mixed forms seem to be attested (Geiger 1941: 193, no. 2911). The month *hīl* or *il* corresponds to November/ December.

§ 81 II, 1: 120, time of Mahallakanāga/Bhātiya II (AD 199-205):

puvaya ba[ti]ya-tisa-maharajaha cata-lagita-paḍama-avanakahi vesaka-cada-puṇamasa-cata-divasa

'On the date: On the fourth day in (the *pakṣa* of) the waxing moon of month Vaiśākha, in the first (year) of the raised umbrella of the great king Bhātiya Tissa.'

Paranavitana reads *puṇamase* against the standard formula. The rubbing is illegible.

§ 84 II, 1: 123, time of Mahallakanāga/Bhātiya II (AD 199-205):

. . . *cata-lagita-visita-avanaka-vasahi* . . .

'in the twentieth year of the passed-on umbrella'.

§ 86 II, 2: 130, time of Kaniṭṭha Tissa (AD 229-247):

puvaya naka-maharajaha puta-maḷatisa-maharajaha cata-legita-paḍamaka-vasahi pusa-pacata-cadahi puṇamasiya-mahapohata-divasa

'At (this) date: (At) the day of the great Uposatha at the full-moon in the later Pusa month, in the first year of the raised umbrella of Mahārāja Maḷatissa, son of Mahārāja Nāga'.

Paranavitana (2001: 128) points out that *pacata*, Skt. *pāścātya*, makes this inscription 'the only Brāhmi inscription in Ceylon so far known to contain reference to an intercalated month'.

§ 91 II, 2: 140, time of Kaniṭṭha Tissa (AD 229-247):

puvaya [maḷi]tisa-maharajaha cata-lagita-sata-avanaka-vasahi baga-cada-avamasiya-sata-paka divasa

'At (this) date: on the seventh *pakṣa*-day of the waning moon of month Baga, in the seventh year of the raised umbrella of Mahārāja Maḷitissa'.

Paranavitana 2001: 141 fn. 18 separates *ava-masiya* and refers the reader to the glossary, where this term is missing. It represents Skt. *āmāvāsya*, the new-moon, through metathesis.

§ 94 II, 2: 146, time of Kaniṭṭha Tissa (AD 229-247):

puvaya maḷi-tisa-maharajaha. . .

'At (this) date: . . . of the Mahārāja Maḷitissa.'

§ 99 II, 2: 160, time of Kaniṭṭha Tissa (AD 229-247):

puvaya sa-avanaka-vasahi majimadina-cada-puṇamisi-cata-pakadivasa

'At (this) date: on the fourth *pakṣa*-day of the waxing moon of the month of Majimadina, in the sixth year.'

Month *majimadina* is called *mädindina* today (Geiger 1941: 132, no. 1962), corresponding to the *phālguna,* i.e. February/March.

§ 100 II, 169, time of Kaniṭṭha Tissa (AD 229-247):

. . . *batiya* . . . *tavanaka-vasahi* . . . *(cada) puṇamasa mahapohata-divasa me likita maparumaka-ramaṇa-maharajaha* . . .

'This has been written on the full-moon day of the waxing moon in the month of . . . in the eighth year . . . (son of) Bhātiya Tissa. . . . Of the great king Ramaṇa, the great lord . . .' (Paranavitana).

§ 103 II, 2: 177, time of Sirināga I (AD 250-269):

(puva)ya sirinaka-maharajaha cata-lagita-(da)sa-(a)va(nakavasahi) visaka-cada-pu(ṇa-masa)

'At (this) date: . . . of the waxing moon in the month of Vaiśākha, in the tenth year of the raised umbrella of Mahārāja Sirināga.'

§ 108 II, 2: 185, time of Goṭhābhaya (AD 309-322):

(B) *me-vavi-dina-puvaya si(ri)naka-maharajaha puta-raja-makavaṇa-abaya-cata-lagita-do-avanaka-vasahi vapa-cada-puṇamasiya-tedasa-paka-di(va)sa dini*

'At the date of donation of this tank: given at the thirteenth *pakṣa*-day of the waxing moon of month Vapa, in the second year of the raised umbrella of King Meghavarṇa Abhaya, son of Mahārāja Sirināga.'

Month *vapa* corresponds to *āśvayuja* or *āśvina* or October/November.

§ 112 II, 2: 195, time of Mahāsena (AD 334-361):

. . . *puviya mahasena-maharajaha cata-legitaka-dasa-avanaka-vasahi vesaka-cada-puṇamasa-dasa-paka-diva(sa)*

'At (this) date: (at) the tenth *pakṣa*-day of the waxing moon of month Vaiśākha, in the tenth year of the raised umbrella of Mahārāja Mahāsena.'

§ 119 II, 2: 209, time uncertain:

. . . *paca-avanaka-vasahi* . . . *dasa-pake-divase*

'On the tenth *pakṣa*-day . . ., in the fifth year . . .'.

INDIGENOUS AND FOREIGN PARTS IN THE DATE FORMULA

These cases present a standard attested from AD 189, onwards and ending with Mahāsena around AD 344, at least as far as the examples given by Paranavitana go. There is one single case of a possible intercalary month, if *pacata* in § 86 stands for Skt. *pāścātya*. The donations are given mainly in the first (4 times), second (twice), third, fourth (twice), sixth, seventh, tenth (twice) and twelfth regnal year, thus putting stress on the first year. Most prominent is month Vaiśākha (four times), then follows Baga (twice). Pusa, Majimadina and Hiri are attested once.

Indigenous are several month names. Home-grown is also the 'raised umbrella', well-known as a concept in the *Mahāvaṃsa*, using *ussāpeti* in numerous cases, whereas *laṅgheti* with the same meaning looks like a local semantic peculiarity.

The term 'date' is foreign; *puvaya*, taken from *etasyāṃ purvāyāṃ*, 'at this date', is found in numerous inscriptions of the Kuṣāṇas and contemporary rulers.

Foreign, likewise, is the splitting of months into *pakṣa*s. This practice is of southern origin. In the north-west, the earliest dates mention Macedonian or Indian names and the respective day, counted from 1 to 30. The Kuṣāṇas at Mathurā deal with days in the same way, but count 4 unnamed months within 3 seasons referred to by name. There are months 1 to 4 of winter, *hemanta* or abbreviated *he*, 4 months of heat, *grīṣma* or *gṛ*, 4 months of the rains, *varṣā* or *vā*. In the Dekkhan, however, *pakṣa*s or half-months play a role from the beginning of time-recording. In an inscription of Gautamīputra Sātakarṇi (around AD 130, Sircar 1965: 197-9), the text ends with *savachare 10 8 vāsapakhe 2 divase 1*, 'year 18, second *pakṣa* of the rainy season, day 1'. Other *pakṣa*s referred to relate to the heat period, *giṃhāna/grīṣma*, and can count up to 7 (Chakravarti 1955-6: 182). That means, inside the Sātavāhana realm the three seasons preserve their names, but each of the four months is subdivided into eight *pakṣas*.

After the Sātavāhanas, e.g. with the Śālaṅkāyanas (4th century) we find phrases like *vijayasaṃvaccharāni terasa 10 3 pauṣa-kālapakkhadasamī*, 'in the year 13 (counted from) victory, the 10th day of the dark half of month Pauṣa' (Hultzsch 1907/8). Nandivarman

II speaks of *pravarddhamāna-vijaya-rājya-saṃvatsarasya daśamasya 10 śrāvaṇa-māsa-śukla-pakṣasya pratipadi*, 'on the 1st day after fullmoon in month Śrāvaṇa, of the on-going 10th regnal year (counted from the date) of the victory' (Subba Rao 1926-7: 101f). In general, after the downfall of the Sātavāhanas, dates in the south are described using month-names and *pakṣa*-names instead of season-names and *pakṣa*-numbers.

In Sri Lanka, therefore, the parallels go with the post-Sātavāhana practice with months referred to by name and the *pakṣa*s uncounted but named as well. The way to name the two *pakṣa*s according to the state the moon is about to assume, i.e. *punamasa* for 'full-moon' and *avamasa* for 'new-moon', seems to be referred to in Ceylon earlier than elsewhere. On the continent the terminology developed into (*vaisākha*)*śuddha*/*śukla*(*divase*) and (*vaiśakha*) *bahula*(*divase*) instead in some parts, and into *āpūryamāṇapakṣe* and *kṣīyamāṇapakṣa* in others (Kielhorn 1900-1: 18).

So we see that several parts of foreign customs were adopted and combined, but not without changes answering to conditions of local climate and taste. Most remarkable is the consistency of the Ceylonese formula, kept unaltered over at least two centuries.

4. SPORADIC INNOVATION

In India many innovations regarding time-keeping took place, e.g. the introduction of dynastic eras and the development of many sorts of astronomical eras, the Śaka era belonging to the latter sort if not being a combination of both (Falk 2002: 94). Many astronomical eras have to do with the 12-year Jupiter cycle, which itself was used for a very short time in India until it was replaced by the 60-year Jupiter cycle, in use at places until the nineteenth century. The 12-year cycle uses the month-names derived from the traditional 27 *nakṣatra* asterisms like *caitra*, *vaiśākha*, *kārttika*, etc., often prefixed by *mahā*: in year (*mahā*)*caitra* Jupiter occupies for one year the same region the sun occupies for one month when the full-moon occurs near the *nakṣatra caitra*.

Now it is remarkable to find a single preserved date of the original 12-year cycle in text § 115 II, 2: 204, its absolute time being regrettably uncertain. The date simply reads *mahapusavasa*, 'the year of Mahāpauṣa', a year when Jupiter stood in the sign Pauṣa, the third month in that system. According to Salomon (1998:197) this system was used 'mostly in the inscriptions of the Parivrājakas', with a start in the late fifth century. The examples known so far come from the early Rāṣṭrakuṭās in Gujarat, the Kadamba king Mṛgeśavarman in South India and king Anantavarman in Kaliṅga. Which area was responsible for the introduction of this era in Ceylon is impossible to say.

NOTE

1. Cf. Geiger 1953: 9, n. 1, where he translates and evaluates the alternative reading *bhātu*, which would make Jeṭṭhatissa a nephew of Sirimeghavaṇṇa.

REFERENCES

Chakravarti, N. P., 1955/6, Brahmi inscriptions from Bandhogarh, *Epigraphia Indica* 31: 167-86.

Falk, Harry, 2002, 'Frühe Zeitrechnung in Indien' in *Vom Herrscher zur Dynastie. Zum Wesen kontinuierlicher Zeitrechnung in Antike und Gegenwart* ed. Harry Falk (Vergleichende Studien zu Antike und Orient, 1). Bremen: Hempen Verlag: 77-105.

Geiger, Wilhelm, 1941, *An Etymological Glossary of the Sinhalese Language*. Colombo: Royal Asiatic Society Ceylon Branch (repr. 1997, New Delhi/Madras: Asian Educational Services).

———, 1953, *Cūlavaṃsa, being the most recent part of the Mahāvaṃsa,* translated, Colombo: The Ceylon Government Information Department.

Hultzsch, E., 1907/08, 'Plates of Vijaya-Devavarman', *Epigraphia Indica* 9: 56-9.

Kielhorn, F., 1900-1, 2, 'Two Kadamba Grants', *Epigraphia Indica* 6: 12-20.

Paranavitana, S., 1983, *Inscriptions of Ceylon*, Vol. II Part I, *Containing rock and other inscriptions from the reign of Kuṭakaṇṇa Abhaya (41 B.C.-19 B.C.) to Bhātiya II (140-164 A.D.),* Colombo: Department of Archaeology.

———, 2001, *Inscriptions of Ceylon*, Vol. II, Part II, *Containing rock and other inscriptions from the reign of Kaniṭṭhatissa (164-192 A.D.) to Mahāsena (276-303 A.D.)*, ed. Malini Dias, Colombo: Archaeological Survey Department.

Salomon, Richard, 1998, *Indian Epigraphy: A Guide to the Study of Inscriptions in Sanskrit, Prakrit and Other Indo-Aryan Languages.* New York/Oxford: OUP.

Sircar, D. C., 1965, *Select Inscriptions bearing on Indian history and civilization,* Vol. I: *From the Sixth Century B.C. to the Sixth Century A.D.*, Calcutta, 1965 (2nd edn., revised and enlarged).

Subba Rao, R., 1926/7, 'Pedavegi copper plates of Nandivarman II', *Journal of the Andhra Historical Research Society* 1: 92-102.

Turner, R. L., 1966, *A Comparative Dictionary of the Indo-Aryan Languages*, London.

CHAPTER 7

Indian Tradition and Time[1]

ALOKA PARASHER-SEN

> The master said, 'Ts'ze, you think, I suppose, that I am one who learns many things and *keeps them in memory?*' Tsze-kung replied, 'yes, but perhaps it is not so?' 'No,' was the answer; '*I seek a unity all pervading.*' (emphasis added)
>
> CONFUCIUS, 15: 2

Most pre-modern ideologies were rooted in looking at the human reality in terms of its relationship with the all-pervading reality of the universe. This resulted in a concern about defining Time and how it was to be gauged. It was critical to see this relationship in terms of change and therefore, the concomitant question arose of how to understand the past, present, and future. There were various interjections on this issue in the western[2] and eastern worlds since the time that the cultivation of the mind became central to human concern. Whereas in the Western knowledge systems the measurement of Time and its various physical features have been well understood, there still remains, even in the hard core areas of advanced theoretical physics, a doubt whether it really exists in a philosophical sense. Critical to all these endeavours was the question of the validity of memory in demarcating Time, especially the terms of its relationship to the past. Needless to say, all these trajectories had an impact on how different societies began to record their pasts and the nature of history that they propounded.

The origin of Time in human thinking can be located in very temporal human concerns that our Stone Age ancestors must have experienced. However, it was only when they realized that they had to recapture the past with the help of memory that they began to manipulate Time. Later, with the development of writing, one can say that the human being tried to conquer Time. With writing, a sort of 'artificial memory'[3] was created of the experience and thoughts of men long dead. Eliade[4] in a study of some ancient myths in fact differentiates between mythical and scared time and profane time: the latter being the continuous irreversible Time of our everyday existence. Primeval myths did play a role in shaping various conceptions of reality in several cultural and philosophical traditions, but in India the concept of *kāla* has to been seen in close association with Action or *karma*. The latter was meant, through rituals and sacrifice, to regenerate Time and re-actualize cosmogony. This meant that the concept of Time was never considered in isolation from the allied concepts of Being and Becoming as change and causality and importantly, at the same time, from the real world of existence. In all the conceptual frameworks and philosophical systems that grew in South Asia there was relevant debate on whether Time was the creator or created, subjective or objective, real or unreal, physical or psychological, empirical or a priori, substantive or attributive and so on.[5] But these debates took place within the given premise that Time, like the all pervasive Being was cyclic and dynamic as it determined and accounted for birth, subsistence and destruction of all empirical beings.

As it will be difficult to discuss in depth all these strands of the Indian tradition, we shall focus towards the end of this paper, only on the Tantric notions. It must be underlined that Tantra did not evolve any system of scientific and philosophical thought independently, but drew freely for its own purposes from various aspects of ancient Indian scientific knowledge. It was also a way of perceiving reality very much rooted in the temporality of life by giving emphasis on the materiality of existence. This syncretic trend made Tantra an elastic and assimilative system and a fusion of many disciplines. It is often suggested that esoteric notions of how Time was reckoned and understood only impacted the few who were learned in society. But our purpose to choose the Tantra traditions to explicate and exemplify is primarily because, unlike some other systems of thought, it also made these notions understandable at a less abstract level and thus affected the community and individual in more ways than one. It is first proposed to give a brief general overview of the way Time was discussed in the overall tradition in ancient India and not exclusively only at the philosophical level but entwined with it in complex ways.

We begin with the perceptive remarks of the well known Hindi writer Agyeya, who writes:

> Literature, as a product of the whole culture of people at a certain time, must necessarily reflect the cosmology of the culture at that time, also the self-view or identity of that people at that time. The cultural significance of even the most direct experience of time will vary from culture to culture . . . the experience with which literature concerns itself is not an isolated experience of an isolated individual organism in *vacuo*, but a multi-layered, multi-faceted complex, determined by more than one coordinate of time.[6] (emphasis added)

As noted above, Indian philosophies delved into the issue of understanding and defining Time over a long historical period and within different textual and ideological situations. Scholars interrogating these issues have tended to give primacy to only philosophical texts and, therefore, have argued that both history and memory had a status of denial in the Indian psyche. Reasons for this are sought in fundamental philosophical doubts generated in the epistemological foundation of these issues. Thus Roy Perrett tells us that in certain Indian philosophical strands memory was considered faulty because it gave no new knowledge; if there was knowledge of something, it could only be remembered to be authenticated—memory was embedded in past experiences and could not validate the true or real object being studied.[7] It would be difficult to survey the entire gamut of these views but from the perspective of the present paper it suffices to point out that a critical differentiation was made between three notions of memory and recording in the textual tradition: *itihāsa* or collective memory, loosely translated as 'history'; *smṛti* or cultural memory; and *saṃskāra* or subliminal impressions produced on an individual's mind by past experiences mental or behavioural patterns. These three terms for particular kinds of 'memory' enables one to differentiate between Time as conceived and applied to a country, nation or any other large entity as framed within *itihāsa*, followed by to a social group, society or *samāja* as articulated in the *smṛti* traditions and then to an individual who was dependant on her/his *saṃskāras*. All three were fostered and written about in the ancient Indian literary traditions. This is important to emphasize for historians. Romila Thapar has pertinently stressed that cosmological discourses do not necessarily exclude one or the other category of reckoning Time so that both the cyclic and linear notions of Time can simultaneously co-exist, indicating that the way the centrality of history is explained in such societies is complex.[8] It thus follows that the idea of change, progress, and modes of narration in these perceptions must necessarily be contrasted with those world-views that only adopt linearity to explain Time. Modern history writing is representative of the latter. In the present context it is the interlinking of the cyclic with the linear notions of Time and the significance of both as it affects an individual's life within the early Indian philosophical traditions that shall be brought to the forefront.

In contrast to the simple generic notion of changing seasonal time (*ṛtu*) mentioned in the early pastoral and agricultural context of the *Ṛg Veda*,[9] a clearly developed metaphysical notion of Time developed, denoted by the term *kāla.* Thus, in the later Vedic context there is considerable elaboration of the idea that Time existed before creation and was the progenitor of the Creator, Prajāpati.[10] In the *Upaniṣads*, while there is much attention paid to the notion of the two forms of Brahma as Time and Timeless, there is only a sketchy outline of the notions of the theory of Time and its calculations.[11] *Kāla* as *mahākāla* was associated with Absolute Time. This was considered the *Time between Creation and Destruction* and within the later Hindu world-view it came to be personified as Goddess Mahākāli.[12] The latter came to be associated with the graphic imagery of the one who had the power to swallow Time so as to bring the play of Time in nature to rest, only to rejuvenate it again and activate the processes of fresh creation. In the context of its continuity, *kāla* was represented through the symbol of the snake in the imagery of Śiva, another of the major deities in the Hindu pantheon. In this context since it was considered the propelling force of the Universe it was said to control the cycle of life and in this way it was the general principle of movement. Its complicated circle is said to be like a snake resting in a coiled posture.[13] As an adornment of Siva it represents the force of destruction, reconstruction and development, but is at the same time a reminder that it cannot influence God and that God is not bound by Time. Time is ageless, timeless, uncreated and imperishable. In such complex intertwining of temporal, divine and cosmic Time much of Hindu mythology reveled.

The *Purāṇas* tell us about the significance of *itihāsa* and remembering the past in terms of a particular notion of Time. As a class of popular literature[14] both *itihāsa* and *purāṇa* are well known and have been used by scholars to construct the notions of history and historical consciousness among the ancient Indians.[15] Both these words occur in the *Atharva Veda Saṁhitā*,[16] but were apparently not given sufficient importance. Earlier, in the *Ṛg Veda*, there is only a sense of allusion to them in the late tenth book.[17] It is only in the Upaniṣads that we learn of the *itihāsa*[18] and *purāṇa* as the fifth veda[19] and sometimes, as two distinct Vedas.[20] In one manner these texts along with the epics can be understood to have encapsulated a way of looking at the past entwined in myth, legend, and events. It reflects how an entire society remembered its past[21] in a way where the value of noting past events (particularly those of political importance) was given the least credit. This, to use Bernard Lewis' words, was its 'inherited historiography' which 'may be described as the collective memory of a community or nation or other entity . . . what it, or its rulers and leaders, poets, and sages, choose to remember as significant, both as reality and symbol'.[22]

Even though from a ritualistic and mystical point of view the interpretations of the Universe gave considerable vent to developing the cyclic notion of time, the etymological root *kāla* from '*kal'* actually was defined as 'to calculate or enumerate'.[23] In fact, it cannot be ignored that there was a substantial development of understanding the mathematical foundations of Time in the class of literature called the *jyotiṣavedāṅgas*, dated by to *c.* 300-200 BC.[24] The brilliance of the mathematical discoveries culminated in the sophisticated *Siddhānta* treatises that developed more fully the concrete aspects of Time calculation and mathematical duration. Discerning Time in this way had great temporal implications. It enabled an understanding of smaller fragments of Time and these understandings happened in the context of defining political Time in the specific locale of different regions. Scholars suggest that though the Indians knew the concept of the zero earlier, Āryabhaṭṭa may not have implemented the regular use of the decimal system.[25] But it is no coincidence that around the fifth century, when the contributions of the mathematician/astronomer Āryabhaṭṭa were being made, Indian rulers started to use eras in decimal notations to define the duration of their rules. According to

D. C. Sircar the earliest inscription recording the date by a system of nine digits and a zero, with place notations for the tens and hundreds, was made in AD 595 in Gujarat.[26] In B. N. Mukherjee's opinion, keeping in mind the authenticity of the records in question, it was the year 847 of the Vikrama era or *c.* AD 789, that saw the earliest date in decimal figures.[27] On the other hand, according to Acharya, the inscriptions of Orissa 'give us a clear insight into the process of the transition from the numeral to the decimal system',[28] a system that stabilized around the tenth century AD. This thus represents for us immediate value given to political time that was so essential for these rulers in a situation when innumerable kingdoms were emerging in the various regions of India.

We wish to emphasize in this context that the maximum development of these ideas happened in the so-called periphery of the subcontinent if we take the centre as the Ganga Valley. Acharya , in fact, points out that it was after the 'cultural unification of the different regions . . . by the Somavaṁśis' that a system of 'dating the epigraphs in decimal' emerged in Orissa around the tenth century.[29] This transition coincides neatly with the growth of regional identities in the form of the assertion of kingdoms rooted in particular political spaces. Despite disagreements on the exact date of the first decimal record, what is worthy to note is that, irrespective of region, a greater concern with historical time and *itihāsa* began to be preserved in the inscriptions. This had important implications of looking at Time not as an independent entity but as being composed of an unending succession of moments within specific spatial parameters.

It cannot ultimately be concluded that these processes in the different regions had no connection with changes taking place at the pan-Indian level. Simultaneously, it was also around the first five centuries of the Christian era that the *itihāsa-purāṇa* as a fund of 'historical' information about the kings that ruled in the so-called Kali Age began to be systematized as a literature much in demand. Although there is no break with the notions of cyclic time, the list of kings that ruled in the Kali Age are indeed given in a sequential order, along with the number of years they ruled. These lists were necessarily prefixed with the legendary dynasties that had ruled during the earlier eras. A further more emphatic co-relation was that the *praśasti* or eulogy section of most inscriptions from the different regions invariably tried to link the actual historical time of their reigns with the meta-narrative tradition of the *Purāṇas* and epics that was rooted in cyclic time. This was done to associate rulers with the mythical and human heroes of bygone days and assert a pure lineage or ancestry that was otherwise blurred in more local and humble origins. Such efforts naturally made exaggerated claims to an imagined past, so as to assert an antiquity that was unique to each of them. Here, then, the more linear notions of Time co-existed with ease with those that apparently had no direct relevance to the immediate concerns of the ruling elites – nonetheless, it enabled particular kings to use civilizational symbols and underscore the fact that the metaphysical notions of Time as a way of looking at their past were equally important as the more immediate linear time establishing their own genealogy and thus authority in a particular region.[30] We thus cannot put forth the view that there was a binary opposition between these two notions of Time, but must conclude that they co-existed. There was indeed a slow progression of viewing different levels of Time within the overall metaphysical notions that was retained throughout Indian tradition and never totally rejected.

Time and memory were co-joined in these notions of *itihāsa* and it must be recognized that its proponents were necessarily selective in choosing the 'actual events' of the past to construct the accounts. Further, in the literary sources in particular they were often mystified into narratives located in the past that were made to appear like stories, legends, and myths. This deliberative move has made some scholars suggest that the *aitihāsik* (historical) mode of explanation was given minimal epistemological weightage *vis-à-vis* the *nairukta* (etymological) mode or that based on interpretation.[31] The main issue for discussion here is how a different authoritative discourse is generated that establishes the normative context in which society as a whole was appended to particular notions of Time. Thus, writes Pollock: 'History . . . is not simply absent from or unknown to Sanskritic culture, it is denied in favour of a mode of truth that accorded history no epistemological value or social significance. . . .'[32] In its place came the power of 'cultural memory' as understood in the rule-boundedness of the brahmanical discourse. This is found in what is commonly known as the *smṛti* tradition that had an umbilical cord relationship with *śruti* or the revealed tradition as memorized in the Vedas.[33] The accessibility of an apparently continuous tradition (*paramparā*) rested on this *smṛti*. A re-articulation of the past in these terms on the interpretation of the meaning that was embedded in the genealogy of knowledge was thus held together in the dominant discourse. The concern was with leaving the meaning open within a given set of rules that lent a certain kind of fluidity but, at the same time, it retained control. Thus history was considered ineffectual as a man-made intervention but this is clearly replaced by 'cultural memory and the record of human achievement' in 'the Vedic model of thought and action'.[34]

In this light Mikael Aktor has elaborated on the notion of Time within the *smṛti* traditions of early India in relation to how the idea of the theory of *varṇasaṃkara* or mixed castes explains the past origins of *jātis*. In this view the production of this literature throws up a model of truth and righteousness as the source of all knowledge and in the process ritualizes Time. In doing so Aktor argues that a 'celebration of a mythical past . . . obscures the present' to create an 'experience of discontinuity in relation to that norm'.[35] That the tensions between the mythical past and the present are indeed resolved brings out an important central point: the theory of decline from the established norm can be integrated with the present ritual and cultural practice, and thereby, establish a continuity of the tradition or *paramparā*. Thus it is aptly concluded,

> By dividing time into concentric scales from macro and micro units, from kalpas and yugas to days and moments, and by establishing connections between them which become events of special importance, the present moment is placed in a history which is directly relevant to present aims.[36]

The above effectively provides us with yet another way in which understanding and capturing the past in the literary traditions of early India was fundamentally related to controlling the present and, in this case, creating social order. In turn this mode of visualizing Time was nonetheless effectively linked to abstract notions of Time as fostered in the philosophical and psychological understandings of it in the dominant ideological system.

This brings us to the last major point of this paper, a closer look at how relatively simple notions of Time coexisted with the complex understandings built on the principle of *saṃskāra* as memory that implicated an individual's life. This connection is not so easily recognizable for those who pursue the social sciences, but cyclic and linear notions of time were also entwined with memory as inherent in the notions of *saṃskāra* and the individual that carried them. According to most Indian philosophies, Tantra included, an object or an event can be perceived in different ways primarily because all our perceptions are supposedly coloured by the *saṃskāra* we carry. It is in the context of this that it is argued that true knowledge of the 'real' is not possible unless one gets rid of *saṃskāra*. Tantra provides one of the methods for spiritual *sādhana* that enables the burning of the very seed of *saṃskāra*, so that the supreme realization of Truth is possible. It is thus elaborated that the visible world that human beings are born into is collectively impressed upon our sensory and mental plates that constantly remain with us and we perceive them when necessary. These embedded things, ideas, and values then change in Time, Space and Individual only to ultimately achieve the highest realization in the eternal, unchanging universal principle when they are supposed to be removed forever.[37] Until then, the evolution and elevation of the human being through various cycles of temporal Time is but the manifestation of the cosmic and the divine in various forms. The individual is thus recognized as the centre of all philosophical contemplation and therefore, the beginnings of understanding the notion of Time rested on how s/he perceived it.

Tantra is an intuitional science, but it is one of those Indian ideological systems that does take into account both material and ideational factors in its formulation of Time and change. The fundamental aim in Tantra is to rouse all the energies in order to discover the body, emotions, and mind so that enlightenment in the state of knowing the truth is achieved. The search for this truth begins with knowing about the origin of things and human beings and their meanings as clearly as possible. To understand this, then, there emerges in Tantra thought a model of the genesis of the world within which, using some of the best scientific knowledge available, mechanisms of explaining change and Time have been formulated. To grasp this explanation of Time has been central to Tantra since, in ultimate analysis, the human being has to comprehend the reverse process of taking him back to genesis as a worthwhile goal. Nature, mind, and body are to be integrated for the realization of reality that is found in the notion of *paramaśiva* or the Absolute. The *Mahānirvāṇa Tantra* informs us that everything has emerged from it: 'the same Brahman is known from his eternal signs, from whom the whole universe has sprung, in whom when so sprung it exists, and into whom all things return.'[38] Thus changes as perceived in the body of the Universe entity is fundamentally related to the temporal body of the human being. *Cakras*, literally circles or wheels, often applied to the diagrams or *yantras*, were used in ritual worship. Importantly, they were also used to define the centres of spirituality within or without the body, as macrocosm and microcosm that were ultimately considered to be one. The lotus within these circles symbolized a centre of energy and the body was itself considered a place of worship and an essential medium for understanding the cycle of Time.

The Tantric conception of he Absolute (Universal Being), *bindu* (point), *nāda* (sound), and *kāla* (Time) were integrated to explain human perceptions and conceptions of Time. Thus it was articulated that *bindu* that is a colourless (*avarṇa*) and formless (*arūpa*) entity is not only a point on a given line but is also the sum total of truth. Therefore, no difference was maintained between zero and the infinite. According to this view every straight line could become an arc of a great circle.[39] Since the human being is ignorant about his 'real' nature and 'being', the institutional and mystic processes involved in Tantric *sādhana* help him to arrive at the nature of truth. Activating the divinity lying dormant in the human body is necessary for this to be initiated. The knowledge of the vague outer world reaches the human sense organs through the framework of space and time. But, it is explained that these are not the true realities and only the mental frameworks of our own creations. The entire process of understanding the true nature of consciousness is then linked to introspection, and this seeing is closely related with memory. This is not the memory of things from the material outer world but that of the inner world which are understood to be with our being even before birth and which must be known before they are to be eliminated so that knowledge of reality can be got. For the modern objective thinker reality is merely crude matter, but not so for the Tantric *sādhaka*, who, recognizing the importance of matter, does not consider it to be without consciousness. In this view, then, all subjectivities and objectivities are a blend of supreme consciousness.[40] Once an altered state of consciousness has been achieved, the ordinary perception of reality changes. Apart from the *yogi* having a holistic perception of reality, his understanding of Time also undergoes a fundamental change. It has been aptly articulated: 'His ascent from one level of consciousness to another alters a normal dimension of linear time-experience as a constant flow of event sequentially organized as past, present and future. This is transformed into an experience that transcends Time and in which all events simultaneously exists in the so-called "infinite present".'[41] Thus, in Tantra this analysis of the present frame of each person becomes the beginning of things beyond his world of experiences and knowledge. It is also important to emphasize that the present life is seen as a series of moments in linearity that have to be grasped before true knowledge is grasped.

To elaborate, in Tantra, recollecting from the past for the origin of things in some imagined space 'out there' is not considered relevant. Memory as closely related to experience is the reality that has to be understood in the clearly defined space of the body. This experienced reality then drives the mind to look back (*parāvṛtti*), to reverse, as it were, the act of genesis. This, as pointed out by Rawson, can be contrasted with the 'common-sense, materialist-scientific view of time most Western people hold'[42] and, one can add, what we today in India have also begun to adhere to. In this understanding we can only look backwards in linear time so that the most distant object looks as though fading from sight and mind. This vision is based on our immediate sense-experience and knowledge, and we begin to look for the origins and beginning of things at some point in the distant past of the outer world, however remote it may be. None of what has gone by could have been experienced from the sense perception of the present moment. Therefore, all these notions of the past have to be made up through mental fictions, occasionally helped out by so-called 'scientific knowledge' that we can only hope takes us back to accurate information. The image of the way Tantra perceives the trail of things and events from the past is not in terms of a 'landscape' full of 'objects', but rather of them being projected out of the 'mouth of the present'. In this image of Time, things did not 'begin' at some imaginary point back in the depths of the past but is being 'projected through each of us . . . vomiting out his world of experience and knowledge.'[43] Thus, what is being projected is the tissue of experience and memory that is intrinsically related to the individual that is also the centre of the Universe from where the true reality is coming. The human being then is merely an instrument of the act of continuous creation, who must then strive to remember, not the outer temporality of things that seem solid in the world around us, but to transcend them, looking beyond the flow of passing time. Around this revolves the essential rituals with the use of *mantra*, *yantra*, and *kāya*.

This understanding of Time in Tantra is not unique to those Tantras that are commonly known as the Hindu Tantras. In fact, in Tibetan Buddhism the notion of the *Kālacakra Tantra* has been clearly articulated. Its discussion is relevant as it is in this system that three levels of Time are clearly discussed and help us focus on the multiple ancient notions of Time. For more than 2,500 years, the *Kālacakra* teachings have been preserved in India and Tibet. We are informed that the Tantric path is the cornerstone of Tibetan Buddhism, blending the Buddhist sacred teachings with those of the Hindu Yoga and Tantra. Padmasambhava in the eighth century took these teachings to Tibet where they have since been preserved. The major purpose of *Kālacakra Tantra* was to assist the initiated into purifying his body, speech, and mind in symphony with the knowledge of the three principal aspects of the Mahāyāna path of Buddhism. These were renunciation of *saṃsāra* expressing the continuing cycle of death and rebirth, and *bodhicitta* or the desire for true, perfect enlightenment for the sake of others and an understanding of emptiness. It is against the background of this understanding of Mahāyāna Buddhism in its Mantrāyaṇa form, that the *Kālacakra* meditational deity Viśvamātā or the 'The Lord of Time' is explained.

The three levels of the *Kālacakra Tantra* were known as external, internal, and alternative, each understood as a wheel of Time. The external wheel of Time was concerned with the laws of Time and space of our three-dimensional, physical worlds that deal with astronomy, astrology and mathematics. This is the Time we normally understand in the procession of the external solar and lunar days. The *internal wheel of Time was concerned with the human body*, including its energy system. The alternative wheel of Time was said to include the doctrine path and initiations of Śrī Kālacakra, its circular *maṇḍala* abode, and its results. Both the deity residing at the centre of the *maṇḍala* and the *maṇḍala* in its entirety were perceived as sacred expressions of the enlightened mind of the Buddha. Each person engaging in the initiation ceremony was nourished through the process of visualizing and contemplating the *maṇḍala*. In fact, there were supposed to be 722 deities in the *Kālacakra maṇḍala,* symbolizing various manifestations of consciousness and reality. In doing so, ultimately the human perceptions would become one with this pure consciousness.

It is important to emphasize that the *Kālacakra Tantra* did not confine itself to the psychological and philosophical aspects of the subject. Rather, the astrological or major basic elements of calculation were seen as an integral part of the highest esoteric elements and this is what made them relevant for the community of people at large. In fact, in what is called the '*Forehead Cakra*' the second type of *Kālacakra* astrology, called an 'implicit' system, deals with the astrological relationships of the internal energies, *cakras*, channels to mental and emotional states, physical organs, and transformative processes. This was then considered a precursor to what is called 'The wheel of Great Bliss' or the primordial element of Time. This Time was to be considered in three ways:

(a) as the mechanism for calculating the motions of the sun, moon and planets,
(b) as the sequential and continually cyclic arousal of mental and emotional states, and
(c) as the primordial sixth element, Time as Bliss, the innermost dimension of transpersonal awareness and 'internal awakening'.

In the final 'wheel of Enjoyment Cakra' the aim of this practice was to integrate mind and body into the primordial consciousness of the Buddha-nature, another way of defining, enlightenment. The nature of this consciousness as expressed in the *Kālacakra* texts was aimed at the freeing of the consciousness from the limitations of the cyclic nature of Time, through a transcendent type of Time termed Bliss. Through the higher Yoga practices these cycles of circulating energy were supposed to be brought into the control of the Yoga practitioner.[44] Needless to add, this subject had many implications that are valuable to anyone with a psychological or spiritual approach to astrology, and present a theory of the astrological interplay with the cyclic states of the everyday, on the one hand, and supernormal levels of human consciousness, on the other.

The ideological notions indeed had a bearing on the way people looked at temporal Time. Its linearity was important for the immediate past, whereas the distant past was rooted in more cyclic versions. The two coalesced at the critical junctures of the present when the individual sought to understand his existence in the world of the everyday. Jan Barmark,[45] in the context of Tibetan Buddhist medicine, has discussed the centrality of this notion for defining the health of the body. To explicate this he elaborates on the biological world of man in nature, his life-world with others, and his inner world. The person is thus divisible into fragments, each manifesting and containing its own cosmologies. However, each is also constituted in terms of relationships and therefore, connected with a larger cosmology. Time is thus ultimately viewed in different dimensions and at different levels, depending on the context, but ultimately can be defined in terms of a large whole. This notion can be contrasted with modern scientific notions where reality is always considered relative and never absolute. It is relative to the Space-Time dimensions as well as to the observation of things thereby overemphasizing the material aspects of what can be experimented upon in its physical entities. This is naturally very different from the emphasis on the mind that the Tantricists articulated.

The epistemological importance given to history as understood in the modern context was rather limited in the early Indian texts. This is not, as Roy Perrrett has pointed out, because the ancient Indians only believed in 'cyclic time'. 'It is true,' he writes, 'that the narratives recounted in the Purāṇas allude to vast cosmic cycles of repeated creation and dissolution (the *kalpas)*, but these are cycles of change *within* linear time.'[46] It is our main argument that this was so not because there was no change in understanding the importance of Time in more specific contexts within the early Indian world-view. In fact, there was more than one valid version of Time embedded in the ancient texts and inscriptions that played a definitive role in the creation and affirmation of cultural and political identity. Archaeologists and anthropologists studying old societies and certain contemporary communities opine that it is not uncommon for some to perceive the passage of their past events in terms of Time not exclusively linear or cyclic.[47] Both could co-exist in defining the complex understanding of different levels of Time and how they were being viewed in particular contexts relevant for those societies.

NOTES

1. A part of this paper 'Time in Tantra' was presented at the National Seminar of "TANTRISM" jointly organized by the Birla Archaeological and Cultural Research Institute, Salar Jung Museum and Osmania University, Hyderabad, 1-3 March 2002.
2. Well summarized in Time Life Books Series on Life Science Library, Samuel A. Goudsmit, Robert Calidorne, *Time*, 2nd edn., 1980. The elusive nature of Time, its remarkable rhythms, its calculations to make calendars, its measurements to define the day and hours and the history of how people the world over have tried to understand it culminating in the notion of relativity as expounded by Einstein have all been comprehensively dealt with in this book that gives a panoramic view of the subject.
3. *Ibid.*, p. 11.
4. Mircea Eliade, 'Time and Eternity in Indian Thought', in Hari Shankar Prasad (ed.), *Time in Indian Philosophy: A Collection of Essays*, New Delhi: Sri Satguru Publications, 1992, pp. 97-124.
5. Taken up for discussion in the Introduction as part of a larger work on Time in all Indian Philosophical Systems in Hari Shankar Prasad, *ibid.*, pp. 1-17.
6. S. H. Vatsyayan, *A Sense of Time: An Exploration of Time in Theory, Experience and Art,* New Delhi: Oxford University Press, 1981, pp. 5-6.
7. Roy W. Perrett, 'History, Time and knowledge in Ancient India', in *History and Theory*, Vol. 38, No. 3, 1999, pp. 317-21.
8. Romila Thapar, *Time as a Metaphor of History: Early India*, New Delhi: Oxford University Press, 1997, p. 44.
9. *Ṛg Veda*, X.42.9; 1.155.6; *Atharva Veda*, XIX.53.1-10.
10. M. Bloomfield (tr.), *Hymns of the Atharva Veda*, p. 224.
11. *Śvetāṣvatara Upaniṣad*, I.2; *Maitrāyaṇa Upaniṣad*, 6.14-16.
12. Inderjit, *Science of Symbols, Deeper View of Indian Deities*, New Delhi: Geetanjali Publications, 1977, p. 121.
13. *Ibid.*, p. 55.
14. Keith informs us that as two classes of literature they are mentioned for the first time in the *Taittirīya Āraṇyaka—Vedic Index*, Vol. I, pp. 76ff.
15. Romila Thapar, 'The Tradition of History Writing in Early India', in *Ancient Indian Social History, Some Interpretations,* New Delhi: Orient Longmans, 1978, pp. 263ff.

16. *Atharva Veda*, XV.6.4.
17. *Ṛg Veda*, X.34 – The story of the gambler's lament.
18. Mentioned along with *purāṇa* in the *Bṛhad Āraṇyaka Upaniṣad*, II.4.10, along with the *Ṛg, Yajur* and *Sāma Vedas* and *Atharvāṅgirasa*. Also mentioned in the same verse are *vidya, Upaniṣads, ślokas, sūtras, anuvyākhyānas. Itihāsa* here is translated as 'legend' and *purāṇa* as 'cosmogonies'.
19. *Chāndogya Upaniṣad,* III.4.1-2. Here the term *itihāsa-purāṇa* occurs conjoined and is translated as 'the reading of old stories'. The editor and translator explains that since it is mentioned with the *Atharva Veda*, which does not have sacrifice proper, the former may be understood as the fifth Veda (SBE, Vol. I, Pt. 1, p. 39, fn. 1).
20. *Sāṅkhāyana Śrauta Sūtra*, XVI.2.21.27; *Satapatha Brāhmaṇa*, XIII.4.3.12-13.
21. Bernard Lewis, *History: Remembered, Recovered, Invented,* Touchstone Edition, 1987 (1st pub. Princeton University Press, 1975), pp. 11-12 defines 'remembered history' as statements about the past that range from 'personal recollections claimed by the elders to the living traditions of a civilisation, as embodied in its scriptures, its classics and its inherited historiography'.
22. *Ibid.*, p. 12.
23. Margaret and James Stutley, *A Dictionary of Hinduism: Its Mythology, Folklore and Development 1500 BC-1500 AD,* Bombay: Allied Publishers, 1977, p. 134.
24. A. L. Basham, *The Wonder That Was India,* 1967, pp. 489-91.
25. M. Winternitz, *History of Indian Literature,* Vol. III, Pt. II (trans. S. Jha), Delhi, 1967, p. 649.
26. D. C. Sircar, *Indian Epigraphy,* Delhi, 1965, pp. 221, 495-7.
27. B. N. Mukherjee, 'The Early Use of Decimal Notation in Indian Epigraphs; in *Journal of the Epigraphical Society,* Vol. 19, 1993, pp. 80-1.
28. Subrata Kumar Acharya, 'The Transition from the Numerical to the Decimal System in the Inscriptions of Orissa', in *Journal of the Epigraphical Society of India,* Vol. 19, 1993, p. 52.
29. Acharya, *op. cit.*, 1993, p. 58.
30. These ideas have been more fully developed in two M.Phil theses done under my supervision and submitted to the University of Hyderabad by A. Aruna, now published as, *State Formation in the Eastern Deccan (7th Century AD-13th Centrury AD)*, Delhi: Bharatiya Kala Prakashan, 2000 and by T. Senthil Kumar, 'Early Medieval South India and Modes of Historical Narration', unpublished M.Phil. thesis, University of Hyderabad, Hyderabad, 2000.
31. Aloka Parasher, 'Absences in History: Towards Recovering History of the Marginal in Early India', Indian History Congress Symposia Papers: 3, New Delhi, 1992, pp. 8-9.

32. Sheldon Pollock, 'From Discourse of Ritual to Discourse of Power in Sanskrit Literature, in *Journal of Ritual Studies*, Vol. 4. No. 2, Summer 1990, p. 333.
33. *Ibid.*, pp. 315-45.
34. *Ibid.*, p. 334.
35. Mikael Aktor, '*Smṛtis* and *Jātis*: The Ritualization of Time and the Continuity of the Past', in Daud Ali (ed.), *Invoking the Past: The Uses of History in South Asia*, New Delhi: Oxford University Press, 1999, p. 259.
36. *Ibid.*, p. 278.
37. Explained in B. K. S. Iyengar, *Light on the Yoga Sūtra's of Patanjali*, Patañjala Yoga Pradīpikā, New Delhi: HarperCollins, 1993, pp. 5, 36-7.
38. III. 9; John Woodruffe (ed.), Madras, 1953, p. 32.
39. Lalan Prasad Singh, *Tantra: Its Mystic and Scientific Basis,* Delhi: Concept Publishing Company, 1976, p. 158.
40. *Ibid.*, for this summary of ideas in Tantra on Space, Time, and Individual Consciousness.
41. Ajit Mookerjee and Madhu Khanna, *The Tantric Way: Art, Science and Ritual*, London: Thames & Hudson, 1977, p. 156.
42. Philip Rawson, *Tantra: The Indian Cult of Ecstasy,* London, 1973, p. 10.
43. *Ibid.*, p. 12.
44. The above ideas on the *Kālacakra Tantra* and Mantrāyana form of Mahāyāna Buddhism Summarized from the web-site listed below: http://www.thewildrose.net/tibetan_buddhism.html
45. Summarized from Jan Barmark, 'Tibetan Buddhist Medicine from the Perspective of the Anthropology of Knowledge', in *Tibetan Medicine*, Series 13, 1991, pp. 25-32.
46. Perrett, *op. cit.*, 1999, p. 314.
47. Robert Layton (ed.), *Who Needs the Past? Indigenous Values and Archaeology*, Routledge, London, 1989, p. 6. Layton notes in this context that the most impressive visions of grand cycles of time are those preserved in Hindu notions of chronology and cosmology.

CHAPTER 8

On Board the Hermapollon: Transporting Gangetic Nard from Muziris

RANABIR CHAKRAVARTI

The long-standing economic image of the subcontinent as exclusively agrarian, steeped in insularity and isolation – especially during the pre-modern times – has undergone a significant shift in historical researches of late. The distinct possibilities of an active non-agrarian sector of the 'traditional' economy are being increasingly illuminated, although the non-agrarian sector remains firmly rooted to the overarching agrarian material milieu. Sustained scholarly efforts have indeed rendered considerable visibility to urbanization, crafts production and trade in early India (up to *c.* AD 1300). Tracing the long tradition of commerce in the subcontinent economic historians have been underlining, roughly from the middle of the 1980s, the significance of the Indian Ocean in the trading activities and linkages of India. The widely believed stigma that early Indians were averse to seafaring with a view to retaining their ritual purity has been effectively negated as such attitudes were available only in the normative Brahmanical lawbooks and at the most, applicable perhaps only to the priestly community. This has resulted in the modification of the dominant historiographical perspective that traditional India was landlocked.[1] 'The argument now made is that there was in pre-colonial times a commercial economy that incorporated many societies of Eurasia and Africa. The economic impact of this trade was not incidental'.[2] The Indian Ocean commerce paved the way not only for movement of men and merchandise on board the sea-going vessels, but for exchange of ideas and cultural traits too among widely dispersed communities.

India's trade with the Roman empire, especially the eastern Mediterranean region (from *c.* late first century BCE to 250 CE), looms large in the history of India's sea-borne commerce, though long-distance overland traffic between South Asia and West Asia was also brisk. The subject concerned has been receiving enduring attention of historians with divergent perspectives of early trade.[3] The availability of a number of Classical texts of the early centuries of the common era, describing this commercial network with an eastern Mediterranean orientation, certainly provides the fillip to the historian's enquiries. Most of the outstanding studies of the trade between the Roman empire and India heavily depend on the *Geographikon* of Strabo (*c.* late first century BCE), the *Periplus Maris Erythraei* by an anonymous mariner (*c.* late first century CE), the *Naturalis Historia* of Pliny (death in CE 79) and the *Geographike Huphegesis* by Claudius Ptolemy (*c.* CE 150).[4] Images of brisk maritime trade and arrival of *yavana* (non-Indian) merchants to ports of South India are offered by the Sangam texts, the earliest Tamil literary creation. The two new translations of the *Periplus Maris Erythraei* in the 1980s, provided a major impetus to the study of this trade.[5] The excavations at Arikamedu near Pondicherry in 1946, established for the first time the archaeological dimension of the empirical foundation of the enquiries into this commerce.[6] To this must be added the large number of Roman coins, often found in South Indian coin hoards, providing the incontrovertible visual and archaeological proof of Roman trade with India.[7] No less significant is the field archaeological evidence of the Mediterranean wares, the celebrated Arretine Ware and amphorae being of outstanding importance, and some other cultural artefacts, as imports to India.[8] Ongoing excavations at a few port sites in the Red Sea (especially Berenike and Myos Hormos/Abu Sharr) which was the major sea-lane linking Indian ports with Alexandria in the Nile delta, immensely enrich our understanding of India's sea-borne commerce in the western Indian Ocean.[9] There is a general consensus among historians that a continuous urge among the rich Romans for procuring luxuries from the East, especially Chinese Silk, fine Indian textiles, precious gems and stones, and exotic spices, was the principal engine that kept the trade in motion for nearly three centuries.

The study of the commerce between the Roman empire and India however has one limitation in that the bulk of the data, except coins and the *Periplus*, are derived from essentially non-economic documents. The long-felt void of a direct trade-document has been filled with the coming into light of a unique loan contract of mid-second century which will be the principal focus of the present discussion. It is a papyrus document written on both sides (recto 24 lines and verso 29 lines), though not in a complete state of preservation, now lying in a museum in Vienna, Austria. First published in 1985, the document has been edited, translated and studied by a few experts, the latest being the one by Lionel Casson which is principally used in our present essay.[10] The purport of this document is to give effect to a contract between two parties concerning the shipment of highly valuable Indian commodities on board the vessel Hermapollon, lying at anchor at the great South Indian port of Muziris on the west coast of India. The transportation of a number of costly commodities from India to Alexandria and various other costs during this protracted journey needed heavy financial investment and that is why a maritime loan had to be contracted. The names of the debtor and the creditor are unfortunately lost; Thur however designates the party of the first part as ego and that of the second part as tu. The debtor was ego and tu the creditor. The contract stipulates that 'in the event of the non-payment by ego of a loan he owes, tu is empowered to take over the security specified in the loan contract. . . , and the security unquestionably consisted of the goods involved in this agreement'.[11] Six parcels of consignment were loaded on to the ship Hermapollon and carried the total price of 1154 talents, 2852 drachmas in silver. The document presents some quantifiable data, so very rare in the study of early Indian economic history. The exported items were Gangetic nard, ivory, elephant tusks and textiles, all of which were, judging their enormous value, certainly luxury commodities of Indian origin. The present paper pays particular attention to the Gangetic nard. Before one moves to a minute study of the Gangetic nard, it is necessary to narrate the actual transportation of these exported Indian products, according to the loan contract document. The destination of Hermapollon from Muziris is unfortunately not known because of the torn condition of the document. But there is little doubt that it should be either Myos Hormos (Abu Shaar) or Berenike, both being premier ports on the west coast of the Red Sea for commercial linkages with the west coast of India. On reaching one of these two ports, goods will be unloaded from the ship and placed on back of camels. Camels would transport these commodities to the famous trade centre, Coptos from where these will be shifted on to boats plying on the river Nile. Thus at Coptos converged important overland and fluvial routes. The riverine trip from Coptos carried the six parcels to Alexandria, the port par excellence of Roman Egypt, where the imported items would have to enter the Roman imperial warehouse and be levied a duty of 25 per cent.

With the increasingly better utilization of the more or less predictable alterations of the monsoon winds, a direct sea voyage from a Red Sea port to a harbour on the west coast of India became regular. Pliny (*Naturalis Historia*, VI. 26.104) suggests the development of this maritime route in four stages, each succeeding stage being shorter and safer than each preceding one. At the most developed stage it was possible to reach Muziris from Berenike/ Myos Hormos in 'forty days' by utilizing the south-west monsoon (Hippalus/Etasian wind/Hypalum of the Classical texts). Casson rightly suggests that such a voyage presumably was undertaken around late August when the south-west monsoon winds were still blowing, but the fury of the monsoon would have been relatively less. Most of the traditional harbours on the west coast of India remain closed during the height of the monsoon, i.e. from June to the middle of August. Casson in fact opines that it was possible to reach a port on the western seaboard of India, especially Muziris, in twenty days, instead of forty days. Pliny, according to him, probably made a miscalculation about the duration of the maritime voyage. A ship is expected to start its return journey from an Indian harbour to its westward destination to a port in the Red Sea or the Persian Gulf in the month of November/ December by taking advantage of the north-east monsoon wind.[12] The Red Sea indeed stole the limelight during the early centuries CE as the major sea-lane linking up the northern sector of the Indian Ocean with the Mediterranean, the *mare nostrum* of the Romans; the erstwhile importance of the Persian Gulf somewhat seems to have receded to background. The Red Sea network too had its typical nautical and navigational features. It indeed provides an opportunity of communications between the Arabian Sea and the Mediterranean, though there was obviously no Suez Canal during the period under review. The Red Sea stretches for about 1,200 miles, with an average width of 120 miles, but also has a number of reefs along the Asian and African shores. Hydrographical studies show that its middle channel offers very safe passages for navigation. The wind generally blows from the north and only during a smaller part of the year the Red Sea experiences the effects of the wind from the south. This has profound effects on navigation in the Red Sea prior to steam navigation. The pre-modern ship plying between the Red Sea area and the Arabian Sea therefore could not take much advantage of the alternating monsoon wind system as it does not match with the patterns of wind movements in the Red Sea area. Thus during the height of the south- west monsoon prevailing winds in the Red Sea blow in an opposite direction, i.e. from the northwest. Sailing southwards in the southern part of the Red Sea, 'during the period of the southwest monsoon, when the wind in all the area is northwest, is a terrible experience, because it follows the movement of the ship'.[13] It is likely that because of these natural hazards of sailing in the Red Sea in a traditional vessel, a combination of sea-voyages, overland trips and fluvial journeys was preferred as one witnessed in the case of the transportation of the Gangetic nard, along with other Indian luxuries, from Muziris to Alexandria. The transportation costs during such a journey must have been enormous which certainly enhanced the price of these extremely precious luxury items.

A striking feature of the loan contract is the conspicuous absence of Malabarese black pepper in the list of Indian exported commodities; black pepper of Malabar was indeed the most sought after Indian spice in the Roman world, figuring very prominently in the Classical accounts and the Tamil Sangam literature alike, and very aptly labelled as the 'black gold'.[14]

The importance of the trade in various types of plant products as spices and fragrances in the Roman empire is well known. A large number of them were imported from South Asia, as amply demonstrated by the *Periplus*, Pliny's *Naturalis Historia* and Ptolemy's *Geography*. During the lifetime of Pliny (death in CE 79) more spices were available in the empire than ever before. Emperor Domitian constructed in CE 92 Rome's own spice quarter, the *horrea piperatoria*.[15] Already by the first century CE, Rome became famous for its conspicuous consumption of spices in the Mediterranean world. Enjoyment of luxury and leading a luxurious way of life by the fabulously rich was projected and lauded in contemporary Hellenistic philosophy.[16] It is in this context that the import of the nard from South Asia, explicitly figuring in the loan contract document, calls for a close scrutiny. The importance of the nard as a dutiable import item to the imperial Roman administration is proved beyond doubt by the loan contract document. A strong confirmation of this system is also available in the list of articles subject to duty upon entry into Alexandria in the *Digest*, a synthetic work of the Roman Law, promulgated by Justinian in AD 533. The list includes spikenard which is the same as the nard.[17] The word nard is derived from Greek *nardos*, referring to oils extracted from certain fragrant grasses, *Nardostachys jatamansi*, invariably described in the Classical texts as a plant grown in the Himalayan mountainous regions in India. In the extremely rich households of Rome it was a custom of ladies to anoint guests at lavish banquets with fragrant oil of nard. The custom of pampering the guest with this exotic and imported oil should certainly be read as a statement of their immense opulence and a commentary on their social status. Nard leaves entered the lavish gastronomical world of the rich Romans as these were used for preparing oyster sauce and another sauce for preparing venison. Rated very high among ointments and plant products, the spikenard is reported to have been tastefully kept in alabaster boxes; it was also widely used as a drug.[18]

The nard was much sought after by the Jewish population in the Roman world too. It was an indispensable ingredient of their ritual and religious practices. The *Talmud* offers as many as sixteen references to the nard, along with myrrh, cassia, saffron and cinnamon, which was an essential item for preparing the incense to be burnt before the altar. The use of these spices for proper worship became an absolute necessity since the exile of the Jews from Egypt. The Rabbinic tradition enjoins upon the extra-ordinary care for preparing the incense and the omission of even a single ingredient marred its ritual purity and hence such an omission was considered a capital offence. The steady demand for imported nard was generated to a considerable extent by Jewish ritual requirements. One has to take into account the fact that the Jews formed nearly 10 per cent of the population in the Roman empire.[19]

The term nard is derived from the Sanskrit word, *nalada*, signifying the name of a plant. Known as early as the days of the *Atharvaveda*, one of the four Vedic *Samhitas* and belonging to the later Vedic literature (*c.* 1000-600 BC), the *nalada* seems to have been recognised important as a medicinal herb in ancient India. The famous Indian medical treatise, the *Susruta Samhita*, was aware of the medicinal properties of this plant.[20] Whether it was as much sought after in India as it was in the Roman world is unknown; but it is unlikely that the nard fetched enormous price and profit in India as an exotic plant product. On the other hand, the nard is invariably lumped together with pearls, pepper and muslin textiles as the costliest imported items to the Roman empire – a point also well driven home by the loan contract document. The nard has its origin and growth in the mountainous regions of the Himalayas, at the altitude of about 17,000 feet. The *Periplus* speaks of three varieties of Indian nard exported from three different ports: from Barabricum, the port in the Indus delta, from Barygaza, the premier port in western India at the mouth of the river Namados (Narmada) and Gangetic nard, shipped from Muziris in Kerala. It is strange to find that Pliny condemned the Gangetic nard for its poor quality and foul odour (*ozaenitis*), as his perception hardly matches all other data on the Gangetic nard. Warmington correctly points out that Pliny must have confused Gangetic nard with lemon/ginger grasses, the latter also known to have yielded oil and loosely called nard. Yet, Pliny himself gives the price of per pound of nard leaves ranging from 45 to 70 *denarii* and the spike (the rootstock) at 100 *denarii* per pound, leaving little doubt that he too considered the nard to be among the costliest imports from India.[21]

As we have already mentioned the nard figures in the *Periplus* in the list of items available at the port of Barbaricum. Interestingly the nard is mentioned therein as one of the 'return' cargoes, that is as a product shipped out from this port to the eastern Mediterranean destinations.[22] The nard transported from Barygaza seems to have reached the port through Ozene or Ujjaiyini (in Madhyapradesh), a major commercial and urban centre in early historical India. 'Through this region there is also brought down from the upper parts, the nard that comes by the way of Proklais, the nard that comes through the adjacent part of Skythia.'[23] Proklais certainly stands for the famous city of Pushkalavati in the northwestern frontier areas to the west of the Indus and identified with the well known site of Charsadda in Pakistan. It is most likely that the nard actually grown in the mountainous regions around Kabul (Kabolitic in the *Periplus*). Skythia of the *Periplus* denotes the lower Indus valley where in fact stood the port of Barbaricum. Thus the supply of the nard at Barygaza came from non-local sources; it will be reasonable to infer that some part of the nard available from the lower Indus country was directed to Barygaza which seems to have been the preferred to Barbaricum in the Indus delta.

The *Periplus* gives an explicit reference to the Gangetic nard. The Gangetic area is located after (that is to the north of) Masalia, identified with the coastal areas of Andhra and located in the deltas of the Krishna and the Godavari rivers. The text mentions the Ganges as the greatest river of India. 'On it is a port of trade with the same name as the river, Ganges, through which are shipped out malabathron, Gangetic nard, pearls and cotton garments of the very finest quality, the so called Gangetic.'[24] The author of the *Periplus* next vaguely speaks of a country farther to the east of Gange, namely Thina or China. The Classical authors had little direct knowledge about China, but derived the information that some Chinese products were shipped 'via the Ganges River back to Limyrike'.[25] In another section the author of the *Periplus* speaks of the shipping network between Limyrike/Damirica and the Ganges country.[26] The Ganges country surely denotes the Ganga delta as it was situated close to the sea (the Bay of Bengal) and as the Ganga reached the sea through it. There is no known port in the region having the name of Ganga, as mentioned in the *Periplus*. However, two ports in the Bengal delta stole the limelight in the maritime scenario of early historical Bengal: one is the famous port of Tamralipta (Tamalites of Pliny and Taluctae of Ptolemy) and the other is Chandraketugarh, not known in any literary/textual material, but a major excavated site in West Bengal. It is difficult to satisfactorily locate the port of Gange, but it seems to have been different from Tamralipta/Tamalites/Taluctae (Tamluk, Midnapur district, West Bengal).[27] This is the reason why its preferred identification is sought with Chandraketugarh. Chandraketugarh has recently yielded a few unique inscribed (in 'mixed' Brahmi-Kharosti script) terracotta seals and sealings on which were depicted representations of sea-going vessels.[28] That Chandraketugarh was a major riverine port in the Ganga delta during the early centuries CE is amply demonstrated by these images of ships on inscribed seals/sealings. The accounts in the *Periplus* also clearly suggest that exportable commodities from the Bengal delta, including the Gangetic nard and the muslin, were first taken to Limyrike/Damirica, i.e. the Dravida country.[29] This coastal zone, corresponding to the coastal tracts of modern Tamil Nadu, had a number of flourishing ports, e.g. Camara, Sopatma, Poduca (Arikamedu near Pondicherry), Kaveripattinam (Khaberos emporium of Ptolemy) and Colchi (modern Korkai). These harbours dotting the coastline from northern part of Tamil Nadu to the deltas of the Tamraparni and Vaigai rivers in the south, were well known to sailors, shippers and merchants of the Roman world.[30] A close perusal of available field archaeological materials and the evidence of the Sangam texts indicates that commodities were carried from the Dravida country westwards to the Malabar coast through Karur, the capital of the Cheras, the present Coimbatore region (Pounata of Ptolemy) and the Palghat pass to Kerala.[31] One may logically visualize the transportation of the Gangetic nard from the Coromandel coastal tracts to Muziris through this overland linkage between the two littoral segments in far South India, after it was brought from the Ganga delta to some Coromandel harbours. This in its turn implies a coastal network along the entire eastern seaboard.

This is particularly illuminated by the distribution of the findspots of a type of pottery, the Rouletted Ware (RW). The RW originally came to scholarly recognition since the excavations at Arikamedu by Wheeler who considered it to be a Roman import. Vimala Begle's extremely significant re-examination and reassessment of this pottery revised its chronology. It is now seen not as a Roman import and therefore not ascribed to a period from late first century BCE to *c*. CE 300. Begle situates it in the date bracket from *c*. 200 BCE to about CE 200. The RW seems to have been of an indigenous manufacturing process, though the technique of rouletting could have been derived from Mediterranean sources of pre-Roman times. The RW is found from a large number of sites along the entire length of the east coast: Tamralipta, Chandraketugarh (West Bengal), Mahasthangarh, Wari Bateswar (Bangladesh), Sisupalgarh, Manikpatnam (Orissa), Ghantasala, Dhanyakatak, Amaravati, Salihundam (Andhra Pradesh), Kanchipuram, Vasavasamudram, Nattamedu,

Arikamedu, Kaveripattinam and Alagankulam (Tamilnadu).[32] The impressive list of the findspots of RW cannot but point to its distinct association with the coastal regions and indicate a coastal network going back to c. second century BCE. Gogte's recent analysis of the clay of the RW suggests that the main manufacturing zone of the RW was the Chandraketugarh-Tamluk area in coastal Bengal as the clay required to produce the RW was peculiar to coastal/deltaic Bengal and was not locally available from elsewhere.[33] Seen from this angle, the RW from the Bengal delta could have reached different sites along the eastern seaboard as regular coastal voyages spread from the Ganga delta to the Tamraparni-Vaigai delta; in other words, the coastal network provided opportunities of linkage and communication along the entire length of the eastern littorals.

One may at this juncture further look for movement of vessels in this area. The inscribed Kharosti-Brahmi seals of early historical Bengal carry images of sea-going vessels visiting and/or starting their voyages from Chandraketugarh. Thanks to the decipherment of the mixed Kharosti-Brahmi script by B. N. Mukherjee, the names and/or categories of these ships have come to light. Thus there were trappaga ships which also figure in the *Periplus* (in the context of the port of Barygaza) and the Jaina text, *Angavijja*. The trappaga, in the light of the descriptions in the *Periplus* appears to be a coastal craft.[34] Two other ships are mentioned in the Chandraketugarh sealings respectively as Jaladhisakra (literally, Indra of the ocean) and fit for Tridesayatra (literally, journeys to three directions, implying possibly long voyages).[35] More or less contemporary Satavahana coins from the eastern Deccan depict figures of double masted ships, distinct from the images of ships appearing on the Chandraketugarh sealings.[36] A merchant named Palita, according to the Jaina *Uttaradhyayana-sutra*, undertook a voyage in a vessel (*poya* or *pota*) from Campa (near Bhagalpur) to reach Pithuda (Pityndra of Ptolemy), located somewhere in between the deltas of the Mahanadi and the Godavari.[37] The Jaina tale points to the possibility of a riverine journey from eastern Bihar to the Ganga delta and from there on to the Kalinga-Andhra littoral by a coastal voyage. The presence of a *mahanavika* or a master mariner in an inscription of *c.* first century CE from Ghantasala (Kontakosylla of the *Periplus* and Ptolemy's *Geography*) strongly suggests an active shipping network in this segment of the east coast.[38] Giving his account of the Damirica/Limyrike ports like Camara, Poduca and Sopatma, the author of the *Periplus* notes the regular plying of the sangara and the kolandiaphonta types of vessels.[39] The sangara, like the trappaga, is an indigenous craft identified with sanghada figuring in the Jaina text *Angavijja*. The kolandiaphonta is explicitly described in the *Periplus* as a large ship plying between Limyrike and 'the Ganges region'. Once again the author of the *Periplus* impresses upon the interconnected coastal voyages linking the Ganga delta with the Coromandel coast. The entire eastern seaboard experienced a lively coastal shipping network in which participated a variety of ships and vessels, e.g. the trappaga, the jaladhisakra, the ship fit for *tridesayatra*, the double masted ship displayed on a particular type of Satavahana coin, the sangara and the kolandiaphonta. These vessels could have operated in specific coastal segments in the eastern sea-board. Thus the trappaga seems to have been common to the Ganga delta, the sangara and the kolandiaphonta associated with the Coromandel coast and the double masted ship associated principally with the Andhra-Kalinga coast. In fact, the above discussions present a lively image of coastal shipping and navigation along the eastern seaboard. Indian shippers and sailors are likely to have been key operators in this coastal linkage. If the distribution of the 'emporia' of Ptolemy in the east coast of India is an indicator of the presence of Greek/Roman merchants therein, then such emporia were mainly in the Tamilnadu coast and did not extend to the north of the Krishna-Godavari delta region. The author of the *Periplus* was certainly more aware of and familiar with the western littoral than the eastern seaboard about which he probably did not command first hand information. Significantly enough, Ptolemy in the mid-second century CE gives us more information of the eastern seaboard and the eastern Indian Ocean than the author of the *Periplus*. This logically implies increased participation and incorporation of the Bay of Bengal trade in the maritime commerce between India and the Roman empire, resulting in the considerable amount of information about and awareness of the significance of the eastern sea-board to someone like Claudius Ptolemy who gathered his information from far away Alexandria.

The export of the Gangetic nard also speaks of the very extensive hinterland of the port of Muziris. This consignment of nard must have started its onward journey from somewhere remote in the north-eastern part of the subcontinent; from there it reached the Gangetic delta for a coastal voyage to the Coromandel coast; from coastal Tamilnadu the nard was brought to Muziris possibly by an overland journey and finally shipped out from Muziris. Commanding such an extensive hinterland/supply zone and exporting its precious local spice (i.e. pepper) Muziris stole the limelight as the premier port of Malabar. That its foreland spread up to the Red Sea port of Berenice and/or Myos Hormos further contributed to its outstanding importance. The Gangetic nard on board the Hermapollon fetched a price of 4,500 silver drachmae, for each of the 60 containers – an enormous price.[40] The total value of the entire imported consignments, according to this loan contract papyrus was a staggering 1,154 talent, 2,852 drachmae, amounting to a massive 7 million sesterces.[41] Estimates of the total budget of the Roman imperial economy are put around 800 million sesterces and about one-eighth of the total budget of the early empire has been suggested to have been siphoned off to the Red Sea area, for the importation of eastern luxuries.[42] The papyrus under review offers an image of the import of Indian luxuries more or less on a comparable scale. The importance of the trade in Gangetic nard in the import of Indian luxuries to the Roman world can hardly be overlooked. Pliny's famous lamentation on the drain of Rome's wealth for purchasing Eastern luxuries naturally comes to our mind in this context. One may justifiably be suspicious that Pliny's figures of the drainage of 50 million sesterces, for purchasing eastern luxuries could have been an exaggeration and it was more a moral statement than an exactly economic one. But in the light of the present papyrus document the total value of the commodities in a single ship, the Hermapollon, stands at an enormous 7 million sesterces. One tends to agree with Parker that Pliny's numbers amounting to 50 million sesterces, 'are still within the bounds of the possible'.[43] The importance of the trade in various luxury items in the commerce between the Roman empire and India has indeed been effectively highlighted by a large number of scholars. The export trade of exotic spices from South Asia to the eastern Mediterranean looms large in the historiography of luxury trade of this period. As the typical instance of this the pepper from Malabar invariably steals the limelight. To this now should be added the nard, especially the Gangetic nard –

the best among all varieties of Indian nard – as one of the most sought after plant-products. The loan contract document certainly furthers our understanding of the port of Muziris which was simultaneously exporting a local plant- product (pepper) and another plant-product (the Gangetic nard) grown in northeastern India. No less significant is the message conveyed by the papyrus that the Bay of Bengal network holds a crucial key to the outstanding rise of Muziris in the western Indian Ocean trade.

NOTES

1. Ranabir Chakravarti, ed., *Trade in Early India*, New Delhi: Oxford University Press, 2001; Ranabir Chakravarti, *Trade and Traders in Early Indian Society*, New Delhi: Manohar, 2002; Romila Thapar, *Early India from Origins to c. AD 1300*, London: Penguin, 2002 highlights the importance of commerce in the making of the civilization and material culture of India.
2. Romila Thapar, *Great Eastern Trade: Other Times, Other Places*, Fourth Vasant J. Sheth Memorial Lecture, Mumbai, 2002.
3. There is a voluminous literature on the Silk Road trade and India's trade with the Roman world. Only a few recent and outstanding works are mentioned hereunder. M. G. Raschke, 'New Studies in the Roman Commerce with the East', in von Hildegard Temporini and Wolfgang Haase, eds., *Aufstieg under Niedergang in der Romischen Welt*, IX, Berlin, De Gruyter, 1978: 604-1361; Xin Ri Liu, *Ancient India and Ancient China AD 1-600*, New Delhi: Oxford University Press, 1986; A. G. Frank, 'The Centrality of Central Asia', *Studies in History*, VIII, 1992: 43-98; Irene M. Frank and David M. Brownstone, *The Silk Road: A History*, New York and Oxford: Facts on File Publications, 1986; Ehsan Yarshater, ed., *Cambridge History of Iran*, III (chapter on economic history), Cambridge: Cambridge University Press,1983; Garry K. Young, *Rome's Eastern Trade, International Commerce and Imperial Policy 31 BC- AD 305*, London and New York: Routledge, 2001; Richard Stoneman, *Palmyra and its Empire*, Ann Arbor: The University of Michigan Press, 1992; G. W. Bowersock, *Roman Arabia*, Cambridge (Mass.): Harvard University Press,1983; Vimala Begley and Richard Daniel de Puma, eds., *Rome and India: the Ancient Sea Trade*, New Delhi: Oxford University Press, 1992 (Indian rpt); J. F. Salles, ed., *Athens, Aden Arikamedu*, New Delhi: Manohar, 1995; F. de Romanis and Andre Tchernia, eds., *Crossings: Early Mediterranean Contacts with India*, New Delhi: Manohar, 1997.
4. Strabo, *Geographikon*, trn., H. L. Jones, Loeb Classical Series, Cambridge, Mass, 1942 (rpt.); *Periplus Maris Erythraei*, trn. W.W. Schoff, New Delhi: Munshiram Manoharlal, 1974 (rpt.); trn. G. W. B. Huntingford, London: Haklyut Society, 1980; also ed. and trn., L. Casson, Princeton: Princeton

University Press, 1989; Ptolemy, *Geographike Huphegesis*, trn., E. L. Stevenson, New York: NY Public Library, 1932.

5. The translation by G. W. B. Huntingford came out in 1980, London: Haklyut Society; this was followed by L. Casson's translation of the text in 1989, see note 4. The present essay cites Casson's translation, as Casson offers an excellent translation along with insights into maritime commerce and early navigational practices.
6. R. E. M. Wheeler and Krishna Deva, 'Arikamedu, An Indo-Roman Trading Station in the East Coast of India', *Ancient India*, II, 1947: 17-124. The site has been re-examined and re-excavated by Vimala Begley, *The Ancient Port of Arikamedu: New Excavations and Researches 1989-1992*, Pondicherry: Ecole francaise d'Extreme-Orient, 1996.
7. A. K. Jha, ed., *Coinage, Trade and Economy*, Nasik: Indian Institute of Research in Numismatic Studies, 1991; P. J. Turner and J. Cribb, 'Numismatic Evidence for the Roman Trade with Ancient India', in J. Reade, ed., *Indian Ocean in Antiquity*, London: Kegan Paul, 1996.
8. Begley and de Puma, eds., *Rome and India* for an in-depth study of these artefacts found in India.
9. Steven G. Sidebotham, 'Ports of the Red Sea and the Arabia-India Trade', in Begley and de Puma, eds, *Rome and India*: 12-38; Young, *Rome's Eastern Trade*, especially chapter 2 on the Red Sea Trade. For the constructions in the Berenike-Coptos road, see pp. 46-7. Information about the ongoing excavations at Berenike appear in the Proceedings of the Conference on South Asian Archaeology. In recent years, Sidebotham has reported about the discovery of nearly 1,500 kgs of peppercorn from Berenike.
10. H. Harrauer and P. Sijpesteijn, 'Ein Neues Dokument zu Roms Indienhandel, P. Vindob. G40822', *Anzeiger der Ostereichischen Akademie der Wissenschaften*, phil-hist, Kl 122, 1985: 124-55; G.Thur, 'Hypotheken-Urkundeeines Seederlehns fur eine Reise nach Muziris und Apographe fur die Tetarte in Alexandreia (zuP. Vindob. G. 40822)', *Tyche* 2, 1987: 229-45; L. Casson, 'P. Vindob G 40822 and the Shipping of Goods from India', *Bulletin of the American Society of Papyrologists*, 23, 1986: 73-9; L. Casson, 'New Lights on Maritime Loans: P. Vindob G 40822', *Zeischrift fur Papyrologie und Epigraphik*, 84, 1990: 185-96. I am grateful to Professor Casson for giving me an offprint of last mentioned article. This is the latest editing and translation of this document. Considering its immense significance its translation by Casson has been reproduced in Niharranjan Ray, B. D. Chattopadhyaya, Ranabir Chakravarti and V. R. Mani, A *Sourcebook of Indian Civilization*, Hyderabad: Orient Longman, 2000; Casson's entire article is also incorporated in Chakravarti, ed., *Trade in Early India*: 228-43.
11. L. Casson, 'New Lights on Maritime Loans': 196.
12. *Idem*, 'Rome's Maritime Trade in the Far east', *The American Neptune*,

XLVIII, 1988: 149-53; L. Casson, 'Ancient Naval Technology and the Route to India', in Begley and de Puma, eds., *Rome and India*: 8-11; also Lionel Casson, *Periplus Maris Erythaei*. The monsoon wind is labelled as Hippalus and Etasian wind in the *Periplus*. Its anonymous author had the correct knowledge that it started blowing from the month of Epiphi (July) onwards. The widely held belief that it was so named after a Greek mariner who discovered it is now seriously questioned. Mazzarino shows that this term, mentioned also by Pliny, is actually a misreading of the term hypalum. His reading therefore suggests that the name Hippalus has nothing to do with the supposed name of a Greek mariner, but was so called because hypalum meant a seasonal south-west wind. S. Mazzarino, 'The Hypalum of Pliny', in Romanis and Tchernia, eds., *Crossings*.

13. Jose Manuel Malhao Perreira, 'The Mighty Red Sea', presented to the International Seminar on Maritime Activities in India with Reference to the Portuguese 1500-1800, Lisboa, 2001: 20.
14. Thapar, 'The Black Gold: South Asia and the Roman Maritime Trade', *South Asia*, XV, 1992: 1-28; however, her statement that the loan contract document under review referred to the shipping of pepper among other cargoes (*Early India*: 241) is not supported by this document . This by no means minimizes the importance of the pepper from Malabar as a premier exportable item from India.
15. Grant Parker, 'Ex Oriente Luxuria: Indian Commodities and Roman Experience', *Journal of the Economic and Social History of the Orient*, XLV, 2002: 40-95, especially 44-6.
16. *Ibid.*, 55-8.
17. *Ibid.*, 41-2.
18. E. H. Warmington, *The Commerce between the Roman Empire and India*, New Delhi: Munshiram Manoharlal, 1974: 194-6; also Parker,'Ex Oriente Luxuria'.
19. Brian Weinstein, 'Biblical Evidence of Spice Trade between India and the Land of Israel: A Historical Analysis', *Indian Historical Review*, XXVII.1, 2000; R.J. Werblowsky and G. Wigdor, *Oxford Dictionary of Jewish Religion*, Oxford: Oxford University Press, 1997: 350; also see, Ranabir Chakravarti, 'Reaching Out to the Distant Shores: Indo-Judaic Trade up to *c.* 1300 CE' (paper presented to the seminar, A View from the Margin: The State of the Art of Indo-Judaic Studies, Oxford, 2002).
20. For *nalada* as a plant name see M. Monier-Williams, *Sanskrit English Dictionary*, New Delhi: Marwah Publication, 1986 (rpt): 530.
21. Warmington, *Commerce between the Roman Empire and India*; also Casson, *Periplus Maris Erythraei*: 236-7.
22. Casson, *Periplus Maris Erythraei*, section 39.
23. *Ibid.*, section 48.
24. *Ibid.*, section 63.

25. *Ibid.*, section 64.
26. *Ibid.*, section 60.
27. Chandraketugarh and Tamralipta both have been excavated and explored. For a general overview of the archaeological data recovered from the two sites see A. Ghosh, ed., *An Encyclopaedia of Indian Archaeology*, II, New Delhi: Munshiram Manoharalal, 1989. Literary mentions of Tamralipta are discussed by P.C. Dasgupta, 'Some Early Indian Literary References to Tamralipta', *Modern Review*, 1953: 31-4; Niharranjan Ray, 'Tamralipta and Gange: Two Port Cities of Ancient Bengal and Connected Considerations', *Geographical Review of India*, XLI, 1979: 205-22; also see Chakravarti, *Trade and Traders*: 129-32.
28. B. N. Mukherjee, 'Kharoshti and Kharoshti-Brahmi Inscriptions from West Bengal, India', *Indian Museum Bulletin*, XXV, 1990, vide especially the catalogue of inscriptions prepared by Mukherjee and accompanying photographs for an understanding of the figures of vessels represented in these inscribed seals and sealings. For an elaborate discussion on these ships see Chakravarti, *Trade and Traders*: 122-9.
29. *Periplus*, section 60.
30. These ports figure in both the *Periplus* and the *Geography* of Ptolemy; many of them are now explored/excavated sites. See R. Champakalakshmi, *Trade, Ideology, Urbanization: South India 300 BC-AD 1300*, New Delhi: Oxford University Press, 1996.
31. Champakalakshmi, *Trade, Ideology and Urbanization*; also R. Nagaswami, *Roman Karur*, Chennai: Brahad Prakashan, 1990; Pounata figures in the *Geography* of Ptolemy as the place from where beryl was available.
32. Vimala Begley, 'Ceramic Evidence of Pre-Periplus Trade on the Indian Coast', in Begley and de Puma, eds., *Rome and India*: 157-96.
33. V. D. Gogte, 'The Chandraketugarh-Tamluk Region of Bengal: Source of the Early Historic Rouletted Ware from India and South-east Asia', *Man and Environment*, XXII, 1997: 69-85.
34. The trappaga figures in the *Periplus* (section 44) as a coaster employed by king Nambanus (Saka ksatrapa ruler Nahapana) to guide non-local ships to the port of Barygaza at the mouth of the Namados (river Narmada). In other words, the trappaga figures as coaster functioning as a pilot vessel. The inscribed Brahmi-Kharosti sealing with the figure of a ship is the first visual representation of this type of ship. See, Ranabir Chakravarti, 'Maritime Trade in Horses in Early Historical Bengal: A Seal from Chandraketugarh', *Pratnasamiksha*, I, 1992: 155-60.
35. Chakravarti, *Trade and Traders*: 122-9.
36. Mala Dutta, *Satavahana Coinage*, Delhi: Hermann Publication, 1990.
37. J. C. Jain, *Life in Ancient India as Depicted in the Jaina Canons and Commentaries*, New Delhi: Munshram Manoharlal, 1984.
38. S. Ghosh, 'A Mahanavika in an Inscription from Ghantasala', unpublished

paper, presented to the Conference on South Asian Archaeology, Paris 2001.

39. *Periplus*, section 60; also see the commentary on this passage by L. Casson.
40. Casson, 'New Lights on Maritime Loans': 200.
41. *Ibid.*, 202; also see Parker, 'Ex Oriente Luxuria': 78-80. Parker however has not used the latest translation of this document by Casson, but cited earlier translations.
42. Parker, 'Ex Oriente Luxuria': 75.
43. *Ibid.* He does also point out that Pliny's statistics could have been suspect because he was probably using them to 'reinforce points motivated by concerns with morality' (p. 78).

CHAPTER 9

A Theatre of Broken Dreams Vidiśā in the Days of Gupta Hegemony*

HANS BAKKER

PROLOGUE

In his monumental *Geschichte Indiens* Hermann Kulke depicts the relationship between the Gupta and Vākāṭaka dynasties as basically an unproblematic one, an alliance that was dominated by the Guptas and secured a peaceful coexistence until their fall.

> Vermutlich in der Phase der Vorbereitung seines Krieges gegen die Kshatrapa gab dann aber Candragupta seine Tochter dem König Rudrasena II. zur Ehe, um den Rücken für seinen Kampf im Westen frei zu haben. Rudrasena starb jedoch schon nach fünfjähriger Regierung etwa im Jahre 390 n.Chr. Auf Candraguptas Rat hin übernahm daraufhin seine Tochter Prabhavatigupta die Regentschaft für ihre Söhne. Während ihrer etwa zwanzigjährigen Regentschaft geriet das Vakataka-Reich zunehmend unter direkten Einfluß der Gupta und gehörte *de facto* bald zu deren Reichsverband. Zwar wurde die Unabhängigkeit der Vakatakas unter Pravarasena II (ca.410 bis 440 n.Chr.), von dem eine große Zahl Inschriften bekannt ist, wiederhergestellt. Doch hatte das Reich der Vakatakas aufgehört, eine potentielle Bedrohung für die Guptas zu sein. Bis zum Untergang der Guptas bestanden statt dessen überaus enge Beziehungen zwischen beiden Reichen, so daß man in der Geschichtsschreibung bisweilen sogar vom Vakataka-Gupta-Zeitalter spricht. Diese engen Beziehungen trugen wesentlich zur Ausbreitung der Gupta-Kultur nach Zentralindien bei. (Kulke 1998, 114)

This representation (including the chronology) reaches back to a powerful, historical theory set forth by A. S. Altekar in a book which he edited together with R. C. Majumdar and which was first published in 1960, under the title *The Vākāṭaka-Gupta Age*. The evidence that has come to light in the last forty years justifies a reassessment of it. In 2002 I investigated the actual lines along which Gupta culture reached the Deccan and how Gupta examples of religious and artistic expression informed those of the Vākāṭakas. This study has confirmed the last quoted statement of Hermann Kulke to the effect that the close relations between both kingdoms significantly contributed to a process of acculturation. The historical question that should next be investigated is for how long, and in which way, these close relations prevailed between both kingdoms. Did they really last till the fall of the Guptas? We shall try to answer this question in the following pages as a tribute to the great historian. We shall focus in particular on Eastern Malwa and its capital, Vidiśā, since this appears to have been the theatre in which aspirations to the Gupta throne were fostered and shattered and in which Vākāṭaka presence made itself most expressly felt.

ACT 1

Rāmagupta

In our reappraisal of the historic image sketched above, we may start on the war of Candragupta II with the Kṣatrapas or Śakas. Candragupta's father, Samudragupta, had extended his home territory—to be located along the Ganges, around Kauśāmbī-Prayāga, with Sāketa (present Ayodhyā) in the north and Pāṭaliputra in the east—towards the west by subduing i.a. the Nāga kingdom and its capital Padmāvatī (modern Pawaya), a kingdom or confederacy which seems to have comprised local Nāga families ruling from the cities of Kāntipurī (modern Kutwar) and Vidiśā (modern Besnagar).[1] The confederacy, if that it was, may have been led by the king of Padmāvatī, Gaṇapatināga, who, according to the famous Allahabad Pillar Inscription, was forcefully dethroned (*prabhasoddharaṇa*).[2] The three Nāga cities, Kāntipurī to the north and Vidiśā to the south of Padmāvatī, mark roughly the broad stroke of land to the west of Bundelkhand, south of the Chambal and north of the Narmadā. The southern part of this country includes the north-eastern Malwa plateau, the fertile land around Vidiśā known as Daśārṇa; its western frontier borders on the central Malwa Plateau with its capital Ujjayinī (Ujjain). This plateau, which came to be called (Western) Malwa, was apparently not annexed by Samudragupta to his kingdom. Behind the tribes of the Mālavas, Ārjunāyanas, and Yaudheyas, listed in the

Allahabad Inscription and said to be ruled by tributary 'frontier-kings' (*pratyantanṛpati*), loomed a more formidable enemy, the Śaka king, probably *mahākṣatrapa* Rudrasena III, who in the same inscription is said to have acknowledged Samudragupta by paying his respect (*sevākṛta*). The city of Vidiśā thus appears to have been some sort of a frontier town by the end of Samudragupta's reign and this may partly explain the great importance attached to control over it and the surrounding country throughout the rest of Gupta history.

It very much probable that the Mahākṣatrapa was unhappy with his subordinate status and his disaffection may have led to a military campaign when he judged the situation to be most favourable, that is, directly before or after Samudragupta's death in *c*. AD 376. That such a campaign and the ensuing Gupta-Śaka war(s) took place, we only know from circumstantial evidence. More than 250 years later a general of Harṣa's army narrates in Bāṇa's *Harṣacarita* the treachery and intrigue that befell earlier kings, among which the renowned act of Candragupta who 'cut down the lord of the Śakas, who desired another man's wife, by disguising himself in her dress'.[3] Rather than remembering an historical event, Bāṇa may have discussed what was known to him from a play, written only a few decades before by a dramatist at the court of one of Harsa's predecessors (the Maukhari king Avantivarman), namely the *Devīcandragupta* of Viśākhadatta.[4] The reconstruction of events directly after Samudragupta's death almost fully depends on an historical assessment of this play, which itself, unfortunately, is lost, but which has been reconstructed from quoted fragments and brief references to it in other sources (among which the *Harṣacarita*). This reconstruction, admirably carried out by V. Raghavan (1963, 858-80), and discussed by many scholars (e.g. Warder 1977, 260-4), may be briefly summarized as follows.

A Gupta rāja, named Rāma, is threatened in his military camp by a ruler (*pati*) of the Śakas. He is forced to surrender his wife Dhruvadevī to the Śaka ruler. His younger brother (*kumāra*), called Candra, is unable to accept the disgrace and resorts to a ruse to kill the Śaka chief. In the disguise of the queen he enters the camp of the enemy and kills the Śaka. This act of boldness (*sāhasa*) earns him the title Sāhasāṅka. For reasons unknown Candra, after his heroic deed, seems to be in danger again, which this time is coming from within the Gupta camp. He resorts to feigning madness. The end of the play is not known.

The main characters of this play are known as historical persons: Rāmagupta, his (younger) brother Candragupta, the latter's wife Dhruvadevī, and the Śakapati, not mentioned by name, but who may have been thought to be Rudrasena III. The play thus seems to have an unusually high historic profile.

The historical assessment is complicated by two allusions made in Rāṣṭrakūṭa inscriptions dating from AD 871 and 933. The *praśastis* of the kings Amoghavarṣa I and Govinda IV seek to elevate their protagonists by comparing their deeds with the miserable behaviour of the foremost of the Gupta dynasty. The two verses run as follows.

After killing his brother, he took (his) kingdom and (his) wife; even so the wretch had recorded surely, a thousand billion times, in the Kali age: 'A member of the Gupta family, he is the donor.' He (on the other hand), who gave his kingdom away more than once, a trifling thing (for him) – not to mention (other) external objects – he blushed, when merely the report went that their donor was the exalted ornament of the Rāṣṭrakūṭa dynasty (i.e. Amoghavarṣa).[5]

Though it was within his power, neither did he contrive outrageous cruelty against his elder brother, nor did he (ever) bring shame (upon himself) by despicable acts such as sleeping with the wife of his next of kin, nor did he betake himself out of fear to demoniac behaviour, irrespective of the holy and unholy alike – by liberality and unequalled acts of boldness that (king Govinda) became on earth a (true) 'man-marked-by-boldness'. (Sāhasāṅka)[6]

To go by these verses, Candragupta not only killed the Śakapati and then feigned madness, but he killed his brother Rāmagupta as well, took his wife, and usurped the throne. There is nothing in Viśākhadatta's play that suggests that its hero Candra in the last, lost act turned into such a villain all at once; as Warder remarks, 'As for Viśākhadatta, it would seem to have been very difficult to have concluded his play with such an action by his hero. He surely arranged the plot in such a way as to free Candra from guilt.'[7]

Although the *praśastis* are arguably blatant propaganda couched in poetry, it is difficult to imagine that the two Deccan kings actually invented such disgraceful acts altogether. In view of what was at stake at this crucial junction, viz., the preservation of the paternal heritage established at great costs, and in the light of similar events later in the Gupta history that we are going to discuss, it seems not wholy unlikely that the Rāṣṭrakūṭa kings did actually divulge an historic stain on the otherwise glorious reputation of the Gupta dynasty. That Rāmagupta ruled for a short period is undeniable. Candragupta's chief wife was called Dhruvadevī, and her husband became master over the Gupta empire, including not only Vidiśā, but, eventually, also the realm of the Śaka kings.

There is therefore every appearance that Samudragupta's old age or death initiated a struggle for power in which at first the elder son, Rāmagupta, who as a viceroy might have been in charge of his father's troups at the western frontier, was on top. To mark his position and to finance it he had begun issuing his own coinage, for which he used the local mints that had earlier struck the copper coins of the Nāga kings.[8] Rāmagupta did not succeed, however, in extending his control over the whole of the Gupta kingdom. As Ellen Raven (1994a, 163 n. 4.66) remarks, 'Perhaps the copper coins of King Rāmagupta also belong to the imperial currency, but the lay-out of their devices does not support such an attribution.' The imperial mints still beyond his reach, in his own power base Vidiśā, Rāmagupta could adorn himself with the grand titles to which he claimed the right. *Mahārājādhirājaśrīrāmagupta* was engraved on the pedestals of three Jaina images found in the village of Durjanpura in Vidisha district, near Besnagar, proclaiming that these three images were ordered (*kārita*) by the 'emperor' himself.[9]

The failure on the part of Rāmagupta to consolidate his power may have been caused by adverse developments in his war against the Śakas. As the *Devīcandragupta* and references to it suggest, Candragupta's coup d'état followed after he had rescued the course of the Guptas. Subsequently, in addition to silver and copper coins minted locally in Malwa, Candragupta, it has been suggested,[10] began issuing his so-called Lion-slayer Type of imperial gold coin to commemorate this victory, though this remains highly conjectural. If Candragupta thus appeared successful where Rāmagupta failed, this may have had to do with the greater political skills of the former. Candragupta was in a better position to hold on to the enemies defeated by his father, because he was married to one of their princesses, Kuberanāgā, on whom he confered the title of *mahādevī*.[11] These Nāgas remained a local force to be reckoned with, despite their subjugation, and their help against their former arch-enemies, the Śakas, may have been a decisive factor. The same political skill, namely to turn old enmities into effective alliances through matrimony, was again displayed by Candragupta when after he had consolidated his power, he married off his own daughter by his Nāga wife to the house of the Vākāṭakas, another old enemy of his father. The marriage between Prabhāvatīguptā and Rudrasena II took place around AD 388.[12] It seems most plausible that especially Candragupta's relation with the Nāgas through his wife secured him victory over the Śakas at long last, whereas his alliance with the Vākāṭakas may have provided the necessary backing, as has been argued by Kulke.[13] This alliance may be viewed as a display of strength rather than of weakness. It not only established family ties between the Guptas and the Vākāṭakas, but also tied together the Vākāṭakas and the Nāgas. In all her inscriptions Prabhāvatī took great pride in her Gupta and Nāga ancestry.[14]

In this way came into being the geopolitical triangle that would determine the ramifications of power in the Gupta empire during the greater part of fifth century: 1) the Gupta homeland along the Ganges, (centring on Kauśāmbī-Prayāga), 2) the strategic southern part of the homeland of the Nāga dynasty (the area around Vidiśā), 3) Vidarbha to the south of the Narmadā, across the Satpura Range (centring on Nandivardhana, residence of the Eastern Vākāṭakas).

ACT 2

GOVINDAGUPTA

Candragupta, thus in charge of the greater part of northern India, appointed another viceroy (*mahārāja*) in Vidiśā to succeed Rāmagupta. There may have been several viceroys during his reign, about whom we do not possess any information at all, but it seems likely that Mahārāja Govindagupta, son by his chief queen Dhruvadevī, was prominent among them. Govindagupta is known from a clay seal of Dhruvasvāminī found at Vaiśālī which reads: 'The illustrious Mahādevī Dhruvasvāminī, wife of the illustrious emperor Candragupta and mother of the illustrious Mahārāja Govindagupta.'[15] The title *mahārāja* may designate the status of governor or viceroy, whereas the fact that the queen-mother mentions him explicitly on her seal seems to suggest that he might even have been heir-apparent.

And there is more evidence. An inscription of a feudatory chieftain (*bhūmipati*) of Skandagupta, Prabhākara, found in Daśapura (modern Mandasor) in western Malwa (dating AD 467-8), makes it probable that Govinda was governor of the western division of Candragupta's empire, Malwa. The *Mandasor Inscription of Malava Samvat 524* reports:

> There was a king that resembled the moon (*candra*) in the firmament of the Gupta lineage by the renowned name of Śrī Candragupta; he captured the eyes of the people like the rising moon. After he had snatched away from (many local) princes (*pati*) their kingship over the earth by brilliant and powerful means, he ensnared the earth with the help of members of his own dynasty; until today it has not yet liberated itself (from these bonds). That Lord of the Earth (i.e. Candragupta), the majesty of whose virtues resembled that of Govinda (i.e. Kṛṣṇa), begat a son who well-deserved the name of Govindagupta and who equaled the sons of Diti and Aditi (i.e. the Devas and the Asuras). When kings bowed their heads to his (i.e. Govindagupta's) lotusfeet – their splendours sinking down – even the Lord of the Gods (i.e. Indra), beset by doubts, ascended the swing of (fearful) deliberation.[16]

The commander of Govinda's army who held these feudatory kings in check, the inscription tells us, was Vāyurakṣita. The chieftain Prabhākara came to employ his son Dattabhaṭa as his general. There is something strange about this inscription. Its author explicitly pledges allegiance to the emperor, who, at Prabhākara's time was Skandagupta, and sings the praises of Candragupta and Govindagupta, but is silent on Kumāragupta, Govindagupta's brother. The inscription strongly suggests that the military services of Vāyurakṣita and his son Dattabhaṭa were not needed during the reign of Kumāragupta. Evidently the family fell into disgrace when Kumāragupta established suzerainty. This is corroborated by the fact that during Kumāragupta's reign another feudatory family was in charge of Daśapura, viz., the Varmans.[17] All this indicates that Candragupta's succession had not been without a struggle. The contender for the imperial throne had again been an elder brother, the viceroy of Vidiśā, Govindagupta. His general, Vāyurakṣita, thus turned out to have been on the losing side.

The *Mandasor Inscription*, though prima facie loyal to Gupta rule, shows some ambiguities that might hint at Prabhākara's uneasiness. First, in this charter this prince speaks of the snares (*pāśa*) laid over the earth (*avapāśita*) by the Guptas, from which it has not yet been able to free itself (*mokṣaṃ samupaiti*); on the lips of a feudatory, this has a dubious ring. Second, he tells us that Indra trembled at the sight of all the feudatories who bowed before Govindagupta. As has been suggested by Thaplyal (1972, 66), the allusion to Indra's (Vibudhādhipa) fear, although a hyperbole not uncommon to this genre, may hint at Kumāragupta, whose *biruda* is 'Mahendra'.[18] The assumed war of succession may have taken place in AD 415-16,[19] too short a period, it seems, for Govindagupta to issue his own coins. Kumāragupta, on the other hand, may have issued a special coin to commemorate his victory and to herald his 'legitimate' ascension to the imperial throne: it showed him (anachronistically) as an invicible (*apratigha*) youth blessed by his parents.[20]

In view of the postulated geo-political triangle, it might be asked what role Vidarbha played in this power struggle. Kumāragupta's sister, Prabhāvatī, ruled as a regent for her minor sons in Nandivardhana at the time. Unfortunately our sources do not allow us to say anything with certainty in this matter. However, considering her close and peaceful relations with Kumāra throughout her life, one may speculate that Prabhāvatī stood on his side and it is not impossible that this may have contributed to his success. Her choice may have ensured that the local Nāgas in eastern Malwa too supported Kumrāgupta's claim to the throne. That Prabhāvatī and Kumāra were two hands in one glove may also be inferred from the following.

ACT 3

GHAṬOTKACAGUPTA

After he had ousted his brother Govinda, Kumāragupta needed another viceroy in Vidiśā. Again it must be noted that there might have been viceroys during his reign on whom we do not possess any information at all, yet it is nearly certain that his younger brother, Ghaṭotkacagupta, was a prominent one among them. This prince is known from the *Tumain Fragmentary Inscription*, which reads as follows:

> The son of the illustrious Candragupta, Kumāragupta, well-nigh the great Indra (Mahendra), protected the whole earth by holding her in his arms of power, as if she were his virtuous, lawful (*dharma*) wife. [. . .] white [. . .],

that moon (*candra*) had risen by the name of Ghaṭotkacagupta, encircled by a halo that is the array of his virtues, [. . .] (illuminating?) the sky and the earth. He, famous for the staunch vigour characteristic of his forbears, after reaping the fame that he had achieved by (his own) arms, [. . .].[21]

This inscription, which records the foundation of a temple in Tumbavana (modern Tumain) by a group of five brothers headed by Śrīdeva in the Gupta year 116 (AD 435-6), indicates that Ghaṭotkaca's station was eastern Malwa, although, just as of Govindagupta, a seal bearing his name was recovered from Vaiśālī.[22] The simile in which he is compared with another rising moon (*candra*) suggests that Ghaṭotkaca too was a son of Candragupta. This is confirmed by the Kevala Narasiṃha Temple Inscription from Rāmagiri:

At all times the conduct of this King (*deva*), Candragupta Lord of the three oceans, was perfect: the sovereign (gave) his daughter (i.e. Prabhāvatī) to the illustrious Rudrasena, (a mine of) virtues. (9) [*one verse lost* (10)] To (this) (sovereign) (i.e. Candragupta)—a great hero, who was like a beast of burden, (carrying) the entire burden of (his) kingdom which was very difficult to bear—[. . .], a son named Ghaṭotkaca (was born) (11).[23]

About this Ghaṭotkaca, the inscription says:

(He pleased) the minds of wise men with refined language, [. . .] of [. . .] whose eyes were like (blue) lotuses [. . .], mendicants with floods of wealth, and the people with (his) fame (15).[24]

Ghaṭotkaca must have been considerably younger than Prabhāvatī, since the inscription suggests he was born after his sister's marriage to the Vākāṭaka King. He therefore was a contemporary of Prabhāvatī's children. When his elder brother Kumāra appointed him viceroy in Vidiśā in AD 416 or slightly later, he may have been about 25 years old. After the death of Rudrasena and Candragupta and Govinda's elimination, Kumāragupta and his sister, the dowager queen of the Vākāṭakas, seized the opportunity to consolidate the geo-political triangle, on which their power was based. They agreed to marry Prabhāvatī's daughter, whose name may have been Atibhāvatī, to their younger brother Ghaṭotkaca, viceroy of Vidiśā. This extraordinary fact is un-ambiguously reported in the Kevala Narasiṃha Temple Inscription.

Then, after he (i.e. Ghaṭotkaca) had seen that niece (*bhāgineyī*) (of his) [. . .], who was a palace Laksmi, [. . .] (this) king paid his respects (to her) and married her. (13)[25]

The stability thus created ushered in three decades of unparallelled cultural bloom. It seems that it is this period in particular (*c*. AD 415-45) that gave rise to the image of a long-lasting, close and peaceful relationship between the Guptas and Vākāṭakas, first drawn up by Altekar and taken over by many other scholars, among which Hermann Kulke, quoted above.

Among the cultural achievements of this time were the plays of Kālidāsa. One of them stages momentous events of a remote past when the Śuṅga general Puṣyamitra usurped the Maurya empire (*c*. 187-151 BC). However, as we will show, the contemporary spectators may have seen through this historic guise the political situation of their own days. In order to facilitate our analysis of this play, its contents may be briefly summarized, with the restriction that we leave the intrigue at the Vidiśā court, which is the play's main plot, for what it is.

A rāja rules in Vidiśā as viceroy, appointed as such by his father who, as commander-in-chief, *senāpati*, is about to consolidate his kingship by a horse sacrifice. To secure the horse the father extends his power to the extreme west, where his army successfully fights the Yavanas. The chief queen of the rāja of Vidiśā is apparently of indigenous Nāga stock—she is called Dhāriṇī, and her signet-ring bears the seal of a serpent (*nāga*). The viceroy of Vidiśā, heir-to-the-throne of the empire founded by his father, with whom relations are good, is at loggerheads with his southern neighbour, the kingdom of Vidarbha. It appears that this kingdom is the domain of two rival branches of a family divided over the question how to deal with the new mighty northern neighbour. One branch had pledged allegiance (*pratiśrutasaṃbandha*) and had wished to enter into a matrimonial alliance, but this was initially prevented by the ruler of the other branch, who was temporarily in power and, through his in-laws, allied to the party that was overthrown by the *senāpati* when he established his rule over northern India.

The rāja of Vidiśā sends his brother-in-law, a bastard brother of Dhāriṇī (*varṇāvara*), to command a frontier post (*antapāladurga*) on the Narmadā, evidently the border between the kingdoms of Vidisā and Vidarbha. After an exchange of unsuccessful diplomatic missions, war breaks out between them. The inimical ruler (pati) of Vidarbha is conquered. The kingdom of Vidarbha is divided into two, and both rulers are installed as joint vassals of the rāja of

Vidiśā, one ruling to the south, the other to the north, of the Varadā (Wardha) river. Peace is sealed by matrimony, when the rāja of Vidiśā marries the co-uterine sister (*sodaryā*) of the friendly ruler of Vidarbha, who thus lives up to her name, Mālavikā, and becomes a princess of the country of Malava.

No doubt the reader has recognized the play as the *Mālavikāgnimitra*, about which Warder remarks that its 'modernity', as claimed by Kālidāsa in the Prologue, perhaps consists in 'this critical presentation of a prince, or perhaps in the presentation in the theatre of the new Gupta-Vākāṭaka politics of marriage alliances and vassal kingdoms, though in the guise of ancient history' (Warder 1977, 129).

The *Mālavikāgnimitra* was written for a Gupta audience rather than a Vākāṭaka one. This is inferred from the fact that supremacy of the northern rulers, though challenged, is gloriously confirmed and the relationship between the sovereign and the viceroy in Vidiśā, despite the latter's moral flaws, is represented as unproblematic, unlike the representation thereof in the post-Gupta play *Devīcandragupta* (see above).

An analysis of the background, against which the play is set, reveals the following elements that reflect the political arena of the first half of the fifth century that we have tried to sketch above.

(1) The major powers of the time are the northern empire and the kingdom of Vidarbha. The border between them was formed by the Narmadā.

(2) The political centre of the western part of the northern empire is Vidiśā, where the heir-to-the-throne rules as viceroy.

(3) This viceroy has tied the indigenous rulers of Malwa to his throne by taking one of their princesses as his chief wife. In Kālidāsa's play this wife is called Dhāriṇī, a name that echos the *gotra* name, Dhāraṇa, of Prabhāvatī Guptā. The signet-ring of Dhāriṇī, which features a *nāga*, and plays an important role in the plot, reinforces this Nāga descent. The historicity of this detail may be illustrated by the signet-ring of Mahārāja Maheśvaranāga, son of Nāgabhaṭṭa (Plates 1 and 2).[26]

(4) The attitude of the Vidarbha rulers (whose coronation names end in Sena) against their northern neighbours is ambivalent. One faction is inclined to come to terms with northern overlordship, the other has not forgotten its allegiance to the

Plate 1: Signet-ring of Mahārāja Maheśvaranāga, son of Nāgabhaṭṭa. Courtesy of the British Museum.

Plate 2: Signet-ring of Mahārāja Maheśvaranāga, son of Nāgabhaṭṭa. Courtesy of the British Museum.

ancient régime, to the rulers who had been overthrown by the new sovereign.

(5) After hostilities between both kingdoms – the Narmadā is crossed – northern suzerainty is established by dividing the Vidarbha kingdom into two vassal states, one ruling to the north of the Varadā River, the other to the south of it.

(6) The establishment of the balance of power is sealed by the marriage of a Vidarbha princess with the viceroy of Vidiśā.

Attempts to read more into Kālidāsa's drama and to connect its protagonists and actions with historical individuals and events are doomed to fail. The play is not an historic drama, and, if one wants to see it as such, it explicitly professes to be one concerned with a distant past. The audiences of the fifth century may have recognized the general political reality of their times, though. It gave the play an exciting dimension, and in that, as Warder remarked, its avowed innovation *vis-á-vis* the works of the poet's predecessors may have consisted.

There is one element in the play that we have not yet encountered. This concerns the internal division within the kingdom of Vidarbha and its partition. Returning from literature to history, we may observe that from the fourth century onwards one branch of the Vākāṭaka family ruled in Nandivardhana (near modern Ramtek), the other in Vatsagulma (modern Wasim). The border between them was the Varadā river (modern Wardha). We do not have enough evidence to know whether the Vākāṭakas were unanimous in their friendship with their northern neighbours. A priori, this seems unlikely, particularly because the dynasty had lost much of its original land to Samudragupta (Bakker 1997, 9-15). We do not know how much resistance there was against Prabhāvatī's regency over her sons and whether there was resentment from the side of these sons against their mother, who seemingly indefinitely postponed (from *c.* AD 405 to 419) their ascension to the throne (Bakker 1997, 15 f.). Is it pure accident that in the aftermath of the power struggle between Govinda and Kumāragupta the Vākāṭaka crown-prince (*yuvarāja*) and eldest son of Prabhāvatī, Divākarasena, vanished from the scene, never to be heard of again?[27] And, finally, we do not know at what costs Prabhāvatī enforced the marriage of her daughter with her maternal uncle, Ghaṭotkaca. What we do know, however, is that after the death of this formidable lady (*c*. AD 443) Gupta-Vākāṭaka relations quickly deteriorated.

About AD 445 Prabhāvatī's youngest son Pravarasena crossed the Narmadā and pitched his army camp (*vāsaka*) in Tripurī (modern Tewar) on the northern bank, i.e. in Gupta territory.[28] To all appearances the tripartite alliance between Guptas, Nāgas, and Vākāṭakas was beginning to erode. This might also have had to do with a new player that had entered the arena, Skandagupta, a bastard son of Kumāragupta. The Gupta emperor was growing old and the jockeying for the best position to succeed him had begun. As far as we know, there were at least three contenders for the throne: 1. Kumāra's legal son by his chief wife Anantadevī, Pūrugupta, who at the time might still have been too young to play a significant part; 2. The emperor's younger brother Ghaṭotkaca, ruling in Vidiśā; and, 3. the outsider, a boy from the harem, Skandagupta.

To stake his claims, Ghaṭotkaca began to issue his own gold coins, on which he wields the imperial Garuḍa standard and takes the *biruda* 'Kramāditya.'[29] For the third time the Gupta empire threatened to fall apart. I have analysed this episode elsewhere (*The Vākāṭakas*, pp. 25-9). Here it may suffice to refer to Skandagupta's *Bhitarī Stone Pillar Inscription* in which, following Mirashi, we may find references to three wars conducted by Skandagupta. The first one records how Skandagupta, while his father Kumāra was still emperor, raised again the faltering fortune of his family (*vicalitakulalakṣmī*) by vanquishing his enemies. Mirashi took this as a reference to the Vākāṭakas and Pravarasena's campaign on the other side of the Narmadā may have had to do with it.[30] I consider it most plausible that in the struggle for power between the centre—the *yuvarāja* Skandagupta (in lieu of Kumāragupta)—and the viceroy of Vidiśā, Pravarasena had chosen the side of his brother-in-law, Ghaṭotkaca. Another ally of the Vidiśā party was in all likelihood the faction of the local Nāgas. The civil war may have dragged on for a decade and may have intensified after the death of Kumāragupta, when Skandagupta's fortunes had reached rock bottom (*viplutāṃ vaṃśalakṣmīm*),[31] but the end was a total defeat of Vidiśā. Skandagupta's *Junagaḍh Rock Inscription* contains a verse in which Skandagupta boasts about how he 'rendered devoid of poison the Serpent Rulers (i.e. the Nāgas) who had uplifted their hoods in pride and arrogance,'[32] and the Kevala Narasiṃha Temple Inscription reports the death of Ghaṭotkaca.

When at a certain time [. . .] he of desirable appearance (i.e. Ghaṭotkaca) [. . .] by/with Indra, [. . .] (her) brother (i.e. Pravarasena) brought the proud woman (i.e. Atibhāvatī) [. . .] back to his own residence with force. (17)[33]

Confronted with defeat, the political triangle on which the stability and power of his kingdom was based in ruins, the Vākāṭaka Pravarasena made the most of a hopeless situation, marched on Malwa, brought his widowed sister back to Vidarbha in a military campaign, and died soon thereafter. In AD 455 Skandagupta officially succeeded his deceased father and proudly declared himself emperor. Frustration concerning his birth may have bred this great pride. In verse 6 of the *Bhitarī Stone Pillar Inscription*, Skandagupta, after his victory (over his uncle Ghaṭotkaca), is said to have run towards his mother, 'which made her weep like Devakī after Kṛṣṇa had killed his enemy', namely his uncle (Kaṃsa).[34] This scene, as has been rightly suggested by Goyal, is depicted on Skandagupta's so-called King-and-Lakṣmī Type of gold coins, on which the lady to the left of the victorious warrior king, smaller than him and without a nimbus, may represent not the goddess Śrī or Lakṣmī, but his anonymous mother.[35]

EPILOGUE

Our reappraisal of Gupta history in the light of the recurrent events in Vidiśā and the role of the Vākāṭakas in them has come to an end. The idyllic picture to the effect that the Gupta-Vākāṭaka relations were close until the fall of the imperial Guptas, i.e. till the end of the fifth century, stands in need of revision. It has emerged that these relations were only intimate and peaceful during the lifetime of Prabhāvatī Guptā. Before and after the long period of more than half a century that this formidable lady dominated the stage (AD 388-443), these relations were marred by conflicting interests, which led to war at least twice, first under Samudragupta, when the Vākāṭakas lost much of their original territory in the Vindhyas, then again under his great-grandson Skandagupta, when they were forced to give up their influence at the court of the viceroy of Vidiśā. Loss of the Malwa connection, and therewith of Gupta support altogether, resulted in

GENEALOGY

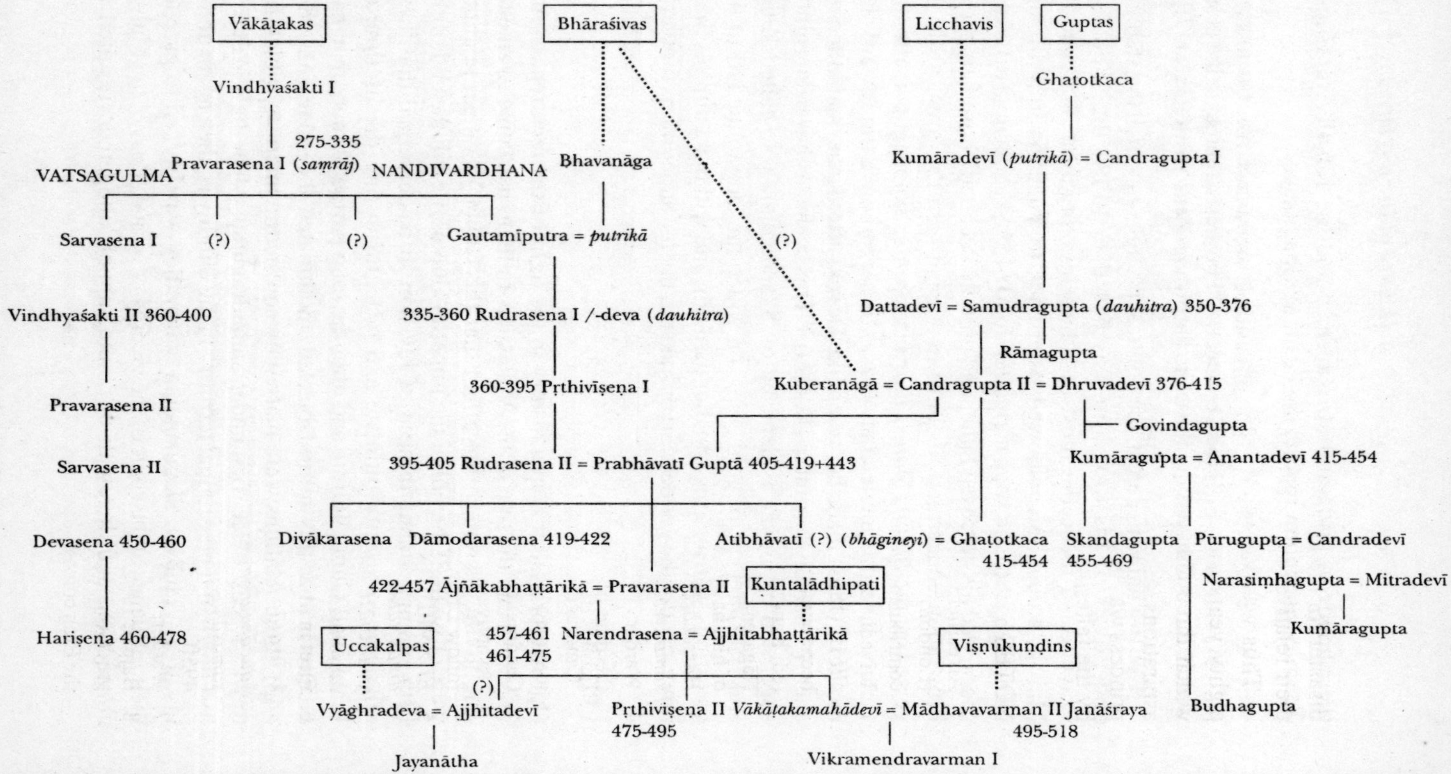

Vākāṭakas
Bhāraśivas
Licchavis
Guptas
Vindhyaśakti I
Ghaṭotkaca
275-335
Pravarasena I (saṃrāj)
VATSAGULMA
NANDIVARDHANA
Bhavanāga
Kumāradevī (putrikā) = Candragupta I
Sarvasena I
(?)
(?)
Gautamīputra = putrikā
(?)
Vindhyaśakti II 360-400
335-360 Rudrasena I /-deva (dauhitra)
Dattadevī = Samudragupta (dauhitra) 350-376
Rāmagupta
360-395 Pṛthivīṣeṇa I
Kuberanāgā = Candragupta II = Dhruvadevī 376-415
Pravarasena II
Govindagupta
Sarvasena II
395-405 Rudrasena II = Prabhāvatī Guptā 405-419+443
Kumāragupta = Anantadevī 415-454
Devasena 450-460
Divākarasena
Dāmodarasena 419-422
Atibhāvatī (?) (bhāgineyī) = Ghaṭotkaca
415-454
Skandagupta
455-469
Pūrugupta = Candradevī
422-457 Ājñākabhaṭṭārikā = Pravarasena II
Kuntalādhipati
Narasiṃhagupta = Mitradevī
Hariṣeṇa 460-478
Uccakalpas
457-461
461-475
Narendrasena = Ajjhitabhaṭṭārikā
Viṣṇukuṇḍins
Kumāragupta
(?)
Vyāghradeva = Ajjhitadevī
Pṛthiviṣeṇa II
475-495
Vākāṭakamahādevī = Mādhavavarman II Janāśraya
495-518
Budhagupta
Jayanātha
Vikramendravarman I

disaster for the Eastern Vākāṭakas, who soon became subordinate to their relatives in Vatsagulma.

Thus was Vidiśā, as we hope to have demonstrated, for at least eighty years (AD 375-455) a theatre of broken dreams, a stage on which three Gupta viceroys paid with their lives for their imperial aspirations, and from which, in a grand finale, a widowed Vākāṭaka princess was hurried away and brought to safety accross the Narmadā by the faltering troops of her brother.

NOTES

* An earlier version of this essay was read before the Vidisha Research Group (London). I am grateful for all suggestions and comments which have contributed to improve its contents.

1. Trivedi, 1957, xxxiii-xxxviii.
2. *CII* III (1888), 7. Many coins of Gaṇapati (Gaṇapatīndra, Gaṇendra) have been found in Pawaya (Trivedi, 1957, 5', xxii-xxiii, 49-54). The *Harṣacarita* (ed. Kane, p. 50, ll. 18f.) mentions as the ruler of Padmāvatī that was killed Nāgasena (who also figures in the *Allahabad Inscription*), but so far no coins of him have been found. Cf. Bakker, 1997, 10f.
3. *Harṣacarita* Ucchvāsa 6, p. 51, ll.10f.: *aripure ca parakalatrakāmukaṃ kāminīveśaguptaś ca candraguptaḥ śakapatim aśātayat.*
4. Warder, 1977, 257. Winternitz, 1920, 210, especially n. 3 with regard to the date of Viśākhadatta in connection with the featuring of the name 'Candragupta' in the final blessing spoken by the chief actor (i.e. Rākṣasa) in some MSS of another of Viśākhadatta's plays, the *Mudrārākṣasa* (in which Candragupta Maurya is one of the principal characters); other MSS read 'Avantivarmā' instead (discussion by Dhruva in his edition, pp. ix-xv). I follow Dhruva and Warder in this matter.
5. *EI* XVIII, 248 (emended): *hatvā bhrātaram eva rāyjam aharat devīṃ ca dīnas tathā, lakṣaṃ koṭim alekhayat kila kalau dātā sa guptānvayaḥ | yenātyāji tanuḥ svarājyam asakṛd bāhyārthakaiḥ kā kathā, hrīs tasyonnatirāṣṭrakūṭatilako dādeti kīrtyām api* ||. Cf. Sircar, *Sel. Ins.* II, 487.
6. Fleet in *IA* XII, 250 (emended): *sāmarthye sati ninditā pravihitā naivāgraje krūratā, bandhustrīgamanādibhiḥ kucaritair āvarjitaṃ nāyaśaḥ | śaucāśaucaparāṅmukhaṃ na ca bhiyā paiśācyam aṅgīkṛtaṃ, tyāgenāsamasāhasaiś ca bhuvane yas sāhasāṅko, bhavat* ||. Cf. Sircar, *Sel. Ins.* II, 495ff.
7. Warder, 1977, 263f.
8. Bajpai, 1992, 84: 'The excavations at Vidisha, conducted by the ASI have also brought to light copper coins of Rāmagupta, similar in size and fabric to the Eraṇ coins of that ruler. . . . After the conquest of the Nāga territories and

after the death of Samudragupta, coins of Rāmagupta were struck in mints of the region previously occupied by the Nāgas.'

9. Gai, 1969, Mirashi, 1982b. The three inscriptions on the pedestals read basically the same: *bhagavato ['']rhataḥ puṣpadantasya* [image A & C: *candraprabhasya*] *pratimeyaṃ kāritā mahārājādhirājaśrīrāmaguptena upadeśāt pāṇipātrika-candrakṣam(aṇ)ācāryakṣamaṇaśramaṇapraśiṣya-ācāryasarpasenakṣamaṇa-śiṣyasya golakyāntyā[ḥ] satputrasya celūkṣamaṇasyeti* ||. It seems that image B (or C) served as an exemplar for the image A, because the irregular saṃdhi between *rāmaguptena upadeśāt* is explained by B, where these words are separated by an image of a *cakra*; similar the irregular saṃdhi between *praśiṣya-ācārya* in A can be explained by the assumption (but the text has been erased here) that in B the word *ācārya* was written on a new line. The reading in A *candra-kṣamācārya* seems haplography of reading in B: *candrakṣamaṇācārya*.
10. Majumdar, 1954, 22. Cf. Raven, 1994a I, 48f., n. 2.125.
11. Bakker, 1997, 11f. See below, n.14.
12. Bakker, 1997, 16.
13. Jain, 1972, 236: 'The great success achieved by the Gupta emperor is indirectly attested to by his coins. The long series of coins testifying to the almost unbroken rule of the Western Kshatrapas, for more than three hundred years, comes to an end between 388 and 397 AD, and is replaced by the coin of a similar design, issued by Candragupta II. The earliest silver coins of Candragupta are of the year 409 AD, issued to replace the coins of the Western Kshatrapas in Malwa.' It would thus appear that Candragupta did not deal the final blow to the Śakas before the middle of the first decade of the fifth century. This is indirectly confirmed by the late date by which Candragupta established his authority over Mandasor (see below, n. 17).
14. *CII* V, 7, ll. 7-8, 36, ll. 8-9: [. . .] *mahārājādhirājaśrīcandraguptas tasya duhitā dhāraṇasagotrā nāgakulasambhūtāyāṃ śrīmahādevyāṃ kuber-anāgāyām utpan-nobhayakulālaṅkāra bhūtātyantabhagavadbhaktā* [. . .].
15. *Archaeological Survey of India, Annual Report* 1903-4, 107: *mahārādhirāja-śrīcandraguptapatnī mahārājaśrīgovindaguptamātā mahādevī śrīdhruvasvāminī.*
16. *EI* XXVII (1947-8), 15 (emended): *guptānvayavyomani candrakalpaḥ, śrīcandraguptaprathitābhidhānaḥ* | *āsīn nṛpo lokavilocanānāṃ, navoditaś candra ivāpahartā* || 2 || *bhuvaḥ patīnāṃ bhuvi bhūpatitvam, ācchidya dhivikramasādhanena* | *nādyāpi mokṣaṃ samupaiti yena, svavaṃśyapāśair avapāśitā bhūḥ* || 3 || *govindavatkhyātaguṇaprabhāvo, govinda-guptorjitanāmadheyam* | *vasundhareśas tanayaṃ prajajñe, sa dityadityos tanayais sarūpam* || 4 || *yasmin nṛpair astamitapratāpaiś, śirobhir āliṅgitapādapadme* | *vicāradolāṃ vibudhādhipo 'pi, śaṅkhāparītaḥ samupāruroha* || 5 ||. Cf. Sircar, *Sel. Ins.* I, 406-9.
17. Viśvavarman (Mālava Era 480 (AD 424): *CII* III (1888), 72-8) and

Bandhuvarman (Mālava era 493 (AD 437): *CII* III (1888), 79-88). This family reigned already in Daśapura before it was annexed by Candragupta to his kingdom, as the earliest inscription of Naravarman seems to show: *Mandasor Inscription of the Kṛta Year 461* (AD 404-5). In this inscription no reference to Gupta rule is found and I doubt whether the epithet *siṃha-vikrānta-gāmin* (clearly a pun on the name of his father Siṃhavarman) 'shows that he (i.e. Naravarman) was a feudatory of Chandragupta II' as Bhandarkar, Chhabra and Gai want us to believe (*CII* III (1981), 263, 264 l. 5; cf. Sircar, *Sel. Ins.* I, 398 n. 1).

18. In the *Tumain Inscription* Kumāragupta, son of Candragupta, is styled *mahendrakalpaḥ* (*CII* III (1981), 278; see below, n. 21. The gold coins of Kumāragupta carry the *biruda 'śrīmahendra'* (Raven . . . 1994a, II, 104ff.).
19. The last dated inscription of Candragupta is from the Gupta year 93 (AD 413) (*CII* III (1888), 29-34: *Sanchi Stone Inscription*), the first of Kumāragupta from Gupta year 96 (AD 416) (*CII* III (1888), 42-5: *Bilsad Stone Pillar Inscription*).
20. Ajit Ghosh in *JNSI* XXII, 180. Raven, 1994b, fig. 12. Cf. Ashvini Agrawal, 1992, who in discussing this type of coin remarks (p. 170): 'The coin in the collection of the British Museum weighs only 115 grains and those of the Bayana hoard weigh between 120.5 and 123 grains, which is the lowest in the series of Kumāragupta's gold coins except for a few specimens of the Archer Type. Considering the fact that there was a gradual increase in weight of the Gupta gold coins till the time of Skandagupta, the Apratigha Type of coins have to be the earliest issues of Kumāragupta I.' For another elaborate discusion in favour and against this interpreation see also Raven, 1994a, I, 41-4. Though the Apratigha coins were issued after the death of Candragupta, his image on the coins served the imperial propaganda by proclaiming that the young prince was elected by his father (and mother) himself. When studying this type of coin in the collection of the British Museum (Allan, 1914, No. 257), I noticed that the female figure to the left of Kumāra, his mother, who extends her right hand towards him, holds a small, indistinct object between her thumb and index-finger. Cf. below, n. 35.
21. *EI* XXVI (1941-2), 118 (emended): *śrīcandraguptasya mahendrakalpaḥ, kumāraguptas tanayas samagrām* | *rarakṣa sādhvīm iva dharmapatnīṃ, vīryāgrahastair upaguhya bhūmim* ‖ 3 ‖ – –⏑–⏑⏑⏑–⏑⏑–⏑– ⏓, – –⏑–⏑⏑⏑–⏑⏑ *(garbbha?)gauraḥ* | *kṣityambare guṇasamūhamayūkhajālo, nāmnoditas sa tu ghaṭotkacaguptacandraḥ* ‖ 4 ‖ *sa pūrvajānāṃ sthirasattvakīrtir, bhūjārjitāṃ kīrtim abhiprapadya* | ⏓ –⏑– –⏑⏑–⏑– ⏓, ⏓ –⏑– –⏑⏑–⏑– ⏓ ‖ 5 ‖. Cf. Sircar, *Sel. Ins.* I, 297-9.
22. *ASI AR* 1903/4, 107. Seal of Ghaṭotkacagupta reading: *śrīghaṭotkacaguptasya*. Cf. Thaplyal, 1972, 66f.
23. Bakker, 1997, 164: *sudurvvahāṃ rājyadhuraṃ samagrāṃ, dhurandharasy(e)<va> supuṅgavasya* | *<prajādhipa> (syā)* ⏑⏑–⏑– ⏓, *<gha>*

ṭo<tka> co nāma suto <babhūva> || 11 || Cf. Bakker and Isaacson, 1993, 53-5.

24. Bakker, 1997, 165: *śuddhair vvacobhir vviduṣāṃ man<ā>* (*ṃ*) <si>, *<pr>ī<nāti nilā> mburuhekṣaṇā(nām)* | ⏓ – ⏑– –⏑⏑–⏑– ⏓ *(s), sādhūn dhanaughair yyaśasā ca lokān* || 15 ||. Cf. Bakker and Isaacson, 1993, 53-5.
25. Bakker 1997, 165: *tām bhāgineyīm atha rājarājo, dṛ(ṣ)<tvā>*⏑– –⏑⏑ *veśmalakṣmi<m>* | ⏓ –⏑– –⏑⏑–⏑– *(d)y<⏓>*, *(u)pāsya pāṇigrahaṇaṃ cakāra* || 13 ||. Cf. Bakker and Isaacson 1993, 53-5.
26. This copper seal in the form of a signet-ring was purchased by Cunningham from a local dealer in Lahore and to date forms part of the Cunningham Collection in the British Museum. It was published in *CII* III (1888), 282 f. and Plate XLIII A. The bull and crescent at top of the seal confirm that the Nāga kings were Śaivas. The name of the king is not known from other sources. It is conjectured that the indistinct tiny objects held in the right hands of the mothers of Kumāra and Śkandagupta are such signet-rings (see n. 20 and n. 35).
27. In the 13th year of Prabhāvatī's regency (*c*. AD 417) Divākarasena was still recognized as *yuvarāja*. *CII* V, 7, ll. 9-10: *yuvāraja[śrī] divākarasenajananī*. The seal of these *Poona Plates of Prabhāvatī* runs (*CII* V, 8): '[By] the enemy chastising order of the Mother of the crown-prince, who is the ornament of the Vākāṭakas and has attained royal fortune by inheritance.' (*vākāṭakalalāmasya [kra]maprāptanṛpaśriya[ḥ] | jananyā yuvarājasya śāsanaṃ ripuśāsa[nam* || *]*). Divākarasena is no longer mentioned as a son or king in the later charters of Prabhāvatī; in his stead two other sons of hers are called Mahārāja in two charters of land donations made in the nineteenth and twentieth regnal year of her son Pravarasena. In these inscriptions (*CII* V, 36 l. 10 (*Riddhapur Plates of Prabhāvatīguptā*); Shastri and Kawadkar, 2001, 135-51 (*Miregāon Plates of Prabhāvatī Guptā, year 20*)), she describes herself as the 'Mother of the Mahārājas of the Vākāṭakas, the illustrious Dāmodarasena and Pravarasena' (*vākāṭakānāṃ mahārājaśrīdāmodarasenapravarasenajananī*).
28. Bakker, 1967, 25.
29. P. L. Gupta, 1946, 316: 'The Leningrad Museum [possesses a coin] with the king on the obverse (nimbate, standing to left, holding bow in left hand and arrow in the right), Garuḍa standard is on the right of the king; beneath the left arm is inscribed *Ghaṭo* with a crescent above. It bears traces of marginal legend ending in (*gu*)*pta*(*ḥ*). On the reverse of the coin is the Goddess (holding lotus in left and and *pāśa* (fillet) in out-stretched right hand) with a symbol on the top left corner. The legend on this side is not certain but seems to be *kramāditya*.' Cf. Altekar, 1954, 310. Another coin was published by Ajit Ghosh in *JNSI* 22 (1960), 120f.
30. Mirashi, 1982a, 70f.; cf. Mirashi in *JESI* (1980), 86ff. The interpretation of this verse is controversial. Fleet in *CII* III (1888), 53-4, ll. 10-11 reads:

samuditaba<la>koṣān pu(ṣya)mitrāṃś ca <j>itvā; he takes this as a reference to the tribe of the Puṣyamitras. Fleet admitted in a note that the second syllable of the name was damaged. Mirashi, 1982a (*IRP* I, 70), following a proposal of Divekar, conjectures the reading: *samuditaba<la> kośā<n yuddhy a>mitrāṃś ca <j>itvā*; that is, 'after having vanquished in battle (*yudhi*) his enemies whose wealth and power had increased,' a reading accepted in the revised edition (1981) of *CII* III (p. 315 vs. 4), but rejected by Agrawal 1989, 211.

31. *Bhitari Stone Pillar Inscription* l. 13 (*CII* III (1888), 54). See below, n. 34.
32. *CII* III (1981), 302. See Bakker, 1997, 27.
33. Bakker, 1997, 165: *tasmin kadācit kamanīyarūpe, ⏓ –⏑– –⏑purandareṇa* | *(t) –⏑(y) –⏑⏑– (s) (sa)mānāṃ, bhrātā balāt svaṃ gṛham ā(ni)nāya* || 17 ||. Cf. Bakker and Isaacson . . . 1993, 53-6.
34. *Bhitarī Stone Pillar Inscription of Skandagupta* (*CII* III (1981), 315, ll. 12-14), vs. 6: *pitari divam upe<te> viplutāṃ <va>ṅśalakṣmīṃ, bhujabalavijitārir yaḥ pratiṣṭhā<pya> bhūyaḥ* (|*) *jitam iti paritoṣan (m)ātaraṃ sāsranetrāṃ, hataripur iva<kṛ>ṣṇo devakīm abhyu<peta>ḥ* <|| 6* ||>.
35. Raven, 1994b, Fig. 2. Goyal, 1967, 265 f. n. 2. This lady, Skandagupta's mother, is depicted with a single braid (*ekaveṇi*), which indicates her widowhood (Bakker, 1997, 114 f.). She holds an indistinct object that seems to stick to the raised index-finger of her right hand, which she extends towards the warrior king, her son. One wonders whether both indistinct, small objects, held in the right hands of the mothers of Kumāra (see above, n. 20) and Skandagupta respectively, notwithstanding the slightly different hand-gestures, might not be one and the same thing. Could it be a signet-ring?

REFERENCES

Agrawal, Ashvini, 1989, *Rise and Fall of the Imperial Guptas*, Delhi.

———, 1992, 'Did Kumāragupta I Abdicate? A study of the numismatic and epigraphic data', in: R. Ch. Chhabra *et al.* (eds.), *Reappraising Gupta History for S. R. Goyal*, New Delhi, pp. 165-72.

Allan, John, 1914, *Catalogue of the coins of the Gupta Dynasties and of Śaśāṅka, King of Gauḍa*, London. *A Catalogue of the Indian coins in the British Museum.*

Altekar, Anant Sadashiv, 1954, *Catalogue of the Gupta Gold Coins in the Bayana Hoard*, Bombay.

Altekar, A. S. and R. C. Majumdar (eds.), 1960, *The Vākāṭaka–Gupta Age* (*circa 200-550 A.D.*), Bharatiya Itihas Parishad, New History of the Indian People, Vol. 6.

Archaeological Survey of India (*ASI AR*), *Annual Report*, 1903-4.

Bajpai, K. D., 1992, 'Coins from Eraṇ Excavations: A Chronological Analysis', in DW. Macdowall *et al.* (eds.), *Indian Numismatics, History, Art, and Culture. Essays in the Honour of Dr P. L. Gupta*, Delhi.

Bakker, Hans T., 1997, *The Vākāṭakas: An Essay in Hindu Iconology*, Groningen, Gonda Indological Studies 5.

———, 2002, 'Religion and Politics in the Eastern Vākāṭaka Kingdom', in *South Asian Studies*, 1-24.

Bakker, Hans T. and H. Isaacson, 1993, 'The Ramtek Inscriptions II: The Vākāṭaka Inscription in the Kevala-Narasiṃha Temple', in *Bulletin of the School of Oriental and African Studies*, Vol. LVI, pp. 46-74.

Bāṇa, *The Harṣacarita of Bāṇabhaṭṭa* (Text of Ucchvāsas I-VIII), edited by P. V. Kane, Delhi, etc., 1965 (2nd edn.).

Corpus Inscriptionum Indicarum (*CII* III 1888), *Inscriptions of the Early Gupta Kings and their Successors*, ed. J. F. Fleet, Calcutta.

——— (*CII* III 1981), *Inscriptions of the Early Gupta Kings*. Revised by Devadatta , ed. Ramakrishna Bhandarkar. Bahadurchand Chhabra and Govind Swamirao Gai, New Delhi.

———(*CII* V 1963), *Inscriptions of the Vākāṭakas,* ed. Vasudev Vishnu Mirashi, Ootacamund.

Epigraphia Indica (*EI*), A collection of inscriptions supplementary to the *Corpus Inscriptionum Indicarum* of the Archaeological Survey. Translated by several scholars, ed. Jas. Burgess [*et al.*] (Vols. III-XV published under the authority of the Government of India as a supplement to the *Indian Antiquary*), Calcutta/Bombay.

Gai, G. S., 1969, 'Three Inscriptions of Rāmagupta', in: *Journal of the Oriental Institute*, M. S. University of Baroda, XVIII, 247-51.

Goyal, S. R., 1967, *A History of the Imperial Guptas*, Allahabad.

Gupta, P. L., 1946, 'Ghaṭotkacagupta', in *Indian Historical Quarterly,* 22, 316-19.

Indian Antiquary (*IA*), A Journal of Oriental Research in Archaeology, History, Literature, Languages, Folklore, etc., Bombay, 1872-1933.

Jain, Kailash Chand, 1972, *Malwa Through the Ages (from the earliest times to 1305 AD)*, Delhi.

Joshi, M. C., 1992, 'Royal Succession in the Gupta Age and the Connotation of the Term *Dauhitra* Occuring in Inscriptions', in R. Ch. Chhabra *et al.* (eds.), *Reappraising Gupta History for S. R. Goyal.*, New Delhi, pp. 111-26.

Journal of the Numismatic Society of India (*JNSI*), 1939, Numismatic Society of India, Hindu University [till 1956: Prince of Wales Museum], Varanasi.

Kālidāsa, *The Complete Works of Kālidāsa*, 1976, The text in Sanskrit and Prakrit, edited with Introduction by V. P. Joshi, Leiden.

Kulke, Hermann, 1998, *Geschichte Indiens. Zweite, verbesserte und aktualisierte Auflage*, München.

Majumdar, R. C., 1954, 'The Expansion and Consolidation of the Empire', Chapter III of *The Classical Age*. Bombay: The History and Culture of the Indian People III.

Mirashi, Vasudev Vishnu, 1980, 'Bhitari Stone Inscription of Skandagupta', in *Journal of the Epigraphical Society of India,* VII, 86-92.

———, 1982a, 'New Light on a Period in Gupta History', in Vasudev Vishnu Mirashi, *Indological Research Papers* (*IRP*), Vol. I, Nagpur, pp. 65-77.

———, 1982b, 'The Rāmagupta Problem Re-examined', in Vasudev Vishnu Mirashi, *IRP*, Vol. I, Nagpur, pp. 56-62.

Raghavan, V., 1963, *Bhoja's Śṛṅgāra Prakāśa*, Madras.

Raven, Ellen M., 1994a, *Gupta Gold Coins with a Garuḍa-Banner. Samudragupta-Skandagupta.* Groningen, 2 vols., Gonda Indological Studies I.

———, 1994b, 'Invention and Innovation. Royal Gupta Gold Coins', in Martha L. Carter (ed.), *A Treasure of Indian Coins*. Bombay.

Shastri, Ajay Mitra and K. D. Kawadkar, 2001, Miregāon Plates of Prabhāvatī Guptā, Year 20, in *Annals of the Bhandarkar Oriental Research Institute* LXXXI, 135-51.

Sircar, D. C., *Select Inscriptions Bearing on Indian History and Civilization* (*Sel. Ins.*), 1942, Vol. I, Calcutta (2nd edn. Delhi/Madras, 1965), Vol. II, Delhi, 1983.

Thaplyal, Kiran, 1972, *Studies in Ancient Indian Seals: A study of North Indian seals and sealings from circa third century BC to mid-seventh century AD*, Lucknow.

Trivedi, H.V., 1957, *Catalogue of the Coins of the Nāga Kings of Padmāvatī*, The Department of Archaeology & Museums, Madhya Pradesh, Gwalior.

Viśākhadatta, *Mudrārākṣasa or The Signet Ring, a Sanskrit Drama in Seven Acts by Viśākhadatta*, crit. edit. with copious notes, translation, introduction and appendixes, indexes, etc., by K. H. Dhruva. 3rd edn. (thoroughly revised and enlarged), Poona, 1930.

Warder, A. K., 1977, *Indian Kāvya Literature*, Vol. III, Delhi.

Winternitz, Moriz, 1920, *Geschichte der indischen littérateur*, Band 3, Leipzig.

CHAPTER 10

Early Medieval Orissa: The Data and the Debate

UPINDER SINGH

The current debate on the nature of the society, polity, and economy of early medieval India has acquired a vintage quality, spanning as it does almost half a century.[1] Historians have come a long way in recognizing that this period was one of profound historical change. However, when it comes to the *nature* of these changes, we are faced with a number of hypotheses that contradict each other in crucial respects. On the one hand, we have the hypothesis of Indian feudalism, which presents early medieval India as a period of fragmentation, an age which saw the transformation of peasants into serfs, the feudalization of power relations and administrative organization, and a decline in urban life and the use of money. The feudalism hypothesis has been applied to both north and south India. For south India, we have another interpretative framework – the segmentary state model, which presents the kings of this period as shadowy ritual figures devoid of the two important props of real power – an organized revenue infrastructure and a standing army. The third major interpretative framework for early medieval India suggests that in many parts of the country, this was not an age of political fragmentation and break-down, but of the emergence and development of state societies and polities. It identifies and emphasizes the forces that made for integration rather than disintegration. We can further connect this interpretation with the marshalling of evidence that the early medieval period was a period of change in urban patterns, but not of urban decay, and that there was a decline in the number of coin types but not of coinage.[2]

This paper has two interwoven aspects, one specific, the other general. The specific focus is on certain features of the history of early medieval Orissa as reflected in the details in the royal land-grant inscriptions about donors, donees, and the gifted land. This discussion is based on an analysis of a little over 300 Sanskrit inscriptions from Orissa and adjacent areas of Madhya Pradesh and Andhra Pradesh, ranging in time from the fourth to the mid-twelfth century AD.[3] The second, general, focus is on the extent to which explanatory models currently used for early medieval India are helpful in furthering our understanding of this period. The overall perspective informing the discussion of these issues is that there are several questions that can be posed regarding both the somewhat euphemistically labelled 'dominant' and 'alternative' interpretative frameworks.[4]

In order to discuss the epigraphic evidence from Orissa, the data can be divided into three overlapping phases, Period I (the fourth to the seventh century), Period II (the seventh to the tenth century), and Period III (the tenth to the twelfth century).[5] Taking a long time-frame divided in this manner makes it possible to identify patterns of historical change. The brevity of inscriptions is offset by their sheer number, and also by the fact that notwithstanding differences of opinion about the initial year of certain eras, they can at least be dated approximately.

ROYAL DONORS AND THE NATURE OF POLITIES

The political history of ancient and early medieval Orissa is fairly complex, and includes the rise and fall of many dynasties. One of the problems in reconstructing a continuous narrative of the political history of this region is the uncertainty that surrounds the initial year of some of the eras used in the inscriptions, such as the Bhauma era and the Gaṅga era.[6] These hurdles are not, however, insurmountable, and it is possible to plot out a broad political narrative of dynastic histories and their geographic contexts.

The thirteenth major rock edict of the Mauryan emperor Aśoka speaks of his successful military campaign against the Kaliṅgas.[7] The administrative centres of Mauryan rule in Orissa were located in or around Dhauli (in Puri district) and Jaugada (in Ganjam district), and the Mauryan administrative infrastructure seems to have been extended in some form to these areas. In about the first century BC, the nuclear area of the Cedi kingdom of Khāravela was located in and around the Mahanadi delta. The outlines of the succeeding centuries remain rather faint. Although there is some numismatic evidence of contact with the Kuṣāṇa empire, the available inscriptional material is scanty. In the fourth century certain parts of southern Orissa and adjacent areas came to be included in the Gupta empire, as is suggested by lines 19-20 of the Allahabad *praśasti* of Samudragupta, which refer to certain kings who were captured and then released.[8] Presumably these kings continued to rule over their principalities with the proviso that they accept Gupta suzerainty. The evidence of the Aśokan edicts and the Hathigumpha inscription, the archaeological remains from Sisupalgarh (which range from the third century BC to the fourth century AD) and the Udayagiri and Khandagiri caves, and the references to a number of political units in the area in the Allahabad *praśasti* are suggestive of a certain level of political and social complexity in some parts of Orissa in early historic times. More archaeological evidence from ancient settlements of this period and a better understanding of the structure of the imperial polities would make possible a more meaningful discussion of these centuries, which otherwise tend to get reduced to an unnuanced story of conquest and encapsulation, as if nothing much else was going on in the area.

From the fourth century onwards, there is evidence of a number of lineages who carved out principalities in different parts of Orissa and contiguous areas, establishing control over a resource base that was in some cases rich enough to permit them to fan out and expand their power through conquests and alliances. Not surprisingly, most of these principalities were located in areas of rich agricultural potential – the river valleys and deltas of the Mahanadi, Brahmani, Vaitarani, Rishikulya, Vamsadhara, and Nagavali. Between the seventh and tenth centuries, we see the Śailodbhavas and Bhauma-Karas carving out fairly large kingdoms. Inscriptions from the highlands of interior Orissa indicate the establishment of principalities in these areas from the ninth and tenth centuries. In Period III smaller kingdoms continued to exist on their peripheries, but the Somavaṁśīs and the Imperial Gaṅgas succeeded in uniting large parts of Orissa through conquest.

When we move to the question of the nature and structure of the polities of early medieval India, we are on more tentative ground.

Part of the problem is one of definition (what exactly do we mean by a state? How do we distinguish between a pre-state and state society?). Another part of it lies in interpreting the evidence from the rather reticent sources to assess the nature of the political system they reflect. These problems are particularly acute when we are looking at the period of transition from chiefdoms to states and also at early, as opposed to mature, states. At a very general level, when we talk of the transition to statehood, we are talking of political elites that had effectively established certain formal mechanisms of power, control, and authority, backed by force, over the resources of certain areas, particularly over land. The political success stories, the large kingdoms, reflect effective extraction and control over a resource base that was rich enough to permit further military expansion.

It is possible to identify certain more specific features of early medieval polities. Compared to earlier centuries, we see higher levels of militarization and many more foci of military power in different parts of the subcontinent. The political narrative of incessant warfare suggests large armies maintained by the great kings of the time. Apart from a central hired core, these armies would have included mercenaries. A large number of Pāla land grant inscriptions (from Bihar and Bengal) address, among others, the Gauḍas, Mālavas, Khaśas, Kulikas, Hūṇas, Karṇāṭas, and Lāṭas. These seem to be references to military contingents recruited from amongst these people into the Pāla armies. The *Rājataraṅgiṇī* of Kalhaṇa also indicates the recruitment by kings of Kashmir of mercenaries from other areas.[9] The core and mercenary troops were supplemented when the need arose by the military capacity of allied and subordinate rulers. The effective mustering and deployment of the mechanism of force led to an unparalleled phenomenon of political and military expansion and the high levels of spatial mobility of a number of political elites virtually all over India. The titles and designations used in the land grants are suggestive of different tiers, ranks, and functionaries in the administrative infrastructure in some of the kingdoms, although it is not always possible to identify the precise meaning of some of the terms.[10] But we see states whose horizontal and vertical linkages are more visible than ever before, and we can connect the emergent political elites with landed groups, some of them created and buttressed by royal land grants.

There is one aspect of the description of the polity of early medieval India in the writings of the feudalism school that is acceptable: the relationship between paramount kings and subordinate kings, between kings and *sāmantas*. However, the other aspects of the thesis, including the idea of political fragmentation and the interpretation of the relationship between kings and the beneficiaries of royal grants is not convincing.[11] The interpretations of early medieval India that highlight the expansion of state society and state formation are better grounded in the empirical evidence from the different regions. Viewing royal land grants within a framework of 'integration' rather than 'disintegration' suits areas such as Orissa well. But certain points can be raised with regard to the integrationist interpretations as well. While state *formation* is often presented as a major theme of this period, once the socio-politics of statehood had made their appearance in an area, the period seems better described as one that saw a *proliferation* of polities. Secondly, the definition of what exactly constitutes the regional level remains problematic and is sometimes assumed rather than defined or demonstrated. And third, although the 'alternative framework' talks about developments at the sub-regional, regional, and supra-regional level, it tends to privilege the regional. It can also be asked whether the configurations of regional culture, whether defined in terms of political units, language or other cultural sign-posts, do not crystallize or fructify only towards the end or even after the end of the early medieval period.

The contours of the kingdoms of early medieval India were fluid and difficult to define. These kingdoms are in fact more easily identifiable by their nuclear areas and political centres than by their boundaries. At the same time, a glance at the narrative of the political history of early medieval India reveals some large empires such as those of the Rāṣṭrakūṭas, Pālas, and Pratihāras, and many more numerous short-lived dynasties with much more modest levels of territorial control, who did not make such a grand splash on the political scene. This makes us pause and consider whether through most of the early medieval period the sub-regional and trans-regional were not perhaps as, if not more, prominent aspects of political formations as the 'regional,' however the region may be defined.[12]

Royal inscriptions represent, among other things, an articulation of royal power. The *praśastis* of the inscriptions give us important clues regarding the antecedents of various lineages, the political geography of kingdoms, and political centres. Most of this period was marked by swiftly changing political configurations – the result of incessant contests for power among various lineages. The continuing process of the redefinition of power equations was reflected in the *praśastis* in an idiom of ranking of power relations, in terms of paramountcy and subordination. In Orissa, some of the royal titles assumed by kings embodied territorial claims (e.g. *Kaliṅg-ādhipati* and *sakala-Kaliṅg-ādhipati*). From the Gupta period onwards, claimants to paramountcy usually assumed the triple title of *mahārājādhirāja*, *parama-bhaṭṭāraka*, and *parameśvara*. Subordinate kings had to be content with *mahārāja*, *mahāsāmanta*, and *rāṇaka*, and were frequently given the epithet *samadhigata-pañca-mahāśabda*' (one who has obtained the five great sounds).[13]

The names and scarcely-brahmanized origin myths of some Orissan lineages (such as the Śailodbhavas, Śulkīs, and Kulikas) betray their local tribal roots and suggest their recent emergence from the stage of tribal chiefdoms to early statehood.[14] On the other hand, there is evidence of certain lineages being migrants into Orissa – the Pānduvaṁśīs came from Mekala (the area around Amarakaṇṭaka), the Bhauma-Karas possibly from Assam, the Tuṅgas from Rohitagiri in Bihar, the Somavaṁśīs from South Kosala (the Raipur, Bilaspur, Sambalpur area), and the Gaṅgas of Śvetaka and Kaliṅganagara from Karnataka. The Gaṅga inscriptions further indicate the fanning out of collateral lineages, while the many groups of Bhañja kings may represent different lineages sharing a common clan affiliation.

The origin myths in the *praśastis* can be seen as an expression of staking and intensifying claims to political power. In Orissa, the elaboration of such myths seems to have particularly come to the fore from about the seventh century onwards. Some of these myths show a complex interweaving of puranic and tribal elements. In the case of the Bhañjas, for instance, it is possible to discern the process of brahmanization. The early Bhañjas of Khiñjalimaṇḍala describe themselves as *aṇḍaja-vaṃśa-prabhava* (the egg-born lineage) but also introduce the *ṛṣi* Vasiṣṭha and the epic hero Rāma into the story.[15] We can see a similar process at work in the Śailodbhava origin myth which traces the origins of the dynasty to the worship of the god Svayambhū by a man named Pulindasena.[16]

None of this sort of thing (miraculous birth from an egg or a rock) for the two major dynasties who came to the fore in Orissa in about the tenth century. Both the Somavaṁśīs and Imperial Gaṅgas anchored themselves quite firmly to the pan-Indian epic-puranic tradition. The Somavaṁśīs claimed to belong to the lunar dynasty. The genealogy of the Imperial Gaṅgas became more and more elaborate and grandiose over time, with the kings of this dynasty ultimately tracing their ancestry to Viṣṇu. This more or less coincides with a shift from Śaiva to Vaiṣṇava affiliations during the time of Anantavarman Coḍagaṅga, which can be seen as an attempt to promote a new sectarian symbol for the expanding empire.

The *praśasti* of the royal grants contains poetic embellishment, conventional rhetoric, and downright flattery. But if examined carefully, the *praśasti*, and the seals and invocations of the grants allow us to reconstruct certain elements that comprised both the ideal and the practice of kingship. The ideal king of the inscriptions of Orissa appears, as he does in literature, in a variety of roles – as victorious warrior, protector of his subjects, maintainer of the social order, giver of gifts, and as one who wards off the evils of the Kali age. Only one dynasty highlights the king as performer of *śrauta* sacrifices. Inscriptions of the Śailodbhavas (who may be placed between the late sixth and ninth century) mention the performance of the Aśvamedha and the Vājapeya sacrifices by Mādhavavarman.[17] Mādhavavarman's inscriptions tell us that he had caused satisfaction to the gods by his performance of the Aśvamedha and other sacrifices, the very mention of which had fallen into abeyance due to the impiety of the kings of the Kali age.[18] However, such boasts are not found in the inscriptions of any other dynasty of early medieval Orissa. This silence indicates that the performance of *śrauta* sacrifices was not an important component of the ideology or practice of kingship in ancient and early medieval Orissa.

Kings of early medieval Orissa established and proclaimed their connection with the religious domain in other ways. The sectarian epithets of kings reflect more than their personal religious predilections, and can also be viewed from the perspective of royal policy. Seen from this point of view, consistencies in and changes in sectarian affiliations assume political importance. The earliest assumption of specific Vaiṣṇava or Śaiva sectarian epithets by kings of Orissa dates to about the fifth century, and becomes quite common thereafter. While *parama-māheśvara* is the usual Śaiva epithet, the Vaiṣṇava epithet *parama-bhāgavata* is replaced early on by *parama-vaiṣṇava*. On the other hand, there are references to certain kings being worshippers of what seem to be tribal goddesses or brahmanized tribal goddesses such as Stambheśvarī.[19] This goddess is mentioned in the Terasingha plates of Tustikāra, and in some of the grants of the early Bhañjas of Khiñjalimaṇḍala and the Śulkīs. The Śulkī inscriptions (the Dhenkanal and Hindol plates of Kulastambha) describe Stambheśvarī as the *kula-devatā* of these kings. Although the specific term *kula-devatā* does not occur in Gaṅga inscriptions, the phraseology of the text suggests that Śiva-Gokarṇa occupied much this sort of position for them.

As far as the exclusive association of a dynasty with a particular deity is concerned, the dynasties that display a consistency in sectarian affiliations (the Śailodbhavas, Ādi-Bhañjas, Śulkīs, Tuṅgas, Somavaṁśīs, the Gaṅgas of Śvetaka and the early Gaṅgas of Kaliṅganagara) were all Śaiva. This is not surprising, as it is well-known that, notwithstanding the proliferation of a large variety of religious cults, until the construction of the Jagannātha temple in the mid-twelfth century, it was Śaivism that prevailed in a big way in Orissa. At the same time, it is interesting to note that although the *praśasti* of kings of early medieval Orissa routinely gives them sectarian epithets, it rarely highlights the king in his role as a builder of temples. This is intriguing in an age which saw the proliferation of temples.

THE DONEES: BRĀHMAṆAS, TEMPLES, AND OTHERS

As elsewhere in the subcontinent, the early medieval period in Orissa saw a systematic and sustained royal patronage of brāhmaṇas and the king–brāhmaṇa relationship was an important aspect of the polities of this period. In spite of evidence of a great variety in vocations pursued by brāhmaṇas from the earliest times, many scholars tend to treat them as a homogeneous social group and persist in routinely translating the word brāhmaṇa as 'priest.' The literary and epigraphic sources of early medieval India present the brāhmaṇas in a variety of roles. As panegyrists and genealogists, they were experts in crafting claims to royal legitimacy, an important skill in times of political turbulence. As ritual advisors to kings, some of them were closely associated with the court circle. As occupants of various official posts, some of them played an important role in the administration of kingdoms. And as the prime beneficiaries of royal grants of land, they emerged as an important landed class and as influential mediators of social and religious values at the village level.

The inscriptions help us break up the category of the brāhmaṇa into its parts by indicating the various bases of differentiation within the community. They also indicate how brāhmaṇa identity was defined over time. *Gotra* appears as the single most consistently specified basis of brāhmaṇa identification in the Orissan inscriptions from the fourth to the mid-twelfth century. From about the seventh century, reference to the *pravara* and *anupravara* of the brāhmaṇas becomes frequent as well.[20]

The Vedic school to which the brāhmaṇa donees were affiliated was another important basis of identity; the terms *caraṇa* (Vedic school) and *śākhā* (recension of a Veda) were often used interchangeably in the inscriptions. A tabulation of the number of representatives of the various Vedic schools among the brāhmaṇa beneficiaries of royal land grants in Orissa indicates that throughout the period under review, brāhmaṇas of the *Yajur Veda*, particularly those associated with the Vājasaneya school, were especially favoured. Brahmanas of the *Atharva Veda*, on the other hand, are almost totally absent among the beneficiaries of royal grants. During the whole period under review, only one inscription – the Neulpur plate of the Bhauma-Kara king Śubhākara – records a grant in favour of *Atharva Veda* brāhmaṇas.[21] The preponderance of *Yajur Veda* Brahmaṇas may have had to do with their ritual expertise, but invoking such an explanation requires further investigation into the precise role and importance of such expertise in the context of what we know about the religion of this period (which was no longer centred on sacrifice but on the temple) and the lack of advertisement of kings as sacrificers in the royal inscriptions.

The routine specification of the ancestry of these donees becomes a regular feature in Orissan inscriptions from about the tenth century, as does the specification of their native place and place of residence. This can be related to the fact that this period saw the influx into

Orissa of brāhmaṇas from other parts of India. There was a flow of brāhmaṇas into Orissa from renowned centres of brahmanical learning in Madhyadeśa such as Ṭākarī, Śrāvastī, Kolāñca, and Hastipada. A few came in from other places in the modern state boundaries of Gujarat, Madhya Pradesh, and Karnataka. Political turmoil and pressures on land have been cited as factors responsible for this spatial mobility, especially from the heartland of the Gaṅga valley to the peripheral areas of the subcontinent. Brahmanical migrations into various parts of India had been going on for many centuries, and the major impetus must have been a search for a better livelihood. There were two things that were new in the early medieval period. One was the intensification of this process and the second was the conjunction of this migration with the proliferation of kingdoms in various parts of the subcontinent.

The brāhmaṇa of the Orissan inscriptions conforms in some ways to his counterpart in the normative texts. There is an emphasis on his Vedic learning. There is also frequent reference to his being a performer of the six acts enjoined on brāhmaṇas in the Dharmaśāstras – sacrificing and conducting sacrifices for others, studying and teaching, offering gifts and receiving gifts (*yajana*, *yājana*, *adhyayana*, *adhyāpana*, *dāna*, *pratigraha*). References to sacrificial expertise occur in a few inscriptions, and epithets such as *dīkṣita*, *agnihotrin* and the less common *upāsanin* also signify this sort of expertise.[22]

The brahmadeyas are sometimes seen as important hubs in the diffusion of temple-based sectarian religion and the *śāsana* brāhmaṇas are associated with the management of temple establishments and estates. The close connection between the brahmadeyas and temples comes out clearly in regions such as Kerala. If we look at the inscriptions of Orissa, a number of things can be noted. There is a virtual absence of references to the sectarian affiliations of the brāhmaṇa donees. The only instances are the Adhabhara plates of the Pāṇḍuvaṁśī king Mahā-Nannarāja, where the donee is described as a *bhāgavata*, the Sirpur inscription of the Pāṇḍuvaṁśī queen Vāsaṭā, where the term *bhāgavata* is used for the two donees, and the Dhenkanal plate of the Śulkī king Kulastambha, where the donee is described as *parama-vaiṣṇava*. The inscriptions associate very few of the donees with temple establishments or *maṭhas*.[23] Either the *śāsana* brāhmaṇas were only marginally involved in the spread of sectarian religion, or the inscriptions are deliberately silent on their association with temples, as this sort of association was not considered particularly prestigious. The *śāsana* brāhmaṇa is consistently presented in his traditionally prestigious role as Vedic scholar.

Howsoever the text of the inscriptions may specifically describe the donees, their contents highlight the brāhmaṇa in the role of the receiver of royal favours and as a land-holder. The brahmanical sources have different opinions on this issue. On the one hand, receiving gifts is one of the six acts considered appropriate for brāhmaṇas and generosity to brāhmaṇas is prescribed as a meritorious act for ordinary folk and kings alike. On the other hand, there are statements to the effect that the acceptance of gifts from kings should be avoided as it diminished the stature of the brāhmaṇa.[24] This sort of tension is not surprising in a tradition that often incorporated and sometimes tried to reconcile divergent points of view. Although the texts reflect different stances on the appropriateness of gift-acceptance, inscriptions from all over the country clearly show that in the early medieval period, certain brāhmaṇa families carved out large landed estates for themselves, benefiting from a series of royal grants of land. The exhortations to avoid such gifts had little impact on this upwardly mobile section of the community.

In Orissa and adjoining areas the majority of royal grants, throughout the early medieval period, were made in favour of brāhmaṇas, but some were made to religious establishments. Literary and archaeological evidence tells us about the prevalence of various Buddhist and Jaina sects in this area. Ratnagiri was a major Buddhist monastic establishment flourishing from about the fifth to the twelfth centuries. The Udayagiri and Khandagiri caves were retreats of both Buddhist and Jaina monks. The earliest extant temples in Orissa belong to the sixth century (the Lakṣmaṇeśvara, Bharateśvara, and Śatrughneśvara temples at Bhubaneswar). Orissa seems to have been a stronghold of the Śaiva Pāśupata sect in this period. The eighth and ninth centuries saw an upsurge in the building of temples, most of which display an amalgam of Śaiva, Sakta, and Tāntric elements. The Liṅgarāja temple at Bhubaneswar was built by the Somavaṁśī kings in the eleventh century. Until the middle of the twelfth century, Orissa was a land of Śaiva temples, and Vaiṣṇava shrines were few and far between. A major shift of gravity from Śaivism to Vaiṣṇavism started during the reign of the Imperial Gaṅga king Anantavarman Coḍagaṅga, who began the construction of the Puruṣottama (later known as Jagannātha) temple at Puri.

Much remains to be understood about the mechanisms, institutions, and patrons that lay behind the early stages in the spread of sectarian religion. The association between kings and temples in India has usually been assumed rather than demonstrated. The sectarian titles claimed by the kings of various dynasties of ancient and early medieval Orissa are not matched by much evidence of their building or patronage of temple establishments until around the tenth century. In comparison with the large number of grants made by the kings of Orissa in favour of brāhmaṇas during most of the period under review, the number of grants to temples is comparatively few. The majority of royal grants to temples benefited Śaiva establishments. There are a few references to the royal patronage of *maṭhas*. Royal grants to Buddhist and Jaina establishments are very few. The inscriptions suggest that during most of the period royal patronage was *not* crucial to the building or maintenance of temples in Orissa. And the patronage of temples did *not* have an important place in royal policy during most of this period. Apart from kings, members of the royal family, and subordinate rulers, there were a variety of other social groups – local land-holders, administrative functionaries, and wealthy private individuals – who extended patronage to temple establishments.

There seems to have been a change as far as all this was concerned in the tenth century. During the reigns of the Imperial Gaṅga kings, there was an increase in the direct initiative of the king in making grants to temples, an increase in the number of secular grants in favour of *nāyakas* or military chiefs, and also a large volume of inscriptions recording temple grants made by members of the royal family. This indicates an important shift in royal policy. With the building of the Jagannātha temple at Puri by the Imperial Gaṅga king Anantavarman Coḍagaṅga in the middle of the twelfth century, the royally-endowed temple emerged as an important component in the practice of kingship.

THE GIFTED LAND

An important part of the land grant charters is the information they give regarding the nature of brahmadeya settlements. One of the limitations of the inscriptional sources is that they tell us little about what was going on in non-brahmadeya villages, which would have outnumbered the brahmadeyas greatly (it is difficult to say what the precise ratio of the two might have been). Details of the extent and location of the holdings, the nature of the land granted, the description of the boundaries (where this occurs), and the terms and conditions of the grants, are crucial in order to understand agrarian structure and agrarian change in early medieval Orissa. The specifications of village boundaries suggest in some cases the clustering of brahmadeya settlements. The evidence from Orissa is significant as it indicates that while *most* of the grants do stipulate that the gift in question was free of the obligation to render taxes to the state (and therefore involved a permanent loss of actual or potential income to the state), *some* royal endowments were not tax free. The latter are known as *kara-śāsanas*, and 13 of them have been found in Orissa.[25] They generally specify the annual rent that the donee was to pay.

An analysis of the inscriptions indicates that the brahmadeyas in Orissa were, in most cases, made free from any kind of state intervention. The privileges granted to the beneficiaries were not restricted to revenue matters. They included comprehensive rights over the natural resources of the area. Some – but not all or even most – of the inscriptions (those of the Pāṇḍuvaṁśīs and Somavaṁśīs) may suggest the grant of certain judicial rights as well: The relevant term is *sa-daś-āparadhaḥ*. But this term can be interpreted in two ways, either as giving the right to punish those guilty of the ten offences or the right to realize fines from those guilty of the ten offences. From the ninth or tenth century, epigraphic evidence indicates an increase in some areas of the control of the brāhmaṇa beneficiaries over sources of revenue other than land. Grants of the Bhauma-Karas, Udayavarāha, the Śulkīs, and Tuṅgas give the donees control over outposts situated in the village, landing or bathing places, and ferries (*sa-kheṭa-ghaṭṭa-nadi-tara-sthān-ādi-gulmakaḥ*). From the ninth or tenth century, some of the inscriptions of the Bhauma-Karas, Ādi-Bhañjas, Śulkīs, and Tuṅgas contain the term *sa-tantravāya-gokuṭa-śauṇḍik-ādi-prakṛtikaḥ* (along with the weavers, cowherds, brewers, and other inhabitants). But this is not a universal phenomenon. It may be noted, for instance, that the grants of the Imperial Gaṅgas do not contain any terms that can be interpreted as transferring judicial rights or rights over the inhabitants of villages to the donees.

The grant of a large number of privileges was offset by what seems to have been the only restriction imposed by the state – that the gifted land was inalienable. This was indicated by terms such as *akṣaya-nīvī dharma* and *a-lekhanī-praveśatayā*. The evidence regarding the nature of the rights bestowed on the brahmadeyas suggests that while these varied to some extent from dynasty to dynasty, the position they created for the donee was one that fell somewhere between that of a landlord and landowner – more than a landlord, and just short of an owner of land in the modern sense of the term. The insertion of a brāhmaṇa landed elite into the countryside initiated a churning process that led to changes in agrarian relations and that had far-reaching impact on many aspects of rural society.

There seems little doubt that the creation of brahmadeya settlements and the terms of the land grants created a class that enjoyed superior rights and control over the inhabitants and the resources of the village. The technical terms of the grants clearly indicate that in economic terms, the relationship between the brāhmaṇa donee and other rural groups was one of exploitation. Whether the substitution of state exploitation and control by the more close-at-hand brāhmaṇa exploitation and control meant increased levels of subjection of the average cultivator is however a more tricky question. One point that can be made, however, is that the degrees of social and economic stratification, dominance and subordination that resulted from royal land grants depended on a number of variables that could differ from region to region and even within regions. These factors included ecology, the availability of arable land, and the existence or absence of competing groups or institutions. In Assam, where cultivable land was not in short supply, and where non-brāhmaṇa groups also held land, the extent of social and economic stratification was not as rigid as in other regions.[26] Levels of social stratification varied greatly between upland Andhra and wet zone lowlands.[27] Corporate organizations of brāhmaṇas such as the *sabhā* furthered the authority of the *śāsana* brāhmaṇas in the Tamil region. In Kerala, the influence of such corporate organizations was enhanced by the absence of competition from corporate organizations of other social groups such as the *nadu* or *nattar*.[28]

THE INTERPRETATION OF ROYAL PATRONAGE

A major point of disagreement among historians has to do with how precisely the act of royal grants to brāhmaṇas and temples is to be interpreted and understood. Part of the problem in the feudalism hypothesis is its understanding of power relationships in overwhelmingly competitive terms. One can question the assumption that an increase in the power and wealth of certain classes (brāhmaṇas) and institutions (temples) necessarily had to be at the *expense* of royal power. If our understanding of the politics of early medieval India gives adequate importance to collaboration and alliances, we can think in terms of the *parallel* increase in power of kings, brāhmaṇas, and temples. Strategies of control, alliances, and collaboration with political competitors and prestigious social groups were crucial facets of the politics of the time.

Another fundamental problem with the feudalism hypothesis is that it rests on a misunderstanding of the politics and economics of patronage. In the post-Gupta period, two different kinds of contexts of land grants can be identified.[29] In certain situations (in fledgling, unstable monarchies) it was part of a quest for power or staking a claim to it. In others (established, more stable ones) it was a proclamation and advertisement of power. *Dāna* – ritual giving – has to be understood within the context of religious practice, social custom, and political precept. It cannot be understood in the way we would interpret a mundane economic transaction in which he who gives without material recompense is the loser. Evidence from many parts of South Asia can be invoked to demonstrate that more and larger gifts were signifiers of more, not less, power. In Orissa, for instance, the maximum number of grants were made by the most powerful dynasties, the Bhauma-Karas, Somavaṁśīs, and Imperial Gaṅgas. If we look for evidence of lavish gifts of land to *hundreds* of brāhmaṇas we find these are absent in Period I, and virtually absent in Period II.[30] There is an increase in the number of such generous grants in Period III and again, we find that it is kings of the most powerful dynasty – the Imperial Gaṅgas – who were making grants to hundreds of brāhmaṇas at a time. Examples of this include the Madras Museum plates of Vajrahasta (in favour of 500 brāhmaṇas), the Galavalli plates of Rājarāja I (300 brāhmaṇas), and the two sets of Korni plates of

Anantavarman Coḍagaṅga (300 brāhmaṇas). Such grants, made at the peak of power of a dynasty, cannot be interpreted as a symptom or a cause of political disempowerment.[31]

The increase of royal grants of land indicates the more systematic and extensive deployment and redistribution of resources by kings. These sorts of equations are recognized for the earlier periods of Indian history. For example, references to kings distributing cows, gold, horses, villages, etc., in the *dāna-stutis* in later Vedic literature are generally seen as an indication of (or at least within a context of) increasing, not decreasing royal power. However, the interpretation is reversed for the early medieval period, where grants are seen as a sort of 'selling out' or disinvestment strategy undertaken by a state that was in the grip of a crisis. In early medieval India (as in the modern world) the more powerful gave to the less powerful, and generous hand-outs did not as a matter of course lead to an erosion of the power of the giver. They arose out of the king's superior control over resources, and also marked a special but unequal power relation between the giver and the receiver.

The importance of land grants in the legitimation of political power has been highlighted by many historians. Political power is mercurial, something that waxes and wanes, that has to be grasped, cemented, claimed, and proclaimed. Legitimation is therefore a constant need, an on-going process involving repeated reiteration and display. However, there are a number of issues related to legitimation that need to be considered carefully. These concern the precise working of the mechanisms of legitimation, the different audiences that the various strategies of legitimation targeted, and the kind of responses they may have elicited.[32] It is also necessary to highlight the connection between legitimation strategies and socio-political alliances, to which they were inextricably linked. Another aspect that can be considered is the reciprocal element of legitimation strategies, enhancing as they do not only the prestige and position of the legitimized but also of the legitimizers.

In the emphasis that is placed on the importance of legitimation strategies, we should not lose sight of the fact that they were a part of political processes in which force was ultimately the most important ingredient. There is also a need to spell out just how the patronage of a socio-religious elite group can be envisaged as an effective strategy in such a situation, which means reflecting more closely on the relationship between power, status, and authority in ancient India.[33] Another question that can be asked is just how effective integrative and legitimizing strategies pursued by early medieval kings actually were. Further, the focus on legitimation should not make us forget the fact that land grants were also about the transfer of land rights that crucially affected agrarian structure and agrarian relations. Therefore, there is a constant need to look beyond the linkages between kings and donees, at the implications that these transfers had for rural society.

In this brief summary of some of the aspects of the history of ancient and early medieval Orissa as revealed in the inscriptions, and how this data impinges on the larger debate, I would like to mention certain areas that require further investigation. There is sufficient ground to question the validity of the hypothesis of a subcontinental decline in urban centres and trade in the early medieval period.[34] There is consequently a need for a better understanding of the precise nature of settlement patterns, urbanization, and trade in early medieval Orissa. There is also a need for a clearer assessment of the administrative organization of kingdoms. The political changes need to be placed within a broader social context that supplements its focus on class with greater attention to caste and gender relations. Clearly, there are still many under-explored areas. Greater clarity about these would help to contextualize the epigraphic evidence of the kind that has been summarized here.

There is no denying that the debate about the economy, polity, and society of early medieval India has been a rich and fruitful one from many points of view. But it has also been constricting, with researchers often trying to fit their data into one or the other explanatory model, and not trying to move beyond them. The debate has also had its share of casualties. The preoccupation with feudalism has led to a dearth of meaningful studies of the literature, philosophical ideas, religion, art, and architecture of early medieval India and a lack of acknowledgement of the cultural richness and vitality of the period. Viewed through the spectacles of a feudal paradigm, all these tend to be reduced to simple and sorry reflections of a decadent feudal order. The alternative hypothesis that highlights integration and state formation is less constrained by a self-imposed theoretical strait-jacket and suits areas like Orissa well.[35] Nevertheless, some of its insights can be stretched further. Finally, when we are dealing with an area as large as the Indian subcontinent, any explanatory framework for the early medieval period will have to have enough flexibility to accommodate and accept regional and sub-regional diversity.

NOTES

1. I refer to the debate on whether early medieval India was feudal or not, not to writings on this period, which obviously go back much further.
2. The literature of this debate is extensive and fairly well-known. Therefore it does not seem necessary to give a detailed listing of the relevant works. However, a few important references can be cited. An important detailed exposition of the Indian feudalism hypothesis was R. S. Sharma's *Indian Feudalism: c. 300-1200* (Calcutta, 1965), which was followed by a number of writings that endorsed, amplified, and sometimes amended the original formulation. The systematic presentation of data to support the hypothesis of urban decay can be found in Sharma's *Urban Decay in India (c. 300-c. 1000)* (New Delhi, 1987). The feudalism model has been applied to early medieval south India by scholars such as Kesavan Veluthat (*The Political Structure of Early Medieval South India*, New Delhi, 1993) and R. N. Nandi (*State Formation, Agrarian Growth and Social Change in Feudal South India*, New Delhi, 2000). The application of Aidan W. Southall's segmentary state model to early medieval South India is undertaken in Burton Stein's *Peasant State and Society in Medieval South India* (Delhi, 1980). The foremost exponents of the 'integration hypothesis' are Hermann Kulke and B. D. Chattopadhyaya. See especially Kulke, 'Fragmentation and Segmentation Versus Integration? Reflections on the Concepts of Indian Feudalism and the Segmentary State in Indian History,' *Studies in History* 4, No. 2 (1982): 237-63 and Chattopadhyaya, 'Political Processes and Structure of Polity in Early Medieval India,' Presidential Address, Ancient India Section, Indian History Congress, 44th session, Burdwan, 1983, reprinted in Chattopadhyaya's *The Making of Early Medieval India* (Delhi, 1997), pp. 183-222. The questioning of the hypothesis of urban decay can be found in Chattopadhayaya's 'Trade and Urban Centres in Early Medieval North India', and 'Urban Centres in Early Medieval India: An Overview', in *The Making of Early Medieval India*, pp. 130-54, 155-82. On the hypothesis of a decline in the money economy in this period, see John S. Deyell, *Living Without Silver: The Monetary History of Early Medieval North India* (Delhi, 1990).
3. A detailed presentation of this data is given in my *Kings, Brāhmanas and Temples in Orissa: an epigraphic study, AD 300-1147* (New Delhi, 1994). A

few of the later Sanskrit inscriptions of the period contain Telugu or Oriya elements. There are several Gaṅga inscriptions in Telugu that have been found in various parts of modern Andhra Pradesh. These have not been drawn on for this analysis.

4. I have only considered the feudalism and the 'integration' models in this paper. The segmentary state model, which has been applied to early medieval south India by Burton Stein is fraught with many difficulties that are fairly well known, and has not been taken up for discussion. In looking at the feudalism and integration hypotheses, the attempt is not to present a comprehensive critique, but to raise new questions.
5. Some of the inscriptions that form part of the discussion here belong to a period a little before what is generally considered to be part of the early medieval period, the sixth to the twelfth/thirteenth centuries AD.
6. The dates that have been suggested for initial year of the Gaṅga era range from the fourth to the ninth century. The dates corresponding to the close of the fifth century seem most plausible. The dates suggested for the initial year of the Bhauma era include 606, 736, 778, and 831. The first of these (which identifies the era used by the Bhauma-Karas with the Harṣa era) seems too early, but those in the middle of the eighth or in the ninth century are more plausible.
7. This was not the first time Magadhan armies had ventured into these parts. The Hathigumpha inscription of Kharavela suggests that the Nandas had already made forays into the area.
8. The relevant references are to Mahendra of Kosala, Vyāghrarāja of Mahākāntara, Mahendragiri of Piṣṭapura, Svāmidatta of Koṭṭura, Damana of Eraṇḍapalla, and Kubera of Devarāṣṭra. The fact that there is no reference to any defeated kings who can be located in northern or central Orissa suggests that Samudragupta's armies may have skirted this area. The Gupta era is used in certain late sixth century inscriptions from these areas such as the Sumaṇḍala plates of Dharmarāja and the Kanas plate of Pṛthivīvigraha, but this need not signify effective political domination, especially since by this time the power of the imperial Guptas had crumbled.
9. The *Rājataraṅgiṇī* highlights the bravery of these mercenaries (M.A. Stein, ed., *Kalhaṇa's Rājataraṅgiṇī*, Delhi, 1960; VIII. 1047, 1082 ff, 1148 ff. Cited in Andre Wink, *Al Hind: The making of the Indo-Islamic World*, Vol. 1, New Delhi, 1999, p. 239).
10. We do not know enough about the administrative organization of the early kingdoms of this period. On the basis of the Midnapore inscription of Somadatta, in which the king claims that he followed the *Manu-śāstra*, Kulke has suggested that the kings of this time organized their rule according to the law books, i.e. Dharmaśāstras ('Royal Temple Policy and the Structure of Medieval Hindu Kingdoms', in A. Eschmann, H. Kulke and G. C. Tripathi, eds., *The Cult of Jagannath and the Regional Tradition of Orissa*,

New Delhi, 1978, p. 127). The extent to which claims of this sort made in inscriptions can be accepted as descriptive of prevailing practices can be questioned

11. Some of the reasons for this are given later in this paper.
12. A further point that merits attention is the simultaneous spread of a pan-Indian brahmanical ideology during this period. See B. P. Sahu, 'Brahmanical Ideology, Regional Identities and the Construction of Early India', *Social Scientist* 29, Nos. 7-8 (July-August 2001), pp. 3-18. An illuminating description and discussion of the interplay between the process of brahmanization and the formation of a regional tradition is Kunal Chakrabarti's *Religious Process: The Puranas and the Making of a Regional Tradition* (New Delhi, 2001). For Orissa, we have the important work edited by A. Eschmann, H. Kulke and G. C. Tripathi, eds., *The Cult of Jagannath and the Regional Tradition of Orissa* (New Delhi, 1978).
13. This seems to refer to the right of enjoying the sound of five instruments – trumpet, tambour, conch-shell, kettledrum, and gong.
14. The problem of definition applies to the term 'tribe' as much as it does to the term 'state'. Ancient Indian historians tend to use both terms in a loose, dichotomous sense.
15. The praśasti of the Ādi-Bhañjas explains this reference by telling us that Gaṇadaṇḍa Vīrabhadra, the progenitor of the lineage, burst out of the egg of a peahen in the great hermitage of Koṭyāśrama, where he was reared by the great ṛṣi Vasiṣṭha. The further elaboration of this story introduces us to the 88,000 sons of Vīrabhadra. It says that due to the prayers of these sons, Vīrabhadra was protected by Rāmadeva and made lord of 88,000 villages.
16. The Śailodbhava origin myth speaks of a man named Pulindasena, famed among the people of Kaliṅga. Although endowed with virtue, strength, and greatness, he did not covet sovereignty, but worshipped the Svayambhū for a man capable of ruling the earth. He obtained this boon, and saw a man emerging from the splintering of a rock. This was the lord Śailodbhava, who became the founder of the illustrious lineage.
17. The Chandeswar plates of Mādhavavarman's grandson Dharmarāja credit Dharmarāja with having taken the purificatory bath on the occasion of the performance of the Aśvamedha and the Vājapeya. While this may represent a second performance or at least a claim to the performance of these sacrifices by a Śailodbhava king, it may also be a reference to or echo of the events of Mādhavavarman's reign. The timing of Mādhavavarman's performance of the sacrifices can be connected to his throwing off allegiance to Śaśānka and his assumption of an independent status.
18. F. Kielhorn, 'Buguda Plates of Mādhavavarman,' *Epigraphia Indica* 3 (1894-5), p. 44, v. 11.
19. On Stambheśvarī, see A. Eschmann, 'Hinduization of Tribal Deities in Orissa: The Śākta and Śaiva Typology', in A. Eschmann, H. Kulke and

G. C. Tripathi, eds., *The Cult of Jagannath and the Regional Tradition of Orissa* (New Delhi, 1978, pp. 79-98).

20. *Gotra* is the patrimonial exogamous clan system of the brāhmaṇas. The *gotras* are divided into *gaṇas*, each of which have their own *pravara*. The *pravara* consists of the name or names (one, two, three, or five) of supposed ancestral *ṛṣis*. The *pravara* of the various members of a particular *gaṇa* have the name of the eponymous *gotra ṛṣi* in common. In course of time, as the boundaries of the *gotra* came to acquire a certain elasticity, the *pravara* came to form a more precise basis for defining the exogamous group. *Anupravara* is a term that we do not encounter in the Sūtra literature. In the inscriptions of Orissa, it seems to have had much the same connotations as the *pravara*.
21. The Neulpur plate records a grant made in favour of 200 brāhmaṇas of the four Vedas, including the *Atharva Veda*. The donees are described as *caturvidya* brāhmaṇas belonging to various *gotras* and *caranas*, representing more or less equally caraṇas schools of the four Vedas (*Bahvrca*, *Vājasaneya*, *Chāndīśa*, and *Atharva*). R. D. Banerji, 'Neulpur Plate of Subhakara', *Epigraphia Indica* 15 (1919-20), pp. 1-8.
22. The inscriptions which associate the donees with ritual expertise are the two grants of Pṛthivi-mahārāja, the Midnapore plate of Śubhakīrti, the Bonda plates of the Pāṇḍuvaṁśī king Tīvara, the Dhenkanal plate of the Śulkī king Raṇastambha, and the Baripada plates of the Nandodbhava king Devānanda.
23. The following inscriptions do make such associations: The Kanas plates of Lokavigraha and Bhānudatta associate Brāhmaṇas of the Maitrāyaṇīya school with the *maṭha* of Maṇināgeśvara. The Indian Museum plates of the Śvetaka Gaṅga king Indravarman associate certain brāhmaṇas with a temple of Mādhava and Svayambhū. The Visakhapatnam plates of the Kaliṅganagara Gaṅga king Devendravarman describe a brāhmaṇa named Somācārya as the superintendent of a shrine of Dharmeśvara-bhaṭṭāraka. The Terundia plate of the Bhauma-Kara king Śubhākara II records a grant to six brāhmaṇas for the upkeep of the *maṭhas* and *maṇḍapas* established by these brāhmaṇas in their native village. The two sets of the Baudh plates of the Bhauma-Kara queen Tribhuvanamahādevī associate certain brāhmaṇas with a temple of Umā-Maheśvara. The Madras Museum plates of the imperial Gaṅga king Vajrahasta associate the Brāhmaṇa donees with a temple of the god Koṭīśvaradeva. The Murupaka grant of the imperial Gaṅga king Anantavarman Coḍagaṅga entrusted the protection of the temple of the deity Narendreśvaradeva to five brāhmaṇas of the village.
24. *Manu* 4. 218 and *Mahābhārata* 13.35.23 state that the food and gifts of a king take away a brāhmaṇa's lustre. The *Yajñavalkya Smṛti* (1. 213) states that a brāhmaṇa, who though entitled, does not accept a gift, attains the highest world. *Manu* 4. 186 asserts that a brāhmaṇa should not frequently

resort to accepting gifts as this leads to the loss of his spiritual power.

25. Two of these instances come from Period I, four from Period II and seven from Period III. In Period I, there are the Bobbili plates of Candavarman and the Ningondi plates of the Māṭhara king Prabhañjanavarman. In Period II, we have the Ganjam grant of the Śvetaka Gaṅga king Prthvīvarmadeva, the Kalahandi grant of the Kaliṅganagara Gaṅga king Vajrahasta, the Chicacole grant of the Kaliṅganagara Gaṅga king Anantavarman, and the Angul plate of the Bhauma Kara queen Dharmamāhadevī. In Period III, there are the following records of tax-paying grants: the Jurada plates of Neṭṭabhañja, the Talcher plate of the Śulkī king Kulastambha, the Puri plate of the Śulkī king Kulastambha, the Talcher plate of the Tuṅga king Gayāḍatuṅga, the Asiatic Society plate of the same king, and the two sets of the Patna plates of the Somavaṁśī king Janamejaya Mahābhavagupta.
26. N. Lahiri, *Pre-Ahom Assam: Studies in the Inscriptions of Assam between the Fifth and the Thirteenth Centuries AD* (New Delhi, 1991), p. 137.
27. Cynthia Talbot, *Precolonial India in Practice: Society, Region, and Identity in Medieval Andhra* (New Delhi, 2001, p. 44).
28. Veluthat, *op. cit.*, p. 209.
29. The literary and epigraphic evidence for royal grants goes back many centuries. In the Gupta period, there are few land grants made by the Imperial Guptas and many more made by subordinate rulers. However, the significant proliferation of land grants in different parts of the subcontinent and their becoming an important component of royal policy are features that can be associated with the post-Gupta period.
30. There are two such instances in Period II. The Chicacole plates of the Kaliṅganagara Gaṅga king Devendravarman record an endowment to 300 brāhmaṇas, and the Neulpur plates of the Bhauma-Kara king Śubhākara records a grant to 200 brāhmaṇas (though 202 donees are actually named).
31. Talbot's analysis of the Andhra inscriptions brings out the close connection between strong polities and high levels of epigraphic production (mostly donative records) in a contiguous region (Talbot, *op. cit.*).
32. This issue has been addressed by Kulke ('Royal Temple Policy. . .'). He talks of vertical legitimation through the patronage of autochthonous deities and horizontal legitimation through the building and patronage of imperial temples. He presents the Gaṅga patronage of the Jagannātha temple as a combination of both kinds of legitimation processes.
33. Kulke has directed attention to Max Weber's important contribution to the understanding of such issues ('Max Weber's Contribution to the Study of "Hinduization" in India and "Indianization" in Southeast Asia', in H. Kulke, *Kings and Cults: State Formation and Legitimation in India and Southeast Asia*, New Delhi, 2001, pp. 240-61).
34. See B. D. Chattopadhyaya, 'Trade and Urban Centres in Early Medieval North India', and 'Urban Centres in Early Medieval India', in *The Making*

of Early Medieval India, pp. 130-54 and 155-82. The evidence from south India does not fit in with the hypothesis of a decline in trade and urban centres. Further, Wink's insistence (*Al-Hind*...) that we look at the Indian subcontinent as part of a broader world that was becoming increasingly knit together through trade and politics is persuasive. Wink, however, seems to go to the other extreme by inflating the role played by the Indian Ocean trade in the political history of the dynasties of early medieval India.

35. Recent studies suggest that it also suits other areas such as Andhra (Talbot, *op. cit.*), Bengal (Chakrabarti, *op. cit.*), and Rajasthan (Nandini Sinha-Kapoor, *State Formation in Rajasthan: Mewar during the Seventh-Fifteenth Centuries*, New Delhi, 2002).

CHAPTER 11

Rabindranath Tagore in Myanmar and His Perception of Southeast Asia–India Relations

SWAPNA BHATTACHARYA

This paper deals with a number of issues, widely spread thematically and chronologically, on Rabindranath Tagore (1861-1941) and his vision of the Hindu-Buddhist past. Interestingly, and not unexpectedly, his vision of a federated and unified Asia never challenged the existence of other religions. But Tagore had a special admiration for Buddhism with all its great and little traditions. We shall first deal with Tagore's deep commitment to Buddhism and his evaluation of it as an alternative religion for Asia, if not for all humanity. His visits to Java, Sumatra, Siam, and Burma as well as his visit to Japan and China, should be taken more seriously than the scholarly world has done so far. In the second part of the essay I have concentrated on his three visits (1916, 1924 and 1927) to modern Myanmar (Burma*). What strikes me is that in contrasty to many Indians, historians included, Tagore's perception of the individuality of the Burmese people is remarkable. While in Burma he felt so much at home that he wanted to stay, taking a respite from the material world, in any of the Buddhist monasteries there. I have tried to prove that the old contact between eastern India (Bengal–Bihar in particular) and Southeast Asia (Java–Sumatra, Siam, Burma) became a source of inspiration for Tagore. He was hopeful that Buddhism, in spite of its untimely 'disappearance' in eastern India, would be rejuvenated solving many problems that British-India had been facing in the 1920s

* Since the article deals with an earlier period, the old name Burma will be mostly used.

and 1930s. The Buddha's message of love, compassion, and tolerance remained his inspiration throughout his life.

I have been motivated by certain academic compulsions in writing this particular piece for Professor Hermann Kulke: I owe my knowledge of the history of early Southeast Asia to him, for he taught me the history of the early Indianized states of Southeast Asia at Heidelberg. Kulke's writings on the impact of the legitimizing principles of early state formation of India on local, regional and imperial cults have considerably enriched scholarly understanding of Southeast Asia in the context of Indian experiences. With just the example of the *Devarāja* (God-king) cult of ancient Cambodia Kulke (1993: 325-79), demonstrated the confluence of religious practices popular in the domains of Śaivism, Vaiṣṇavism and Mahāyāna Buddhism, which found their home in Angkor Wat and Bayon. Research on influences on the *Devarāja* cult from India, China, Yunnan, Chenla, Champa and Indonesia from the very early period, and its continuity into the modern period, only prove the spiritual and material creativity of ancient Cambodia. Whether Kulke writes on pre-colonial states of India (1997) or Southeast Asia (1990, 1993), the question remains the same: how 'small' or 'big' they were in the early medieval period. So far I understand him he said that the early state was neither big nor small, but it was operative at many levels because of its religious and moral authority. That is why it was a legitimized state (Kulke 1993: 294-379) and Kulke would certainly agree that direct contacts with India in many ways kept the legitimating traditions alive at lower levels and at the level of empire. Necessary monetary resources were kept flowing to remind the people of the kingdoms (Angkor of the ancient Khmers, the Śailendras and Śrīvijayas) that Buddhism was not to be imprisoned in the rigid Theravāda monastic principles. Hinduism did not mean only the supremacy of a certain cult or a particular caste, but it was the confluence of faiths coming from a country where the Buddha was born. The popularity of Mahāyāna Buddhism in ancient Burma, Indonesia, and Cambodia not only made Śaivism and Vaiṣṇavism acceptable but these faiths penetrated deeper into the societies (also Tarling 1992, Vol. I: 286-304).

RABINDRANATH TAGORE'S EXPERIENCES IN SOUTHEAST ASIA AND HIS PERCEPTION OF A COMMON HINDU-BUDDHIST PAST

During his long life Rabindranath Tagore (1861-1941) came to feel impelled to discover for himself how India was present in the societies of Southeast Asia. Had he been an orthodox Hindu, Tagore would not have done that, or would have done it with a strong prejudice, but he was born into a family in which Buddhist values were upheld and honoured. Many important writings on Tagore (in Bengali) highlighting his Buddhist background have remained neglected, even partially forgotten. I have had the privilege to see and hear a number of scholars who had enjoyed Tagore's patronage in their studies on Pali, Buddhism and Sanskrit, at Viśva Bhāratī. Many historians are oblivious of the fact that Rabindranath Tagore widely travelled across Asia and wrote important accounts of what we call the 'Indianized states'. I attempt here to bridge the gap between early and modern Southeast Asia, placing Tagore in the middle in his role as a nationalist and internationalist, as a propagator of Pan-Asianism and Western rationality, as a lover of 'Indianization' and 'Indigenization' (Mabbett 1977).

Tagore's Vision of a common Hindu-Buddhist past of Asia (Dutta and Robinson 2000: 277, Aronson 1978: 47) in the context a pan-Asian nationalism has not been adequately studied. It went back to a past when a federation of Asia stretching from Burma to Japan was united in close ties with India. Tagore (1985: 35). As Dutta and Robinson have stated, his visit to Holland in the early 1920s and his exposure to Dutch scholarship on that region provided an impetus for that. Tagore was concerned not only with the awakening of India from the deep slumber of colonialism, he was equally concerned with other countries in the same state of colonial domination (for example, Indonesia and Burma). He believed that India, on its way to freedom, could make common cause with Burma, Ceylon (Sri Lanka), Indonesia, Malayasia, China, and Japan. Indeed, in this endeavour he was so keen that he established a centre for Chinese studies in Santiniketan in the year 1937 (Woodman 1969: 14). He deeply wished that China should become a partner in India's mission for the achievement of an Asian unity.

Tagore had earlier been fascinated (Tagore 1985: 29-57) by Japan's cultural and economic strength in not succumbing to western colonialism; but to China his suggestion was to come closer to India. He wanted the people of China to remember that past in which Chinese pilgrims had come to India to study Buddhism. Siam or modern Thailand fascinated him too, and later he developed a very close relation with that country. Like Japan, Thailand also had that political will not to succumb to colonial pressure, though we know that it could 'save' itself only under extreme political constraints (Tarling 1992, Vol. 2: 291-3). Tagore admired the wealth of Buddhist values traditionally existent in the societies of Burma and Ceylon. And even though Islam came to 'conquer' Malaya, Java, and Sumatra, he was fascinated by the way those countries assimilated the plurality of faiths in a most spontaneous and syncretic way. Hindu Bali reminded Tagore of a Hindu past (*Rabīndra Rachanāvalī*, Vol. 12: 293 ff).

Even so, Tagore was not primarily concerned with 'religion' as such. He saw things beyond religions and in those countries what fascinated him was how Hinduism and Buddhism amalgamated with each other without entering into conflict. I strongly believe that the old contact between the Śailendra dynasty of Java and the Buddhist centre of Nalanda played on his mind (Bhattacharaya 1985: 154, Inscription no. 33). In fact throughout his life he felt committed to remind the Bengalis that Bengal had a pluralist and liberal religious tradition, in which the impact of Buddhism and Vaiṣṇavism occupied a special position. By this he denied the existence of both orthodox Islam and orthodox Brahmanism (Hinduism) in pre-colonial Bengal.

Rites and rituals that he saw for himself in Bali reminded Tagore of a past that India herself had forgotten (*Rabīndra Rachanāvalī*, Vol. 12: 95). What fascinated him was how the people of Bali moulded the Indian epics according to their own choice, not binding themselves in obligation to follow the Indian version. Indian religion and Indian customs found new expressions in Java, Sumatra, and Bali. Tagore's remark about the people of Bali ('their style is Indian but their bodies are indigenous', *Rabīndra Rachanāvalī*, Vol. 12: 293) indicates his deep understanding of the indigenous psyche of its people. The address given by Tagore in the farewell reception organized by the Greater India Society on the eve of his journey to Java is also noteworthy in this connection. On the one hand, he was overwhelmed by the occasion, on the other hand he cautioned his countrymen against certain prejudices. Let me translate a portion of his critical speech:

> When people are really poor, they search for outside glory. They engage in futile academic exercises quoting *ślokas* from obscure manuscripts. We should feel ashamed if we make a noise about our past glory. We would only insult the truth if we take pride in an irrational manner. If we search for our glory outside the boundary of our country, it should be done in the interest of our own satisfaction. Before going to Java I must free my mind from all pride and prejudices. I must be honest to myself why I am undertaking this trip. I must find the *mantra* of the *Maitree*, which was the eternal *mantra* of our country. Thus, my mind would be able to clear the jungle and build the temple; when desert will turn into oasis, my life will be fulfilled. (*Rabīndra Rachanāvalī*, Vol. 13: 670-1)

The Greater India Society, established in 1926 to make Indians aware of their cultural contribution to the countries east of India, had a difficult mission. In this academic forum Tagore urged Indians to 'look east' to discover their own virtues, instead of proving only the merit of their virtues in the form of the cultural debt of the peoples of Southeast Asia.

With these ideas he visited several countries. One should not forget that the Indian business community, also deeply committed to promote Hindu-Buddhist-Muslim harmony not only in India, but also in countries beyond the geographical boundary of India, was also interested in promoting Tagore. It is known that Sri Jugal Kishor Birla undertook the expenses of Tagore's 1924, tour to Burma, China, and Japan (Dutta 1993: 995). An atmosphere of communal harmony (Rothermund 2000: 1-35) was needed in India and abroad. Nationalism (Rothermund 1970) developed in a different and difficult way in India as two different consciousness – one Hindu and the other of a large section of Muslim Indians. This kind of religious polar-ization was not visible, however, in Southeast Asia. Burma, with the largest Indian population there (Chakravarty 1971; Bhattacharya forthcoming), had as many Hindus as Muslims. Tagore was aware that not only India, but also Buddhist majority countries east of India had also non-Buddhist Muslim and Christian populations. While he was much impressed by the pluralist ethnic composition and relative calm and harmony of those societies, he was particularly impressed by the Buddhist tradition of Siam and Burma.

Burma's attachment to British India, in which position it remained until April 1937, has made things related to Burma 'less interesting' for historians and laymen (see Bhattacharya 1996). Separation meant only administrative separation; the British needed Burma for India and India for Burma until both got their independence (Taylor 1987). Tagore was disappointed to see that the Indians had nearly forgotten that India had a Buddhist past, he saw that the Buddha's message of sacrifice and tolerance could solve many knotty problems in the country. Of course, there were other issues around which three trips of Rabindranath Tagore to Burma (1916, 1924 and 1927) were organized. He saw in Burma a very living Buddhism; the same he saw also in Siam (Thailand), when he visited Bangkok in October 1927. He was given a tremendous ovation at the Chulalongkorn University when he visited it to deliver lectures (Barua 1967: 65).

Tagore seemed to be impressed by royal patronage to brahmans, in these countries, even as brahmanic domination remained absent (see Ray 1998: 133). More attractive to Tagore was the way people of those countries followed the path of Lord Buddha, whom Rabindranath called the supreme human being ever born in this earth (*Rabīndra Rachanāvalī*, Vol. 11: 255-7).

Tagore sent scholars from Santiniketan to Buddhist countries like Thailand, Burma, and Ceylon in particular. With this mission Nityananda Vinod Goswami, an eminent Pali and Buddhist scholar and teacher at Patha Bhavan, was sent to Ceylon and Burma. With the spirit 'charity begins at home' Tagore asked his son Rathindranath to learn Pali with Vidhusekhar Shastri. Prabodh Chandra Sen (1962) describes the impact of Buddhist philosophy on Tagore. His son Rathindranath translated Aśvaghoṣa's *Buddhacarita* into Bengali in 1906. Sylvain Lévi, was one of the Indologists promoting Buddhist studies in Santiniketan in the early 1920s. Tagore's deep commitment to Buddhism made him a frequent visitor to Bodhgaya. At least two visits are known to us – in 1904 and again in 1914. Krishna Kripalani, the noted biographer of Rabindranath Tagore, observed: 'only once in his life, said Rabindranath, did he feel like prostrating himself before an image, and that was when he saw the Buddha at Gaya'. (Barua 1967: 45). Barua has shown that in several writings, Tagore would suddenly bring up the subject of the Buddha and His life. The Buddhist kingdoms of Asia captured his mind. In his famous novel

Shesher Kavitā, one of the characters, Shobhanlal, was described as interested in tracing the old Buddhist route to India from China via Afghanistan (Barua 1967: 175; O. von Hinüber in Bechert and Gombrich 1993: 99-107). For historians it is interesting to note that just two years before the publication of *Shesher Kavitā*, Tagore had been in Java, Bali, and Siam. During that trip (1927) he also was for the last time in Burma.

Tagore was not only aware that Afghanistan played an important role in the mission of preaching and practising Buddhist values, he was also aware of the sea route through which Buddhism wandered – from the South China Sea into the Indian Ocean – via the Indonesian Islands and Ceylon to the Indian ports. Tamralipti of Bengal (Tamluk in Midnapore district) was a well established port of disembarkation from travellers from the Far East (Dutta, 1988: 295). In the famous Kalyānī Inscription from the period of King Dhammaceti of Burma (1472-92) reference has been made that one of the four theras, well-versed in the *Tripiṭaka*, who came to lower Burma to rejuvenate the Buddhist spirit, hailed from Tāmalitti (the others were from Kāñcīpuram and Laṅkādvīpa.) There is no doubt that Tāmalitti is the Tamralipti port which carries the memory of a Buddhist heritage nurtured by, among others, maritime contact between eastern India and lower Burma (Bhattacharya 1997: 60).

Rabindranath Tagore extensively read the Buddhist *Avadāna*, *Jātakas* and *Dhammapada*. His mission of promoting the spirit of Buddhism among the people of India was so serious that he wrote a number of poems, short stories, and dramas using Buddhist plots, moulding the stories in his own unique way (Das 1967; Barua 1967). In this mission he was influenced by Rajendralal Mitra's *Sanskrit Buddhist Literature of Nepal*. Tagore composed such pieces to preach the message of tolerance, love, and compassion. No less interested he was in protesting against caste oppression and the meaningless rituals which had made Buddhism unintelligible to the masses. He was quite aware that an overdose of Tantric rituals (Bechert and Gombrich 1993) and esoteric rites brought about the decline of Buddhism in Bengal in the twelfth and thirteenth centuries (Niyogi 1980). Protest against this ritualism and esoteric practices and also against orthodoxy in all religions in general became clear in Tagore's famous *Achalāyatan*. The message was to create a new edifice of human relations by destroying the old structure. This, one of his most symbolic works, has been interpreted by Barua as one of the very few in which the decadence of contemporary Buddhism was denounced (Barua 1967: 163).

Chaṇḍālika attests to Tagore's commitment to Buddhism – which does not tolerate untouchability. In *Chaṇḍālika* (The Untouchable Maiden) Tagore narrated the story of Prakriti, who belonged to the Caṇḍāla caste. Ānanda, the famous disciple of Lord Buddha once drank water served by this girl and she felt so confident after this that she tried to drag the monk from his renunciation to an abject desire for her. She lost all religious scruples of fear, for she owed nothing to her religion, which had disowned her. She forced her mother to exercise her art of magic on Ānanda. This indicates that Tagore was aware of the 'might' of magic, wonders, and external rituals that had entered the domain of Hindu-Buddhist society. Initially Prakriti's mother was successful and Ānanda was dragged to their door with a distorted face full of shame. But suddenly things changed: his face became full of joy – joy at winning over the Māra in himself and also winning the girl. Prakriti cursed herself, but ultimately surrendered and fell at Ānanda's feet.

Tagore's commitment to Buddhism was the most inspiring factor in his engagement with the Greater India Society. This Society was born in Calcutta in 1926, with eminent Indian scholars as members: B. N. Puri, R. C. Majumdar, B. C. Chhabra, N. K. Sastri, K. Nag, P. C. Bagchi, and others who felt that India's religious and cultural influence in countries east of India should be studied in the context of a 'greater Indian perspective' (see, for example, Majumdar 1991; Nag 1926).

Tagore did not feel complacent about the Indian influence; instead, he admired the way the people of Southeast Asia had moulded their own cultures, not actually rejecting their indebtedness to India. Concerned with the common roots of South and Southeast Asian civilization, he saw the dangers in overdoing the exercise of tracing influences, especially at a point of time when those countries were struggling for their own political emancipation from colonial power. Tagore was against ultra-nationalism and the physical boundaries of nations were not his concern. His major concern was crushing the geographical barriers by creating a more natural boundary of humanity. He said:

India has never had a real sense of nationalism. Even though from childhood I had been taught that idolatry of the nation is almost better than reverence for God and humanity, I believe I have outgrown that teaching, and it is my conviction that my countrymen will truly gain their India by fighting against the education which teaches them that a country is greater than the ideals of humanity. (Macmillan Pocket Tagore Edition 1988: 105)

If we compare a few words from Tagore's essay 'Buddhadev' (*Rabīndra Rachanāvalī*, Vol. 11), we find that his vision went much beyond Southeast Asia. He saw 'India' in Japan, China, Mongolia and Tibet, writing that it was the Buddha who took the message of *Bhārat* to various parts of Asia.

In Java, Tagore remarked that he had seen an element of *bhakti* (*Rabīndra Rachanāvalī*, Vol. 11: 256-7) expressed in the creation of hundreds of images of the Buddha, depicting various stories from *Jātakas*. Those who toiled for days and nights to create these images had shown how much they revered Buddha and his messages. The greatest message of love and compassion was shown by the truest disciple, king Aśoka, who through his inscriptions preached the supreme *dhamma*, the spirit of *ahiṁsā*.

THREE VISITS TO BURMA

Rabindranath went to Rangoon en route to Japan and America in 1916. His *Jāpanjātrī* (*Rabīndra Rachanāvalī*, Vol. 12: 149-90; first pub. 1919) was dedicated to Ramananda Chattopadhyay, the editor of *Modern Review*. In this we have some two or three pages containing impressions of Rangoon. He was on board a Japanese ship with William Winstanley Pearson and Charles Freer Andrews, two English missionaries, who were life-long disciples of Rabindranath, and the famous artist Mukul De.

Tagore's first view of Rangoon shocked him: long chimneys of mills raised their heads to the sky. Ships from various parts of the world swallowed the beautiful Burmese city quite mercilessly, while long rows of jetties were sucking its blood. Rangoon was so dominated by this heartless cruel commercial goddess (*Vānijyalakṣmī*) that one could easily say that it was 'existent in the map of Burma, but not in Burma itself' (*Rabīndra Rachanāvalī*, Vol. 12: 156). This metropolitan city had not grown from its own soil, it had come floating from elsewhere, and thus, Tagore gave the epithet 'obstruction' to it

(Mukhopadhyay 1961: 451). Tagore drew parallels between Rangoon and Calcutta. In Calcutta also he saw the presence of the same brutal goddess of commerce.

Yet, in Rangoon was a corner where Tagore could find the entire country accredited. This was the precinct of the Shwedagong pagoda. Entering the pagoda premises Tagore felt that Rangoon suddenly became smaller. He understood that Shwedagong was the fulcrum of the past, present, and the future of Burma, but somehow was 'disappointed' with the inner and outer atmosphere of this great pagoda (*Rabīndra Rachanāvalī*, Vol. 12: 158). He was amazed to see the calm and the peace in Burmese people, but found them 'too easy going' (*ibid.*) even though he was aware that the hearts of the Burmese people were burning for freedom from the British. He saw Burmese Buddhist women doing their own business of selling candles, flowers and other articles for *pūjā*. Around the Pagoda he saw stationery shops run by Burmese Muslims, comfortably at home with their business in Burma. People visiting the Pagoda were free to eat meat, fish, or whatever they wanted. Everywhere he saw a spirit of freedom, and the courage to crush useless social barriers. Tagore asked one of his Burmese friends about this freedom of activity in and around the religious sacred premises. He was told that the Buddha never said 'no' to anything. Buddha merely said what he himself found 'good' and what he found 'bad'; thus there was no sense in restricting anything externally. The real *mukti* would come from inner soul. Therefore, it hardly mattered whether someone ate meat or fish or anything else in the surroundings of the pagoda. Genuine freedom would come from the inner soul. This left a deep impression on Tagore's Buddhist mind.

During this short visit to Rangoon, Tagore once was impressed by the women of Burma, moving on streets, in commercial centres, in temple premises-indeed everywhere he went around. This was not yet a commonly sight in India. Tagore remarked that it was not merely that they went out of the home, but that they could undertake whatever work they wanted. That was what made them so unique.

On the day of the departure from Rangoon Tagore was writing to his daughter-in-law, Pratima Devi, that his inner soul did not permit him to leave this beautiful country. He wished he could spend a few months in one of the monasteries of Burma, withdrawing from the world. He was also writing about the reception given to him by the people of Rangoon. The Burmese aesthetic sense and art of engraving had impressed him greatly. He also wrote about the gentleness of the Burmese people (Pal 1997: 174).

The second visit to Burma took place in March 1924, on the way to China. From China Tagore went to Japan again. Accounts of this visit are found in *At the Crossroad: Autobiography of Nripendra Chandra Banerji*, and in Kalidas Nag's *Kavir Saṅge Akśodin* ('Hundred Days with the Poet'). N. C. Banerji was the editor of *The Rangoon Mail*, a newspaper run by the Indians in Burma, publishing matters relating to Congress politics at the national level. Bengal politics too had good coverage in this paper. N. C. Banerji, who was called from India to work as the editor of *The Rangoon Mail* (1924-7) was Rabindranath's host in Rangoon. Other personalities who accompanied the poet on this trip were Kalidas Nag, Leonard Elmherst, Miss Green, Prof. Kshiti Mohan Sen, and Prof. (artist) Nand Lal Bose. But the 'Tagore Reception Committee' was formed with other eminent members from various communities as well. Burmese professors, a few lawyers, leading Gujarati businessmen, some Europeans and Chinese residents of Rangoon were also included in the Committee (N.C. Banerji 1974: 160). The *Rangoon Mail*, the *Rangoon Daily News* and other Burmese news agencies did their job in giving coverage to this visit. The *Rangoon Mail* wrote: 'May we in India and Burma rise to a proper comprehension of Rabindranath's message and his work! In honouring such a personality, in helping the cause which he holds so dear, Burma will only be honouring the best in her own soul' (Dutta 1993: 995). Kalidas Nag (1986) informs us that intellectuals and philosophers of both countries came together on the occasion of this visit. Discussions were held on Indo-Burmese relations, Bengal's contact with Burma, Buddhist psychology, philosophy, and religion.

The third visit of Rabindranath Tagore to Burma took place in October 1927, on his way back from Malaya, Bali, Java and Siam. The eminent linguist Suniti Kumar Chatterji was invited to accompany the poet on this journey, which took three months. Though accounts of this trip were published in Bengali journal *Pravāsī* and later also in *Viśva Bhāratī Patrikā,* the most detailed account in a single work is found in *Rabīndrasaṅgame Dvīpamay Bhārat O Shyāmdesh* (S. K. Chatterji 1980).

What purpose did Tagore's visits to Burma serve? Apparently, India–Burma relations had reached a point of 'no return' in the 1920s, leading to the separation of India from Burma in April 1937 (Cady 1960). Tagore was quite sure that Burma would find her way to freedom on her own, no matter whether the country administratively remained attached to India or not. Therefore, he was more concerned to promote a robust and sustaining friendship between the two countries – a mission in which both the countries could depend upon their Buddhist past.

CONCLUSION

Rabindranath's experiences with Burma appear to be an extremely interesting chapter of his life. On the one hand, he was free of many prejudices that occasionally influenced one or the other 'Greater India' enthusiasts. N. R. Ray's book *Sanskrit Buddhism in Burma* (1936) as well as his other books and articles on Burma bear testimony to his deep appreciation for Burma's continuity in sustaining the Buddhist heritage. But, in a way, he was an exception. K. Nag, a scholar on Asia, looked at Burma and Ceylon with a certain prejudice, bringing the two counties too much under the shadow of India. Tagore did not do that; instead, he saw in Burma many things which appeared to him admirable and worthy to be followed by India. The position of women in the Burmese society, for example, impressed him. Unfortunately Tagore did not make any observations on old Burma. One wonders why he did not pay a visit to the Buddhist sites in Pagan. Nevertheless, his sharp observation on the rapid and crude urbanization of Rangoon is remarkable. Describing the city of Rangoon as an 'obstruction' he felt sorry for the local people, who were cornered by the dominating business groups whether Indian, Chinese, Burmese or English. In fact, Rangoon appeared to him a 'City of Protest'. The Bengali residents, of whom there were thousands, making Rangoon (modern Yangon) their home, responded tremendously to Rabindranath. When he arrived in 1916, for the first time, a crowd shouting 'Bharat Mata ki Jai, Rabindranath ki Jai,' received him. For Bengalis, both from India and modern Bangladesh, it is significant that for the first time Tagore was received outside India by a welcome address in Bengali.

It is known to Myanmar scholars that Thakin Kodow Hmaing, the great poet and patriot of Burma, is called the 'Tagore of Burma' (Kyi 1991: 115; Dutta 1993: 998). Following Tagore's rejection of a Knighthood, he rejected a similar British offer (Dutta 1993: 998). In the years following the independence of Burma, Tagore's *Gītāñjali*, *Sonār Tarī*, *Janmadin*, and *Sphuliṅga* were translated into Burmese. It is often argued that the Burmanization (or the appointment of Burmese in public posts and vacancies) process in colonial Burma isolated the domiciled Indian community, causing the deterioration of Indo–Burma relations. If one considers that Rabindranath was in the forefront of the national education movement (Sen 1947), for education in the vernacular and freedom of thought in education, one certainly understands why Burma in the 1920s honoured Tagore. In 1916, he said, the Nation was the highest evil for the nation (*ibid.*: 134). Not bogged down by the developments during the First World War, Tagore went on with his mission for universal brotherhood, founding his dream institution, Viśva Bhāratī, in 1918.

Thus, we see that his visit to Burma in 1916 took place in a very critical and creative phase of his life.

One of the most urgent issues, which occupied the young Burmese nationalists in the 1920s, was national education. The entire Boycott Movement in 1920 (Aye Kyaw 1993: 20-34) against the University Bill was aimed for issues, so dear to Indain nationalists. For this cause Tagore stood always in the forefront. Both countries were on the same mission of achieving self-rule through promotion of national values. Indeed, as Aye Kyaw has shown, the Indian National Congress also supported the University Boycott Movement in Rangoon. In conclusion I must remind the reader that U Ottama (Chakravarty 1977: 36-42; Maung Maung 1980), the forerunner of the Pongyi (monk)-led nationalist movement of the 1920s, was an admirer of Tagore. In *His Message from Burma*, Bhikkhu Ottama wrote: 'As a messenger of peace and a missionary of human brotherhood, [Tagore] has travelled far and wide, and he has worked strenuously to bind the East and the West together with the golden tie of Love. His life and ideals will long inspire all workers in the cause of humanity' (Bhikkhu Ottama 1931: 186).

Readers must have noticed that in this contribution I am engaged not so much in the debate of Indianization, for I believe on reading

Tagore carefully many debates on the issue become superfluous. I am more concerned with the aspiration to link the past of Southeast Asia with the present.

In this exercise, Kulke's writings on the early city and state of Indonesia and Cambodia (1990, 1993) deserve special mention. He has divided the process of state formation in three phases: chiefdom or local principality, early kingdom, and imperial kingdom. Using Sanskrit names for territorial units, the rulers of Śrivijaya and Śailendra kingdoms of Java and Sumatra created their own realms of power. It is interesting to note that Kulke has not forgotten to stress the old contact between Bengal and Indonesia. Referring to a central Javanese inscription of the year 782, he says that the inscription itself 'reports the consecration of a Mañjuśrī image by a Śailendra king and his *guru* who had come from Bengal (*gauḍidvīpa*)'. The image was installed by the king in order to protect 'his *deśa*' (*deśasya tasya*). Kulke is of the opinion that *deśa* here means the king's *Stammland* or *watek* (Kulke 1993: 317). No matter how big or small the king's actual domains was, his conviction about Buddhism and his regard for Bengal's Buddhist heritage is remarkable. The Boddhisattva Mañjuśrī was a popular deity as early as the Gupta period. N. Dasgupta's work (in Bengali) testifies to her popularity. Even during the Pāla period this particular deity of the Buddhist pantheon, representing wisdom, was widely worshipped in Bengal (Dasgupta: 136). Dutta's path-breaking *Buddhist Monks and Monasteries in India* legitimately stresses the role of *bhakti* among the Buddhists of Asia. *Bhakti* to Boddhisattvas was common among the population of India and the Buddhist kingdoms of Southeast Asia. It was seen as a fruitful way to achieve the *nirvāṇa* (Dutta 1988: 179). When Rabindranath was in Borobudur (constructed between AD 760-860) in the autumn of 1927, looking at the hundreds of Buddhist images taken from the *Jātakas* he wondered how much *bhakti* the people of this ancient state had for creating such a monument *Rabīndra Rachanāvalī*, Vol. 11: 257). I have referred to Kulke's observations regarding the popularity of Mahāyāna Buddhist beliefs accommodating comfortably pluralism in religious faiths in Cambodia. His conclusions are based on hard historical sources, namely inscriptions, while Tagore's observations are in their major part expressions of his immediate reactions. To my understanding, both converge and uphold the central *bhakti,* which bound all sections of the people of South Asia and Southeast Asia, giving them an unique religous identity. The *bhakti* movement played a powerful role challenging sometime the dominance of brahmans or at least making them uncertain. This happened in all parts of India. Bhattacharya's valuable *Bāṅglār Vaiṣṇava-bhāvāpanna Musalman Kavi* (1962) bears evidence that even Muslim poets of eastern Bengal and Assam were inspired by Vaiṣṇavism. They wrote *padāvalīs* as naturally as they embraced Islam. It was this syncretism and tolerance that gave Tagore the inspiration for his several journeys across the world.

ACKNOWLEGEMENTS

I am thankful to Supriya Ray, Librarian, Rabindra Bhavan, University of Visva Bharati in Santiniketan, and Subimal Lahiri of Visva Bharati Granthan Vibhag (Publication Centre), Kolkata, for their assistance in locating some sources used in this paper.

REFERENCES

Aronson, Alex, *Rabindranath through Western Eyes*, Calcutta: Riddhi India, 1978a (1st pub. 1943).

Aye Kyaw, *The Voice of Young Burma*, Ithaca: Cornell University Press, 1993.

Banerji, Nripendra Chandra, *At the Crossroads 1885-1946: The Autobiography of Nripendra Chandra Banerji*, Calcutta: Jijñasa, 1974 (1st pub. 1950).

Barua, Sudhangsu Vimal, *Rabīndranāth O Bauddhasaṁskriti*, Calcutta, BE 1374 (CE 1967).

Bechert, Heinz and Richard Gombrich (eds.), *The World of Buddhism,* London: Thames & Hudson, 1993 (1st pub. 1984).

Bhattaçharya, Jatindra Mohan, *Bāṅglār Vaiṣṇava-bhāvāpanna Musalman Kavi,* Calcutta: Calcutta University, 1962 (1st edn. not mentioned).

Bhattacharya, Swapna, *Landschenkungen und Staatliche Entwicklung im frühmittelalterlichen Bengalen (5.bis 13.Jh.n.Chr.)*, Wiesbaden: Steiner-Verlag, 1985 (Beiträge zur Südasienforschung, No. 99).

———, 'Traditions of Myanmar Studies in India', in: *Traditions in Current Perspective. Proceedings of the Conference on Myanmar and Southeast Asian Studies*, Yangon: Universities Historical Research Centre, 1996: 10-24.

———, 'Some Observations on Mahāyāna Tantric Beliefs in Ancient Myanmar', in: *Journal of Ancient Indian History* (Calcutta University), 20 (1997): 52-67.

———, 'Indian Diaspora in Myanmar', in: *Indians in Diaspora*, volume to be ed. by Prof. Sarvadaman Singh and published by the Maulana Abul Kalam Azad Institute for Asian Studies, Kolkata (forthcoming).

Bhikkhu Ottama, 'Message from Burma', in: Ramananda Chattopadhyay (ed.), *The Golden Book of Tagore: A Homage to Rabindranath Tagore from India and the World in Celebration of His Seventieth Birthday,* Calcutta: Golden Book Committee, 1931: 186.

Cady, John F., *History of Modern Burma*, Ithaca: Cornell University Press, 1960.

Chakravarty, N. R., *The Indian Minority in Burma: The Rise and Decline of an Immigrant Community*, London: Oxford University Press, 1971.

Chakravarty, S. R., 'Bhikkhu U Ottama - An Advocate of Indo-Burmese Friendship', in: *Quarterly Review of Historical Studies*, 17, 2 (1977): 36-42.

Chatterji, Suniti Kumar, *Rabīndrasaṅgame Dvīpamay Bhārat O Shyāmdesh,* Calcutta: Prakash Bhavan, 1980 (1st pub. 1940).

Das, Asha, *Rabīndranāth O Bauddhadharma*, Calcutta: Kallol Prakashani, BE 1374 (CE 1967).

Dasgupta, Nalininath, *Bānglay Bauddhadharma*, Calcutta: A. Mukherjee & Co., undated.

Dutta, Bijit, 'Brahmadesh O Rabīndranāth', in: *Paschimbaṅga*, 1993 (BE 1400), Barsha 26, Nos. 42, 43 and 44 (Department of Information and Culture, Govt. of West Bengal), pp. 991-8.

Dutta, Krishna and Andrew Robinson, *Rabindranath Tagore: The myriad-minded man,* Calcutta: Rupa & Co., 2000 (1st Paperback edn. London, 1997).

Dutta, Sukumar, *Buddhist Monks and Monasteries of India*, Delhi: Motilal Banarsidass, 1988 (1st pub. London, 1962).

Kulke, Hermann, 'Indian Colonies, Indianization or Cultural Convergence? Reflections on the Changing Image of India's Role in South-East Asia', in: *Onderzoek in Zuidoost-Azie. Agenda's voor de jaren negentig*, ed. H. Schulte-Nordholt (= Semaian, 3), Rijksuniversiteit te Leiden, 1990: 8-32.

———, *Kings and Cults: State Formation and Legitimation in India and Southeast Asia*, New Delhi: Manohar, 1993.

——— (ed.), *The State in India 1000-1700*, New Delhi: Oxford University Press, 1997 (1st pub. 1995).

Kyi, Aung San Suu, *Freedom from Fear and other Writings*, New York: Penguin, 1991.

Mabbett, I. W., 'Indianization of Southeast Asia: Reflections on the Historical

Sources', in *Journal of Southeast Asian Studies* VIII, 1 (1977): 1-14, 2: 143-61.

Majumdar, R. C., *Hindu Colonies in the Far East*, Calcutta: Firma K. L. M., 1991 (1st pub. 1944).

Maung Maung, *From Sangha to Laity: Nationalist Movements of Burma 1920-1940* (Australia National University Monograph on South Asia, No. 4), New Delhi: Manohar, 1980.

Mukhopadhyaya, Prabhat Kumar, *Rabindrajībanī O Rabindrasahitya Prabeshak,* Vol. II, Calcutta: Visva Bharati, BE 1368 (CE 1961; 3rd enlg. edn.).

Nag, Kalidas, 'Greater India', in: *Greater India Society Bulletin* 1, 1926.

———, *Kavir Saṅge Akśodin*, Calcutta: Papyrus, BE 1394 (CE 1986).

Niyogi, Puspa, *Buddhism in Ancient Bengal*, Calcutta: Jijñasa, 1980.

Pal, Prashanta Kumar, *Rabijībanī, 1914-1920* (Vol. 7), Calcutta: Ananda Publishers, 1997.

Ray, Himanshu P., *Winds of Change: Buddhism and the Maritime Links of Early South Asia,* New Delhi: Oxford University Press, 1998 (1st pub. 1994).

Ray, Nihar Ranjan, *Sanskrit Buddhism in Burma,* Calcutta, 1936.

Rothermund, Dietmar, *The Phases of Indian Nationalism and Other Essays,* Bombay: Nachiketa Publishers Ltd., 1970.

———, *The Role of the State in South Asia and Other Essays*, New Delhi: Manohar, 2000.

Sen, Prabodh Chandra, *Bhārat Pathik Rabīndranāth*, Calcutta: A Mukherjee & Co., 1962.

Sen, Sachin, *The Political Thought of Tagore*, Calcutta: General Printers and Publishers Ltd., 1947.

Tagore, Rabindranath, *Nationalism,* Madras: Macmillan India, 1985 (appeared in 1950 and 1976).

———, 'Jāvāyātrīr Patra', in *Rabīndra Rachanāvalī*, Vol. 12, Calcutta: Govt. of West Bengal, 1990.

———, 'Jāpānyātrī', in *ibid.*

———, 'Buddhadev', in *ibid.*, Vol. 11 (1990).

———, 'Kālāntar', in *ibid.*, Vol. 13 (1990).

———, *Lectures and Addresses. Selected from the Speeches of the Poet by Anthony X. Soares*, Madras: Macmillan Pocket Tagore Edition, 1988.

Tarling, Nicholas (ed.), *Cambridge History of Southeast Asia*, Vols. 1 & 2, Cambridge: Cambridge University Press, 1992.

Taylor, Robert, *The State in Burma,* London: Orient Longman Ltd., 1987.

Woodman, Dorothy, *Himalayan Frontiers: A Political Review of British, Chinese, Indian and Russian Rivalries*, London: Barrie and Rockliff, The Cresset Press, 1969.

PART III

Politics of Identity and Culture

CHAPTER 12

The Oriya Movement and Singhbhum

NIVEDITA MOHANTY

The Oriya movement in the twentieth century seeking unification of all the Oriya speaking territories progressed in phases. The important achievements in the course of the movement were: 1905 when Sambalpur was united with the core Orissa, and 1936 when the province of Orissa was created in-corporating Ganjam, 1948-9 when twenty-four out of the twenty-six of the Orissan princely states were merged with Orissa. Of the important tracts that were left out were Midnapur, some pockets in western and southern Orissa and Singhbhum along with the two princely states of Seraikella and Kharswan. Seraikella and Kharswan and the rest of Singhbhum had all along occupied a special place in the hearts of the Oriyas and therefore their exclusion caused discontent. This sentiment found a strong expression in the form of a 'Boundary Agitation' when the States Reorganization Commission's verdict in 1956 went against the return of Singhbhum, especially that of Seraikella and Kharswan to Orissa. This was for all intents and purposes the last upsurge by the Oriyas that the century witnessed. When in November 2000, the new state of Jharkhand was constituted, one did hear some rumblings relating to the possible amalgamation of Seraikella and Kharswan with Orissa, but they never gathered any serious momentum.

This paper traces the history of the Oriya movement in Singhbhum, analyses its salient features, and attempts to identify the reasons for its failure. Such a study warrants some knowledge of the history of the region.

A BRIEF HISTORY OF THE REGION

Singhbhum constitutes the south-eastern part of the newly formed Jharkhand state and shares a border with Bengal on the east and with Orissa on the south and south-west. It can be identified with three current districts, viz., East Singhbhum, West Singhbhum and Seraikella-Kharswan. Believed to be a part of 'Utkala in earlier times,[1] the region was divided into the chiefdoms of Singhbhum and Dhalbhum in the medieval period named after their respective ruling chiefs.

THE LAND OF THE SINGHS

The chronicle of the Singh ruling dynasty known as the 'Vamsa Prabha Lekhana' is recorded on palm leaf in Oriya language; it is said to be maintained by a family of Dogras.[2] The original palm leaf manuscript having been affected by moth, was copied in AD 1643, by Maguni Rout Dogra. The chronicle traces the origin of the Singhs to the Rathore Rajput stock from Marwar. It mentions that there was an earlier Singh rule in the seventh century AD, although a chronological record is available only from the thirteenth century onwards. The record also informs us that in 1205 the first Singh ruler Darpa Narayan Singh was made the king of Venugarh by the 'Bathudi', 'Kat' and 'Paudi' clans of the Bhuiya tribe. Ten years later, one of his successors named Kasi Ram Singh built a new capital and called it Porahat after a cowherd, 'Puda'. He then brought the Bhuiyan idol Pauri Devi and made her the presiding deity of the chiefdom.[3] There are also numerous other legends regarding the origin of the Singhs which are dealt with, at length, by O'Malley and Dalton.[4] The Bhuiyas, the earliest and the largest group of settlers of the land are associated with most of these legends.

In 1620, the chief of Singhbhum, Arjun Singh III, gave his uncle Kumar Bikram Singh the fiefdom of 'Singhbhum Pir', a tract spread over 50 square miles with 12 villages. This was in recognition of Bikram Singh's services to him as his regent, when he had lost his parents early. Ambitious and powerful, Bikram Singh made Seraikella his capital and soon annexed Kharswan and Asantalia to his territory, which he gave away to his second son; his eldest son remaining first in the line of succession to Seraikella. He took away many temple grant lands and also wrested the lands from the neighbouring chiefs. Soon he declared his independence of Porahat. Later Seraikella even took away Porahat's state deity Pauri Devi, and would eventually eclipse the parent state.

The Land of the Dhals

The Dhal Chronicle, known as 'Dhalbhum Bivaran', was written in 1928 by the Oriya 'Vaisnavite Rajguru' of the Dhals.[5] The chronicle talks of one Adisura, who, emerging from the *yajna* at the bank of Vaitarani in Jajpur, came to the north at Dharanagar and founded his kingdom during the post-*Mahabharata* era. One Jagaddeb Pramar of his lineage once went on a pilgrimage to Puri. There he had a dream of a young woman who directed him to go to north and gain a prosperous land on the banks of Subarnarekha. He arrived in Ghatsila in Dhalbhum, and defeating the warring factions in the land, who were low caste Hindus, founded the present Dhal chiefdom in 1231. His priest friend Balaram Ojha changed his name into Jagannath Dhal. The chronicle identifies him as an Agnivamsi kshatriya, while Dalton believes him to be of Bhumij origin. Apparently, Dharanagar (identified with the Dharagiri in Dhalbhum) provided the Bhumij chief who was hinduized through the rituals at Jajpur. The Bhumij deity Rankini became the presiding deity of Dhalbhum.[6]

These hinduized chiefdoms were formed by the indigenous settlers of the land with the help of the Oriya speaking Sukla Yajurvedi brahmins from Jajpur. They had local presiding female deities who were subsequently influenced by the Viraja traditions.[7] The brahmins were not only the chief priests of the rulers, they also continued to hold key positions and controlled the overall administration. Their exposure to the advanced Hindu rule in Orissa further helped them manoeuvre the reins of power. Gradually, other Vedic brahmins were brought in, and 'sasana' villages in the tradition of Puri were set up. The brahmins who came subsequently originated in several places in Orissa: Sambalpur, Mayurbhanj, Ganjam, Cuttack and Puri. Simultaneously, streams of brahmins also came from Bankura, Puruliya, Midnapur (now in Bengal), where they had settled earlier, having migrated from Orissa. The British occupation and the Maratha raids also prompted the movement of brahmins to these regions in the nineteenth century. In the Oriya movement in Singhbhum it was this community that would take a leading role.

British Rule: The Administrative Changes

Soon after the East India Company received the Diwani of Bengal, Bihar and Orissa in 1765, it started breathing hard on the necks of the numerous independent chiefdoms to the north and west of Midnapur. By 1767, the British forces had subjugated many of them.

With great difficulty the British forced Dhalbhum to submission and its old ruling chief was sent to the jail in Midnapur. His nephew Jagannath Dhal VII was installed with the agreement that he would pay the revenues periodically. Soon after the forces left, Jagannath Dhal ignored the agreement and continued a decade long guerilla war with the British. The latter, fearing that the disturbances could spread farther, returned the chiefdom to Jagannath Dhal in 1777, with a much lower revenue in the bargain. The overall administration, however, was controlled from Midnapur. In 1800, Dhalbhum came under the Permanent Settlement.

As soon as the British gained a foothold in Dhalbhum, they looked beyond, to the west, and desired to possess Singbhum. In 1793, the chief of Seraikella entered into an agreement with them regarding the surrender of fugitive rebels. In 1803, when the Company was at war with the Marathas, the Governor-General wrote a friendly letter to the chief of Seraikella, Kumar Abhiram Singh, seeking his aid and assistance. The help sought was in the nature of preventing the Marathas from passing through his state into the Company territory. In exchange he was assured of friendship in future: the English would never march into his territory or demand tribute. During the 1818, Maratha war, Seraikella took greater care in its border territories to prevent the infiltration of the Marathas. In 1823, Seraikella and Kharswan formally declared their allegiance to the British government.

In 1767, the Singhbhum chief had approached the British for protection against the continuous plunder of his neighbours. After the Maratha war, Ghanashyam Singh of Porahat apprised the British of the rights of his forefathers in Singhbhum, and desired that their paramountcy be restored with British help. He also needed help to restore Pauri Devi and sought their aid in suppressing the Ho insurgency. By the agreement of 1820, Porahat became a tributary of the British; while the request for paramountcy was ignored, the Seraikella chief was asked to return the deity. When he refused, it was forcibly taken away and returned to Porahat.[8]

When the office of the Residents and Political Agents were established at the conclusion of the Maratha Wars, Singhbhum came under the South-West Frontier Agency in which the three Singhbhum states, Porahat, Seraikella and Kharswan, were treated as independent of each other. In 1833, when the Jungle Mahal was broken up, Dhalbhum was transferred to Manbhum under the same agency.

In 1836, Kolaan was constituted as the Ho territory to contain this militant tribe. This was done by taking away slices of land from Porahat, Seraikella, Kharswan, and Mayurbhanj. The new territory came under the direct administration of the British under a Principal Assistant Commissioner placed at Chaibasa. In 1848, Dhalbhum was added to Singhbhum and was administered by the same Principal Assistant Commissioner. In 1854, Seraikella, Kharswan and Porahat came under the jurisdiction of the Deputy Commissioner of Singhbhum, subject to the general supervision of the Commissioner of Chhotanagpur. Thus, by the second half of the nineteenth century, for the first time Singhbhum could be identified as a single entity under the Commissionership of Chhotanagpur, though the administration of its internal units differed from each other.

There were further changes in its internal territorial units after 1857. During the rebellion Seraikella and Kharswan supported the British and attempted to influence them against Porahat. Raja Arjun Singh of Porahat was found guilty of instigating mutiny that reached its heights during the alleged Chaibasa treasury loot. In 1859, he was exiled to Banaras with a sum of Rs. 400 per month until he died in 1890. The government made free grants of parts of the Porahat lands to those subordinate chiefs who had rendered them assistance in 1857.

Seraikella received the sub-state of Keraikella and special gifts called 'Khellut' for its loyal services. The Kharswan chief, who had already become a trusted ally of the British during the Bhumij Revolt of 1832, known as the 'Ganga Narayan Hangama',[9] received four villages of the Porahat chiefdom and also 'Khellut' in recognition of his services during the Mutiny.[10] By the proclamation of 1892, Porahat was declared subject to the Lt. Governor of Bengal and by the Porahat Estates Act II of 1893, it was declared that the estates should be a part of the District of Singhbhum. It was incorporated in Bengal by a proclamation of 1894. Arjun Singh's infant son, Narpat Singh, upon attaining adulthood appealed to the government in 1895, for the restoration of the estate to him. He was given back the shrunken estate and was given the title of raja in 1901. On his death in 1934, with no male heir to succeed, this was made a part of the British territory. The Seraikella chief Aditya Pratap Singh Deo's memorial to the Viceroy in 1932, and again in 1934, claiming the Porahat estate as a reward for all his past services to the British, was ignored.[11]

The primary reason for this was that, in 1915, in deference to the joint memorial to the Government of India by Seraikella and Kharswan, they were in 1916, transferred to the Orissa States Agency. The inclusion of Porahat, therefore, would have meant a transfer of territory from Bihar to Orissa that was a highly sensitive issue at that time.

THE ORIYA MOVEMENT

Singhbhum had been taken over piece-meal by the British. Following several administrative changes, when the land came under the Chhotanagpur Commissionership in the province of Bengal, no undue attention was given to such an arrangement by the Oriya speaking people, as their mainland too was attached to Bengal. Besides, Cook's report in 1895, as well as the Risley Circular of 1903, had been sympathetic to the Oriya cause. These people therefore already expected Singhbhum's inclusion with Orissa as only a matter of time, in order to complete the unification. No special initiative to create a popular demand thought necessary.

The overall impact of the formation of the Utkala Sammilani in 1903, on Singhbhum was negligible. Thus while ten delegates went from Midnapur to attend the inaugural session of the Sammilani, Singhbhum was represented only by Krushna Chandra Acharya of Kharswan and the landlords of Bera, Iccha and Sonua. Similarly, while as many as 381, associations were formed in all the outlying Oriya speaking areas, in the feudatory states and in Calcutta as well, not a single one was formed in Singhbhum. For its part, the Utkala Sammilani, the National Assembly of the Oriyas, too had no agenda for this outlying tract.

GOPABANDHU DAS AND THE BIRTH OF THE IRREDENTIST STRUGGLE IN SINGHBHUM

In 1912, when the Bihar–Orissa province was formed, the transfer of Chhotanagpur including Singhbum to Bihar disconcerted the Oriyas. So far Bihar and Orissa had been in the same boat, subservient to

Bengal. Now in the new province not only did Bihar become the dominant partner, it also remained in possession of the Oriya speaking outlying tract. This created a souring of relationship between the different groups.

The realization now dawned on Oriya leaders that an appropriate opportunity to retrieve the dismembered Oriya tracts in the north had been missed. In 1911-12, Gopabandhu was the legal advisor in Mayurbhanj State. During this time he came into contact with some of the prominent Oriyas of Singhbhum. He was also dealing with some documents relating to the mines owned by Mayurbhanj at Gorumahisani, which supplied ore to TISCO. Proximity to Singhbhum provided him with the opportunity to get familiarized with the region well. In the Puri session of the Utkala Sammilani in 1913, he gave a vivid description of the problems Oriyas were facing in Singhbhum.

Singhbhum's major non-tribal language was Oriya. In the early days of British rule Oriya was recognized as a vernacular of the district.[12] Gradually, when Bengali and Hindi speaking people held key administrative positions and dominated the region, the Oriya speaking people progressively started facing problems. For example, prior to 1862, Bengali was practically unknown in the villages of Dhalbhum. The Bengali speaking officers recruited in the estate had to learn Oriya for official work. In some cases they even added Oriya surnames to their original Bengali ones. There was no Bengali medium school in Dhalbhum until 1864-5.[13] The same year, two Bengali medium primary schools were opened in Kokpara and Baharagora.[14] Hindi schools had already been opened with government aid in Chaibasa and Seraikella by 1856. Soon Hindi and Bengali vernacular schools opened throughout the district with the support of the British government. Dalton, the Commissioner of Chhotanagpur, after his tour of Singhbhum in 1868, encouraged Hindi and Bengali schools in place of Urdu and Oriya[15] By July 1871, in the Singhbhum district there were 13 vernacular and English schools, with a total of 829 students. These schools did not teach Oriya. The Oriya elementary schools, 'Chatsalis', where Oriya children went for preliminary education, were unaided and ignored.

By the 1870s, the non-Oriya language groups, especially the Bengali speaking people, became greatly influential both in the mainland Orissa as well as in the frontier region. Dalton writes, 'The Headmaster of the Chyebasa school, Babu Sarada Persad

Gungopadhya, who is also Secretary to the aided and Model Schools, is a very superior person.'[16] Attempts were made to claim Dhalbhum as a part of Bengal, whereupon the chief had to defend his estate's language as Oriya in a written document.[17] The census reports of 1891 said that Oriya was spoken throughout Singhbhum district; in 1901 it was recorded that Oriya was spoken over the greater part of the district; but the 1911 census said that in Singhbhum there were three languages, Oriya, Bengali, and Ho. The replacement of Oriya by Hindi and Bengali posed insurmountable obstacles for the Oriyas. Often they could not understand correctly the contents of summons, proclamations, or other processes issued by the courts in Hindi or Bengali, suffering incalculable loss and injury on this account. Their children spoke Oriya at home but had to learn either Bengali or Hindi at school.

Gopabandhu realized that although Singhbhum was historically, culturally, and linguistically connected to Orissa, linguistic onslaughts due to the geographical and administrative separation would weaken its historical links. Rich in mineral resources, Singhbhum had a great potential for the economy of Orissa. Singhbhum's mines had attracted ancient men, and later Jain traders, who had extracted copper and iron extensively. The Mughals, including Akbar, had been enamoured by the gold and diamonds of this area. In modern times, many industries sprang up in the region, the most important being TISCO in 1907. Hailed as the national pride TISCO drew wide attention and attracted extensive and continuous migration that was to change the demographic picture. It was inevitable, therefore, that Singhbhum would soon become a bone of contention between Bihar and Orissa and that Bengal would play a crucial role.

The Language Agitation

Gopabandhu Das, fully seized of the plight of the Oriya people, drafted a charter of demands that aimed at the unification of the dismembered Singhbhum tract with the rest of Orissa. His priority was to save the Oriya language.

In 1913, the Utkala Sammilani in Orissa formally approved of the initiatives for the movement in Singhbhum and passed resolutions for the introduction of Oriya in the courts, for official use, and in schools in Singhbhum. In the next session, 1914 at Parlakhemundi, Ananta Mishra was appointed as the roving missionary to carry on the propaganda work in the outlying Oriya tracts. In December 1915, in the eleventh session of the Sammilani held at Sambalpur, the chief of Kera, Lakshmi Narayan Singhdeo, a descendant of the Porahat raja and a friend of Gopabandhu, was chosen as President. Thus a formal identification of Singhbhum's problems with the Sammilani's main programme began in earnest.

A memorial submitted by all ranks of people of Singhbhum to the Lt. Governor of Bihar and Orissa in 1916 complained about the use of Hindi and Bengali in official documents and communications. 'Thus under the influence of Bengalee and Hindi speaking officers, Oriya gradually lost its place in schools and Government offices, and Hindi and Bengali became the two recognised vernaculars in the district, though Oriya still continues to be taught in some solitary private schools and pathsalas and used by private parties in the writing of their deeds and documents.'[18] This memorial was signed by the rajas of Porahat and Dhalbhum, the Thakur Saheb of Anadapur, the Zamindar of Chainpur, and Krishna Chandra Acharya, and many others. A telegram was also despatched by Krishna Chandra Acharya to the Lt. Governor of Bihar–Orissa on 7 January 1914 requesting protection of the interests of the Oriyas.[19]

The Singbhum Oriyas became increasingly vocal about their demands. The press gave a great deal of coverage as well as financial support to the region which encouraged the local leaders.[20] By 1916, a host of regional associations had emerged. The same year the 'Singhbhum Utkala Sabha' was formed. Some of its founding fathers included Pandit Iswar Chandra Hota, Suresh Chandra Sarangi, Purna Chandra Tripathy, Kahnu Kisore Pani, Braja Mohan Tripathy, Krushna Chandra Acharya, Kamal Krushna Pradhan, Gati Krishna Sarangi, Anandapur Thakur Saheb, Udit Narayan Singha Deb, and Iswar Sarangi. The immediate focus of the association was the re-introduction of Oriya in schools and courts. Its endeavours were supported by the chiefs of Seraikella-Kharswan, Porahat, and Dhalbhum. 1916 also turned out to be an eventful year as Seraikella and Kharswan were transferred to the Orissa States Agency. The Oriya language was restored in these states with the initiative of the rulers.

Gopabandhu Das, an elected member of the Bihar-Orissa Council in 1916, availed the opportunity to present the plight of the Oriya speaking people in Singhbhum. He also highlighted the injustice of artificially tagging them with Bihar. He understood the strength of the tribal support, and made a conscious effort to win it to his cause. His interaction with the tribal leaders, including the Ho leader Dolmanki, convinced him that they were familiar with the Oriya language and given an option they would prefer to be taught in Oriya.[21]

Das was encouraged by the sympathetic views of the Deputy Commissioner of Singhbhum, A. Garret '. . . that Porahat and Dhalbhum are essentially Oriya area when they are not aboriginal, is undeniable . . . every step that has been taken in the direction of abolishing the Oriya language in these tracts is based on the efforts of the wrong that has been done in the past and is still being perpetuated' and the Commissioner of Chhotnagpur, B. Foley's suggestion that 'if it is desirable to exclude Bengalis as much as possible and to give more power to the Oriyas it would seem advisable that Singhbhum should be transferred to the Orissa Division'.[22]

Gopabandhu's dream was not only to preserve the language but to spread education in the traditions of his legendary school at Satyabadi. He requested his Satyabadi colleagues to open up branches of the school in the outlying Oriya speaking areas. Along with his close associate, Godavaris Misra, who was one of the finest teachers of Satyabadi, Gopabandhu arrived at Chakradharpur in Singhbhum in 1919, with the intention of translating his ideas into reality. He was supported in his endeavour by Oriyas as well as generous non-Oriyas. Local youth also came forward to work with the famed personalities from Satyabadi. One Oriya vernacular school was opened at Chakradharpur. Many alumni of Satyabadi joined here as teachers and Gopabandhu also deputed teachers from Puri. Soon the school became a High School. The *puruna basti* (old settlement), where the Porahat royal palace was located, became his headquarters.

In March 1919, a 'Singhbhum Oriya Education Fund'came into being. Ananta Mishra brought out a newspaper from Singhbhum. Das often visited these areas and with the local leaders constituted a committee to organize the spread of the Oriya education and to strengthen their movement. At the end of 1919, there were 140 Oriya vernacular schools in Singhbhum and a High School at Baharagora. The Secretary of the Utkala Sabha, Purna Chandra Tripathy, and

Dhalbhum residents including Suresh Chandra Sarangi and Trilochan Mishra collected funds for the Baharagora school. Dharani Dhar Mishra of Sambalpur sent from his Banaprastha Press's profits a hundred rupees. The local Oriyas also donated generously.

There was a spurt of literary activity. Iswar Chandra Hota's lyrics were on the lips of every Oriya in Singhbhum then, the most popular of them being

> Oriya is our voice
> Our soul is Oriya
> Born in the Oriya land
> Oriya we make grand
> Read and learn shall we Oriya
> Sing Oriya songs
> Orissa our motherland
> Orissa we make grand.[23]

Gopabandhu's stature was already on the rise and in April 1919 he presided over the annual session of the Utkala Sammilani at Cuttack. His *The Samaj*, a weekly founded in the same year, devoted its attention to the Oriya movement in the outskirts. His suggestions to the government were to discontinue the recruitment of non-Oriya teachers in Oriya schools and also to appoint an Oriya Deputy Inspector of Schools to deal with the problems of the Oriyas and the Oriya-speaking Hos. When the Managing Committee of the Chaibasa School wanted to withdraw Oriya on the plea that the number of Oriya students was not sufficient enough, Gopabandhu recommended not the removal of the language, but to intensify its spread. However, the Oriya language and schools survived, and it was expected that government grants would be forthcoming.

Thus by 1920, having succeeded in preventing the annihilation of the Oriya language, the Oriyas strongly believed that their claim for amalgamation would become stronger. In order to finalize the course of action for the amalgamation movement and to strengthen the relationship between the Oriyas in Singhbhum and those in the mainland Orissa, it was decided that the sixteenth session of the Utkala Sammilani would be held at Chakradharpur.

By then Gopabandhu had been deeply influenced by Gandhi and

he was convinced that the linguistic division of the provinces advocated by Gandhi would soon be a reality. Thus in 1920, when the Nagpur Congress passed the resolution supporting the cause, Gopabandhu identified the aims and goals of the Utkala Sammilani with those of the Congress. However, Gopabandhu inadvertently created an explosive situation: the Congress had declared non-cooperation, but the Oriya schools needed the support of the government! The situation became even more volatile, because the anti-Oriya elements would certainly be more active consequent upon the Congress decision of provincial division on the basis of the language. Gopabandhu's image was that of a messiah in Singhbum; therefore the region did not react against his decision; but in mainland Orissa, there was a distinct cleavage now.[24]

The Singhbhum Oriya movement that had spread at the grass roots level faced a serious setback. The High Schools at Chakradharpur and Baharagora changed into National Schools and the teachers became busy with Congress party work, at which they not only missed the government grant, but also became the targets of governmental wrath.

With Gopabandhu moving around like a hurricane and inspiring his fellow workers, no one thought that any thing would go wrong. When the Congress provincial units were decided on the basis of the language, though Bihar claimed that the Singhbhum District Congress unit should function through the Bihar Provincial Congress Committee, the famous 'post card ballot' in 1921 decided it in favour of Orissa.[25] This turn of events gave a fillip to the hope of the Oriyas and added to their complacency. The Biharis, meanwhile, never accepted it as the final decision and worked hard to destabilize the situation. 'From 1921 onwards the Biharis came to the fore in manipulating census returns to minimise the strength of Oriya speaking population and to swell their own, as a result of which the Oriya speaking population which actually is about 40% of the total population was reduced to a mere 20%.'[26]

The image of Chakradharpur School, the symbol of Oriya nationalism in Singhbhum, faded. The Bihari business community who had extended support for the school withdrew their support. By the end of 1922, many of the leaders in Orissa were behind bars and Gopabandhu's arrest in 1923 hit the last nail into the coffin. The

Oriya movement in Singhbhum became rudderless; Godavaris left Singhbhum.

Amalgamation Movement

On the eve of the Simon Commission's arrival in 1928, attempts were made to organize an amalgamation movement, but it was not successful as the Congress had boycotted the Commission. Ananta Mishra, on the personal level made extensive campaigning. The Singhbhum Utkala Sabha carried on vigorous propaganda work. Fresh faces from Orissa emerged in the region and new associations sprang up in Jamshedpur. The Simon Commission went by the Attlee Sub-Committee Report and did not include Singhbhum and Midnapur in its recommended province for Orissa. Instead it recommended establishing of a committee to go into the details about the boundary of Orissa, if it were to become a province. Disappointed with the Simon Commission's report, and with the hope of convincing the forthcoming Boundary Commission about Orissa's legitimate claims, the real amalgamation movement began in Singhbhum.

The situation was now entirely different, mainly because Gopabandhu, the father of the Oriya Movement in Singhbhum had died in 1928 leaving a vacuum in the leadership. Before his death he had brought Gandhi closer to Orissa. In 1925, he had also brought C. F. Andrews to Jamshedpur and had acquainted him with the Oriyas and their problems in Singhbhum. In his absence now, Orissa did not have a single leader of stature at the national level or at the All-India Congress to influence decisions. Besides, Jamshedpur because of TISCO had become the promised land of wealth and prosperity and Bihar and Bengal would now stake their claims more vigorously than ever before.

The amalgamation movement during this time concentrated more in and around Jamshedpur. Godavaris Misra returned to the scene to organize the Singhbhum Oriyas. Donations were collected and the statements on the Oriya Problem were widely distributed. The Golmuri Oriya Samaj, the Binapani Club, and Santiniketan were significant associations to organize the movement.[27] The Singhbhum Orissa District Congress Conference, the all Orissa Women's Conference and the Students Conference held in Jamshedpur in 1930 had their impact as well.

Nevertheless, in TISCO itself it was Bihari and Bengali employees who dominated, and by the 1930s, there were first generation settlers already in Jamshedpur from the above provinces. National leaders like Subhas Chandra Bose, J. M. Sengupta, and Rajendra Prasad who often came to iron out the labour problems of the Company, supported the anti-Oriya stand.[28] The Bengali organization called the 'Singhbhum Hitaishini Sabha' was making wide publicity about its claim and various rumours were spread that the plight of the Oriyas would be more if they went to Orissa. In villages the Oriyas were harassed and the local tribes were instigated against them. Dhalbhum, which includes Jamshedpur on its northern point, also came more under Bengali influence because of its new ruler. One of the Dhal offshoots in the Chilki Gara Raj in Bengal won a court case against the Dhals of Dhalbhum and ousted them. Thus while the former Dhals still supported the Oriya cause, little hope was there from the new ruler Jagadish Chandra Dhabal Deb.

Lakhsmidhar Mohanty's demand of reviving the Oriya language in courts and schools in Singhbhum in the Bihar–Orissa Legislative Council was opposed by both the Director and the Education Minister of Bihar and Orissa.[29]

Under such circumstances, the Oriyas were looking forward to their meetings with the Orissa Boundary Committee to explain the entire situation. But veterans of the Orissa Congress including Nilakantha Das who would have proved their points were debarred by the All-India Congress to meet the Committee, for the Congress then was declared illegal by the government. The local Oriya leaders were no competitions for the senior Bihar or Bengal leaders who adopted various ways to influence the Committee. The Utkala Sabha as the mouth piece of the Singhbhum Oriyas presented a memorandum to the Orissa Committee, but the inevitable happened.

Singhbhum did not come to Orissa in 1936. By then, it was clear that the British government had no particular interest of seeing to the Oriya cause in Singhbhum; instead they had thought it necessary to convert the region into a localized frustrated zone for the Oriyas to undermine the growth of the Congress movement. After 1930, it was the Congress wave that the British were really worried about. Thus, in order to suppress the national movement 'they tried with all the might to set up Biharis and Bengalis against the Oriyas and to bring about stagnation and ultimate cultural and political death by supplanting Oriya schools by Hindi and Bengali ones'.[30]

THE MERGER OF THE PRINCELY STATES AND SERAIKELLA-KHARSWAN

With the formation of the Orissa province in 1936, the provincial legislature elections kept the leaders busy. Soon after, the focus of the Orissa Congress was on the 26 princely states and their ultimate integration. The resistance of these states and the Congress-supported Praja Mandal movements were frontline issues. The demand for the amalgamation of the Oriya speaking regions, consequently, receded to the background.

In Orissa, the Garjat Praja Sammilani that was formed in 1931, to bring about an improvement in the condition of the people in the Orissa princely states, was rechristened the Orissa States Peoples' Conference in 1937. Soon it branched out into Praja Mandals in the princely states, with the aim of demanding a change from the existing semi-feudal rule. The States Enquiry Committee chaired by Mahtab in 1939, recommended the dissolution of the contract between the British and the state rulers in view of the inherent inability of the said states to support popular enlightened administration. The Committee further recommended bringing the chiefs as well as the people under the jurisdiction of the autonomous province of Orissa.[31] It was but natural that the rulers of the princely states would not accept such proposals that would appreciably diminish their power and influence, although some of them were ready to introduce progressive reforms. The recommendations of the Mahtab Committee, however, had to be shelved due to the outbreak of World War II.

Of all the princely states of Orissa, Seraikella and Kharswan represented a unique situation. Comprising an area of 449 square miles and 157 square miles respectively, they were not geographically connected to Orissa, except through another princely state, Mayurbhanj. Positioned as such in Singhbhum, these twin princely states had all along supported and participated in the Oriya Language Movement and had also worked for the protection of the interest of the Oriyas who constituted the bulk of their subjects.

In the 1940s, the Freedom movement of the Congress intensified in the Singhbhum district as in other places. During this time, the radical element of the Congress was also working in tandem with the Praja Mandals in the princely states, which had its impact on Seraikella and Kharswan. In order to assuage the feelings of their subjects, the chiefs of Seraikella and Kharswan immediately took some reformative measures. In 1943, the Seraikella raja conferred enlarged powers on the 'Praja Parishad' that had been constituted by his proclamation in 1939, and made it more representative with a view to bringing the people into closer touch with the administration. The Parishad consisted of the Vice-President of the State Council, who was the heir-apparent, and 28 members of whom 18 were elected. The rest were nominated by the ruler. The organization met from time to time to discuss current issues. 'It will now be for the Seraikella public to make a proper use of these rights and thus prove worthy of the trust and confidence reposed in them by the Rajah Saheb of Seraikella' wrote the editorial of the weekly *Indian States and Zamindaries*, 24 October 1943. Considering the rising prices due to the war, the salaries of low income groups received a raise.[32] Socio-cultural activities were sponsored too. In June 1945, Kalindi Charan Panigrahi, the eminent Oriya writer, was invited to speak on 'Utkala Kala O Sahitya'. The raja also encouraged womens welfare activities and a Mahila Mangal Samity was formed in 1945. With all these the raja of Seraikella was hailed by many as an ideal and benevolent ruler.[33]

Kharswan, almost a shadow of Seraikella, was always known for its enlightened administration. Under the 'Kharswan Praja Sabha' Order 1940, the state was divided into five constituencies. The Sabha consisted of 5 elected members of whom one was an aboriginal and 5 nominated members, besides the 'Dewan' as the Chairman. Matters concerning agriculture, water supply, primary education, sanitation, medical relief and communications were the main subjects discussed by the Sabha.

Simultaneously the princely states were expected to provide for the war needs too. A National War Front was inaugurated in Kharswan under the leadership of the Kharswan Yuvraj. During the years of 1942-4 the 'grow more food' campaign was pursued by the raja.[34] Dearness allowance and special allowances to low income group were also granted in view of the cost escalation. Nevertheless, economic problems including the short supply of essential items led to a volatile situation in these states.

Nehru's presidential address to the All-India States Peoples' Conference at Udaipur on 31 December 1945, 'all these ancient and harmful relics will have to go if the people as a whole are to raise themselves out of the morass of poverty and degradation'[35] made the rulers of the princely states uncertain. They thought about introducing further reformatory measures as well as forming closer groups among themselves.

The rulers of Chhattisgarh and of Orissa had been making several plans for forming a regional union to safeguard their interests. Some of them including those of Sonepur, Patana, Kalahandi, Seraikella, Korea, Bamra, Khandpara, Khairagarh along with K. C. Neogy (earlier Dewan of Mayurbhanj state and subsequently a Minister in the Government of India's Interim Ministry), met at Sonepur House in Calcutta in April 1946. Following the meeting, the raja of Seraikella, on behalf of these rulers wired Gandhi for an interview along with the Raja of Korea (Chhattisgarh). The purpose of meeting Gandhi was for an exchange of views regarding the future status of the princely states 'and also to impress upon him the undesirability of the Orissa Congress leaders taking a hostile attitude by carrying an anti-state propaganda'.[36] Gandhi had shown his dissatisfaction over the violent happenings in the princely states in the late 1930s and exhorted the subjects to carry on the satyagraha through non-violence.[37] He also had pleaded with the rulers to see the writing on the wall and mend their ways. He did not intervene in the states, because he did not favour class war. Further, he needed the united strength of rulers and subjects to fight the British.

Pyarelal, Secretary to Mahatma Gandhi, replied that 'Gandhiji is of opinion that in this connection they should see Pandit Jawaharlal Nehru who is the proper authority to be consulted on the question of the Indian States'.[38] The Seraikella Raja A. P. Singh Deo then requested B. C. Roy, the Chief Minister of Bengal, to arrange a meeting with Gandhi.[39]

During this time, the Congress Ministry in Orissa under the Premiership of Mahtab began working intensely towards the programme of integration of the Orissan princely states. Responding to Mahtab's letter, dated 9 May 1946, the Seraikella chief mentioned his disapproval of 'certain press reports about 'your efforts for amalgamation of Orissa states with the province and certain news comments coupled with an effort to foment agitations in the states'.

Reminding the Orissa Chief Minister of the deep connection between the states and the Orissa province, he desired a cordial relationship and wished the people of Orissa well. The chief requested Mahtab for a public and official contradiction of the statements appearing in press in Orissa against the rulers. He also suggested the withdrawal of agitations in the states for a successful negotiation between the State Authorities and the Congress.[40]

Meanwhile, Seraikella was also directly approaching the Congress leaders for a negotiation. Replying to his letter of 24 May 1947, Nehru wrote, 'The Rulers of most of the States seem to be completely oblivious of what is happening in India and in the world. On no account and whatever happens, we are not going to leave the people in the lurch.'[41]

With no encouraging words from Nehru and with their relationship with the Orissan government turning bitter, the rulers of Seraikella and Kharswan tried hard to prevent their integration within the province of Orissa. They were also confident that their plan for an Eastern States Union would be a reality soon. On the 30 July 1947, the Seraikella chief wrote to the Resident, 'Singhbhum with its rulers were never within Orissa, but was a part of Bihar. . . . The Congress of Orissa . . . is casting a covetous eye on the resources of these States in order to enrich the provinces quickly. . . . To hand over the States to such unscrupulous people of narrow minded vision and low capacity will be a most treacherous and unjustified act and a gross exploitation of the true interest of the States. . . .'[42] The next day, the Eastern States Union began to function with Seraikella as president.

Some rulers of the Eastern States Union were in Delhi from 29 November 1947 till the 6 December 1947 and saw senior Congress leaders like Mahatma Gandhi, Sardar Patel, Rajendra Prasad and Pattabhi Sitaramaya; they presented their notes expressing a willingness to modify the Eastern States Union Constitution according to the advice and desire of the Dominion Government.[43]

During this time, the internal situation in Seraikella was in a state of turbulence. The British had left India with the fate of the princely states still hanging in balance. The Praja Mandal agitation that had started in Seraikella in 1946, essentially by the Oriya Congress members, embraced all sections of the people, including the adivasis. Now in mid-1947, it assumed the character of a mass movement.

Several leaders including Pabitra Mohan Pradhan, Sarangadhar Das, Nabakrishna Choudhury, Malati Choudhury and Surendra Nath Dwivedy, who were the brains behind the Praja Mandal movements in the princely states elsewhere in Orissa, came to organize similar activities in Seraikella and Kharswan. Bijay Kumar Pani of Kharswan assumed the leading role and the residence of Jagadish Chandra Mohanty in Jamshedpur became the non-official headquarters of the movement.[44] The rulers of these states tried hard to control the destabilizing situation. The Seraikella raja attempted to win over the adivasis by various attractive promises. He made a proclamation on 7 December 1947 that steps would be taken at the earliest to set up a representative body for framing the constitution of his state and for the transfer of power to his peoples' representatives.[45] The Kharswan ruler also conceded some demands of the Praja Mandal.

The situation, however, did not improve either in these two states or in the rest of the princely states. The rulers appealed to Gandhi, who referred the matter to Sardar Patel, then Home Minister. The Orissa government too requested Patel to intervene. Patel visited Orissa, conferred with the princes, and asked them to give their consent to the merger. On 14 December 1947, the twenty-five princely states of Orissa signed an agreement to merge with Orissa province. It was decided that on 1 January 1948, the Orissa government would formally take over the administration of these states. Mayurbhanj did not sign the agreement on the grounds that it had already introduced popular representative government.

As the Singhbhum area remained outside the province of Orissa and the state of Mayurbhanj remained independent, Seraikella-Kharswan was not physically connected to Orissa but to Bihar instead. Such an opportunity could not be ignored by Bihar and it attempted to make the arrangement permanent one. In the meantime, politics in southern Bihar had undergone a sea change.

THE ADIVASI MOVEMENT AND THE MERGER ISSUE

The emergence of Birsa Munda in Chhotanagpur during the last decade of the nineteenth century had brought about an awareness among the adivasis that created a lasting impact in the subsequent period. In the beginning of the twentieth century, various reform movements as well as agitations against the exploitation of the adivasis were noticed. Slowly they grew into a movement for separate statehood in south Bihar. The Simon Commission was presented with the memorandum to that effect by the Chhotanagpur Improvement Society constituted by the Christian adivasis of the region. In 1938, an Adivasi Sabha was formed that assimilated all the factions and became the umbrella organization. In 1939, Jaipal Singh Munda was made its president and it soon assumed an all-India stature and became an Adivasi Mahasabha. With the emergence of Jaipal, the adivasis of Chhotanagpur were united as never before and were seriously planning to agitate for the formation of a separate state that would be called 'Jharkhand'. The Oxford-educated Munda soon became a high profile leader and member of the Constituent Assembly. When he presented his agenda, Orissa's position *vis-à-vis* Singhbhum weakened. The territories claimed by the Adivasi Mahasabha for the Jharkhand province were Chhotanagpur, the Santal parganas and ten princely states including Seraikella and Kharswan.

While Bihar and the Centre were unresponsive to the claim for Jharkhand the Eastern States Union encouraged Jaipal, ostensibly to win adivasi support for their cause. Jaipal argued that Seraikella and Kharswan were to be included in Bihar instead of Orissa; once the Jharkhand province was formed, as a part of Jharkhand they would have more freedom and all their traditional royalties would be restored. The Eastern States Union saw nothing to lose from this argument. They propelled the case of Seraikella and Kharswan and won Jaipal's support to strengthen their own movement. Jaipal worked hard to destabilize the Orissa claim on Singhbhum by influencing the adivasis of the region. Bihar leaders appreciated Jaipal's stand in Singhbhum, for they knew that this would ultimately be to Bihar's advantage. Mahtab thus sent some influential persons who were also related to the rulers of Seraikella and Kharswan to persuade them in favour of Orissa.

On the other hand, in Seraikella and Kharswan, the adivasis were already greatly influenced by their own rulers as well as by some of the local Oriyas,[46] by the Jharkhand leaders and by the Bihar Congress stalwarts to prevent an administrative takeover by the Orissa government. The adivasis were told that they should never allow the states to be integrated within Orissa, as those were rightfully theirs and soon they would have a province to themselves. Sensing trouble, the Centre asked the Orissa government to send a police force to these states and to bring the situation under control in order to take over the administration, as agreed, on 1 January 1948.

On that date adivasis from all over Chhotanagpur assembled in Seraikella and Kharswan. There was a long procession of these people and a meeting at the market place in Kharswan in the afternoon. They expected their supreme leader Jaipal to come to lead them in their agitation. But Jaipal abstained and the inevitable happened. In Seraikella, extra care had been taken and no untoward incident happened. But the mob frenzy could not be controlled in Kharswan and there was firing, causing death and destruction.

SERAIKELLA AND KHARSWAN LOST TO ORISSA

Although, Seraikella and Kharswan came under the Orissa government, much was made of the Kharswan incident as was planned to discredit the Orissa administration. The Government of India thus appointed the Baudekar Tribunal in February 1948 to decide on the future of the above two states. This, however, did not meet. Meanwhile, Seraikella and Kharswan continued to be centres of political manipulation and chaos; it was indicated by the appointment of the Baudekar Tribunal that the handing over of these two states to Orissa was not final and that the arrangement might change. The 'Praja Samiti' that had been formed by the prince Bhoopendra Narayan Singh Deo, the third son of the Seraikella chief, to counter the Praja Mandal movements was now activated. It worked against those Oriyas who desired merger and also against the officials of the Government of Orissa who were appointed to look after the administration of Seraikella.[47]

During this time, the Singhbhum Oriyas, on the other hand, tried to press on the authorities their claim to the entire Singhbhum, not the two states alone. A memorandum entitled 'Singhbhum' by the Dhalbhum Oriyas prepared by Tarapada Sarangi gave details of the historical, geographical and cultural connections of the region with Orissa. The memorial also invoked the Congress pledge to the provincial redistribution on a linguistic basis.[48]

Jaipal Singh had taken up Seraikella and Kharswan as the testing ground for the entire Jharkhand movement. In his presidential speech at the Adivasi Mahasabha's annual session at Ranchi in February 1948, he said, 'I have, ever since the Kharswan massacre on 1 January, been trying to probe into the deeper reasons for the promiscuous merger, and I am more and more inclined to the view that there has been some conspiracy either at the Centre or in the Provinces to create the present situation with a view to administering a rude shock on the Adivasi Movement'.[49]

The Eastern States Union issued an appeal where they said that they had never been averse to cooperation between the states and neighbouring provinces in matters of common concern. 'Complete merger was never the intention of anyone and that idea must be removed once for all.' They had presented three alternatives to the government of India regarding their status.[50] Their demands having been ignored, they wanted to begin a mass movement and appealed to the people of the states, to 'unite, to organize and to be ready to fight for their right'.[51]

Sardar Patel observed that these two Oriya states were going through a lot of confusion in the administration and they formed only an island territory in the district of Singhbhum. He decided to transfer them in May 1948 to Bihar, as a temporary expedient on the grounds of administrative convenience.

It is believed that the Seraikella Raja met Mahtab soon after, expressed his regrets for the past action and sought his help for rejoining Orissa. This plea was relayed to Patel,[52] but was ignored. After the merger, Seraikella and Kharswan did not receive any special status in Bihar. In contrast, their counterparts in Orissa enjoyed high profiles in politics and society. Besides, there was no Jharkhand in sight and in the following days, the Eastern States Union weakened. Frustration, therefore, soon set in.

On January 1949, Mayurbhanj followed the footsteps of other princely states and merged with Orissa. At this juncture, the Oriya leaders had hoped, the case of Seraikella and Kharswan would be reopened as a result of the direct corridor of connection with Orissa being now available. But this aspiration was thwarted.

A joint statement of the Premiers of Orissa, C. P., West Bengal and Bihar accepted the decision of the Government of India in regard to the then distribution of former native states of the Eastern States

Agency.[53] With the Constitution of India coming into force on 26 January 1950, Seraikella and Kharswan became an integral part of the province of Bihar. In July 1950 Seraikella appealed to the Supreme Court of India against the Governor-General's 'States Merger (Governor's Provinces) Order, 1949' as wrong, and pointed out that the plaintiff-state was illegally merged in the province of Bihar under the said order. The Supreme Court, however, dismissed the allegations.[54]

THE STATES REORGANIZATION COMMISSION

The Government of India set up a States Reorganization Commission (SRC) in 1953 to study in detail the administrative boundaries of the provinces and to recommend reorganization wherever required. This raised new hopes among the Oriyas. The memorandum from Orissa government to the SRC was prepared by Radhanath Rath, then Minister-in-charge of Finance, Education and Welfare.

Apart from the government memorandum, there were also wide-scale preparations in Orissa and Singhbhum to represent their cases to the Commission. In Orissa, the princely states that had championed the cause of the Eastern States Union now formed an alliance under a new party called The 'Ganatantra Parishad'. This Party led the opposition in the Orissa Assembly where the Congress was in power. The almost defunct 'Utkala Sammilani' was now revived to work for the amalgamation of the Oriya speaking tracts.

An important meeting was held at Seraikella under the auspices of the local branch of the Utkala Sammilani on 7.2.1954. R. N. Singhdeo, maharaja of Patana and the second son of the then ruler of Seraikella, Member of Parliament and President of the Utkala Sammilani, presided. He was accompanied by several stalwarts from Orissa that included Godavaris Misra, Syamsunder Misra, member servants of the India Society and the Kalahandi Raja, deputy leader of the opposition in the Orissa Assembly. They exhorted the people to put up their wishes strongly before the SRC and get organized for the amalgamation movement. Unfortunately, hired hooligans alleged to be from Bihar turned violent and created chaos in the meeting.

In Singhbhum, two branches of the Utkala Sammilani were formed, the 'Dhalbhum Utkal Sammilani' with Mrutyunjaya Das as the

President, and the 'Singhbhum Utkala Sammilani' with the Tikayet of Seraikella as the President. These branches worked hard to unite the Oriya speaking people of Singhbhum and agitate for the amalgamation. The Dhalbhum branch also functioned occasionally in tandem with its counterpart in Midnapur. The Tikayet of Seraikella, Nrupendra Narayan Singhdeo, prepared a monograph, 'Singhbhum, Seraikella and Kharswan – Through the Ages' – with a foreword by the famous historian, Radha Kumuda Mookerji. 'It is to be hoped that the Commission appointed for the re-organization of the States of India on the basis of linguistic, cultural, economic and administrative considerations will go fully into the case of these two States for their incorporation in the state of Orissa in the light of the very relevant documents and material presented in this book,' wrote Prof. Mookerji. The book concludes thus: 'In Peace and Prosperity, in War and Adversity, in Calamity and Catastrophes, in Habits and Customs, in Ceremonies and Obsequies, in Hopes and Disappointments, in Dress and Demeanour, in Culinary and Coiffure, in Dance and Drama, in Art and Literature, the people of Seraikella-Kharswan-Singhbhum express themselves in the same way and in same details as their brethren in Orissa.'[55] This sentiment was expressed in some form or the other by the Oriyas all over when they presented their case to the SRC with regard to Singhbhum. The President of Singhbhumi Students' Union in Cuttack, Bibekananda Pati, who was the Principal of the Radhanath Training College, compiled and presented a memorandum to the SRC on behalf of the Union.[56]

Some interesting tactics were employed by the leaders from Bengal during the SRC. They tried to lure the Oriya leaders with the promise that if they endorsed the transfer of Dhalbhum to Bengal, then they would support the case of Seraikella and Kharswan for the merger with Orissa. The Dhalbhum Oriyas, especially brahmins from the 'sasana' village of Baharagora, vehemently protested against such a move. The leaders of Bihar then gave the impression that they supported the Dhalbhum Oriyas and advised the latter not to pay heed to the words of the Bengal leaders. However, as it turned out, being the administrative authority over the area, they could also use provincial machineries to marginalize the Oriya agitations.

The SRC Report, released in November 1955, brought large scale disappointment to Oriya speaking people. The Orissa Assembly sent its disapproval and requested for a reconsideration. Moving a motion in the Lok Sabha, R. N. Singhdeo said that the Commission had done a blatant injustice to Orissa by denying even an inch of land to her.[57] In 1956, after probing into the report thoroughly a high-level four member committee headed by the Prime Minister gave the final verdict: no change in its decision on Orissa. It said, 'language by itself does not, in our opinion, provide sufficient justification for breaking up a district', and 'above all, in view of the recommendations which we make for the transfer of part of the Manbhum district to West Bengal, the transfer of Seraikella subdivision, or any portion thereof, to the state of Orissa will convert the Dhalbhum subdivision in the east into an enclave which will not be physically contiguous to the rest of Bihar'.

This decision, compensating Bengal and minimizing the damage to Bihar, irked the leaders in Orissa. The Orissa Provincial Congress Committee resolved to condemn the Central government and the Ministry offered to resign. Confident of the support of the ruling party, leaders all over Orissa called upon the general public to join a protest. In January 1956 there were serious demonstrations in Puri. The fire spread; there were picketing and strikes around the province of Orissa. Widespread violence and firing resulted in three persons being killed in Cuttack and Puri. The Ministry that had announced its resignation continued with the orders of the Prime Minister.

There were attacks and counter attacks on the floors of the Orissa Assembly and in the media. The ruling party was accused of inefficiency and betrayal; the opposition for instigating the violence. The SRC and its aftermath remain a permanent stigma on the Orissa Congress.

CONCLUSION

The Oriya irredentist struggle in Singhbhum did at some stages show sign of success, but its ultimate goal of the territorial unification with Orissa remained elusive at the end of it all. The inclusion of Seraikella and Kharswan in 1916 into the Orissa group of states and their continuation till 1948, was the only territorial success, albeit briefly. This happened due to the initiative of the chief of Seraikella, Udit Narayan Singh Deo.

Ironically, for the secession of Seraikella-Kharswan from Orissa, it is his grandson, Aditya Pratap Singh Deo, who is largely held responsible. The latter who ruled Seraikella from 1931 to 1969 was an ambitious man. He was admitted to the Chamber of Princes in 1940 which enhanced his stature among his peers. He encouraged education in Oriya medium and patronized Oriya literature and culture. His contributions to the large developmental projects in Orissa such as the setting up of the Utkal University and the Hirakud Dam are well documented. His leading role in forming the Eastern States Union was ostensibly to perpetuate the royal traditions that the rulers all over were trying to retain. In the final analysis, it would therefore appear that his move was not anti-Oriya, it was largely against merger and was against the loss of the royal identity.

From the point of view of Bihar, to retain Dhalbhum, it was necessary to fight for Seraikella and Kharswan for otherwise with Manbhum having gone to Bengal, Bihar would have no possible access to the region. Bihar leaders were of the view that, if Dhalbhum would be allowed to remain as an island, it would be lost in no time to Bengal, already eyeing this region. Interestingly, however, there was a small strip of land connecting Dhalbhum to Bihar, but that was ignored.[58]

Concentrating on Seraikella and Kharswan alone in the 1940s and thereafter, turned out to be a weakness in the strategy of the Oriya leaders. In retrospect, the loss of Singhbhum territory to Bihar disconnected Seraikella and Kharswan from Orissa once Mayurbhanj deferred its decision on merger.

After Gopabandhu, there was no consistency in approach to the problem of Singhbhum from the leaders of either mainland Orissa or of Singhbhum. There were only sporadic movements on the eve of some specific events, such as review by any Government Commission. One is tempted to remember Lord Curzon's observations in 1912, that the callous indifference of the government for the Oriya cause was primarily due to the fact that 'the Oriyas are a non-agitating people'.[59]

In the 1930s Oriya struggle in Singhbhum went to the grass roots in the course of its language agitation and amalgamation movement, all sections of society participating. It was essentially a different kind of political game during the time of merger and thereafter, for which the Oriya leaders had no specific strategy and as such, wilted before the Machiavellian politics of the more influential leaders from the neighbouring provinces.

It also was apparent that the Congress leaders were keen to strengthen their own political position and enhance their image in Orissa by effecting the merger as early as possible. Any farsighted politician from Orissa should have understood the sensitive position of Seraikella-Kharswan and should have tried to win them with better offers. The backing of Praja Mandal movements in these two states by the Congress leaders from Orissa caused further damage, as it eventually alienated the rulers of these states.

In retrospect, it could be said that although the Oriya movement in Singhbhum did not reach its ultimate goal of amalgamation, it did achieve a landmark through its language agitation. The Oriya language in Singhbhum was preserved and with it, a significant part of Oriya heritage was saved from extinction.

NOTES

1. N. K. Sahu, 'Historical Geography', in M. N. Das (ed.), *Sidelights on History and Culture of Orissa,* Cuttack, 1977, pp. 36-7.
2. Tikayet Nrupendra Narayan Singh Deo, *Singhbhum, Seraikella and Kharswan - Through the Ages,* Calcutta, 1954, p. 24.
3. *Ibid.*, p. 20.
4. L. S. S. O'Malley, *Bengal District Gazetteers*, Vol. XX, *Singhbhum, Seraikella and Kharswan*, Calcutta, 1910, p. 221.
   E. T., Dalton, *Descriptive Ethnology of Bengal*, Calcutta, rpt. 1973, p. 185.
5. Krishna Chandra Raul, *Dhalbhum Bivaran* (Bengali), Midnapur: Madhabi Press, 1928.
6. Nivedita Mohanty, 'The Jungle Civilizatión, Dhalbhum—A Case Study', in S. Mahapatra (ed.), *Rethinking of Indian Culture, Challenges and Responses*, Cuttack, 1999, pp. 341-2.
7. *Ibid.*, p. 343.
8. It is believed that the image of Pauri Devi returned was a faked one (Deo, Singh N. N. Tikayet, *Singhbhum*, p. 85). Since that day, the deity housed in the temple of the Seraikella Palace daily accessible only to the Bhuiyan priest, the ruling chief and the queen, the heir apparent and his consort, and the queen mother. The other members of the royalty are allowed the 'darshan' only on special occasions.
9. Dalton, *Ethnology*, p. 181.
10. P. C. Roy Choudhury, *Singhbhum Old Records*, Patna, 1958, p. 278.

11. Memorial to the Earl of Willingdon, Viceroy and Governor-General of India. Through Lt. Colonel A. S. Meek, C. M. G., Agent to the Governor-General of India. On behalf of Raja Aditya Pratap Singh Deo, Ruling Chief of Seraikella, 1934 (Private Papers, Seraikella Palace), p. 3.
12. In 1821, the Mundas and Mankis (headmen) of Kolhan had entered into an agreement with the British government which envisaged the question of education to the Hos in Oriya or Hindi.
13. *Log Book, Kokpara School*, 21.2.1914, copied in 1953 (Bengali).
14. The Dhal Raja's adopted son, Madhusudan Samal, opened a Bengali Lower Primary School in 1864-5 in his village at Kokpara, apparently to please his wife from Midnapur. His grandson, G. K. Samal, one time general Secretary of Utkal Sammilami of Dhalbhum and married to the great-granddaughter of Fakir Mohan Senapati, the father of modern Oriya literature, never forgave his grandfather for this conduct.
15. Letter from Dalton, the Commissioner of Chhotanagpur to the Deputy Commissioner of Singhbhum, W. H. Hayes, dated Camp Bandgaon, 26.2.1868, Old Correspondence, Singhbhum, 1867-8.
16. Letter from Dalton to Rivers Thompson, officiating Secretary to the Government of Bengal, Chhotanagpur, 31.7.1871, Old Correspondence, Singhbhum, 1871.
17. Raja Satrughna Dhal's submission in Land Registration Case, dated 17.6.1887.
18. Two Bachelors of Arts, *The Oriya Movement*, Aska, 1919, p. 109.
19. Nayak, Lakshmidhar, *Ṣinghbhumira Gopabandhu* (Oriya), Jatani, 1977, p. 45.
20. *Asa* (Oriya newspaper from Berhampur, Orissa), 26.6.1916.
21. *The Samaj* (Oriya newspaper from Cuttack), 22.7.1931.
22. Letter of the Commissioner of Chhotanagpur Division, Mr. Foley, I.C.S., to the Secretary, Government of Bihar and Orissa, Judicial Department, No. 868J, dated Ranchi, 26.3.1919.
23. Dipak Sarangi, 'Upantaru lekhuchi' (Oriya), in: *'Gopa' Memorial Volume*, Baripada, 1978, p. 140.
24. Nivedita Mohanty, *Oriya Nationalism, Quest for a United Orissa*, New Delhi, 1982, pp. 100-6.
25. Godavaris Misra, *Arddha Satabdira Odisa O Tahire Mo Sthana* (Oriya), Calcutta, 1970, p. 223.
26. Memorandum to the States Reorganization Commission on behalf of Singhbhumi Students' Union, Bibekananda Pati, President, Singhbhumi Students' Union, Prajatantra Press, Cuttack, 1954, p. 7.
27. *Prajatantra* (Oriya News paper from Cuttack), 24.11.1926.
28. *The Samaj*, 30.9.1931.
29. *Ibid.*, 8.7.1931.
30. Memorandum to SRC, Singhbhumi Students' Union, p. 7.

31. *The Enquiry Committee, Orissa States*, Cuttack, 1939.
32. *Nabeen* (Oriya Weekly from Berhampur), State Supplement, 25.1.1944.
33. *Odia* (Oriya weekly from Berhampur), 12.11.1945.
34. *Indian States and Zamindaries*, The Leading Illustrated Weekly Journal for Indian Princes, Chiefs, Zamindars, State Officials, etc., Vols. 17 & 18, Nos. 54 & 1, 26.12.1943 and 2.1.1944.
35. *Amrita Bazar Patrika*, 2.1.1946.
36. Letter from A. P. Singh Deo to the Maharaja Saheb of Kalahandi, Bhawanipatna, Kalahandi, dated the 12.5.1946 (Private Papers, Seraikella).
37. *Harijana*, 3.12.1938.
38. Letter from Pyarelal, Valmiki Vihar, Reading Road, New Delhi, dated 29.4.1946, to the Secretary to the Raja of Seraikella (Private Papers, Seraikella).
39. Letter from A. P. Singh Deo, Seraikella, dated the 19.5.1946 to Dr. B. C. Roy, M.R.C.P., F.R.C.S., the Chief Minister of Bengal (Private Papers, Seraikella).
40. Letter from A. P. Singh Deo, Seraikella, dated 20.5.1946, to Mr. H. Mahtab, Chief Minister, Orissa, Cuttack (Private Papers, Seraikella).
41. Letter from Jawaharlal Nehru, 17 York Road, New Delhi, dated 31.5.1947, to Raja Aditya Pratap Singh Deo, Raja of Seraikella (Private Papers, Seraikella).
42. *Bruhattara Utkala Gathanare Badha Bighna* (Oriya), Orissa Public Relations Department, 1956, p. 12.
43. *An Appeal of the People of the Eastern States*, 1948 (Private Papers, Seraikella), p. 2.
44. Dipak Sarangi, Manuscripts, The Praja Mandal Movement in Seraikella and Kharswan, pp. 2-3.
45. 'Proclamation of Maharaja Aditya Pratap Singh Deo, Ruler of Seraikella. This Seventh Day of December, One Thousand Nine Hundred and Forty Seven in the Seventeenth Year of My Rule' (Private Papers, Seraikella).
46. Nilamani Routray, *Smruti O' Anubhuti* (Oriya), Cuttack, 1986, p. 193.
47. *Bruhattara Utkala*, p. 6.
48. Tarapada Sarangi, *Singhbhum*, Jamshedpur: City Press, 1948.
49. Presidential Speech by The Honourable Mr. Jaipal Singh to All India Adivasi Mahasabha at Ranchi on 28.2.1948.
50. Letter from the chiefs of Patna, Dhenkanal, Korea and Seraikella, dated 30.1.1948, to Mr. Menon, *An Appeal of the People of the Eastern States*, Annexure A., pp. 11-13.
51. *Ibid*., p. 10.
52. *Bruhattara Utkala*, p. 48.
53. *Ama Satabdi* (Oriya fortnightly from Bhubaneswar), 15.6.2000, p. 27.
54. Original Jurisdiction, Civil Suit No. 1 of 1950 , The State of Seraikella as

Plaintiff *versus* The Dominion of India, The Province of Bihar as Defendants (Private Papers, Seraikella).

55. Deo Singh, N. N. Tikayet, *Singhbhum,* p. 117.
56. Memorandum to the SRC, Singhbhumi Students' Union, Cuttack, 1954.
57. Report of SRC, Lok Sabha Debate, 23 December 1955, pp. 1295-7.
58. Press Statement of Bhoopendra Narayan Singh Deo, Leader of the Seraikella- Kharswan People's Deputation to the Eastern Zonal Council Meeting, dated 29.12.1960, Calcutta, p. 2.
59. Two Bachelors, *The Oriya Movement*, p. 42.

CHAPTER 13

Blurred Boundaries: Religion and Politics in Orissa

ISHITA BANERJEE-DUBE

Notions of separation between religion and politics are premised upon universal definitions of the two categories. To start with, the universal definition of religion came into being through a chequered process in post-Reformation Europe, its 'universal' applicability suspect since its inception. The demarcation of politics from religion owes its origin to the same legacy, although it is widely accepted and acknowledged that mutations and fluctuations in the realm of the political are governed by conditions of history. Religion, on the other hand, continues to be seen as something constant and unchanging through the ages, notwithstanding searing critiques of the idea.[1] It has been persuasively argued that there can be no universal definition of religion even for Europe and Christianity, because the elements and relationships that constitute it are historically specific, and because the definition itself is the product of historically shaped discursive processes.[2] The attempt to come up with a definition valid for all ages inevitably leads to a search for and identification of an 'autonomous essence' that makes particular categories at once ahistorical and transcultural. It also fosters an understanding of traditions such as Islam or Hinduism as 'different' in that the demarcation of religion and politics do not hold in them. My analysis of the relationship between the temple of Jagannath in Puri, the indigenous rulers who were its servants and patrons, and the colonial and postcolonial state of Orissa will draw upon and take forward this critique. It will, however, not dismiss or underestimate the significance of the gradual processes of secularization that came to pass in Europe in the centuries following the Reformation. The essay will also engage with Hermann Kulke's examinations of the interface of the *kṣetra* and *kṣatra* in Oriya history and, as befitting a true homage, will try to critically extend the understanding of religion and politics in modern Orissa.

Several studies of India have underscored the embeddedness of religion in politics. Orissa offers a striking example. In 1230, king Anangabhima Dev of the Ganga dynasty ritually dedicated his kingdom to Purushottama-Jagannatha of Puri, declaring him to be his divine overlord as well as the state deity of Orissa. Anangabhima completed the construction of the temple of Jagannath in Puri begun by his predecessor Chodaganga Dev, and placed the worship of the deity on a firm footing by introducing different and distinct ritual services (*seba*), each assigned to a particular group of functionaries. The *chattisa-niyoga* – thirty-six categories of temple servants – owe their origin to this decision of Anangabhima Dev. The king reserved the privileged position of the *adya sebak*, the first servant/prime servitor, for himself. Anangabhima and his successors ruled as the son (*putra*) or deputy (*rautta*) of the Lord of the Universe, in accordance with his divine order (*adesh*).[3] This divine order is what qualified the kings to exercise *danda*, defined as an ensemble of 'power, authority and punishment'.[4] The rulers of Orissa also commanded supreme authority over the affairs of the temple, and supervised the ritual services offered to Jagannath by different categories of temple servants. The monarch thus became the font of both ritual and political authority, giving the lie to the division between the religious and the temporal, and rendering inapplicable the theory of *dharma* encompassing political power in South Asia.[5] Although successive rulers paid varied degrees of allegiance to the 'deputy ideology', Jagannath remained the *rashtra devata* (state deity), at times legitimizing the claim of a usurper to the throne, and at others neutralising the challenge posed by ambitious priests and recalcitrant subjects.[6] As central authority weakened and political control came to be concentrated in the Khurda region, the rulers clung to Jagannatha with greater zeal. The strategy worked. In the sixteenth century, the Raja of Khurda was recognized by Man Singh, General of the Mughal Emperor Akbar, as the successor to the 'imperial' Gajapatis of Orissa.[7] This perception persisted in the eighteenth century, although Khurda's political authority suffered considerable decline first under the direct rule of the powerful Nawabs of Bengal and their *subahdars* in Orissa and then at the hands of the Marathas (of Nagpur) who conquered

Orissa from the Nawab of Bengal in 1751.[8] The Marathas in fact virtually reduced Khurda to the status of a *zamindari* by bringing both its feudatory states and the administration of the temple of Jagannath under their control.[9] The kings of Khurda, as the first servants of Lord Jagannath, managed to retain their symbolic superiority over the Oriya princes of the tributary states.[10]

East India Company rule was introduced in Orissa in the early nineteenth century against this background. British officials, aware of the position of Jagannath and the importance of his abode, took care to placate the priests of the temple in Puri. With this began a process by which subtly and steadily the Raja's authority was bypassed and his power over the temple servants effectively reduced. When the troops of the East India Company crossed the borders of Orissa in 1803, the secretary to the Governor-General forwarded to the officers leading the campaign, a letter addressed to the priests written by a famous pundit of Bengal. In it the pundit assured the priests of the basic religious tolerance of the British and their 'profound benevolence' toward their subjects. Wellesley, the Governor-General, instructed his officers to offer 'the most ample protection' to the pilgrims to Jagannath and to treat them with every mark of consideration and kindness. From the beginning, then, the colonial state tried to take on the role of the 'protector' of the temple, its ritual functionaries and pilgrims, in an effort at once to pre-empt hostility, and to underscore its supremacy over the Indian prince. What was implicit in this was the superiority of a 'modern' state that was secular and yet afforded protection to religious specialists and institutions, as opposed to the outmoded authority exercised by the king in the name of a divinity. The priests of the temple seized upon the special importance accorded to them by the invading colonial power. They readily switched their loyalty and without qualm upheld the British conquest of Orissa as an act sanctioned by the state deity.

The Raja of Puri jeopardized his position by joining the Marathas in resisting the British troops that marched into Orissa in 1803. He was imprisoned, his territories seized, and the management of the temple of Jagannath wrested from his control. The temple was placed under the care of a committee of Brahman pundits. However, the arrangement did not work. Within a few years, the king of Puri was released from prison and re-instituted as the Superintendent of the temple of Jagannath.[11] A new and unique designation, that of Raja-

Superintendent, was created for him. If this underlined his subservience to the Company's government, it also acknowledged his right to be in charge of the affairs of the deity, of whom he was the first servant. Indeed, the choice of the Raja as the Superintendent was based almost entirely on proof of efficient management unearthed by the investigations of the British Collector at Puri. The Collector held the Marathas responsible for the 'total anarchy' that prevailed in the temple at the time of British take-over. Under the Raja's direct management and vigilant supervision, commented the English official, every single instance of deviation from duty on the part of the temple functionaries was punished 'either by fine or corporal chastisement'.[12]

The authority of the re-instituted Raja was seriously circumscribed. His designation, Superintendent, underscored his acknowledged submission to the British masters. Colonial officers kept a hawk-like watch over the administration of the temple and despite their proclaimed policy of non-interference in the internal affairs of the temple, often intervened in the interest of 'law and order'. The duty to protect 'the life and limbs of the pilgrims resorting to the temple', frequently provided the colonial government with a valid reason to interfere. Moreover, the income and expenditure of the temple was brought under direct British supervision and comprehensive lists of temple properties were drawn up.

All this produced interesting and contradictory consequences. The long, continuous and visible presence of the colonial state made the Raja's subordination an established fact. The complete control he exercised by virtue of a combination of executive-judicial functions deriving from his divine overlord, became confined to that of a weak executive, working under the guidance of a sovereign political power. This steadily weakened his hold over the ritual functionaries of the temple, the Brahman and non-Brahman servants (*sebȧks*). Indeed, some of these servants had, since the sixteenth century, slowly begun to shake off the complete control of the king by turning to newer sources of income that helped increase their influence.[13]

In effect, then, the temple of Jagȧnnath came under the close surveillance of a temporal authority that in no way depended on the shrine or its presiding deity for its political strength. Nor did it seek any symbolic tie with the temple and the deity for legitimacy. Indeed, its proclaimed faith in the separation of religion and politics, supplemented by a constant campaign of Protestant missionaries against the connection of the East India Company's state with the temple of Jagannath, stopped the colonial state from taking over the administration of this Hindu temple. The Raja continued as the Superintendent with conferred autonomy in the internal affairs of the temple, in spite of recurrent charges of negligence and mismanagement levelled against him by British officers.

To state that British rule functioned on the basis of a demarcation of the domains of the religious and the political is not to posit a clear distinction with an essentially different West. To reiterate my point made in the introductory paragraph, the delineation of the two realms was the consequence of a long, laboured and tortuous process in post-Reformation Europe.[14] Yet, the challenge posed by the Reformation to the universal church set in motion a trend by which slowly but steadily, religion came to be viewed as an essentially private affair. The separation between the state and the church, and religion and politics had become, at least in theory, entrenched in English society by the nineteenth century.

At the same time, the colonial state could not sever its ties with the temple. Its secular duties of 'protection' and maintenance of law and order made a mockery of its proclaimed policy of non-interference in the affairs of religious institutions.[15] Here then was a paradox. The total control that the Hindu kings sought to exercise on their subjects and territory by claiming to be the first servants of the Lord of the Universe was accompanied by a belief that the well-being of the kingdom depended on the pleasure of the Lord. Proper conduct of ritual services and ceremonies of Jagannath was an obligation voluntarily taken. The colonial government could not be further from this notion. Its claim to superiority and modernity rested on its distance from religion. Yet, the distance often turned out to be elusive. The secular duty of 'management' prompted the rational colonial state to step in to ensure the proper conduct of rituals and services, for the protection and benefit of the votaries of this 'public trust'. Vigilance over the functioning of a Hindu a religious institution was made out to be a necessary duty of a 'secular' legislating executive. The state in its role as the 'protector' superseded the Indian prince, who ruled in the name of a sovereign deity.

As indicated earlier, the resourceful ritual functionaries of the temple were quick to grasp the new realities. Actuated by a new confidence deriving from the great trust placed in them by British officials as the repositories and representatives of Hindu 'tradition', they used the judicial authority of the colonial state to improve their position *vis-à-vis* the Raja.[16] Complaints to colonial administrators against the Raja-Superintendent became a common occurrence in the nineteenth century. Even those who remained loyal to the prince and stood by him in times of distress recognized the limited nature of his power as the executive head of the temple. Gradually but irreversibly, the *sebaks* grew in strength, they slipped out of the 'iron-grip' that the Raja is presumed to have had over them prior to the rule of the Marathas. Equally, these functionaries juxtaposed the foreignness and distance of a Christian government to the proximity of the Hindu prince to the deity, and cleverly manipulated the British notion of separation between religion and politics to stave off total control of the temple by the state.

The temple suit of 1886 provides an impressive instance of this tactic. In the 1880s, the British government tried to take advantage of the imprisonment and indictment of Raja Dibya Simha Deb on a charge of homicide, to put an end to the 'mismanagement' of the temple. The Collector of Puri instituted a case in the court of the District Judge, Cuttack, against the Raja. The purpose was to wrest the temple from the sole superintendence of the Oriya prince and place it under the supervision of a committee of five trustees with the Raja. The colonial state initially was successful. Following this, Oriya nationalists and temple servants made common cause to save the Raja, the symbol of indigenous and Oriya dignity, pride, faith and authority. The opposition was fierce enough to make the British government backtrack. It decided to work out a compromise with Rani Suryamani, the guardian of the minor Raja.[17] The ritual functionaries of the temple played a very significant role in the affair. Even before the actual suit was instituted, they had petitioned the British Commissioner against the proposed move. The petition declared in no uncertain terms that the temple servants could serve only under the Raja of Puri, 'the most respectable person among the Hindoos of India'. They were willing to accept punishment when it was due from this 'most respectable person'. To serve under the members of the proposed committee would be nothing but humiliating.[18]

The state of independent India inherited a curious and conflicting legacy. As an avowedly modern, secular state, it subscribed to the 'separation-of-power' model.[19] At the same time, the Constitution, an extremely detailed and intricate document, granted the judiciary enormous power as the overall arbiter. This arbiter was to exercise 'regulative oversight' to ensure the smooth functioning of various social controls, in particular religion. Articles 25 and 26 of the Indian Constitution established the primacy of public interests over religious claims and granted a wide scope to governmentally sponsored reforms. The Constitution thus disposed of the notion of a preordained separate religious sphere entailed by the separation-of-power model. The state and its legal machinery took on the new role of the reformer with gusto. Alongside, they carried on the task, initiated by British rule, of systematization and classification of knowledge, convinced of its efficacy as a mode of exercising governance. The treatment of religious institutions as public trusts continued, as did the stress on their efficient 'management'. All this brought about significant changes in the fortunes of the Raja of Puri and the temple of Jagannath within a few years of independence. The colonial state's insistence on 'improvement' and 'protection' combined with belief in a vague notion of *dharma*, moral duty, to make the take-over of the management of the temple by the state of Orissa in 1955 legitimate and necessary.

I have indicated that the power and authority of the Oriya prince was severely restricted by the pronounced presence of the colonial state. The eagerness of British officials to codify customs and usage, and rights and duties of temple functionaries, prompted ritual servants to use these written customs as 'inalienable rights'. This they used with equal success against both the colonial and the postcolonial state, and against the king of Puri. Moreover, the treatment of the temple as a trust by the government of the Company and the English crown that gave no recognition to the sovereign personality of the deity and his capacity to confer 'legitimate authority' on his deputy – the king – made the *sebaks* completely independent of the Raja. The continuity of their service no longer depended on the will of the first servant. The triangular relationship of indirect exchange between kings, priests, and deities that Chris Fuller has shown to exist in the temples, was broken.[20] The crown, emptied of political dynamic and authority, became 'hollow'.[21]

And it was precisely the fact that the king of Puri had no control over the other servants of the temple, which made him 'unfit' to supervise the running of that religious institution in independent India. The 'secular' government of the state of Orissa, even more than its colonial predecessor, felt the need for legislative action to save the temple from decay. The Minister of Law and Home, in his speech in the State Legislature, dwelt at length on the 'lawlessness' that prevailed in the temple to urge for the necessity of legal intervention.

> In the absence of any guidance from the Raja and sufficient contribution from him for the regular expenses of the Temple, the scheduled and disciplined performance of the Nitis has suffered beyond imagination and the Raja has practically lost all control over the different sebaks and other temple servants. Economic rivalry and moral degeneration of the servants and sebaks has divested them of all sense of duty and cooperation. Specific endowments are regularly misapplied and misappropriated. . . . the nonavailability at the appointed hours of the Mahaprasad coveted by millions of pilgrims is always there these days. The lapse into unorthodoxy has resulted in extremely unhygienic conditions inside the temple and commission of heinous crimes even within the temple precincts is not rare; even the image of the deity has at times been defiled and its precious jewellery removed.[22]

The Minister was convincing. The Jagannath Temple Administration Bill was introduced in the State Legislature and the Shri Jagannath Temple (Administration) Act (No. XIV of 1952) was passed. The Act provided for the appointment of a Special Officer who was to draw up a list of 'the rights and duties of different Sebaks and Pujaris and such other persons connected with the Sebapuja or management of the Temple and its endowments'. This list was expected to bring order into the administration of the temple. The Special Officer drew up a Record-of-Rights and submitted his report on 15 March 1954. This report once again urged reform, highlighting the mis-management prevailing in the temple. The Shri Jagannath Temple Act of 1955 took away the superintendence of the temple from the Raja and vested its administration and governance in the Shri Jagannath Temple Managing Committee, with the Raja of Puri as its Chairman. A provision of the Act appointed an administrator as the Secretary of the Temple Managing Committee and gave him the virtual power of administration.

Ram Chandra Deb, the Raja of Puri, did not accept the decision.

He, and subsequently his son Bir Kishore Deb, filed suits in the High Court of Orissa and then the Supreme Court of India that challenged the constitutional validity of the Shri Jagannath Temple Act.[23] The Rajas lost the suits. A powerful and autonomous judiciary came to the aid of the state. Through elaborate verdicts, the High Court of Orissa and the Supreme Court of India granted sanctity to the measures taken by the state of Orissa with regard to the temple of Jagannath and upheld the validity of the Act of 1955. The arguments of the Raja were squashed as 'untenable' and his appeals dismissed.

I will not rehearse the details of the verdicts here.[24] Rather, I will examine the assumptions that underlay the rulings of the courts and explore their implications. The decisions of the High Court and the Supreme Court underscored the new confidence the judges had acquired following the elevated position granted to the judiciary by the Constitution. The judges had become both the custodians and creators of ideology. Interestingly, in this secular role they came very close to the Hindu king as the supreme judge, who according to Dumont, served as the essential link between the brahmanic world of *dharma* and the empirical world of men over which the dharmic order was to prevail. The guardians of justice of independent India carefully identified and constituted the sphere of religion within which neutrality was to operate, and simultaneously defined what religion, in this case, Hinduism is. The definition was in tune with the idea of a unified and uniform Hinduism held by middle class Hindu intellectuals.[25]

The claim of the Raja(s) of Puri that worshippers of Jagannath formed a distinct religious group was summarily dismissed. Jagannath was the Lord of all Hindus. Hadn't British administrators and scholars sung the praises of the syncretic cult that drew its adherents from all Hindu sects? The administration of the temple of Jagannath, a public temple that belonged to all Hindus, could thus be placed in the hands of a managing committee comprised exclusively of Hindus, without violating any clause of the Constitution.[26]

The verdicts also brought to the fore the legal system's reliance on 'precedents' – a reliance that made individual court cases part of a seamless history and devoid, at times, of 'context sensitivity'. Moreover, the judgements used the colonial period as the constant and near exclusive reference. The history of intervention by British rule in the management of the temple was reproduced to highlight the subordination of the Raja to the higher state authority. The government take-over of the temple was strongly endorsed.

The dubious dichotomy of the religious and the secular was applied to distinguish between the rights and privileges of the Oriya prince as the first servant of Jagannath and his duties as the Superintendent. This came very close to the distinction made by Dumont between status and power to argue that in India the spiritual and the temporal were separate with the temporal submitting to the spiritual. Interestingly, the delineation of the ritual from the political by the judges was used to establish the superiority of the state, the decidedly temporal, over the jumbled authority claimed by the king of Puri. His rights and prerogatives as the prime servitor of the deity were shown to be religious and 'traditional' – based on 'ancient custom and usage as recorded in Madala Panji and Niladri Mahoday and as permitted by tradition'.[27] The Raja's power as the Superintendent, on the other hand, was purely secular, and owed its origin to the munificence of a higher authority, the 'modern' colonial state.[28] It 'derived solely from the grant made by the ruling power by Regulation IV of 1809'.[29] It followed, then, that it was perfectly legitimate for the postcolonial state to supervise and, if necessary, intervene. All that the Shri Jagannath Temple Act had done was to substitute the position of the Raja as the sole Superintendent of the temple by his chairmanship of a committee of eleven members. It had carefully safeguarded the Raja's rights, privileges and perquisites as the first servant. The task of the committee of eleven was to arrange for the efficient organization of the *sevapuja* and the 'daily and periodical Nitis' (rituals and ceremonies) of the temple and supervise the activities of temple servants.[30] This was a purely 'secular' function that had no bearing on the religious part of the services. Indeed, it was a duty of the secular state to ensure the proper management of the temple and an efficient performance of their services by the ritual functionaries for the benefit of the 'users' of the public institution. The inextricably bound ritual and political powers of the Oriya prince were overwritten by a polarization of the sacred and the secular that pronounced the omnipotence of the bureaucratic state and undermined the legitimacy of the king.

The take-over of the management by the state of Orissa has not improved its administration. The effort of the secular state to combine colonial ideas of protection and improvement of the temple – a public trust – with the Hindu notion of *dharma* to implement its supreme authority, has been foiled by the resourceful servants of the temple. These ritual functionaries cleverly divorce status from the power of the secular state to dodge its attempts at control. The state, not in any way related to the deity, does not have the legitimacy that the Hindu Raja had as the deputy and the first servant of the sovereign lord. The Raja was eligible to exercise *danda* – the authority to govern and punish his subjects in general and the temple servants in particular. The state of independent India, though more powerful than the Raja, lacks the king's moral authority to arbitrate in matters of religion. Hence it cannot appropriate the role of the king in relation to the temple. In actual practice, the ritual specialists and pilgrim traders connected to the temple frequently circumvent the authority of the Temple Administrator, an official of the state's civil services, by resorting to his superiors. This has made it possible for the present Raja of Puri to articulate his displeasure at the state's 'negligence' of its duties toward the temple. Positions stand reversed, while the problems and contradictions of the entanglement of religion and politics continue.

NOTES

1. For an important formulation of a theory of religion as a system of symbol and meanings within anthropology see, Clifford Geertz, 'Religion as a Cultural System', in Geertz, *The Interpretation of Cultures* (New York: Basic Books, 1973), pp. 87-125.
2. Here I draw heavily upon the arguments of Talal Asad advanced in 'The Construction of Religion as an Anthropological Category', in Talal Asad, *Genealogies of Religion: Discipline and Reasons of Power in Christianity and Islam* (Baltimore and London: The Johns Hopkins University Press, 1993), pp. 27-54.
3. The several works of Hermann Kulke provide detailed and incisive analyses of the relationship of the cult of Jagannath and the Gajapati kings of Orissa. See, for instance, 'Early Royal Patronage of the Jagannatha Cult', in Eschmann, Kulke, Tripathi (eds.), *The Cult of Jagannath and the Regional Tradition of Orissa* (New Delhi: Manohar, 1978), pp. 139-56; *Jagannatha-Kult und Gajapati-Königtum. Ein Beitrag zur Geschichte religiöser Legitimation hinduistischer Herrscher* (Wiesbaden: Franz Steiner Verlag, 1979);

and 'King Anagabhima, the Veritable Founder of the Gajapati Kingship and of the Jagannatha Trinity at Puri', in Kulke, *Kings and Cults: State Formation and Legitimation in India and South East Asia* (New Delhi: Manohar, 1993), pp. 17-32.

4. Jan Gonda, *Ancient Indian Kingship from the Religious Point of View*, cited in Ranajit Guha, 'Dominance without Hegemony and its Historiography', in Ranajit Guha (ed.), *Subaltern Studies,* VI: *Writings on South Asian History and Society* (New Delhi: Oxford University Press, 1992), p. 238.
5. For a statement, elaboration, and analysis of this theory see Louis Dumont, *Homo Hierarchicus: The Caste System and its Implications* (trans. Mark Sainsbury, Louis Dumont and Basia Gulati, Chicago and London: The University of Chicago Press, 1980), in particular pp. 68-71, 75-8. Dumont makes a clear demarcation between status and power, and between spiritual and temporal authority, to argue that in India the supremacy of the spiritual was never expressed politically, and that while in actual practice (secondary level), the king counterbalanced the brahman who was ritually purer and higher in status, at the primary level (of theory), kingship submitted to priesthood. This separation of the spiritual and the political, and the supremacy of the brahman (*dharma*/status) over the king (temporal/ power), falls through once the king combines the spiritual and the political by claiming to rule in the name of a sovereign deity, and legitimizing his power by drawing upon status. This instance, very common in ancient and medieval India, has not been taken into account at all by Dumont.
6. Kulke, 'Jagannātha as the State Deity under the Gajapatis of Orissa', in *The Cult of Jagannath*, pp. 199-208.
7. *Idem*, 'Ksatriyaization and Social Change: A Study in Orissa Setting', in *Kings and Cults*, p. 86.
8. The Nawabs of Bengal became virtually independent in the 1730s and 1740s with the decline of Mughal authority.
9. Kulke, 'Kṣetra and Kṣatra: The Cult of Jagannātha of Puri and the "Royal Letters" (*Chamu Citaus)* of the Rājās of Khurda', in *Kings and Cults*, p. 54.
10. *Idem*, 'Kshatriyaization and Social Change', pp. 86-7.
11. A letter from the Secretary to Government notified the Magistrate of Zillah Cuttack that 'the Honourable Governor General in Council has been pleased to resolve that the Rajah of Khoordah be released from confinement'. Secretary to Government to Magistrate, Zillah Cuttack, 5 March 1807, Jagannath Temple Correspondence, Part I, p. 71. Regulation IV of 1809 vested 'the superintendence of the temple, its internal autonomy, the conduct and management of its affairs and the control over its priests and officers' in the Raja.
12. Report of Charles Grome, the Collector of Southern Division at Puri,

10 June 1805, Department of Revenue, 26 January 1805 to 10 July 1805, Orissa State Archives, Bhubaneswar.

13. The hold of the Hindu Rajas over the landed estates assigned for the meals of Jagannath and the temple servants weakened in the sixteenth century with the defeat of Pratap Rudra Dev. This was aided by a different factor – the move of Caitanya to Puri. Caitanya's message of love and devotion transformed the lofty Lord-of-the-Universe into a pliant personal god, and his *prasad*, graced left-over – the reserve of a select few – into the unpollutable *mahaprasad*, the 'great grace' of a universal god that erased social distances among his worshippers. From this time on, the grant of *amruta manohi* (nectar-feeding) lands for the food offerings made to Jagannath and a share in his *prasad* no longer remained the prerogative of the ruler. Greater accessibility of the *mahaprasad* resulted in an increase in the number of patrons. Pilgrims to Jagannath were encouraged to donate lands for the food of the Lord. This was also the time when enterprising temple servants initiated the 'Jatri business' (pilgrim trade). For a critical analysis of this process see Ishita Banerjee-Dube, *Divine Affairs: Religion, Pilgrimage, and the State in Colonial and Postcolonial India* (Shimla: Indian Institute of Advanced Study, 2001), pp. 96-125.
14. Indeed, studies have shown that even Elizabethan England revealed a marked ambivalence and anxiety toward this separation, while the rule of James I saw a prevalence of the notion of divine kingship. Deborah Kuller Shuger, *Habits of Thought in the English Renaissance: Religion, Politics, and the Dominant Culture* (Berkeley: University of California Press, 1990).
15. Ranajit Guha argues that the transition of Britain's occupation of India from its predatory, mercantilist beginnings to a 'regulated empire', was marked by a corresponding shift from an idiom of conquest to an idiom of order. Ranajit Guha, 'Dominance without Hegemony and its Historiography', p. 234.
16. The seven volumes of Jagannath Temple Correspondence that cover the period of colonial rule in Orissa, abound in instances of British officials consulting and seeking the advice of its pundits in matters relating to the ritual services, ceremonies and festivals. They turned to the pundits as persons well versed in the scriptures and customs of the Hindu tradition, urged on by a belief that the Raja-Superintendent was not doing his job well. For an incisive analysis of the process by which colonial knowledge on India was generated through the joint efforts of the colonizers and the colonized see, Bernard Cohn, *Colonialism and Its Forms of Knowledge: The British in India* (Princeton: Princeton University Press, 1996); Nicholas B. Dirks, 'Introduction', in Dirks (ed.), *Colonialism and Culture* (Ann Arbor: The University of Michigan Press, 1992), pp. 1-25.
17. For an analysis of this law-suit and its implications, see Banerjee-Dube, 'Travails of the Lord: Disputed Claims of the Khurda Rajas of Puri as

Custodians of the Jagannath Temple', in Joseph T. O'Connell (ed.), *Institutional and Organisational Aspects of Religious Movements* (Shimla: Indian Institute of Advanced Study, 1998), pp. 29-34; and Banerjee-Dube, *Divine Affairs*, pp. 66-76.

18. To the Commissioner of Orissa, the petition of the servants of God Juggernath of Pooroosattam Khetter, 8 July 1882, Jagannath Temple Correspondence, Part VI, pp. 1384-5.
19. It has been rightly argued that there is disagreement over the meanings and implications of a secular state. It can stand for 'a severe aloofness from religion, a benign impartiality toward religion, a corrective oversight of it, or a fond and equal indulgence of all religions'. Marc Galanter, *Law and Society in Modern India* (New Delhi: Oxford University Press, 1992), p. 237.
20. Christopher J. Fuller, *Servants of the Goddess. The Priests of a South Indian Temple* (Oxford: Oxford University Press, 1991).
21. I borrow this from Nicholas Dirks. Taking the example of a Hindu kingdom in south India, Dirks provides an incisive analysis of the wide ranging processes set in motion by colonial rule that transformed indigenous kingship into a 'hollow crown'. Nicholas B. Dirks, *The Hollow Crown. Ethnohistory of an Indian Kingdom* (Cambridge: Cambridge University Press, 1987).
22. N. R. Hota, *Final Report on Ekhrajat Mahal 1953 to 1965* (Cuttack, 1965). Also cited in Banerjee-Dube, *Divine Affairs*, p. 77.
23. It is interesting to note that the lawyers of the Rajas argued that the Act of 1955 contravened Article 26 of the Indian Constitution. This article, in their opinion, granted distinct religious bodies the freedom to manage their own affairs and to administer the properties of the temple in accordance with law. This is an instance of different interpretations of the same clause of the Constitution by distinct groups.
24. For detailed analyses of the verdicts see Banerjee-Dube, 'Travails of the Lord', and *Divine Affairs*, pp. 79-86.
25. A legal scholar has argued that the decision-making habits of Supreme Court Judges are not much different from those of middle class metropolitan Indians, 'technically unpredictable, not uninfluenced by imitative cosmopolitan habits'. Rajeev Dhavan, *The Supreme Court of India: A Socio-Legal Analysis of Juristic Techniques*; *idem*, 'Introduction', in Marc Galanter, *Law and Society in Modern India,* p. xxix.
26. I do not mean to suggest that the judges were wrong in declaring Jagannath to be the god of all Hindus. What I wish to emphasize is the authority with which they made the pronouncement. This case was a part of several others in the 1950s and 1960s in which the Supreme Court made confident statements regarding what did and did not constitute Hinduism. See, for instance, Chandra Mudaliar, *State and Religious Endowments in Madras*

(Madras: Madras University Press, 1976), pp. 250-78; Marc Galanter, 'Hinduism, Secularism and the Indian Judiciary', in Galanter, *Law and Society*, pp. 237-56.

27. On Appeal from the High Court of Orissa, Supreme Court Appeal, No. 31, Part I, Record of Proceedings in the High Court of Orissa, No. 6, Judgement, 30 April 1958, p. 159.
28. Note the pervasive presence and uncritical acceptance of binaries – tradition/ modern, religious/secular – in this argument.
29. *Ibid.* (see n. 27).
30. *Supreme Court Decisions*, Vol. 4, 1964, p. 763.

CHAPTER 14

Problematizing Heritage: Region, Religion and the Making of Cultural Identity

YAAMINEY MUBAYI

Mention the word 'Kashmir' in a South Asian gathering and the reaction could be explosive. Contending claims to this 'paradise on earth' have made the nationalistic rhetoric in the two antagonistic states a 'lifeblood' issue. Amidst the official jargon, however, a pattern of geopolitical inter-linkages is discernible which would appear to cause both countries to appropriate the valley in a spirit of a larger cultural consciousness. It is this consciousness, with highly elastic boundaries, that denotes a culturally constituted region and its heritage.

Such a heritage, ubiquitous in South Asia, is a pluralistic entity, where multiple communities as stakeholders each assert their claims, but essentially co-exist in a shared socio-cultural space. Problems arise, however, when the dynamics of contemporary majoritarian politics seeks to engulf this entity. Heritage comes to be appropriated by a single community or a group. This situation confronts South Asia today, when the historically evolved dynamics of shared cultural spaces have been subverted by the politics of numbers, and 'region' and 'identity' have come together as areas of contention and exclusivity.

'Region' is a problematic term, simply because of the variety of structures it subsumes. Regions can be instituted, created at the stroke of a pen, or denoted with administrative or geographical intent. It is, however, the experienced region where material and symbolic space is designated as such by its own inhabitants that we are concerned with. Amongst such a mix of communities, their environment and their historical relationships with each other, the people's 'shared reaction' to their own space contributes to the creation of particular cultural patterns that can be collectively viewed as their heritage.[1]

Social status, folk traditions, village rituals, local histories and dialects, belief systems, food habits and attire, are interwoven into the complex cultural tapestry of the region, and can be drawn upon to mobilize the collective identity of its inhabitants when required. This is the essence of that elusive entity, heritage, an amalgam of identities, attitudes, property, resources and relation-ships. This highly fluid complex can only be identified when called upon in relation to a comparable socio-political system, when the particular community requires its concerns to be expressed. It is not devoid of internal logic, however, or of inherent conflict and the means of its resolution.

Different communities in India have focused and drawn upon their collective identities in response to social and political changes in their habitat. The outbreak of tribal rebellions in the Chhotanagpur region in the nineteenth century, for example, beautifully illustrate the coalescing of heritage and identity, forming the core of the physical spread of the movements. The proclivity to loot, plunder and pillage by the Bhils of Khandesh in the eighteenth and nineteenth centuries, has been regarded as an expression of an alternative sovereignty, endorsed by their identity as 'jangli' (wild). Such practices came up sharply against the dominant model of governance, the 'rule of law' that was being imposed by the colonial state at the time. Instances of conflict between custom and law are best expressed in the case of the management of the Jagannatha temple lands along the eastern coast. Here, the multiple nuances of rights and obligations inherent in the notion of *seba*, were curtailed and circumscribed by colonial efforts at 'systematizing' temple management and extracting maximum revenue from the land. The legal and social changes initiated in this period find fuller expression in post-colonial India, where litigation over temple lands has in fact led to revenue *minimization,* temple impoverishment, and losses to the state.

Historical, political, ethnic and social motivations can be observed as coming together to define a community's response to the changing needs of its habitat in a cultural sense. The awareness of who we are and what is ours, underlie the definition and defence of a particular heritage. The heritage in question, whether status, right to territory or material wealth, has been a problematic area with blurred boundaries, with multiple and contending claims in the past. These blurred and feeble linkages, however, could suddenly sharpen focus and create a powerful channel for the transmission of the past to the present with terrifying force.

FUSING REGIONAL CONSCIOUSNESS, IDENTITY AND HERITAGE

Historically, heritage has been selectively drawn upon to define cultural identity while expressing the concerns of communities in situations of violence and conflict. The tribal rebellions of Chhotanagpur and the practice of ritual plunder amongst the Bhils of Khandesh illustrate the fusing together of cultural identity around issues of territorialism and land rights.

Tribal and Peasant rebellions of the nineteenth century, particularly the Santhal (1855) and Kol (1832) movements, the Birsaite *ulgulan* (1898) and the Paik rebellion of coastal Orissa (1817), were in retaliation to the dis-possession of landed groups by colonial revenue policies, the Permanent Settlement (1793), and the Bengal jagirdari system. The common motif running through the different uprisings was the central issue of territoriality, the drawing upon of a common lineage and physical habitat by the rebels to further their cause.[2]

By defining the 'self' against the 'other', the rebels projected their concerns as victims of duplicity and oppression by *dikus* or foreigners.[3] Within the ethnic space created for themselves, the rebels spread solidarity through common concerns, such as the 'innocence' of the tribal peasantry exploited by the perpetrators of the new revenue systems, the spoliation of their physical habitat, the 'forests and rivers . . . trees, fish, lands, jagirs . . .' taken away by *dikus*, so that they could no longer live in harmony with their environment.

Violence was also an intrinsic part of the internal social dynamism of certain communities. The Bhils of the Khandesh forest tracts of central-western India which was under Maratha rule actively raided villages to establish their authority over the countryside as an alternative power centre. They considered it their privilege to plunder the settled peasant communities of the Gaekwad-Maratha territories. The Bhil raids, or *dhads*, were symbolic of authority over the region, and they claimed the plundered wealth as tribute, picturesquely termed *hak* (right). Such *haks* were regarded as *giras* (mouthful), and were a direct claim to the plunderers' status as brigand chiefs. In fact, the ritually higher castes of the region, such as the Koknis, often identified with the Bhils in order to claim a share of the authority of plunder possessed by the 'jangli' Bhils.[4]

Adopting a persona of wildness that gave them their particular status in the country's political and material hierarchy, the Bhils also called themselves 'Mahadev's thieves', thereby giving themselves a ritual sanction for their raiding activities. They were an important part of the balance of power in the region, a check to the authority of the kings, who depended upon their support and honoured their *haks*. During the accession of the British administration, the Gaekwad *killedars* fought to retain their alliances with the Bhil chiefs, sometimes even by offering them *haks* independently of the colonial rulers. The necessary presence of the Bhil chiefs at the coronation of the Gaekwad rajas indicates their significant role in maintaining the ritual-political structure of governance in the region.

The presence of alternative foci of power was not a threat to the state in pre-colonial society – rather it was the notion of shared sovereignty that energized the peculiar socio-political order. The power of the sovereign was reinforced, not diminished, by multiple claimants to authority. Alternatively, the acknowledgement of *girasiya* rights by Gaekwad officials was a way of controlling or channelizing the wildness of the Bhils. When the region came under British dominance, however, the Bhils and their activities came to be regarded as 'wild' and 'aberrant', and the *dhads* were termed 'criminal'. The colonial state operated through a system of centralized revenue collection – the notion of shared sovereignty with its multiple foci of power became anachronistic in this milieu. Revenue gained ascendancy over status as a form of the exercise of power.

THE RITUAL OF POWER AND THE INTERPLAY OF STATUS, SEBA AND THE STATE IN TEMPLE COMMUNITIES

When the mainstream institutions of state and society are viewed, there is need to explore the issues underlying identity-building and the exercise of power over the land. In pre-colonial India, temples and their communities formed a space for the interplay of status, ideology and politics, as also being the focus for the exchange of wealth into status. Temples were a microcosm of the social reality around them.

The relationship between a temple and the local kingship was a highly nuanced one. Kings patronized temples and related institutions by mobilizing people, resources and materials in their building and development, and utilized the networks of pilgrims and devotees to project their authority, in relation with the temple's popularity, beyond their territorial frontiers.

Another dimension to the temple-state's structure of authority in and beyond the region was provided by *mathas*, affiliated institutions that linked the temples to trans-regional ideological and material networks. *Mathas* proliferated as corporate institutions with monastic traditions bearing sectarian affiliations. They were important centres along the 'information highways' of the pre-modern world, viz., trade and pilgrim routes, market towns, and temple centres, where their *dharmashalas* attracted the exchange of ideas and information through itinerant traders, monks, and pilgrims.

The Kautuka *matha* in Sanjan, a trading town on the Konkan coast, founded in AD 900 under the patronage of the ruling Rashtrakuta dynasty, depicts an interesting instance of the type of checks on the role of the state in its interaction with religious institutions of the time.[5] The *matha* administration was entrusted by the Rashtrakuta kings Krsna II and Indra II to the Arab governors of the region, highlighting the significance of the Arab trading community in the political and economic affairs along the Konkan trade routes. There is evidence of Arab assimilation into the cultural mainstream through marriage alliances, and the Arab governor is recorded as having donated land for the upkeep of Pancagaudiya brahmins in the *matha* as well. The *matha* thus stood for a cosmopolitan and pluralistic setting with respect to its management, activities, and connections with the land.

A dispute developed between the *matha* and a nearby Visnu temple that was patronized by low-caste Bhillamala traders who had recently migrated to the region from Rajasthan. The conflict arose over a plot of land belonging to the temple that was enclosed within the *matha* compound. To decide the issue, a *vyavastha* (judgement) was issued by the Rashtrakuta king, representing a mutually acceptable agreement whereupon the *matha* would pay 40 silver *madhas* to the temple annually as rent for the enclosed plot.

The case is interesting because it highlights the restrained exercise of royal authority by the Rashtrakuta kings in a manner that defused the tension between the two institutions without making any major structural changes to the disputed property. The *matha* represented a well-entrenched cosmopolitan tradition involving trade as well as landed connections. The temple was under the patronage of a newly-migrated trading community, who had possibly not yet fully established their credentials in the local society. The *vyavastha* tactfully dispersed any potential rivalry between the two trading groups and represented their interests in a mutually satisfactory manner.

The prominence of status as a perceived power was seriously challenged by colonial rule, wherein the monetary value of land and resources gained ascendancy over ideological factors. Land became a means for extracting maximum revenue through commodification and alienation, rather than as an expression of authority through access and control.

An excellent example of this clash of perceptions is the Jagannatha temple at Puri, regarded as the largest land-owning entity in eastern India. It is impossible to estimate the exact extent of lands donated and managed under its name. A popular proverb describes the temple as owning property in every taluk and village along the east coast. An exact estimate of the property was not relevant to temple functioning, however. All the required material for rituals and maintenance were procured through established grants, *matha* networks, and royal patronage. Thus the notion of *Amritamanohi* lands, viz., those yielding 'ambrosial food' for the deity was more an amorphous idea indicating the extent of the temple's influence in the region. The actual property was scattered over vast distances so that it was neither practical nor efficient to claim revenue from them. Their value lay in the status that the donations accorded to the devotees, and to the peasants who worked the lands as privileged tenants of a divine landlord.

The colonial administration, after establishing a Board of Revenue at Cuttack in 1803, began a programme for the systematization of revenue collection that included the tabulation of all lands, their resumption and redistribution as zamindaris. The Jagannatha temple was viewed by the officials as a tremendous potential source of revenue through the amount collected as Pilgrim Tax, a traditional cess imposed on pilgrims to Puri, as well as the *Amritamanohi* lands.

Under the overarching structure of revenue maximization policies such as the Permanent Settlement and the Sunset Laws, the colonial administration in Orissa began to reclassify all territories that were not directly under princely rule. Having assumed the direct administration of the Jagannatha temple in 1803, they proceeded to separate the *Amritamanohi* lands, which were to be kept aside for temple maintenance, from other lands which could be put up for cultivation under zamindars. This was not easy, given that the *Amritamanohi* lands were not clearly demarcated entities. Traditional ownership of land included multiple usufructory rights, alternatively and simultaneously termed *dhana*, *adhikara*, *bhoga*, or *svamitva* in the classical texts on jurisprudence.[6]

Specifically, difficulties arose when the colonial authorities tried to separate lands endowed to *mathas* for temple services, from *Amritamanohi* lands. For instance, in the case of the Sataishazari Mahal, or the 'fund of 27,000', a traditional endowment for the maintenance of particular rituals, we see the full extent of the clash between alternative perceptions of order, the indigenous and the colonial. The 'fund of 27,000' symbolizing a notionally appropriate figure demarcating the resources for temple use, was based on a quit-rent collected from the prestigious Brahmin settlements around Puri, called *sasanas*, and was used to maintain the *kotha bhoga*, or the 'household expenditure' of Jagannatha. It indicated certain areas for collection but was essentially a symbolic entity, both in terms of the amount of revenue collected and extent of property. The British government had initially assumed direct administration of the Jagannatha temple in 1803, a proposition that became increasingly difficult to carry out, owing to the contradictory policy of 'non-interference' in local affairs espoused by the East India Company management at a higher level, and the efforts of the Company's officials to intensify control over affairs on the ground.

What that translated into was this: the 'direct' administration of the temple by the Company involved the deployment of large-scale funds, approximately Rs. 53,000 per annum, for its maintenance. These were to be defrayed from the revenue collected as Pilgrim Tax. In the 1820s and 1830s, there was mounting pressure on the Company's Directors from the Evangelicals as well as the Free Trade lobbyists in Britain, to dissociate themselves from 'idolatrous' institutions like the Jagannatha temple. This led to the abolition of the Pilgrim Tax in 1840. Now that a lucrative source of revenue was unavailable, and their obligation to maintain the temple continued, the government made over some lands including the Sataishazari Mahal to the temple in 1858.

However, this did not prevent the administration from interfering in the management of temple lands. In fact, the rhetoric of 'withdrawal' from temple affairs by colonial authorities masked the intensification of their control through details of regulation, particularly through fiscal management. For instance, the origins of the Sataishazari Mahal were carefully investigated, and it was discovered that there was 'no sunnud' recording the grant in history, simply a revenue amount that was fixed by custom.[7] The property included some *inam* lands as well, which were to be excluded from the category of *Amritamanohi*. Other lands, whose revenues could not be ascertained, were also excluded from the grant and clubbed together as 'tahseel alahida', literally 'lands', etc. Besides revenue management, the Company administration took charge of flood control, health services, law and order and other administrative mechanisms that ensured their control over the lands. The temple became another 'department' under the Company administration, and the sacredness of the temple lands, the status of the various users, the diverse nature of their multiple claims, were submerged by the minutiae regarding revenue types, the details of collection, the fixing of boundaries and the 'freezing' of land tenures.[8]

The penetration of the realm of temple property and status by colonial revenue and legal processes did not pass unchallenged by the populace. These were not only changes in revenue collection, they symbolized the overturning of an entire worldview, and subverted the identity of thousands of land-users, an identity that was directly related to their status *vis-à-vis* the temple. One form of protest was the rebellion by the dispossessed landed militia, the Paiks of Puri, in 1817 (as mentioned earlier). However, a more subtle and far-reaching resistance to the changes may be found in the flood of litigation in the newly-established colonial courts, wherein multiple claimants to the land and its products emerged to stake their claim to the newly settled properties. Interestingly, since the new laws gave an equal hearing to all claimants, a number of petitions that would customarily have been deemed invalid, were entertained in the courts, and some even granted. For instance, there is a case in the Sadr Diwani Adalat Records of Bengal wherein the right of succession of a *mathadhari*, the supervisor of a *matha* in Puri, was challenged by a rival office-bearer who produced a 'deed of succession' in his own favour, that was ostensibly signed by the previous supervisor. Later, this document was found to be forged. The dependence of the colonial courts on documentary evidence as the major guideline for legal procedure, as opposed to custom and popular perception, often led to such contradictions. This was the point at which the dichotomy between the imposed legal and revenue structures and the prevailing reality of perception regarding property, and through property, social status and identity, began to intensify. This dichotomy has not been rationalized to this day, and much of the Jagannatha temple property is under litigation, a major factor in the contemporary resource crunch faced by the institution.

CONCLUSION

The roots of conflict over property, status, and identity are often found in the contradictions between the present and the past, when modernity is imposed on, and has not evolved from, tradition, through a process of logical elimination of anachronistic practices. In such a situation, constitutional processes, laws, and bureaucracy can become instruments for exploiting the system for personal gain by vested interests. The colonial government created a situation wherein institutions were preserved as figureheads, disconnected from the political and economic linkages that acted as checks and balances and connected them to the land and the people. The princely states are an important example. Temples and other sacred spaces too, were a victim to such a disjuncture, and their management was completely entrapped by Acts, Special Committees, Management Reports, minutes, memos and, finally, litigation.

It is unfortunate that the post-independence state in India has done little to remedy such anachronisms, and in the matter of heritage, has largely followed the institutional framework dating back to the time of Lord Curzon. For example, the Jagannatha Temple Act of 1961 places the management of the temple in the hands of a Temple Committee, headed by an SDM level civil servant, of which the Puri Raja, traditionally regarded as the *rautta* (deputy) of Jagannatha himself, is simply the Secretary. The dichotomy between the power of custom and the mechanisms of state authority have continuously prevented any sustainable effort in temple management, particularly with reference to financial management. Instead of becoming a self-sustaining and even profitable institution, the temple has become a financial liability for the state, with its lands under litigation and its donor funds not being channelized for development purposes. The colonial spirit of the state subsidizing, yet dissociating itself from developing of, the temple, continues.

Such a state-centred model for managing heritage is simply not sustainable, as it first and foremost divides the community from its cultural legacy, and secondly, deprives it of the right to participate in its development. It thereby throws open the situation to exploitation by vested interests, to the exclusion of the community. The identification of a people with notions of region and identity has to be addressed in a manner which promotes inclusivity and celebrates plurality. This can only be done when policy formation takes place in a culturally sensitive and logical manner, taking contemporary material and social conditions into account.

NOTES

1. Karine Schomer *et al.* (ed.), *The Idea of Rajasthan: Explorations in Regional Identity*, New Delhi: Manohar, 1994.
2. Ranajit Guha, *Elementary Aspects of Peasant Insurgency in Colonial India*, New Delhi: Oxford University Press, 1983, pp. 278-337.
3. A term encompassing not merely the British administration, but also Bengali zamindars, moneylenders, tahsildars, outsiders in general, looters, deceivers, and so on.
4. Ajay Skaria, 'Being Jangli: The Politics of Wildness', in *Studies in History*, Vol. XIV, 1998.
5. Ranabir Chakravarti, 'Merchants, Monarchs and a Matha in Northern Konkan (*c*. 900-1053 AD)', in *IESHR*, Vol. 27, No. 2, 1990.
6. J. D. M. Derrett, *Introduction to Modern Hindu Law*, New Delhi: Oxford University Press, 1963.
7. O. W. Malet, Esq., Officiating Collector of Pooree, to The Commissioner for the 19th Division, Cuttack, No. 86, Dated Pooree, 23 February 1842, JTC, Vol. 3.

8. Y. Mubayi, *Altar of Power: The Temple and the State in the Land of Jagannatha (c. 16th-19th centuries)*, New Delhi: Manohar, 2004.

REFERENCES

Appadurai, Arjun, *Worship and Conflict under Colonial Rule,* Cambridge: Cambridge University Press, 1981.

Chakravarti, Ranabir, 'Monarchs, Merchants and a Matha in Northern Konkan (*c.* 900-1053 AD)', *IESHR*, Vol. 27, No. 2, 1990.

Cohn, Bernard S., *An Anthropologist among the Historians and Other Essays*, New Delhi: Oxford University Press, 1987.

Derret, J.D.M., *Introduction to Modern Hindu Law*, New Delhi: Oxford University Press, 1963.

———, *Religion, Law and the State in India*, London: Faber and Faber, 1968.

Guha, Ranajit, *Elementary Aspects of Peasant Insurgency in Colonial India*, New Delhi: Oxford University Press, 1983.

Jagannatha Temple Correspondence (JTC), 1804-1832, Orissa Research Project (ORP), Mss. 130, Orissa State Archives, Bhubaneswar and The Orissa Archive, South Asia Institute, Heidelberg.

Mubayi, Y., *Altar of Power: The Temple and the State in the Land of Jagannatha (c. 16th-19th centuries)*, New Delhi: Manohar, 2004.

Presler, Franklin A., *Religion Under Bureaucracy: Policy and Administration for Hindu Temples in South India*, Cambridge: Cambridge University Press, 1987.

Schomer, Karine, et al. (eds), *The Idea of Rajasthan: Explorations in Regional Identity*, Vol. 1, New Delhi: Manohar, 1994.

Skaria, Ajay, 'Being Jangli: The Politics of Wildness', *Studies in History*, Vol. XIV, 1998.

CHAPTER 15

Mapping the Mahatma: Literary Tracts and Rumours in Late Colonial Orissa

CHANDI PRASAD NANDA*

This paper explores popular perceptions of Gandhi and the diverse forms of interplay of the Gandhian imagery with popular consciousness in colonial Orissa. It focuses on some Oriya literature on the theme and symbolism associated with Gandhi. It is worth pointing out that there was an upsurge in the publication of such texts after 1920.

Further, this paper also examines the nature and significance of rumours that developed around the 'Mahatma' and the way the concept of swaraj was sought to be given a dominant Gandhian flavour in the context of the mobilization and varied patterns of popular initiatives amongst the tribals of Koraput district of Orissa during the period of 1937-42. In delineating these above aspects, this paper highlights the complex interaction between the conventional understanding of Gandhian leadership in terms of message and style, and the popular images of Gandhi.

II

We begin with an examination of the nature and content of popular Oriya literature on Gandhi, published in the 1920s, specifically coinciding with Gandhi's call for Non-Cooperation. These tracts were authored by small-time 'hack' writers, and belonged to the world of popular literature, in contrast to the middle class nationalist literature. Composed mostly as poems and *bhajans*, these tracts sought to identify Gandhi as a new *avatar* born to liquidate evil from the earth, and whose birth signaled the arrival of a new age.

A tract entitled *Gandhi Avatar O Gandhi Bhajan* depicts Gandhi as the 'partial incarnation' of God.[1] The poet begins by articulating that it was due to the blessings of Sarala Das (fifteenty-century low-caste Oriya poet), Gandhi and Jagannath, that he could venture to pen his *bhajan*, which he refers to as the *Bharat Swaraj Purana*.

The poem points out that when the burden of 'sins and exploitation' weighed heavily on 'mother India', her deceased sons congregated in heaven to draw the attention of Vishnu and Laxmi to the miserable state of affairs caused by foreign rule. They appealed to the gods in order to decisively intervene to mitigate the sufferings of Indian people. The 'almighty', once convinced and realizing the urgency, promised to appear on the earth in a sort of 'partial incarnation' instead of a 'full incarnation' which would have been a time consuming process. Further, the 'almighty' consoled the devotees that He would be born in Gujarat, the land of piety, with which He had been earlier associated (in the *avatar* of Krishna). He also assured the devotees that in his Gandhi *avatar*, he would remove the misery of the Indians, through the *charkha* (spinning-wheel) and weave the 'Hindus-Muslims into one thread'.

The other crucial component of the poem is that it holds foreign rule, modernity, and Western civilization to be responsible for creating anarchy in Indian society and eroding its 'traditional values'. The poem is in fact set in the context of a critique of modernity and extols the 'glorious past' of India. The section on Gandhi *bhajan* as distinct from the Gandhi *avatar* exhorts devotees to continuously take the name of Gandhi along with Tilak and Gokhale and become involved in the making of Swaraj, discarding anything associated with British/ Western culture.

Similarly, another tract entitled *Gandhi Mahatmanka Gita* (songs about Gandhi Mahatma) begins with the depiction of India's glorious past, equating it with the land of heroes like Ramachandra, Yudhistira, Arjuna, Valmiki, Vedavyasa, Kalidasa and Shivaji.[2] The poem points out that the multi-faceted glory of India underwent a process of decline with the onset of 'foreign rule' and India was transformed into a 'mine of illiteracy and coal' in contrast to the 'progress of science and knowledge' of the past. In order to correct this anomaly, a Mahatma was born in Gujarat as Gandhi.

The poem goes on to describe the life and activities of Gandhi in

South Africa, Kheda and Champaran, wherein he took up causes and fought for the interests of the 'Indian brothers and sisters' and thus was deemed as God by one and all. It elaborates on the nature and programme of the Non-Cooperation movement waged by Gandhi against British rule, and exhorts people to realize the importance of the message as well as the futility of imitating the values associated with foreign rule. The poem refers to the Gandhian spinning wheel as the *sudarshan chakra* with whose support a person could be made economically independent and overcome the miseries of life. Interestingly, it refers to the 'cow' as the 'god' of the Hindus and holds the Hindus responsible for cow-slaughter as they – after utilizing the cow in cultivation – finally disposed it off to the butcher. Thus, while cautioning Hindus not to sell cattle, and absolving Muslims of the 'sin' of cow-slaughter, it preaches the cardinal Gandhian principle of Hindu-Muslim unity.

In a characteristic style, a few lines refer to the past glory of the 'land of Utkal' and its present predicament. Finally, the poem appeals to the Oriyas to seize the golden opportunity and to 'jump headlong into the rising tide of nationalism' like the people of Bengal, Bihar, Madras, and Bombay in order to ensure a solution to the 'crisis of the present' and to restore the lost glory of the Oriya 'race'. The inclusion of a passage dealing with the problems of Orissa assumes significance in the context of the politics of Utkal Sammilani (a regional political outfit launched in 1903 to champion the cause of amalgamation of Oriya tracts lying scattered in different provinces and to demand a separate province for Orissa) which remained basically opposed to the ideas of Congress nationalism.

We come across two other interesting tracts under identical titles – *Kali Bhagabat*. The first, published in 1925, is a general description of life and society in the age of Kali,[3] the last and most degenerate of the four *yugas*. The *Kaliyuga* literature invariably reflects a sense of acute anxiety prevailing everywhere in society due to terrible failures on the part of the people to conform to the right ritual and conduct. In other words, what such literature portrays is the reversal of order in terms of caste, gender, and age that threaten the natural hierarchy and social order during the period of Kali. Interestingly, the last two sections of the this tract focus on Gandhi as the conqueror of Kali. The poem goes on to narrate how Gandhi, as an 'extraordinarily intelligent' and a 'widely loved' person, was born in India and afterwards mastered several disciplines, travelled many countries, 'earned money profusely', and thus became prominent.

Sensitive to the cause of the starving millions and armed with a religion to serve humanity, Gandhi sought to protect the interests of the 'coolies of Champaran' and Africa. He travelled extensively in India and found that people were dying of starvation and disease. Gandhi immediately took up the campaign of administering medicine to the people in the countryside and thus saved many souls. He kept on explaining to the people that Hindus and Muslims were like brothers and that people should remain united and follow the path of non-violence. He further advised them to be self-reliant and give up jobs and lead a balanced 'household life' discarding away greed and obsessions.

The ninth chapter of the poem concludes that Gandhi was born on this earth for the well-being of humanity and to conquer Kali. It also points out that those who listen to this Gandhi Mahatma *charita* would turn out to be extremely 'good and pious'. The tenth chapter discusses the evils associated with Kali whose dominant feature is violence and contrasts it with that of ahimsa dharma. It also describes how the 'wicked, crooked and foolish' people (who were both Hindus and Muslims) had forgotten the religion of non-violence and had taken to violence and fought amongst themselves. This had forced Gandhi to undertake a fast. As a result of Gandhi's fast, the Ganga and Yamuna got flooded. This massive flood swept away many villages and towns, destroyed buildings and temples, human beings and animals. The poem ends by suggesting that the apocalypse was the result of the erosion of the values of non-violence.

The other noteworthy text under the same title (viz., *Kali Bhagabat*) was authored by a wandering Vaishnavite mendicant, Abhiram Paramhansa. Born into a lower middle class family in 1905, Abhiram was adopted by Arjuna Patnaik of Koromolo, Puri. In course of time, he emerged as a *lokaguru* who moved around the towns and the countryside to preach to the illiterate and uneducated masses the message of the *Gita* and bhakti, through *bhajans* and songs.

What merits critical attention here is the fact that Abhiram initially stationed himself in Calcutta and began his career as a religious preacher. But afterwards, he was back in his village to establish a seat of learning named the Shanti Anandashrama at Koromolo. From 1927 to 1933, he undertook extensive tours in the rural areas of the Cuttack district and set up his first ashram to popularize his religion. During this phase, he sought to perform many miracles for his lay disciples. Moreover, this phase coincided with the Civil Disobedience movement and Abhiram assumed the status of a patriotic *sanyasi* – a local version of Gandhi in popular perception.

Abhiram's supposed power to perform miracles during his walking tours and *Kali Bhagabat*'s predictions of a sudden and total transformation, with the termination of the *Kaliyuga* – which in many ways mirrored cyclical concepts of time and engineered myths about the 'golden ages' of the past like *Satyayuga* where just kings ruled – were clearly tied up with future-oriented impulses. Such millenarian hopes were invariably built up around those leaders who religiously stood for the virtues of truth and sanctity, whether Gandhi or the mendicant Abhiram Paramahansa.

Abhiram's composition was published around 1933.[4] This text was proscribed by the colonial authorities and he was sentenced to imprisonment for a year on the ground that he sought to excite 'hatred, contempt and disaffection' against the king emperor. *Kali Bhagabata,* which is defined as a 'story of strife and salvation' by the author, assumed the form of dialogue between Chaitanya and King Mana or the mind personified. Chaitanya points out that those who are foreigners are bent upon destroying swaraj, and then proceeds to valorize the virtues of Congress *satyagrahis* and the Mahatma. The repeated reference to Mohan in the text and its identification with the person having *mahat* (noble) and *atma* (soul) is suggestive of Gandhi's leadership. It is against this backdrop that Chaitanya predicts the unfolding of an 'Indian drama' over the 1939-42 period. As suggested, in this drama the *satyagrahis* would be grouped under the leadership of Mohan who would command the armies in the first war against George V. The Indian drama or the war in India would be characterized by the cries of 'beat' and 'seize', and at the end of the day the emperor along with all foreigners, would leave. As suggested, since the king would not come to his senses and realize the gravity of the situation in 1939, at 40 he was not likely to be able to see any better, as people develop eye problems in their 40s. Consequently, he would not sit on the [throne]; and in 41, he would 'not be present'.

This finally paves the way for 42, when Kali is 'conquered' and 'gone' and vices removed from society with the removal of the foreigners. As elsewhere, Gandhi emerges as the conqueror. The text locates George V as a merchant and associates the European armies with all the vices of colonialism and modernity: lust, evil, wickedness, and egotism.

Yet another tract entitled *Mahatma Gandhinka Katha* contains a series of instructions of Mahatma Gandhi in connection with the Non-Cooperation movement.[5]

In our motherland of India, in Gujarat, a Mahatma has been born,
His name is Mohan Das Karamchand Gandhi,
He is always preoccupied to mitigate our sufferings,
He is willing to sacrifice his life, if that could serve our interests,
He is a supreme soul and extremely knowledgeable,
If we follow his advice, we can protect our religion and we can live happily forever,
The Mahatma has given a few instructions for our wellbeing,
If we follow what he says, then we will not have misery or sufferings,
And, sins and dissatisfactions will be removed. . .

The tract then proceeds to provide various instructions given by Gandhi concerning the khadi programme, the boycot of courts, Congress membership, the anti-liquor drive, Hindu-Muslim unity, cow-protection, emphasis on traditional education as against English education, self-purification, etc. The book ends with the note: 'If we follow the path of honesty and truthfulness and dedicate ourselves to the service of the nation by sacrificing a little bit of our petty interests then we will attain swaraj within this year. We will definitely get back our lost glory and happiness.'

Similarly, an activist of the Bharat Sevak Samaj and a noted social reformer of Orissa, Laxmi Narayan Sahu, published a biography of Gandhi wherein he clearly expounded the ideological viewpoints of Gandhi.[6] Noting that the name of Gandhi was being chanted throughout the villages of India, he concluded that 'he is undoubtedly second to none in India'.

Another Gandhian nationalist of Orissa, Gobinda Chandra Mishra, who was also an inmate of the Sabarmati Ashram, came out with a biographical sketch of Gandhi in 1921.[7] This was followed by another tract entitled *Swaraj Miliba Kipari?* (How to attain Swaraj?).[8] The latter spelt out Gandhi's ideas on swaraj in vivid detail and says, 'Unlike other countries, where one needs arms to establish swaraj, Indians only require God's blessing backed by self-sacrifice to attain swaraj'.

While dispelling popular misconceptions that swaraj meant Gandhi *raj*, the book exhorted people to join the religious war for swaraj, since Krishna was their guide. It further cautioned that those who would lose this opportunity would suffer terribly. It also emphasized that those who would die in this war for swaraj would attain salvation.

Two more tracts published in the 1930s also merit attention at this stage. A text entitled *Gandhi Budha* (Gandhi, the Old Man) written by the noted nationalist leader of Orissa, Nityananda Mohapatra, focused on Gandhi as the conqueror of *Kaliyuga* and compared his arrival with the beginning of *Satyayuga.*[9] There was also a satirical tract on Gandhi written under the penname of the Nirdhum Dhumaketu Mistry.[10] Even though the author makes it clear in the preface that the intention was not to develop a critique on personalities like Gandhi or Malaviya, the poem contains an interesting reference to how a childless couple was blessed with a son by organizing Gandhi *puja*. When some of the relatives of this couple were arrested because of their involvement in the Satyagraha movement, the couple held Gandhi *baba* responsible for their imprisonment. This spelt doom for the family. In the meanwhile, their son took to English education, became a lawyer and married a Christian. He was attracted to nationalist activities and joined the Gandhi *dal* along with his wife. However, in due course of time, he was also arrested causing serious shock to his parents. The parents realized that all these unfortunate developments were because of their condemnation of Gandhi. They resolved to organize a Gandhi *puja* once more and undertook a fast as a result of which the son could come back to them divorcing his Christian wife and leaving the job of politics in the town and finally returned to his village and religion.

As can be seen, these literary tracts constructed ideas and visions on Gandhi, along with a host of other complexities at the popular level. Perhaps their wide circulation in the rural areas imparted a distinct possibility about the emergence of Gandhi *raj* as an alternative source of power and authority *vis-à-vis* colonialism. Moreover, given the relative absence of Congress networks in rural Orissa in the

1920s,[11] these tracts served to carry ideas about Gandhi to the people at large.

As has been noted above, the tracts fall into two categories. The nationalist literature on Gandhi emphasized on the need to emulate the programmes, content and style of Gandhian leadership as well as the concept of swaraj. On the other hand, the popular tracts on Gandhi sought to image Gandhi on diverse ways: as an avatar; a partial incarnation; the conqueror of Kali; or, as a messiah, whose arrival saw the dawning of a new *Satyayuga*. The theme of reward/punishment is also visible in some of these tracts. Thus, any defiance of Gandhian advice resulted in floods. Further, Gandhi is also seen as the supreme soul who cured specific ills by administering medicines to the diseased or removing the exploitation of the oppressed 'coolies of South Africa and Champaran'. Some of these tracts also assume the tones of millenarianism where Gandhi is bracketed with a sudden miraculous total transformation or reversal. The *Kaliyuga* tract of Abhiram Paramhansa brings out this theme quite powerfully, where attainment of swaraj is predicted through Gandhian intervention. What needs to be mapped while dealing with these tracts is the complex pattern of interaction between the official, conventional understanding of Gandhian leadership which was sought to be pushed through by the Congress leadership and the popular autonomous imagining of Gandhi at popular levels.

It is worth pondering about the way Gandhi's visit to Orissa (his first visit to Orissa being in 1921) influenced the production of such literature. In fact, the report regarding Gandhi's first visit to Puri in 1921 in one of the nationalist dailies ran as follows, 'The whole town seems to be tense and greatly excited. Everybody here talks about the Mahatma.'[12]

III

In the following section, the paper seeks to examine the nature of popular perception *vis-à-vis* Gandhian swaraj in a tribal tract of Orissa which had its specificities and differed from the coastal tract of Orissa. The literary texts on Gandhi as discussed in the foregoing section, it may be emphasized, were authored and produced in the coastal districts of Orissa. In fact, these coastal districts came under the spell of nationalist ideas much earlier than the other areas, particularly the tribal tracts of the hinterland. It is worth mentioning that the post-Civil Disobedience movement in Orissa not only witnessed progressive radicalization of the anti-imperalist struggle but the phase was also conspicuous by the broad horizontal and vertical reach of Congress.[13] This finally resulted in the climax of anti-imperialist politics in terms of Quit India movement.

Against this backdrop, we will here briefly sketch how Gandhi and the notion of Gandhian swaraj were understood in a predominantly tribal tract, Koraput district, during 1937-42 and how such understanding fuelled a process of radicalization of popular protests often backed by considerable popular initiative and militant methods. It may further be pointed out here that the popular perception of Gandhi based on the literary tracts described above could not possibly have spurred the imagining of Gandhi in the tribal region of Koraput in the late 1930s or early 1940s. However, it is pertinent to observe here that the noticeable shift in the understanding of Gandhi as we will come across in this tract may be attributed to the broad radical transformation of the ongoing anti-Imperialist movement.

In fact, while examining this aspect during the period of 1937-42, one can hardly ignore the fact that the said period was preceeded by two powerful mass movements, the Non-Cooperation and Civil Disobedience movements, the structuring of a broad left ideology within the Congress Movement, and the politics of the Krushak Sanghas and its significant coincidence with the Congress ministry of 1937-9.

And so to Koraput. During 1937 elections that petitions addressed to Gandhi were discovered in the ballot boxes in Jeypore estate, perhaps backed by rumours among the tribals that if they cast their vote in the yellow box (the colour of the Congress), then Gandhi would be their Maharaj and they would not have to pay any rent in future.[14] Similarly, around July 1937, there was a suggestion to appoint Gandhi Gumasthas for every 25 villages, to whom the villagers could report their grievances in Jeypore estate.[15] The mobilization of tribal people was facilitated by the circulation of brief letters, drafted by the Gandhi Gumasthas and Gandhi Naikos who headed the rural units.[16] These 'Gandhi notes' called upon people to assemble at particular points to picket markets. It is interesting that when the

DCC of Koraput hastened to suspend the campaign for such picketing in May 1938, hoping for a government order in this regard and advising people to be 'law-abiding', it had to use similar Gandhi notes/letters instructing people not to picket without the permission of the local leaders.[17] Even then, the tribesmen of Hat Konga (Jeypore), Chikima (Nowrangpur) and Awarda (Padwa) continued to picket, carrying Congress flags and putting on Gandhi caps. This is suggestive of the tribal people's growing perception of Congress flags and Gandhi caps as weapons that provided immunity against attack. Besides, the very existence of a Congress ministry made the tribal people conceive of an imminent Gandhian *raj*.

Similarly, we come across rumours which sought to be spread in Koraput during 1938, suggesting that Gandhi would tour the district, from house to house, and those who could not produce the Congress ticket which they must buy, would die. The Khonds of Kerada village were told to construct a house so that Gandhi who would visit the district would stay there. More so, the materials for the construction of the house were taken from the estate without permission. These types of rumours, apart from suggesting how the name of Gandhi was used to mobilize tribal people, also points to a predominant notion prevailing at popular levels as regards the power and authority of Gandhi.[18] What merits critical attention here is the fact that in the context of divergent trends obtaining at popular levels of the movement, the DCC leadership of Koraput planned to organize various tribal training centres in the district. Accordingly, a training camp for congress volunteers was opened at village Nuaput near Jeypore on 6 November 1938.[19] The camp imparted training in scouting, lathi drill, and physical exercise apart from lectures on spinning, homeopathy, country medicines, animal husbandry, etc. The organization of the Nuaput camp indicates the 'controlled mobilization' in the backdrop of divergent understandings of Gandhi and Gandhian swaraj at popular levels.

We also come across yet another form of moblization of tribes in 1939 under the symbol of Gandhi. A Gandhi *khatoli* (small wooden apparatus on which image of Gandhi was seated) kept moving from village to village in Koraput district. People in the village kept the *khatoli* for a number of days and made offerings it before passing it on to the next village. The *khatoli* was said to have originated in

Madras Presidency. The purpose of the circulation of the *khatoli* was to mobilize and indoctrinate the tribals with Gandhian ideology.[20]

What appears clear from the developments in this tribal tract is the fact that during 1937-9, popular consciousness came to be invested with a radical vision of swaraj. This accelerating phenomenon was further reinforced by the call of Quit India or with the spread of the Gandhian *mantra*, 'do or die', in 1942. What we can see during 1942 in Koraput was the distinct transformation in the call of *Gandhi ki jai* almost amounting to violent attacks on the markets, thanas, and shops. Herein, one notices the transformation of adoration and adulation to the fierce cry for militant action.

For instance, we can consider the following incident when the tribals of Pottangi village marched to attack a market in 1942.[21] They went in a procession, carrying Congress flags and lathis. Entering the market, they shouted: *Mahatma Gandhi ki Jai*, *Congress ki Jai*, *Swadhinata Miligala*, *Kehi Loka government ku sistu Diana*, *Raja ku sistu Diana*, *Government Bhangigala*, *Ae Sarkar Bandara bala hoigala*. [Victory to Gandhi/Congress; We have achieved Swaraj, Don't pay rent to the Government, Don't pay rent to the Raja/ Maharaja, The Government is gone; This Government is not worth one public hair.]

After shouting slogans, the people almost ransacked the market, looting the eatery and grocery shops, burning mill-made clothes, and forcibly taking away the receipt books of the *sahukar* (moneylender). Thus the popular perception of Gandhi, his 'orders', and his supposed authority as well as the notion of imminent Gandhi *raj* were significantly in opposition to those of authorized Congress version of the Mahatma and contested the basic ideas of Gandhism itself. In the backdrop of such developments, it is perhaps worth arguing that the militancy which rocked the tribal tract of Koraput district during 1937-42 was rooted in this paradox.

NOTES

* I am grateful to the Charles Wallace (India) Trust and in particular to Dr. F. H. Taylor for a fellowship that enabled me to consult materials in the India Office Library, London. This paper was first read and discussed at the 2nd annual conference of the Centre for Gandhian Studies, Rabindra Bharati University, Kolkata (7-8 January 2002). I am grateful to Sekhar

Bandopadhyay, Raj Sekhar Basu, Sanjukta Das Gupta for their comments on the paper. In particular, the author also gratefully acknowledges the comments on the paper by Biswamoy Pati. Even though it has not been fully possible to respond to his comments, this paper can be seen as a preliminary draft on the proposed theme of discussion.

1. Krushna Chandra Mohanty, *Gandhi Avatar and Gandhi Bhajan*, Calcutta, 1921, India Office Library, London.
2. Krushna Chandra Ray, *Gandhi Mahatmanka Gita*, Cuttack, 15 Aug. 1921; India Office Library, London.
3. Sadasiba Panda, *Kali Bhagabata*, Cuttack, 1925; India Office Library, London.
4. Judicial Proceedings against Abhiram Paramhansa, Ganjam, Case No.15 of 1934, Government Press, Madras.
5. Chintamani Das, *Mahatma Gandhinka Katha*, Cuttack, 1922; India Office Library, London.
6. L. N. Sahu, *Mahatma Gandhi*, Cuttack, 1921; India Office Library, London.
7. Gobinda Chandra Mishra, *Mahatma Gandhinka Jiban Charita*, Cuttack, 1921; India Office Library, London.
8. Gobinda Chandra Mishra, *Swarajya Miliba Kipari*? Cuttack, 1921; India Office Library, London.
9. Nityananda Mohapatra, *Gandhi Budha*, Bhadrak, 1937.
10. Nirdhum Dhumaketu Mistry, *Sangeeta Jobra Karakhana*, Cuttack, 1921; India Office Library, London.
11. The spread and impact of Gandian ashrams in the countryside and the emergence of an organized Gandhian cadre was relatively limited in this phase, as compared to 1930s.
12. *Amrita Bazar Patrika*, 29 March 1921.
13. For a detailed understanding of the process of transformation of anti-colonial politics in Orissa, refer, Chandi Prasad Nanda, *Towards Swaraj*, New Delhi, 1998; also Biswamoy Pati, *Resisting Domination: Peasants, Tribals and National Movement in Orissa (1920-50)*, New Delhi, 1993.
14. Chandi Prasad Nanda, 'Mobilization, Resistance and Popular Initiatives: Locating Tribal Perception of Swaraj in the Jeypore Estate of Orissa (1937-38)', in: *Proceedings of the Indian History Congress*, 58th Session, 1998, p. 544.
15. Home Political Files (HP), 10.7.37, Orissa State Archives (OSA), Bhubaneswar.
16. HP, Report of S. P. Koraput, 28.4.38, OSA, Bhubaneswar.
17. HP, Orissa Police Abstract Intelligence (OPAI), 7.6.38, OSA, Bhubaneswar.
18. For detailed reference see, Nanda, 'Mobilization . . .', *op. cit.*
19. HP, OPAI, 18.11.38.
20. HP, Fortnightly Report, Koraput, 13.5.39, OSA, Bhubaneswar.
21. HP, Special Report 14/42, OSA, Bhubaneswar.

CHAPTER 16

Decolonised Orissa: Issues and Problems

BISWAMOY PATI

This paper focuses on Orissa, exploring the way this region interacted with several complexities that emerged after the end of the Second World War. These ranged from the prospects of India gaining independence, electoral politics, the rise of the mass movements, the liquidation of the feudal enclaves (princely states), and the abolition of landlordism and the introduction of land reforms. It examines the very conceptualization of the 'future' before and after 15 August 1947. What was Orissa supposed to be in the imagination of those who were saddled with the power to shape its destiny? How did they negotiate with popular expectations/politics, and locate the diversities that together constituted Orissa? In this sense, this paper is also concerned with the evolution of the alternative order that emerged over this period and focuses on certain specific issues related to elite politics, administration, the unification of the Province, planning and development, and caste and communalism. In fact, these offer clues to the 'future' – in a phase when anti-imperialist rhetoric was increasingly losing its meaning.

THE 1946 ELECTIONS AND AFTER

In 1945, the end of the Second World War coupled with the victory of the Labour Party in the General Elections in Britain offered fresh possibilities for ending the political deadlock in India. By this time most of the political prisoners in Orissa had been released. Soon after assuming office the Labour Government declared that the elections to the various legislatures would be held in early 1946. One of the first was the elections to the provincial legislatures.

As the PCC machinery harnessed itself to fight the elections and Mahtab attempted to, as he claimed, keep the big landlords 'at least . . . neutral' he promised the Congress High Command that he would prevent any 'organized party' from contesting the 1946 elections.[1] His success on both counts was not really a result of his individual ability, but a fall-out of the post-1937 election attitudes of landed sections.[2] Thus at freedom's doorstep one observes a strengthening of this alliance. In this contest the prominent Congrees leader, Biswanath Das, stated that the landlords were anxious to join the Congress. Thus the son of the Kanika *zamindar* was selected as a candidate of the Congress for the Central Legislative Assembly.[3] Some like Motilal Pandit, a landlord, became Congressmen just before the 1946 elections and drew their legitimacy from the new power structure to exploit their peasants.[4] However, this was not a one-sided affair. Congress was as eager as the landlords to have the landlords on its side. Here one can cite the selection of Ranjit Singh, son of the Raja of Borasambar, as a Congress candidate. Ranjit had served in the Royal Air Force during the Second World War and his selection violated at least one of the three basic norms that had been formulated by the Congress High Command to select candidates for the 1946 election.[5]

The PCC's victory in the 1946 elections in Orissa was not surprising, and unlike at the 1937 elections the colonial bureaucracy did not expect anything else to happen.[6] In 37 constituencies out of the total 60 PCC candidates were elected unopposed and the overall position gave the PCC 47 seats.[7] It is worth pointing out at this juncture that the organizational strength of the PCC had declined considerably, as the Table 1 illustrates.

This was because of the repression and the fact that the PCC was legalized only in 1945. Yet the mass appeal and popularity of the PCC had, if anything only increased, and it continued to rouse popular enthusiasm and aspirations in Orissa.

The formation of the ministry saddled the Congress with fresh responsibilities. One of its first tasks was to release some of the remaining political prisoners and implement the promise to institute

TABLE 1: UTKAL PCC: NUMBER OF PRIMARY MEMBERS[8]

1929	1935-6	1937	1938	1945-6
6,945	6,829	5,760	1,98,325	1,03,216

enquiries into the excesses during the Quit India movement. C. M. Trivedi, the Governor, seems to have exerted considerable pressure to stall any move to institute an enquiry into the 1942 excesses, and sought Mahtab's cooperation for a cover-up.[9] At the same time, Mahtab was against the setting up of a general enquiry into the conduct of government servants as this would lower their morale. In fact, he strove to allay fears by a public statement that for acts done in obedience to orders of a higher authority no blame would be given to any officers if they had not gone beyond the reasonable scope of such orders.[10] This was a clear signal about the dependence on the bureaucracy for the management of administration, which increased in this period of transition. Thus, at the doorstep of freedom Mahtab asked for the retention of the Governor's advisers and for more senior ICS officers.[11] The new ministry also abolished the tax on salt manufacture – something that was widely appreciated.[12]

Mahtab's vision of the future was conditioned by a need to unite the princely states with the Orissa province (since otherwise nothing could be done to improve things) and to improve the conditions of the adivasis (as only during the earlier Congress government had anything been done to improve their lot). He recognised the fact that Orissa was an extremely poor province where people lived in semi-starvation. He felt that the solution to all problems lay in the establishment of a representative government at the centre, which implied a more favourable centre-state relationship.[13]

The Congress ministry also planned to improve the supply of essential commodities, for which some schemes were planned. Besides, two laws were adopted to accord equality to untouchables in services and institutions maintained by the government and allowing them to enter temples. An agrarian reforms committee was also set up.[14]

On the threshold of freedom the links between the Congress and the landlords were sought to be further strengthened. The PCC which had fired popular aspiration in the late 1930s now talked of how 'the actual abolition of *zamindari* present[ed] practical difficulties' and began speculating whether or not to compensate the landlords.[15] The abolition of the *zamindari* system began to be shelved and was seen as a step to be taken only after independence. It was no more considered 'a simple matter . . . as if the Ministers have to go . . . to the Secretariat, ask for a slip of paper and just write on it that the *zamindari* system is abolished'. There was a clear attempt to side-track the issue that had been so 'central' to the PCC's politics since 1936-7. By March 1947 it was made adequately clear that the government was in no hurry to abolish the *zamindari* system as 'with all its ills' it had been in existence for several centuries.[16] We also get references to Congressmen intervening as arbitrators to settle disputes between landlords and peasants.[17] The landlords evidently realized that the Congress was the lesser evil and were happy to have a Congress ministry in power.[18]

In this phase we also witness an attempt by the Congress to strengthen its links with 'rich' peasants. For example, the idea of increasing the procurement prices of grain and demanding a re-classification of different varieties of rice for the purpose of promoting a large number of varieties in the 'superfine' category was for the benefit of the landlords and the rich peasants who came next in the rural social hierarchy.[19] Besides, within months following independence the system of control imposed on foodgrain was removed. Mahtab wrote to Gandhi rationalizing it as a step meant to benefit the agriculturist.[20] This policy, along with the high prices of foodgrain in the 1947-8 phase, meant that the landlords and rich peasants having surplus grain stocks made huge profits.[21] Similarly the conceptualization of a ceiling on the agricultural income tax for those whose income was more than Rs. 5,000 annually[22] was aimed at strengthening links with small landlords as well as rich peasants.

The new 'rulers' desired to build a new capital and this figured prominently in the 'Post-War Development Plans', with the Governor mentioning that the sanctioned amount of Rs. 40 lakh was inadequate.[23] Bhubaneswar was finally accepted as the site of the new capital.[24] The demand was for Rs. 2 crore, though Rs. 1.32 crore were sanctioned by the Government of India.[25] On laying the foundation of the new capital, Nehru had expressed the hope that Bhubaneshwar would not be 'a city of buildings for officers and rich men without relation to common masses. It will accord with our idea of reducing differences between rich and poor'.[26] As described in 1951, the financial implications stood at Rs. 5.40 crore,[27] an astoundingly high amount for a poor province like Orissa.[28]

And the same Congress which had only a few months earlier criticized the arming/fencing of the police stations, increased the budgetary allocation for the police force. This was rationalized as a feature associated with the very process of 'development' itself. Interestingly, the Congress in Orissa seemed to depart from the Mahatma when it came to planning for development. 'To bring Gandhi into the day-to-day business' such as the strength of the police force began to be frowned upon as obstructing 'big development all round'.[29]

Steps had to be also taken to check the corruption of government servants and traders. In 1946-7 there were 500 cases and a majority of the guilty were convicted. The trend of bureaucratic corruption worsened with independence, government officials being sometimes caught red-handed with bribes.[30]

The need for developmental projects also made the ministry contemplate means to acquire land for private companies.[31] The development projects included an iron and steel plant, survey of the mineral resources, improving the communication links by building two bridges on rivers Kathjuri and Kuakhai, a broadcasting station, the question of the princely states and a greater share of post-War developmental grants to Orissa 'in view of her backwardness'.[32] Mahtab seems to have been quite clear that Orissa would not 'participate' in large-scale industries and in the 'state control of industries in Orissa'[33] – features which were a legacy of the anti-imperialist struggle. Simultaneously, proposals like setting up an industrial credit corporation and a central bank were aimed at encouraging the regional capitalist sector.[34]

As the development of Orissa was being planned, one of the first efforts was to implement the plans to build dams at Hirakud, Machkund and Duduma. Related primarily to the issue of technology transfer in the years of de-colonization, this saw the entry of the US as a player in India.[35] The problem of dam construction remained a rather contentious issue over this period. Clearly noticeable were the eagerness and haste to adopt a technology that would, it was hoped, solve the problems of flood control, electricity generation, and irrigation – without looking into the problems that could ensue. There was also an unwillingness to look at the displacements that would result, and the issues of rehabilitation and compensation.

This plan received stiff opposition due to a variety of reasons. One has to bear in mind here the background of a colonial society grappling to adjust to rapid changes in the direction of capitalism and largely unprepared for the changes which were being planned. This can be perhaps illustrated by the appearance of certain 'ill omens' that raised doubts in the minds of people about shifting to the alternative site offered by the government at Machkund. Local leaders like Laikman Hontal (Khorsapada) and Mongal Hontal (Chicanput) gave expression to the fears of the adivasis whose land was to be taken over for the dam.[36] There was a belief current in Sambalpur at the time that power generation would siphon out all the important properties from the water, making it useless for agriculture.[37] Campaigning in the Duduma area by Radhakrushna Biswasroy (the PWD, Labour and Commerce Minister of Orissa), a popular leader of the Koraput area, failed to improve the situation.[38]

One also observes that this contributed to sharpen elite level political polarization between the coastal tract and western Orissa. Some of the western Orissa princes (especially Patana) sought to fuel an agitation against the Hirakud dam project in order to demand the secession of western Orissa from the province. Prominent Congress politicians of western Orissa such as Bodhuram Dube and Laxminarayan Mishra made common cause with them. Centred around the idea of secession of Hirakhand (which comprised western parts of the province) from Orissa, it caused a lot of embarrassment for the Congress.[39] This opposition to the Hirakud dam was backed by the urban middle classes (whose landed interests associated with the *guntia* system was threatened), along with the microscopic business interests of western Orissa. What was harped upon was the genuine problem of Sambalpur's/western Orissa's backwardness and to mobilize those threatened by displacement. After all, there was the immediate question related to displacements and a genuine fear about due compensation.[40] This effort was quite successful, since the problems posed by the construction of the Hirakud dam had been altogether ignored. Governor Trivedi's concerns on this front were restricted to the files that were allowed to gather dust.[41] In fact, an undated document 'Questions and Answers on the Hirakud Dam', framed for the purpose of propaganda, listed 26 questions and answered them without touching on the central aspects related to the displacement, rehabilitation, and compensation.[42]

Thousands of 'objection petitions' were filed against the proposed land acquisition in connection with the construction of the Hirakud dam.[43] On 12 November 1946, 40,000 people marched around

Sambalpur and assembled for a meeting where the construction of the Hirakud dam was opposed.[44] In fact, even officials who toured some of the concerned areas were 'impressed' by the 'success' of the anti-dam agitation.[45] The form of the opposition, of course, changed with the Communists joining in and opposing both the dam as well as secessionist politics.[46] May 1947 saw the launching of a *satyagraha* against the dam which was criticised by the Communists as an attempt by the princely rulers to divert the attention of the people from the struggle for independence.[47]

There were, of course, some problems which need to be spelt out. The polarization of communal and caste identities began in this phase. Although in many ways these can he traced back to the nineteenth century, they can also be associated with the politics of the anti-imperialist struggle itself as well as the 1943 famine.[48] Talking of specifics, we can mention the growth of the Rashtriya Swayamsevak Sangh (RSS) in 1946[49] and the problem of rabid communalists within the PCC organization itself.[50] One should also refer to the way some Congressmen rallied round the cow during their opposition to the 'grow more food' programme by labelling it the '*gorumara*' (cow-killing) food programme.[51] Along with this was the communalized perception of the bureaucracy which looked upon Orissa as a 'Hindu province'.[52]

Badly hit by the famine, Bhadrak (in Balasore) had a Muslim population composed of poor wage-earners; while the Hindus formed the landowning section.[53] During crises the sharpening of class relations took a communal turn with communalists playing their role. The happenings outside Orissa hardened communal identities. The colonial administration's inept handling of the situation triggered off a police firing on a 'Muslim' gathering which obstructed a 'Hindu' procession. The death of three people created a stir in Orissa.[54]

These features were reinforced by the fears perpetuated by communal organizations like the RSS. Thus, when it observed its first anniversary at Jharsuguda (in Sambalpur) on 13 April 1947, about a hundred Hindu and Muslim families left the place fearing a communal riot. Similarly, a 'highly inflammatory' anti-Muslim leaflet circulated in Cuttack on 6-7 May which contained 'lurid' accounts of the 'atrocities' perpetuated by Muslims on Hindus in Punjab and East Bengal and incited 'Hindus to take up the challenge'.[55]

Another feature was the strained caste relations. Like communalism, it was associated with class tensions, between rich and poor, a fall-out of the 1943 famine. There were attempts at assertion by outcastes like the Pana labourers of Cuttack, who demanded higher wages. What followed was a social boycott imposed on them by caste Hindus, and a subsequent clash. From Balasore we get a reference to the development of a class conflict, with the Harijans boycotting caste Hindus and not working in their fields since the latter had excommunicated their brahmin priest. When the Brahmins employed labourers from a neighbouring village a clash resulted. We also get references to fishermen in some neighbouring villages who resolved not to carry the palanquins of high caste people.[56] The downtrodden desired to go before the presence of the gods and goddesses 'stolen' by the upper castes. This concept was something rooted in the popular tradition and was also linked to the 'temple-entry' question focused upon by Congress and Gandhi in Orissa.[57] Thus independence came to be associated with the advent of freedom for the outcastes to go to the presence of the gods and goddesses. This explains the momentum gained by the temple-entry agitation and inter-caste dinners that saw the participation of some ministers.[58]

In this phase some castes like Khandayats and Sundhis got organized. The Khandayats attempted to unite and agitate in order to improve their conditions and enable themselves to meet the dominance sought to be exercised by the 'Brahmin-Karana' ministry. The Sundhis appealed to their caste people to take to professions other then their traditional selling of liquor, and to give up customs like child marriage. Consequently we also witness the emulation of the dominant castes in several ways, including minor attempts at social reform. In some cases this led to inter-caste tensions as in the case of Goudas (cowherds) and caste Hindus at Puri, when the former sought upward mobility.[59]

The threshold to freedom was also marked by an increase in crime. Table 2 illustrates this phenomenon.[60]

In the 1947-9 phase crime increased from about 60 per cent (1947) to about 84 per cent (1949). Incidentally, the peak for the 1939-46 period was about 55 per cent (1946).[61]

Although it is extremely difficult to establish links between this increase in crime and popular expectations of *swaraj*, 15 August 1947 was viewed as 'freedom from fear of the police and magistracy and in the *zamindari* areas, of estate officials'. Popular aspirations located

TABLE 2

Rise of crime in the first quarter of 1947		Triennial average
Murder	5	20.3
Dacoity	14	8.3
Robbery	25	20.3
Rioting	39	24.0

independence as the end of authority itself,[62] given its close association with colonialism. We witness strained relations between the landlords and peasants in all the districts of Orissa, including the estates, in 1947.[63] Among the people there was also the hope of a future without landlords and moneylenders, and therefore without the *zamindar-sahukar-sarkar* nexus. One can cite here the perceptions of Ramchandra Barik, a domestic servant, originally from coastal Orissa but who at this time was working for his master, posted in East Pakistan. Barik asked his master's son if with independence, his loans would be written off and his mortgaged lands returned to him by his village *sahukar*.[64]

This perhaps also explains the acts of some 'unimportant Congressmen' who 'instigated' people not to pay land revenue, asked *naikos* to report cases to them before going to the police, urged people not to go to the police, and pronounced that in future *chaukidars* and union presidents would be appointed only from among Congressmen.[65] Given this perspective one can perhaps also explain the difficulty in comprehending why the price of rice should go up with the advent of freedom.[66]

It was in response to such trends that Mahtab's *Prajatantra*, funded by the landlords, carried a signed editorial by him 'advising . . . [and] exhorting the public to realise the responsibilities of Independence and switch over from political agitation and an attitude of negation and obstruction to constructive activities'.[67]

THE MASS MOVEMENTS

The unresolved nature of the contradictions led to a spell of mass movements especially in the coastal tract, including Ganjam, and some of the princely states. What does appear impressive is that even in the face of certain definitely divisive trends, the politics of the Kisan Sangha as well as the Prajamandal movement united the peasants and adivasis in a struggle against their oppressors. The strength of these movements in 1947-8 normally goes unnoticed, unless one takes care to link them with the land reforms that were instituted (howsoever weak and limited they might have been),[68] the disappearance of certain feudal practices which were exploitative,[69] and, last but not least, the integration of the princely states with the province of Orissa.[70]

The Coastal Tract

Let us begin with the coastal tract. The Kisan Sangha occupied the centre of the Communist Party's activities during the phase of transition. The problem was the Congress' declaration of 'war' on the Communists in the early months of 1947, forcing some activists to go underground.[71] This trend intensified in the post-independence context, leading to the arrests of 70 activists by 1949 and prompting Nehru to write to Mahtab to stop these arrests and the banning of organizations as they had earned a bad name for the Congress.[72]

Inspite of the difficulties, by the beginning of 1947 the Kisan Sangha focused forcefully on the abolition of the *zamindari* system which was being side-tracked by the Congress.[73] Its activities sought a link with the workers and students. On 18 March 1947, a Trade Union Day was celebrated and resolutions were passed asking for the abolition of the *zamindari* system along with demands of workers.[74] In May 1947 the Communists held a mass rally at Cuttack, which was attended by representatives from the different districts and also from the princely states on the occasion of the first session of the Orissa Assembly. The basic objective of this rally was to demand the abolition of the *zamindari* system as well as the improvement of the conditions of peasants.[75]

Besides this, the Kisan Sangha also tried to build a *bhagachasi* (sharecropper's) movement demanding the amendment of tenancy laws in order to fix the share of the *dhulibhag* (produce rent) tenants at three/fifths of the gross produce, and the grant of written leases to cultivators. Attention was also given to the abolition of reserved forests and the distribution of essential commodities to village committees.[76]

The 'Kisan March' to Cuttack (March 1947) was a massive attempt to mobilize the peasants and adivasis of coastal Orissa. It originated from Ganjam on 20 March 1947, and the marchers reached Cuttack on 27 March. Numerous meetings were held on the way which had an electrifying effect on the countryside of coastal Orissa. At these meetings the basic perspective of the Kisan Sangha was outlined and the people were urged to join the marchers. A systematic campaign was unleashed to abolish the *zamindari* system without compensation, for reduction of rent, tenancy rights over *inam* lands, prevention of encroachment by landlords on *heta* lands, exemption of rent of small peasants, confiscation of land from those who had more than thirty acres of land and its redistribution among the landless, subsidised sale of paddy to poor consumers, better irrigation facilities and more satisfactory procurement and distribution of controlled commodities.[77]

When the Kisan Sangha marchers met at Cuttack on 27 March 1947, a resolution was passed by the 1,000 peasants present which called for the abolition of the *zamindari* system, forced labour and *bhagchas*; restoration of ownership of lands to tenants; and amalgamation of the princely states with Orissa. Most of the speakers condemned the compromising character of the Congress and its sympathy with capitalists.[78] These activities paved the way for the sharecroppers' movement.

The *bhagachasi* movement developed in Khurda (Puri) and spread to the entire Puri district. The forms of protest included the non-payment of rent in cash or kind for lands cultivated under the *bhag* system, as well as sharecroppers entering and cultivating the lands of *zamindar*s.[79] In an attempt to counter the *bhagachasi* movement a large number of activists were arrested at Puri.[80] Gradually the *bhagachasi* movement spread to the districts of Cuttack and Balasore. In Cuttack the rural rich were deprived of their grain stocks and the lands of *zamindars* were 'forcibly' cultivated by the *bhagachasis*.[81]

In November 1947 the pressure of the movement had forced the Congress ministry to issue a communiqué which led to the enactment of the Sharecroppers' Act. This gave three-fifths of the produce to the sharecropper and two-fifths to the landlord. However, the problem was one of actual implementation of this Act and the strength of the peasant movement was, ultimately, the only factor which could ensure its implementation. In areas where the peasant movement was weak the peasants were forced, through false cases and threats of eviction, to surrender half the produce.[82]

After independence the *bhagachasi* movement spread to the entire coastal region, developing rapidly even under extremely repressive conditions. This was the context in which the Kandhas (adivasis) of Takarada in Ganjam rose to fight landlordism and its exploitative practices and scarcities, especially of water. A major irritant was the absence of land rights of the *raiyats* (agricultural labourers) who worked on the *inam* lands of the *inamdars* (the landlords who had the *inam* lands). This meant that they were forced to surrender three/fifth of the produce to the *inamdars*. The sweep of the peasant movement and campaigns by prominent Congress leaders like Biswanath Das made them decide to pay the reduced rent. A major movement developed to end landlordism, backed by the Kisan Sabha. The Congress government, keen on backing the landlords in this volatile context, retaliated by using force that ended with firing in May 1948. This was the first occasion when state violence of this nature was directed against a peasant movement in Orissa after independence. It demonstrated the extent to which the government could go to in order to protect its class allies.[83]

The *bhagachasi* movement continued in 1948 in an attempt to assert the rights of the sharecroppers in the face of the brutal repression and terror unleashed by the police and the rural rich. Meetings and conferences of the Kisan Sangha were banned.[84] Ironically, the Congress government stood by the landlords and resorted to arrests of Kisan Sangha activists, most of whom were implicated in a host of false charges.[85] However, the pressure of the Kisan Sangha and the movement of sharecroppers forced the Congress government to accept that the Sharecroppers' Act would remain valid till January 1949. Nevertheless, what needs to be pointed out is that independence failed to solve the problems of Orissa's sharecroppers.[86]

The Princely States

As for the princely states, this last phase saw a popular upsurge. There was close collaboration between these feudal chiefs and the retreating colonial power. The first indication of this was the restoration of the Chiefs of Nilgiri and Dhenkanal (1946). The feudal chiefs, pampered by the colonial bureaucracy, began to examine the possibilities of staying out of the Indian Union. This drive led to two meetings – one of the Orissan and Chhattisgarh Chiefs at Puri (May 1947) under the aegis of the Resident Eastern States and the Political Agent and the other, of Orissan Chiefs at Bhawanipatana (September 1947). In a national context charged with communalism these chiefs decided to raise an army of Muslims, Pathans, and Gurkhas, with the obvious aim of splitting the Prajamandal Movement.[87]

As the chiefs planned to ensure a transfer of power from the Resident of the Eastern States and the Political Agent to themselves, the Prajamandals prepared to face the challenge. In August 1947 a conference of various Prajamandal activists was organized at Cuttack, in which the Communists were actively involved. This called for a merger with Orissa and asked the people to resist the undemocratic rulers.[88] The uncertainties and ambiguities of the Congress also created confusion. Its initial response to the aspirations for the merger of the princely states was to drag its feet. Mahtab, the PCC chief spokesman and known as a champion of the merger movement, initially talked about a mere administrative merger. This was turned down by the Congress High Command, and was followed by a policy of ambivalence.[89]

After independence, the popular upsurge in some of the princely states assumed extremely militant forms. Realizing the intensity of popular pressures, the position of the PCC began to shift.[90] And it is precisely at this juncture that we should turn to the spell of mass movements in the princely states which led to the integration of these bastions of feudal control with Orissa.

The most visible enclave of this was Nilgiri. With the restoration of the Raja, the durbar began to take steps to counter the Prajamandal. In its attempt to divide the state people the durbar turned to a section of the adivasis trained to oppose the Prajamandal. A conscious effort was made to create an Oriya-tribal dichotomy harping on the theme that the Oriyas would grab the lands of the adivasis and the only way of preventing this was to unite with the durbar. Given the fact that most of the adivasis were agricultural labourers, the durbar projected itself as their 'saviour'. The Raja linked his activity primarily to the Bathudi tribals, whom the Communists had not been able to win over politically.

In this context the Communists of Balasore met at Madapadia (Nilgiri) on 6 April 1946, where it was decided to counter the new offensive of the Raja. The Communists took the initiative to organize numerous meetings of the Prajamandal all over the state. They tried to emphasise how the durbar exploited the adivasis as well as the non-adivasis. Besides political propaganda, the Communists also began training their cadre to face the Raja. Funds were collected and a *bundh* was built by about 800 people, who got together at the call of the Communists, planted red flags, and worked to complete the structure. Although these activities helped in uniting the state people and made the durbar uneasy, the Communists failed to wean away the Bathudi tribals from the influence of the durbar.[91]

Around this time the Communist Party decided to mobilize the state people to assert their fishing rights. According to the prevailing system waterways of the state were auctioned and everybody had to part with a portion of their catch to the auctioneer. At this juncture a massive movement developed, with thousands of people fishing all over the state. The durbar's desperate attempt to smother the movement by arresting some of the leaders failed to achieve any success.[92]

The conference of the Balasore District Communist Party was held at Agasti Nagar (Nilgiri) where the prospects of a sharecroppers' movement were discussed. The most important outcome of this conference was the expansion of the base of the Communists. Thousands of sympathizers were recruited as members of the Communist Party and plans were made to increase the membership of the Kisan front.[93]

However, the elections for the Praja Sabha created differences between the Congress and the Communists. Things were complicated when the Praja Sabha had its first meeting (3 August 1947) since some adivasis joined in demanding representation and raising anti-Oriya slogans. It was in this situation that on 15 August 1947, the Prajamandal organized a huge meeting of about 20,000 people to celebrate independence.[94]

After independence, things took a serious turn when the Raja-backed loyalists began attacking non-adivasis, derailing the plans to launch a share-croppers' movement. In some cases the Raja-backed adivasis cut grain from the fields of non-adivasis. The Communists made serious appeals for a united struggle to meet this new problem but failed to get a response from the Congress. The situation became extremely critical as the attacks mounted.[95] Initially, the Communists were in a dilemma since they had a strong base among the adivasis. However, as the attacks continued they decided to retaliate, and drifted from their original plan of taking over the palace and surrendering it to the Orissa government. In fact this decision to retaliate was also influenced by Mahtab. Tragically, several tribal villages were burnt down by the Communists.[96]

The PCC which had been observing everything sitting on the fence at last decided to intervene.[97] Kailash Chandra Mohanty and Malati Choudhury met the Nilgiri Communists. Arms were distributed to a general gathering of people, including the Communists. At a time when the popular upsurge had thoroughly undermined its authority and credibility, the Orissa government sent in troops (November 1947) to merge the state with Orissa. This was the first princely state to be merged with the Indian Union and the PCC harped on it to tell the Rajas what awaited them in the future.[98]

Interestingly, after merger the defence of forest rights continued to occupy an important theme with the Prajamandal and the Kisan Sangha. In 1949 the Congress government sought to impose restrictions on the use of forests. Large-scale mass violations followed forcing the government to abandon its policy.[99]

The merger of Nilgiri paved the way for the merger movement itself. When Patel and Menon discussed the issue with the Rajas of Orissa (December 1947),[100] they were speaking from a position of strength – the basis for which had been created by the popular Communist-led upsurge at Nilgiri, as well as the momentum gained by the merger movement some of the other states. Faced with the popular movements the Rajas felt quite insecure. In such a context Patel's intervention made it clear to them that those Chiefs who did not agree to merge would be responsible for maintaining law and order in their state as the Congress government would not help them in any way.[101] Thus as can be seen, on the one hand the Congress was not in favour of an offensive against the princely states; on the other it hoped to draw its strength from the strength of the popular upsurge sweeping the states.

As for Dhenkanal, we find that after independence the merger movement gathered considerable momentum. The restored Raja (August 1946) decided to resort to caste politics in order to salvage himself. He rallied brahmins, promising that their land grants (*brahmottar*) would be made permanent; simultaneously, he promised land to the landless outcastes. Besides, outcastes were mobilized to cut away standing crops from the fields of Prajamandal activists. Several dismissed officials were re-instated and a Praja Sammilani was established to campaign against amalgamation with Orissa. In order to terrorize the people the state recruited forty Gurkhas and procured arms and ammunition.[102] A rumour was circulated that if the state merged with Orissa, the price of rice would go up.[103]

In this context the Prajamandal took a bold position for the merger with Orissa.[104] The Communists established secret contacts with the Eastern State police who agreed not to open fire if and when the palace was taken over.[105] The climax of the popular upsurge saw 20,000 people, led by the Prajamandal, marching to Dhenkanal town and demanding responsible government.[106] This scared the Raja as well as the PCC. The latter began negotiations with the Chief.[107] The state *bandh* call of the Communists was opposed by PCC leaders like Sarangadhar Das, who in fact pressurized the administration to enforce Section 144.[108]

In the events that followed the Raja fled to Delhi. The Prajamandal occupied the palace and the administrative buildings. With this the ground was prepared for merger. However, even in early 1948 the officials of the Raja resorted to arrests of Prajamandal activists.[109]

As for Talcher, Prajamandal activists like Pabitra Mohan Pradhan had refused to surrender, although from about 1945 they had been advised to do so, among others, by Gandhi.[110] In July 1947 all the warrants were cancelled. After Independence a massive demonstration was organized by the Prajamandal in which 20,000 people joined in to demand amalgamation with Orissa.[111] Consequently, when the Raja of Talcher met Patel in December 1947, he was under considerable pressure.

At Ranpur, the arrests and repression following the death of Bazellgate had left the people demoralized. This phase saw fresh initiatives by the Communists, resulting in meetings and much discussion and debate. In panic the durbar announced a ban on Prajamandal meetings, which proved ineffective.

In an attempt to reach the people of the state the Prajamandal would stage a play on Bazellgate after every meeting.[112] Very soon slogans like 'Victory to the Prajamandal' and 'Victory to Mahatma Gandhi' echoed from different parts of the state. People began to gather at the Ranpur *garh*. This set the ground for a massive gathering at Chandapur (4 November 1946). People joined in, giving token food payments as membership. Among those present were Radhanath Rath (the editor of the *Samaj*, the organ of the PCC who presided), leaders of the Orissa Prajamandal organization, Congressmen like Banamali Pattnaik and Sarat Pattnaik (Secretary of the Communist Party of Orissa). Madan Mohan Pradhan (Secretary of the Orissa State People's Conference) called for a fight against the imperialists and the Rajas and that only struggle could ensure freedom. Radhanath Rath appealed to the rulers 'to hear the call of their subjects' and expressed that 'we will not take away all the powers of the Rulers if they cooperate with us'.[113] This position reflected how the PCC was uncertain about its position *vis-à-vis* the states.

The Ranpur Prajamandal was finally re-organized, with Ramchandra Ram as president. A resolution was drafted which, among other things, demanded unconditional merger with Orissa, abolishing of all princely states and the release of prisoners accused of Bazellgate's murder. Besides, there were a number of economic demands: the standardization/reduction of land revenue, the abolishing of illegal dues, rights over forest and pasture, the supply of essential commodities, a system of control over moneylenders to medical and educational benefits. The Communists pressed for the aboilition of *jagirs* and their allotment to the landless peasants.[114]

These developments led the durbar to set up a parallel Prajamandal. Interestingly, this was composed of oppressive state officials and unscrupulous businessmen who started wearing *khadi* caps. This organization made no secret of its anti-Communist position. What is indeed fascinating is the way the Communists had been able to consolidate their position in the Prajamandal. Popular perceptions distinguished the real Prajamandal, the 'Ram Ram' Prajamandal, after Ramchandra Ram, the Secretary.[115] This shows the selectivity of popular consciousness and how it distinguished between 'good' and 'evil'.

In its attempt to divide the people, the durbar set up a so-called representative body for which elections were held. The 'Ram Ram' Prajamandal swept the elections, losing only one seat inspite of the fact that the durbar spent lavishly, misused the administrative machinery, and sought to secure promises of voters by serving *mahaprasad* to win the elections. The elected representatives boycotted the Raja at the first meeting itself. These activities prepared the ground for the merger of Ranpur with Orissa.[116]

The struggle climaxed with the merger of twenty-four princely states with Orissa.[117] Significantly, a clear compromise had been struck with these feudal chiefs. Each were given a privy purse exempt from tax, besides various other concessions. The basic idea was that 'the government of India should not create as an aftermath of merger any social or economic problems for rulers'.[118] Many ex-Rajas thronged the Congress, some of them sought advice from Congress leaders about their business prospects.[119] Some others like Rajendra Narayan Sighdeo (of Patana) accepted the emerging reality and took up the unresolved issues and problems – many of which were a fallout of the bankrupt policies of the Congress – and in the 1952 elections reaped an impressive political harvest.[120]

ORISSA: BETWEEN CHANGE AND CONTINUITY

The independence of India did mark a major shift in the balance of forces. In specific terms, Orissa saw the demise of the princely states. However, there were problems in the way the new ruling class responded to the Prajamandal movement and the princes, as well the land reforms that were tailored over the 1946-52 period. Thus its indeed amazing that it took five years to implement many of the points that had been raised since the Congress campaign of 1936 and the setting up of a Committee in 1946. On the face of it, the basic thrust was to remove the landed intermediaries, which included the *zamindars* and the *guntias* (in western Orissa and the ex-princely states). The absence of land struggles in western Orissa and, with some exceptions, in most of the princely states,[121] implied that the foundation of the *guntia* system was almost left intact in this belt. Nothing illustrates this better than the way it was implemented through 'compromises' in the ex-states like Patana. Similarly, the Orissa Debt Bondage Abolition Regulation I of 1948 failed to produce any significant impact in western Orissa. In fact, both these were admitted in official circles in the 1960s.[122] As discussed, the abolition of landlordism and the *guntia* system took a very long time and centred on the basic paradigm of compromise. Besides illustrating Oriya ruling-class links with land and landed interests, it explains, at least partly, the perpetuation of these problems.[123]

The way the new ruling class negotiated with communalism and divisive politics – cutting across party lines – also needs to be borne in mind. Similarly, its utter insensitivity is clearly visible in its vision, priorities and the way it located human beings in the process of development in this phase of transition. Apologists of post-colonial ruling classes tend to over-emphasize the colonial past while assessing post-colonial societies like India. These need to be critiqued, especially since many of the problems remain, and in many ways they have been reinforced since independence.[124]

NOTES

* An earlier version of the paper 'Independence & After: Orissa, 1946-1952', was published in the *Indian Historical Review*, Vol. XXIX, Nos. 1 & 2, January-July 2002, pp. 198-223.

1. Durga Das (ed.), *Sardar Patel's Correspondence*, Vol. 2 (Ahmedabad, 1972), p.163; Mahtab to Patel, 21/11/1945.
2. See Biswamoy Pati, *Resisting Domination: Peasants, Tribals and the National Movement in Orissa* (New Delhi, 1993), Chap. 3, 'Of Movements, Compromises and Retreats: Orissa, 1936-39' for details.
3. Home Political, National Archives, New Delhi (hereafter HP), 18/10/1945; 18/12/1945.
4. All India Congress Committee, Private Papers, Nehru Memorial Museum and Library, New Delhi, File No. G-42/1947-8 (hereafter AICC); from Mathurananda Mohanty, Cuttack, to Bapuji (Gandhi), 12.4.1947.
5. Who's Who Compilation Committee of Freedom Fighters, Orissa (hereafter WWCC), Accession Number 50, January 1946, mentions that the Congress Parliamentary Board had adopted three basic criteria: (1) loyalty to Congress principles during the Quit India movement; (2) capacity to do legislative work; (3) influence in the constituencies. Ranjit's selection violated the question of loyalty to the Congress.
6. One is tempted to refer to the prediction of H. J. Todd in 1946 about who the new rulers of Orissa would be. Thus, he expected them be from the ruling families, 'the . . . Orissa Zamindars and . . . the . . . Congress'; cited in H. K. Mahtab, *The Beginning of the End* (Cuttack, 1972), p. 83.

7. AICC File No. 3/1942-6. One should mention the position of the other political formations here: Muslim League 4, Independents 4, and the Communists 1; and there were 4 non-elected members. Whereas the Congress polled 66,281 votes, the Muslim League polled 4,336, the Independents polled 554 and the Communist candidate polled 2,234 votes.
8. AICC File No. 3/1942-6.
9. H. K. Mahtab Private Papers, Nehru Memorial Museum & Library, New Delhi, Subject File No. 3, Ist Instalment, Governor of Orissa to Mahtab, Prime Minister, Orissa, 24 May 1946.
10. AICC File No. ED1 (KW-3)/1946-7, 'Orissa and the Congress Ministry 1946-7'.
11. Mansergh *et al.* (eds.), *Transfer of Power* (London, 1973), Vol. VII, Document No. 17, reports one meeting between Wavell, Cabinet delegation and Provincial Governors, 28/3/1946. In fact, this heavy reliance on the bureaucracy in Orissa continues even today.
12. HP 18/3/1947.
13. Mansergh, *op. cit.*, Vol. VII, Document No. 62, Report of meeting between Wavell, Cabinet delegation, and Mahtab, etc., 6/4/1946. The question of centre-state relations was also expressed by Sarangadhar Das in the Orissa Legislature Assembly; as he put it: 'Being a poor province we did not ever have money. Now for 2-5 years we have the opportunity to get money from the Indian Government and if we do not take advantage of this now, when will we?' (my translation from Oriya), *Orissa Legislature Assembly Proceedings* (hereafter *OLA Proceedings*), Vol. III (Cuttack, 1947-8), p. 360. Mahtab, *Sadhanara Pathe* (Oriya, Cuttack, 1972), p. 296, also hints at centre-state relations when he mentions that no one was bothered about Orissa in 1946.
14. AICC File No. ED1 (KW-3) 1946-7, *op. cit.*; the Committee was expected to, among other things, make land revenue uniform, remove intermediaries, prevent fragmentation of holdings, make provisions for common land and improve agricultural production; the amendment of laws were planned to grant security of tenures, to simplify sale laws and introduce a rent ceiling; an agricultural income tax was planned; some steps were also planned to help small holders; and finally, laws were also contemplated to make it easier for government to acquire land for private companies 'in the interests of planned economic development'.
15. *Ibid.*
16. *OLA Proceedings,* Vol. II; III (Cuttack,1946-7; 1947-8), pp. 339; 367.
17. HP 18/6/1946; 18/7/1946; 18/11/1946; 18/12/1946.
18. Mahtab, *Sadhanara Pathe*, *op. cit.*, p. 301, mentions how he got funds to set up the *Prajatantra* newspaper around November 1947. This should be borne in mind while discussing how the landlords felt safe with the Congress in power and responded by patronising it.

19. Interestingly, even Congressmen and the official organ of the Orissa Congress – the Samaj – ridiculed Mahtab's demand for a higher procurement price for rice than what was fixed by the Government and his idea that only five per cent of the people had to buy rice from the shops. As the Samaj put it, Mahtab did not know what he was talking about; HP 18/2/1946.
20. Mahtab Private Papers, S.F. No. 7; Mahtab to Gandhi, 31/12/1947.
21. Board of Revenue, Cuttack, file subject 'Land Revenue Administration Report 1945 to 1948-49'; the Report for 1947-8 mentioned how 'agriculturists', who had surplus for sale, profited by the prevailing high prices of food grain. Given the state of things these features helped the zamindars and the rich peasants. See Shakti Padhi, *Land Relations and Agrarian Development in India: A Comparative Historical Study of Regional Variations* (Thiruvananthapuram, 1999), to get an excellent idea about the land system/social structure in both coastal and western Orissa and grasp who the real beneficiaries of such steps were.
22. AICC File No. ED 1(KW-3)/1946-7. This drive to strengthen the links with the 'rich' peasants also implied certain land reforms, and, in fact, the PCC's post-1947 moves to abolish the zamindari system should be seen in this light.
23. Mahtab Private Papers, S.F. 3; Governor of Orissa to Eric Coates, Finance Member Viceroy's Executive, 17 August 1946.
24. *Ibid.*, Governor of Orissa, C. M. Trivedi to Mahtab, Prime Minister of Orissa, 9 September 1946, where he suggested New Cuttack as the new capital, like New Delhi.
25. Mahatab Private Papers, S.F. 31, from A. C. Bose, Deputy Secretary Government of India to Government of Orissa, 23 July 1947.
26. S. Gopal (ed.), *Selected Works of Jawaharlal Nehru*, Vol. VI (New Delhi, 1987), p. 489; speech at foundation-laying ceremony Bhubaneshwar, 13/4/1948. Needless to say, this ideal remained unrealized.
27. Address of V. P. Menon, Governor of Orissa, on 11 July 1951, *OLA Proceedings* 1951 (Cuttack, 1953), p. 5.
28. This was frontally criticised by Baidyanath Rath (Communist) in the Assembly on 12 July 1951, as 'wasteful' and 'extravagant', *ibid.*, p. 31.
29. See Madhusudan Mohapatra's position in *OLA Proceedings*, Vol. II (Cuttack, 1946-7), p. 361, while he debated the 'Orissa Military Police Bill, 1946'.
30. AICC File No. ED1(KW-3)/1946-7; Mahtab, Private Papers, S.F. 11.
31. AICC File No. EDI (KW-3)/1946-7.
32. Mahtab Private Papers, S.F. 3, from Governor of Orissa, C. M. Trivedi, to Mahtab, Prime Minister of Orissa, 15 September 1946. Over the 1946-51 period effort was also directed to develop roads in Orissa. Thus, Governor V. P. Menon's speech to the Orissa Asembly on 11 July 1951 referred to

this aspect; for details *OLA Proceedings* 1951 (Cuttack, 1953), p. 2.

33. Mahtab Private Papers, S.F. 3, Prime Minister Mahtab to Governor, Orissa, 13 October 1946, and Governor to Mahtab, 25 June 1946, where he wrote that Mahtab had mentioned this idea to him 'more than once'.
34. Mahtab Private Papers, S.F. 3, from Nityananda Kanungo, Revenue Minister, to Mahtab, Prime Minister, Orissa, 29 June 1946, where he specifically raised these issues.
35. See for example Sanjoy Bhattacharya and Benzamin Zachariah, '"A Great Destiny": The British Colonial State and the Advertisement of Post-War Reconstruction in India, 1942-45', *South Asia* 19, 1, 1999, p. 71-100, to grasp the dynamics of this dimension. HP 18/3/1947 refers to an American engineer, Mr. Savage, who came in to see and give his opinion on the Hirakud dam in March 1947. Interestingly, Sanjoy Bhattacharya, *Propaganda and Information in Eastern India 1939-45: A Necessary Weapon of War* (Richmond, 2001), p. 127, refers to one G. R. Savage, who was a Central Intelligence Department Officer in 1944-5; if it was indeed the same person, we can perhaps see how the retreating colonial power attempted to encourage separatist politics in the area.
36. A Miscellaneous note in Mahtab Private Papers, S.F. 10.
37. From my childhood I have heard this point about water losing its properties if electricity is tapped from it.
38. Mahtab Private Papers, S.F. 3, Trivedi, Governor, to Biswasroy, 24 June 1946.
39. Mahtab, *Sadhanara Pathe*, *op. cit.*, pp. 309-10; Mahtab, Private Papers, S.F. 3; 7; 10. For a detailed and valuable account of the consequences of the dam see Balagovind Baboo, *Technology and Social Transformation: The Case of the Hirakud Multi-Purpose Dam Project in Orissa* (New Delhi, 1992). As pointed out, there has been an increase in the frequency of floods from 11.8 years in 1956 to 3.75 years in 1988; cracks have appeared in the dam which he attributes to the improper 'curing' of concrete that was used; the Public Accounts Committee was not satisfied with the financial handling of the project; and the high rate of silting which affects irrigation (p. 143). But most importantly, he refers to the human cost, viz., displacement, inadequate or non-payment of compensation, and rehabilitation that was hopeless and inadequate (especially Chap. 6, and pp. 144-8). In fact, from what I gather, many people are yet to get the compensation for their lands that had been taken over during the construction of the Hirakud dam.
40. Mahtab Private Papers, S.F. 34, Note of the Governor, 18/11/1946, who met some 'prominent citizens' of Sambalpur lists the points raised by them. A Miscellaneous note in Mahtab Private Papers, S.F. 10, March 1947 and HP 18/3/1947, described meetings in the Machkund area where it was resolved to oppose all attempts at evacuation until details related to definite amount of compensation, arrangements for re-settlement and future benefits

from the scheme were made available. Apprehensions were also expressed that if the evacuation took place before the rains agricultural activity would get affected.

41. Mahtab Private Papers, S.F. 31, C. M. Trivedi, Governor of Orissa, to Mahtab, Prime Minister, Orissa, 19 April 1947, where he was very keen to discuss the question of publicity with regard to the Hirakud dam.
42. Mahtab Private Papers, S.F. 36.
43. HP 18/9/1946.
44. HP 18/11/1946.
45. HP 18/1/1947.
46. HP 18/2/1947; the Congress' position matched the opposition to the secessionist movement, HP 18/6/1947.
47. HP 18/5/1947.
48. For details Pati, *Resisting Domination*, *op. cit.*, Chaps. 1 and 5.
49. HP 18/11/1946; 18/12/1946; we get references to the circulation of rumours, leaflets and an increase in communal tension from November, 1946.
50. Mahtab Private Papers, S.F. 11; Mahtab wrote to Nehru thus: 'If I may say so, some of our Congressmen are more communal than the communalists themselves.' 3/11/1947.
51. HP 18/7/1945
52. Mansergh, *op. cit.*, Vol. VII, Document No. 235; C. Trivedi, Governor of Orissa, to Wavell; 9/5/1946.
53. HP 33/17/1943.
54. HP 5/6/1947 refers to the intervention of Muslim and Hindu communalists of Bhadrak.
55. HP 18/4/1947; 18/5/1947.
56. HP 18/4/1947; 18/5/1947.
57. For details Pati, *Resisting Domination*, *op. cit.*, Chap. 1. Although rooted in the nineteenth century it was championed both by Gandhi and the Congress in the 1920-47 period. Thus, Gandhi had never entered the temple of Jagannatha and the two Congress ministries of Orissa had attached considerable importance to this question; see for example K. M. Patra, *Orissa Legislature and Freedom Struggle, 1912-1947* (New Delhi, 1979), pp. 140-1; 255-8, for details. In fact, as mentioned earlier, the 1946 Congress ministry formulated a bill to facilitate the entry of Harijans.
58. HP 18/2/1947; AICC File No. 18/1946-9 mentions how Malati Choudhury led Harijans of Angul to enter a temple on 12 October 1947 which reflected perhaps a climax of the temple-entry movement.
59. HP 18/4/1947; we can add that there was a Khandayat conference in April 1947.
60. HP 18/5/1947.
61. C. M. Wright-Neville, *Report on the Administration of Police in the State of Orissa for the Year 1949* (Cuttack, 1954), Intro., Chart No. 1.

62. HP 18/7/1947.
63. Board of Revenue, Cuttack, 'Land Revenue Administration, Report 1945 to 1948-49', mentioned the strained relations between peasants and landlords in all the parts of Orissa.
64. I am thankful to Prof. Partha Sarathi Gupta for this reference. As he put it, Barik remained silent, perhaps not entirely convinced, when answered in the affirmative.
65. Mahtab Private Papers, S.F. 3; from C. M. Trivedi to Mahtab 16/7/1946.
66. Mahtab Private Papers, S.F. 7; from Mahtab to Gandhi, 31/12/1947. We can add here the mixed feelings of the Communists regarding independence and how this led them to speak of the 'farcical' nature of the freedom. They failed to grasp that an independent country had been born. Our evidence suggests, however, that in Orissa the Communists joined in the all-party celebrations in all the districts; *Peoples' Age*, 31/8/47.
67. WWCC Acc. No. 97, 1st half of August 1947.
68. See for example, Government of Orissa, *Report of the Land Reforms Committee Orissa 1958* (Cuttack, 1958), to get an idea of this dimension; perhaps the most significant recommendation was the suggestion to have a land ceiling, which was to be 7 acres (p. 15).
69. Here I am referring to certain feudal obligations, including forced labour. However, the problem of bonded labourers remains in Orissa even today.
70. The integration of the princely states does not seem to be properly grasped by scholars like Ian Copland, *The Princes of India in the Endgame of Empire* (Cambridge, 1997), who focus on this to illustrate the triumph of nationalism.
71. HP 18/2/1947;18/2/1947 refers to *Muktijuddhya* where an article appeared about the government's 'declaration of war' on the Communists. The Socialists seem to have died out in this phase.
72. Mahtab Private Papers, S.F. 11; Nehru to Mahtab, 8/6/1948; Mahtab to Nehru 1/7/1949. This is rather interesting since repression was the all-India policy of the Congress *vis-à-vis* Communists in this period.
73. HP 18/1/1947; 18/2/1947; 18/3/1947.
74. HP 18/3/1947.
75. WWCC Acc. No. 28; the rally also demanded improvement of the conditions of low paid workers
76. HP 18/1/1947; HP 18/4/1947; 18/7/1947. One can see the obvious parallel between the demand for 3/5th share of the produce of the Kisan Sangha and the Tebhaga Movement in Bengal in this phase.
77. HP 18/3/1947; the meetings also focused on the demands of workers and salaried employees.
78. HP 18/3/1947; the abolition of the *bhagchas* implied granting of land rights to share-croppers; connected with the demand for the abolition of the *zamindari* system and ownership rights for tenants, this seems to be the logical corollary.

79. HP 18/4/1947; Biswanath Sahu, *Land Utilisation in Orissa* (Cuttack, 1951), p. 198.
80. HP 18/5/1947.
81. HP 18/4/1947; Bishwanath Sahu, *op. cit.*, p. 198.
82. *Peoples' Age*, 6/6/1948.
83. Gurucharan Pattnaik, *Ganjam Re Rakta Prabhat* (Bloodbath in Ganjam, Oriya), Nabajuga Press, Cuttack, 1972, provides perhaps the best account of this peasant movement. In fact, HP 18/10/1946 refers to a meeting at Jakar in Ganjam (October 1946) which was presided by Biswanath Das, where one of the resolutions passed called for a reduction of produce rent in the Ganjam *zamindaris*.
84. *Ibid.*, *Muktijuddhya*, 6/11/1948.
85. *Ibid.*, for details; *Muktijuddhya*, 6/11/1948, referred to how the Congress government got Kisan leaders of Balasore like Nityananda Deb arrested, how certain *zamindars* like Jadunath Mahapatra and Radhanath Mahapatra terrorised peasants through middle-men and how in Rahanga village Mohunts (Upendra Panda and his brother) used *goondas* to threaten Abhimanyu Panda, a Kisan leader.
86. *Peoples' Age*, 6/6/1948.
87. WWCC Acc. No. 28, 99; Peoples' Age, 6/7/1947. The central points discussed included the establishment of a communication system (linking-up the different states telephonically) and raising a joint police force. The concept of a Mahakosal (i.e. Federation of States) was discussed.
88. WWCC Acc. No. 28.
89. All India State People's Conference (hereafter AISPC) File No. 129; P. Sitaramayya wrote to Mahtab: 'You contrast the scheme of amalgamation by which you describe your proposals. . . . But how do you call your scheme a scheme of amalgamation when you retain the princes with their autocratic powers in their own states and offer them in addition the chances of becoming ministers with you. . . . Even now I say that so long you recognise the autocratic heads of individual States a scheme of amalgamation would be a misnomer' (21/7/1947).
90. See for example, Mahtab Private Papers, S.F. 7. In response to a letter from Sarat Pattnaik, Secretary of the Communist Party of Orissa (18/9/1947) to Mahtab, seeking to work unitedly. Mahtab replied positively. As he put it '. . . I think the time has come when all political parties should frame a common policy towards the States problem'.
91. Nilgiri Praja Andolana Compilation Committee, *Nilgiri Praja Andolana Ra Itihasa* (Oriya, Balasore, 1982), pp. 131-5 (hereafter, *NPARI*); WWCC Acc. No. 99. Its worth mentioning how this bears some resemblance with Gandhian constructive work; *ibid.*, pp. 135-8; WWCC Acc. No. 100; the durbar's uneasiness prompted it to arrest some Prajamandal activists.
92. *NPARI*, p. 138. We do not have clear evidence for Nilgiri, but around this time, fishermen in some of the princely states asserted themselves *vis-à-vis*

high caste people and refused to carry their palanquins; HP 18/5/1947.

93. *NPARI*, pp. 139-42.
94. *Ibid.*, pp. 145-8; *People's Age*, 31/8/1947; at these meetings the national flag was unfurled. People came in large numbers carrying red and Congress flags. We can add that on 15 August the durbar released many prisoners, including some criminals, with whom the Raja negotiated to counter the Prajamandal.
95. *NPARI*, pp. 152-62.
96. Personal communication Banamali Das (Nilgiri, May 1982).
97. Mahtab had offered arms to the Communists which they had refused and had instead asked for some money which was never received; personal communication, Sarat Pattnaik. However, given the existing popular upsurge the PCC decided to intervene by November 1947.
98. *NPARI*, pp. 168-74; personal communication Nanda Pattnaik (Cuttack, June 1987); WWCC Acc. no. 99; 47; after the merger of Nilgiri the *Samaj* and *Prajatantra* dropped hints that a similar fate awaited the other Rajas; WWCC Acc. No. 47.
99. Personal communication Banamali Das.
100. WWCC Acc. No. 99; two separate conferences were held - one with the rulers of 'B' and 'C' class states and one with those of 'A' class states.
101. Harekrushna Mahtab, *Beginning of the End* (Cuttack, 1972), p. 30.
102. AISPC, Nehru Memorial Museum & Library, New Delhi, File No. 129, 'Allegations Against Raja of Dhenkanal during his twenty years of Rule' (undated); Sarangadhar Das, 'A Review of the Political Situation in the Eastern States' (27/11/1947).
103. Personal communication Sarat Pattnaik (Cuttack, June 1983); I have already referred to the increase in the price of rice in Orissa around the end of 1947.
104. AISPC file no. 129, Krutibas Mishra's (Secretary, Dhenkanal Prajamandal) statement articulated the popular feeling: '. . . the Dhenkanal Prajamandal requests the Government of India not to effect any compromise settlement with the Rajas, but to direct them to hand over all powers to the people' (n.d.).
105. Personal communication Sarat Pattnaik; Baishnab Pattnaik (Dhenkanal, June 1985).
106. Sadasiv Pradhan, *Agrarian and Political Movements* (New Delhi, 1986), p. 148.
107. Personal communication Baishnab Pattnaik; he told me that Mahtab used to go to the palace to conduct negotiations which appeared strange.
108. Personal communication Sarat Pattnaik.
109. AISPC File No. 129; Sarangdhar Das, 'Report on Orissa and C.P. States Merging with Orissa' (2/2/1948).
110. Pabitra Mohan Pradhan, *Mukti Pathe Sainika* (Oriya; Cuttack, 1979),

pp. 242-3; Pradhan also mentions Mahtab who on 8/4/1946 had advised him at Delhi to surrender to the Raja. The Talcher Raja made Pradhan's case a prestige issue and only in July 1947 was the warrant for his arrest cancelled; AISPC File No. 164.

111. Sadasiv Pradhan, *op. cit.*, p. 147; it seems Gandhi advised the Raja to merge.
112. Ramachandra Ram, *Sangramee* (Oriya; Cuttack, 1986), pp. 158-61; the leading Communist activists like Ram moved around the state, cycling 10 to 15 villages a day to mobilise the people. For details on the Bazellgate case see Pati, *Resisting Domination*, *op. cit.*, Chap. 3.
113. *Ibid.*, pp. 163-4; Mahtab Private Papers, S.F. 13; Ramprasad Singh and Srivasta Naik, Secretary States Students Conference, also expressed similar anger against the Rajas.
114. Ram, *op. cit.*, pp. 164-71.
115. *Ibid.*, p. 172.
116. *Ibid.*, pp. 175-7; we should add here that at the so-called democratic elections the durbar did not allow political prisoners and women to cast their vote.
117. One should note here that two of the princely states—Kharsuan and Singhbhum—merged with Bihar.
118. V. P. Menon, *The Story of the Integration of the Indian States* (Madras, 1961), p. 154.
119. Mahtab's correspondence 141/44, Nehru Memorial Museum & Library, with the Raja of Dhenkanal; the Raja wanted his advice for joining the Bengal Breweries (20/8/1950) and Mahtab's Private Secretary replied to the Raja (22/8/1950) expressing Mahtab's inability to advise him.
120. Mahtab Private Papers, S.F. 31, contains R. N. Singhdeo's statement after the 1952 elections which shows that the Ganatantra Parishad (the party of the ex-princes) contested 58 Assembly seats and won 31 seats in the first general elections.
121. For details, Pati, *Resisting Domination*, *op. cit.*, Chap. 3.
122. Government of Orissa, *Land Tenure and Land Reforms in Orissa 1962* (Cuttack 1962), pp. 81-96. One should also add that both these are institutions exist even today.
123. For a brilliant analysis of this aspect see Padhi, *op. cit.*, especially Chaps. 10 and 11.
124. A classic example is Bipan Chandra, *Essays in Colonialism* (Hyderabad, 1999), where he asserts the need to see 'colonialism as the constant backdrop' while studying any major aspect of a post-colonial society (p. v).

CHAPTER 17

The Pure Spring: A Cosmogram at Khallikot

JOANNA WILLIAMS

Majestic ancient buildings such as Konarak and Borobudur lend themselves readily to interpretation as images of a world-view. Yet a small, carefully wrought spring, still intact in one of the former minor states of southern Orissa and created 250 years ago when the region was dwarfed by outside powers, is of equal interest. I shall argue that this represents a significant cosmological vision, that it indicates a moment when patron as well as advisors felt challenged, and that it merits attention – both intellectual and visual.

This spring is a part of a palace complex on the western outskirts of Khallikot at a site known as Nirmal Jhar (or Pure Waters) from the spring that surfaces from the low hills here. The palace buildings include pavilions that catch the summer breezes, a shrine to the right in Plate 1, and a large tank still in use for bathing. From an inscription set into a wall of the palace, we know that the complex (*prāsādādi*) was built at the end of the reign of Aparājita Balukeśvara, around 1750 CE (Plate 2).[1] In lines 5 and 6 of the inscription, Balukeśvara is credited with praiseworthy public works (*kirtti*), including a reservoir (*sāgara band*) and a brahman village (*śāsana*), both bearing his name; the latter is presumably the present hamlet Balukeśvarpur, on the eastern side of Khallikot.

The mid eighteenth century might not seem a promising climate for architecture in Orissa. The once proud province had for two centuries been under Mughal rule. In the last stage, Taqi Khan, governor in Cuttack of the Nawab of Bengal, had in 1733 led to the temporary removal of the Jagannātha triad from Puri to Aṭhgarh, adjoining Khallikot, where a the stone temple of Mārda was erected in two months to house them. [2] As Hermann Kulke has argued importantly, that entire episode seems to reflect, not Muslim

Plate 1. General view of Nirmal Jhar complex from northwest corner.

Plate 2. Inscription on palace wall.

persecution of that cult but rather a power struggle for control over the growing pilgrimage economy.[3] At Khallikot, Balakeśvara's grandfather, Sri Ram Hari Śaraṇ, is supposed to have been given the seemingly backhanded title Chhoṭe-rāya (as it appears in the Nirmal Jhar inscription), meaning small overlord by the ruler of Parlakhemuṇḍi, his neighbour to the south, after conflict and reconciliation between the two.[4] Balukeśvara retained this title along with the more grandiloquent one, Mārda (again the inscription's spelling, apparently a variant on *marada* or virile) Rāja, given him by his overlord in Puri/Khuruḍha. The later eighteenth century saw the presence of the Marathas and the British in parts of Orissa, although neither left an impact in Khallikot visible today. In short, this was a time of turmoil when cultural patterns and authorities were called in question.

The Nirmal Jhar water-works may be seen as a response to such conditions. On the one hand, in practical terms they make a natural water source accessible to a populace who faced the constant spectre of drought.[5] Today local people continue to use the large tank in the foreground of Plate 1. This is fed by a vividly functioning *makara*-spout that brings water from within the palace buildings. On the first raised terrace a plain basin, roughly ten feet square, is locally identified as Prayāg, the site of the union of north India's two great sacred rivers, bringing to mind the linkage between a benevolent ruler, ritual purity, and the practical benefits of water.

A third basin, seven and a half feet square at ground-level, its maximum dimension, is located behind the temple and a plain hall on axis with both temple and palace (Plate 3).[6] This miniature *kund* constitutes an image of one version of the complex myth of the descent of the river Ganga to earth. This caught the attention of the British zoologist and anthropologist Nelson Annandale, who published it in 1924.[7] His diagram, our Figure 1, elucidates the story succinctly. The initial source of the river is the feet of Narāyaṇa or Viṣṇu, seated in a niche that dominates the basin, with four arms and his customary attributes (Plate 4). Thence it flows counterclockwise to the five heads of the smaller, submerged figure of Mahādeva Śiva. The channel continues to the two-armed figure of a sage (Plate 5) on the same scale as Narāyaṇa, whom he faces across the basin. From there the water flows to the summit of a hill (Plate 6), from which it would

Plate 3. Small *kund* east of temple from northeast corner.

Plate 4. Nārāyaṇa, west side of *kund*.

Plate 5. Sage Jahnu, east side of *kund.*

Plate 6. Mt. Meru, north side of *kund.*

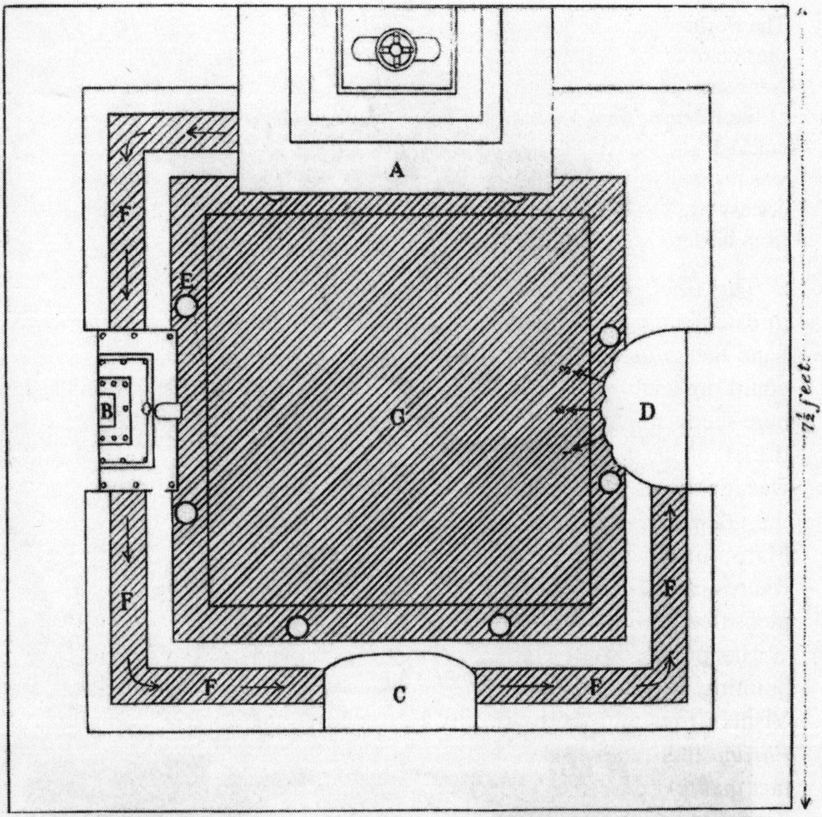

Notes: A. Shrine of Nārāyaṇa; B. Five-headed Māhādeva; C. Sage Jahnu; D. Mt. Meru with streams of (1) the Ganga (2) the Jamuna (3) the Saraswati; E. One of the Aṣṭābakra; F. Channel representing the primeval Ganga.

Figure 1. Plan of the small *kund* at Nirmal Jhar, Khallikot, after N. Annandale.

issue in three streams visible in the dry season when the water level is low.

Annandale's account includes the explanation of a local *sadhu*, whose words were translated by his photographer:

> The world was out of tune and everything was in decay, for the Rāgiṇīs, who preside over the modes of music, had grown old and forgotten how to sing. Narāyaṇa, the Creator, summoned the Gods to a feast and called on one of the Rāgiṇīs, now decrepit like her sisters, for a song; but her voice was cracked. Then the five-headed Mahadev lifted up his voice and sang. Harmony was restored to the universe, the Rāgiṇīs grew young again and Narāyaṇa in ecstasy was dissolved in perspiration, which flowed down his body and issued from his left foot in a mighty stream.[8]

This flood, even mediated by descent on the head of Mahādeva , threatened the earth. It was swallowed by the sage Jahnu, whose left hand the *sadhu* saw as making a gash in his thigh so that the water could proceed to earth through a pure orifice. The figure in Plate 5 here seems to me to hold a rosary in his proper right hand and to rest the left on his thigh and/or the sole of his right foot. And the mountain was identified as Mount Meru, whence the sacred river divides into the Ganga, Jamuna, and Saraswati, flowing into and out of lake Mansarovar, the *kund* itself. Within the water stand eight hunched figures, their heads just visible in Plate 4 , whom the local informant identified as *aṣṭabakra* or Eight Deformed Ones.[9]

Hariprasad Shastri appended a note to Annandale's account, pointing out that in the *Viṣṇu Purāṇa* the Ganga also arises from Viṣṇu's foot, but that it is only in the very late *Brahma Vaivarta Purāṇa* that this is linked to the god's delight at celestial music. In fact that text describes Ganga originating in the limbs of Rādhā and Kṛṣṇa; as an interloper on his throne she became a target of Rādhā's jealousy.[10] Shastri also notes that Jahnu appears in the north-western and some southern versions of the *Rāmāyaṇa* where it might be a later interpolation.[11] Yet Ganga is known as the daughter of Jahnu in other classical sources.[12] I would prefer to imagine a pool of variants co-existing in the past as they do now. This *kund* gives concrete, visible form, to one eighteenth-century oral tradition, leaving some questions open if we insist on correlation with verbal texts as they survive today.

The modern mythographer may be surprised to find Narāyaṇa's

role emphasized over Mahādeva's, as in the version familiar in the south, where the royal penitent Bhagiratha plays a role comparable to Jahnu's, sometimes following the Jahnu episode.[13] The temple at Nirmal Jhar (Plate 7), today identified as a Rādhā-Kṛṣṇa shrine, is distinctly Vaiṣṇava. On either side of the door that leads into the sanctum are images of two childhood forms of Kṛṣṇa in which the *gopis* play the general role of a chorus (Plates 8, 9). In the mid eighteenth century, Chaitanya's impact had not yet brought the cult of Rādhā to this part of Orissa.[14] *Bhakti* is loosely thematized in the playfully worshipping generic female bodies and in the nursing cows and calves beneath the Govardhana-dhara. That mountain is defined by the same swirling forms that shelter plants, animals, and sages as at play on Mt. Meru (Plates 6 and 8). The crisp, angular, slightly squat style of figures indicates likewise that the *kund* and the temple were executed at the same time.

In today's oral version of the story of the Descent of the Ganga, local people point up to the temple roof in reference to the Rāgiṇīs who have forgotten how to sing, recalling the no longer active *gharānā* of Parlakhemundi and the lost traditions of the temple dancers of Puri. Can this sense of loss be read back to Khallikot in 1750? Then

Plate 7. Rādhā-Kṛṣṇa Temple from north side.

Plate 8. Kṛṣṇa Lifting Mountain (*Govardhanadhara*) by shrine door.

Plate 9. Kṛṣṇa Having Stolen Gopis' Clothes (*Cirahāra*) by shrine door.

the basic forms of the temple might recall another crumbling relic of Orissa's past, the Sun Temple at Konarak, roughly 60 miles to the east. The presence at Nirmal Jhar of a separate structure to the east, which I hypothesize to be a *nāṭa mandapa* as at Konaraka, set apart rather than joined to the porch as would have been the norm by the eighteenth century,[15] might be explained by emulation of Konarak. The roofs of both porch (*jagamohana*) and shrine (*deul*) also bear unexpected resemblance to the notable Sun temple. There of course the original form of the shrine roof had the tall, curving profile of the traditional *gaṇḍi,* distinct from the pyramidal *piḍha deul* of the porch. A sliver of the Konarak *gaṇḍi* survived in the early nineteenth century, as documented in British drawings.[16] The Khallikot builders, had they been motivated by archaeological accuracy or simple archaism, might have chosen that form, but their bulbous pilasters and lobed arches reflect familiarity with Islamic architecture in India. The *piḍha* roof seems to have become an acceptable form for shrines in Orissa by this point, so that the choice here may be seen as a version of the contemporary norm and at the same time a tribute to the surviving parts of Konarak.[17]

If so, the recasting of the female musicians and dancers on the roof of the Sun temple's surviving porch as Rāgiṇīs unable to sing is of significance. The Konarak figures seem to play a part in the movement of the Sun's chariot, comparable to that which *mahari/ devadasis* play in the Puri Jagannātha temple as well as the male priests who strike gongs and sing on the carts of the Ratha Yātrā today. Nirmal Jhar does not make specific reference to a wooden chariot, and hence the figures have lost a rationale that is more than generically auspicious. While reduced in size, like the entire edifice, and in number, they remain an attractive embellishment, whose raison d'etre can be connected to the most vividly novel part of the complex, the small *kund.*

Invoking the trope of the Ganga identified with a local river is not without precedent. Rivers of south India had been compared with the great northern and celestial river both under the Pallavas (most graphically in Mahendra's inscription and rock-cut relief at Tiruchirapalli) and under the Colas (Rajendra's temple Gangaikondacholapuram). The small stream issuing from the hill at Nirmal Jhar may seem puny by comparison. Yet what we see here is another case of the mapping into a local situation of a theme widely known in diverse versions from literature.

In 1750, Khallikot was in a weak position with competing local overlords and with more distant threats, political and climatic. I have already alluded to Kulke's role in recasting the study of the eighteenth and nineteenth centuries in Orissa. First, he took this period seriously and saw its role as developing patterns from a 'classical' past. Thus he saw its records as an important part of our understanding of that past. Moreover he saw the last two centuries as a richly pluralistic moment, even in the seemingly isolated region of Orissa, rather than in terms of communal conflict and Orientalist decline. The visual evidence bears this out at Nirmal Jhar, where Islamic details are welcomed in an inventive if archaizing Hindu shrine. In the same way, Maratha dress and British material culture contribute to the illustrations of the local genre of illustrated palm-leaf manuscripts.[18] We will understand these things only if we cease to use terms like 'crude' and 'confused' to describe the period.

Finally, the intellectual ambitions of the elegant complex at Khallikot illustrate another of Kulke's major topics, the parallel between 'Hinduization' in India and 'Indianization' in South-East Asia. Almost seven centuries earlier, Jayavarman VII had constructed a comparable water monument, Neak Pean, at Angkor. This recreated a cosmological schema in which a lake in the Himalayas was the source of four rivers that define the universe . There of course the theme was given a Buddhist twist. The central shrine bore relief images of Avalokiteśvara, and the horse Balaha rescuing devotées in the water constituted in part an *avatāra* of the Bodhisattva. The entwined serpents that gave rise to the name Neak Pean are identifiable with the *nāgas* Nanda and Upananda, who produced the Buddha's lotus seat in some textual versions of the Great Miracle at Sravasti. Yet serpents may also evoke indigenous ancestral spirits. Bernard Philippe Groslier suggested with tantalizing brevity that this site was connected to Jayavarman's *abhiṣeka* and that the significance endures in the modern Cambodian water festival, which celebrates the annual reversal of the course of the Tonlé Sap.[19] The empire of Jayavarman VII required vaster scale, with more strident political implications, which he had already developed in the third phase of the Bayon by including sixteen chapels that housed the gods of the provinces of the Khmer state. I do not mean to claim that Aparājita Balukeśvara of Khallikot was in this league of actual power and architectural ambition. Yet the complex at Nirmal Jhar remains a testament to local initiative, weaving together courtly ideas and an imposing ancient monument as partial model, with stories surely known in part in oral, folkloric form, all realized by local artisans' abilities. Kulke's clarion call to recognize indigenous initiative in this process has encouraged a fundamental shift in our understanding of how such cultural processes are shared in structure and shaped by local conditions.[20]

NOTES

1. This statement masks several small uncertainties. A. Vadivelu asserts that Balukeswara Deo 'discovered the waterfall, known as Nirmal Jhar, where he also built some temples', *Aristocracy of Southern India* (Delhi: Mittal Publ., 1984), Vol. 1, p. 107). The local historian Baikoli Mohopatra concurs that Balukeśvara was responsible for the tank; he quotes the inscription accurately in Oriya, although several parts permit variant readings. *Oḍiśā Itihāsare Khallikotara Sthāna* (Cuttack: Sahadev Pradhan Publ, 1981, p. 21). This local view is based on the inscription, which was added by one of Balukesvar's descendants , Rajasinha, who died in the 1750's. The list of Khallikot rulers in Vadivelu and Mohopatra coincides, except for the period following Balukeśvara, apparently because he had several grandsons who quarrelled. A second Balukeśvara, without the epithet Aparājita, appears late in the nineteenth century.
2. A. K. Rath, *Studies in Some Aspects of the History and Culture of Orissa* (Calcutta: Punthi Pustak, 1987, p. 220). A temple by this name exists south-east of Polusara. The altar with three empty bases (albeit smaller than the present Puri triad), the absence of detailed carving (indicating haste), and the proximity of the sculptors' village of Mathura all fit with this account.
3. H. Kulke, *Jagannātha Kult und Gajapati-Kìnigtum* (Wiesbaden: Franz Steiner, 1979) especially Ch. VIII.
4. Vadivelu, op. cit, p. 107.
5. Orissa is reported to have suffered ten drought years during the first half of the ninteenth century. Krushna C. Jena, *Socio Economic Conditions of Orissa* (Delhi, Sundeep Prakashan, 1978), p. 86.
6. It is tempting to think of this hall as a dance pavillion (*nat mandap*) linking sacred and secular structures. In Plate 1, the head of the sage (seen from behind at the left of Plate 3), appears as a small dark bump between temple and plain hall.

7. 'A Working Model of the Origin of the Ganges in a Temple in Ganjam', *Memoirs of the Asiatic Society of Bengal* VIII, 4 (1924), 251-4. Two of Annandale's photos and the gist of his note are reproduced in Steven G. Darian, *The Ganges in Myth and History* (Honolulu: University of Hawaii Press, 1978), pp. 27-30.
8. *Memoirs of the Asiatic Society of Bengal* VIII, 4 (1924), 254. This is followed by a note on the mythology by Hariprasad Shastri and a brief note by Percy Brown addressing the date, which he suggests is a very recent copy of an old design. These authors describe the carving as mannered and crude and the programmatic mythology as confused and funny.
9. Their heads are better visible in Annandale's dry-season photographs. The authoritative Oḍiya Lexicon, *Pūrṇachandra Orḍiā Bhaśākośa* (Vol. I, p. 728) cites Astābakra only as the name of a single sage, bent in eight places as cursed by his father.
10. *Brahmavaivarta Purāṇa*, tr Shanti Lal Nagar, ed. Acharya Ramesh Chaturvedi (Delhi: Parimal Publications, 2001), Vol 1, p. 206 (Prakrti-khanda, Ch. 10, verse 178).
11. *The Rāmāyaṇa of Vālmiki*, Vol. I, tr. R. P. Goldman (Princeton: Princeton University Press, 1984), p. 363, n. 24.
12. Kalidasa frequently alludes to the Ganges by the epithet *Jahnukanyā*; C. Śivaramamurti, *Rishis in Indian Art and Literature* (New Delhi: Kanak Publications, 1981), pp. 49, 224. The release of the river through an exceptional, non-polluted orifice occurs in full accounts of the event, although in many this is the ear. It is possible that the sage's name, Jahnu, has been conflated with *jānu* or leg in the version where a gash is made in the thigh.
13. M.-E. Adiceam, 'Les images de Śiva dans l'Inde du sud: XV. – Gangādharamurti', *Arts Asiatiques* CCCII (1976), 99-138.
14. P. Mukherjee, 'Chaitanya in Orissa', in A. Eschmann, H. Kulke, G.C. Tripathi, eds, *The Cult of Jagannatha and the Regional Tradition of Orissa* (New Delhi: Manohar, 1978), p. 318.
15. Thomas Donaldson, 'Development of the Nāṭa-Mandira in Orissan Architecture', in *Kaladarsana*, ed. J. G. Williams (New Delhi: Oxford/IBH, 1981), pp. 41-4.
16. K. S. Behera, *Konarak, the Heritage of Mankind* (New Delhi, 1996, vol. I, p. 130 (drawing dated 1809); also 132 (1820), 138 (1837). Some aspects of the Konarak temple were obviously altered because of the Vaiṣṇava focus of this shrine: enigmatic Saivite figures, dancing figures in boats above the lowest tier of the roof are eliminated and Garudas added atop the shrine roof as at Puri. Annandale asserts that most of the temple and the spout of the large tank are made of laterite (*op. cit.*, 252-3); to this untutored eye they appear close to the khondalite of Konarak, their pinkish tone accentuated by annual re-painting with ochre.

17. Thomas Donaldson, in his magisterial *Hindu Temple Art of Orissa*, includes the *pidha* shrine of the Jagannātha temple at Palur on Chilka Lake, which he describes as 'late in date', immediately following a temple datable to the sixteenth century (Leiden: E. J. Brill, 1986), Vol. II, 740-1, Fig. 1825. These later temples remain to be studied with the rigour accorded to early ones.
18. Cf. J. P. Das and J. Williams, *Palm-leaf Miniatures: the Art of Raghunath Prusti of Orissa* (New Delhi, Abhinav Publications, 1991), pp. 83-6.
19. *Inscriptions du Bayon, Publications de l'École francaise d'Extreme Orient, Mémoires archéologiques* III, 2, Paris: EFEO, 1973, 291-302.
20. H. Kulke, 'Max Weber's Contribution to the Study of "Hinduization" in India and "Indianization" in Southeast Asia' (*Kings and Cults*, New Delhi, Manohar, 1993, 240-61), provides a succinct guide to the historiography of these ideas.

CHAPTER 18

Kondh Classification and Mythology in Macpherson's 'Account'

GEORG PFEFFER

Soon after conquering the coastal region in 1803 British led troops must have contacted Kondh settlements in Orissa. In 1835 the British also had their first encounters with the 'mountain Khond',[1] somewhat different from the peaceful tribes of the plains. The occasion was the usual confrontation.

In the British version of history, the Zamindar of Goomsur, nowadays known as the G. Udaigiri region, had rebelled against them and subsequently taken refuge in the mountains among his allies, the 'rude' tribes. Troops of the Madras Presidency, led by Lieutenant (later Captain) Charles Macpherson, followed him, in the course of these persecutions contacting a culture altogether unknown to them and, *horribile dictu*, practising human sacrifice. This the Europeans would not tolerate. The so-called '*Meriah* Wars' ensued, terminating in the subjugation of the Kondhmals (or Kondh mountain) region. Thus at a rather late stage of colonial history, Macpherson, as well as his successor, predecessor, fierce rival and fellow Scotsman John Campbell,[2] had an opportunity to join the coveted ranks of 'empire builders', even though the climate in that part of the empire – rugged mountains, impenetrable forests, swampy woodlands and tracts of open plain – was and is 'pestilential'. He divided Orissa 'into an alpine, a semi-alpine, and a maritime region' (218). With decreasing altitude tribal life was progressively reduced from independence to servitude.

Since the campaign had to be financed, the officer in charge was bound to submit descriptive reports on the situation, composed in the famous 'no nonsense' style of the Raj. After the successful wars in the mountains, Macpherson's account was published by the *Journal of the Royal Asiatic Society* and read by some of the founders of a new discipline called 'ethnology' in some and 'social anthropology' in other quarters. In this case, fellow Scotsmen had discovered the importance of the data. John Ferguson McLennan[3] was the first to utilize the recent publication, generalizing the ethnographic findings with regard to 'primitive marriage', i.e. the Kondh affinal (or marriage) rules of exogamy (or marrying out) and endogamy (or marrying within a specified unit), as well as the conflicts between the two 'sides' involved in affinal exchange, just as he applied the supposed Kondh practice of 'female infanticide' in his argument. MacLennan's work, marred by the usual logical faults in the 'origin of' hypotheses of his time, must nevertheless be counted as the foundation stone of all further anthropological inquiry into inherited affinity as a guiding principle of social classification all over the world.

The second classic to adopt Macpherson's ethnography was James George Frazer in his *The Golden Bough.*[4] This vast exotistic assemblage of global comparisons, involving bits and pieces of culture in the field of magic and religion, introduced an ever growing public readership to Kondh human sacrifice and other strange customs, without any reference to the source, so that Frazer himself, who never left the armchair of his library, is the usual reference. Thus the theoretical aspirations of two founders of social anthropology have been informed by Kondh socio-religious ideas, even though this influence has hardly ever been noticed in the history of the discipline.

Later anthropological work on Orissa also owes much to Macpherson. Bailey[5] quotes the Scotsman and probably chose the same northeastern Kondhmals region for his fieldwork because of the pioneer publication. He does not, however, discuss Kondh religion at length, whereas Niggemeyer's[6] substantial study of the Kuttia Kondh in the Belghar region does refer to Macpherson. Perhaps via Frazer, this museum man must have identified this sample of an ideology (of human sacrifice) that could fit into the Frankfurt school of 'culture morphology' prevalent in that university department until the 1960s. Macpherson – more than the accounts of the later Kondhmals pastors and administrators – received detailed attention in the work of Barbara Boal,[7] a Scotswoman fluent in the (generally untaught) Kondh language, who had served for decades as a missionary among the christianized Malia Kondh and was therefore well acquainted with everyday life in a Kondh village. Through her countryman's ethnography, she had developed a deep regard for the original Kondh religion, even though she did not conduct any prolongued fieldwork among its practitioners and, being an amateur, found it difficult to select a comprehensive form for the many excellent ethnographic details of her study.

The first highly professional and extended anthropological field-work among the mountain Kondh has been conducted by Roland Hardenberg in intervals since the spring of the year 2000. This colleague has been living in the mud hut of an isolated village for more than eighteen months by now and will continue the work from January 2003 onwards. Apart from his excellent knowledge of Oriya, he has, on his own, also mastered the difficult – hitherto absolutely unknown – language of the mountain people. During one of my usual spring excursions, he led me to some of the many *Meriah* sacrifices he has witnessed, so that I could compare it to the – in many ways different – Kuttia Kondh *Meriah*, i.e. the ritual of another Kondh people of another high mountain range which I had observed during excursions in 1981 and 1990.

Hardenberg's monograph will certainly present a completely new picture of Kondh society and religion. This must be pointed out, because Macpherson's account of the mid-nineteenth century, guided by commonsensical considerations of his time, had been taken as the standard version by the subsequent authors. None of the later publications on Kondh religion – including those of many Indian colleagues – has had the benefit of being based upon the participant observation of extended fieldwork or upon relevant anthropological theories. None bears witness of the multiple socio-religious networks, none makes sense of the standard ritual antagonisms. Indian authors have reported what local informants had explained to them and Western writers have been content with the logic of Macpherson's account rather than analyzing the 'total social fact' observable in contemporary society. The discovery of the gruesome human sacrifice did attract many more readers than the socio-cultural logic of about a million Kondh of our times. The latters' neighbours do, of course, frequently suspect the original practice to continue, and, once during the past 22 years of my highland Orissa excursions, an old and trusted Kondh friend (who was also an influential religious functionary) informed me of two human sacrifices during an exceptional event, one victim having been an infant, the other one an adult volunteer.

Given the ethnographic preoccupation with human sacrifice, nobody will be astonished to find Macpherson's general introduction to Kondh religion being practically ignored by later authors. The officer had, however, over the years conducted extensive inquiries into this subject and employed a fairly large staff of local experts for this undertaking, particularly one Dr. Cadenhead, Principal Assistant of the Orissa Hill Agency, and Soonderah Sing Deo, 'the Hindu gentleman . . . whose services . . . cannot be overrated' (222-3). Macpherson also saw the vast variety of Kondh local traditions and, therefore, deliberately restricted his findings to Goomsur in the northeastern Kondhmals. Any overall statements would have been unwise in view of the Kondh complex as a whole being located in the hills between the Mahanadi in the north and the Srikakulam district of modern Andhra Pradesh in the south, a vast area that incorporated numerous linguistic and social-cultural sub-units. The following debate on Kondh religion in general will be confined to Macpherson's data.

KONDH GENESIS

Whereas the Judeo-Christian Book of Genesis initially has a human male include and oppose a human female, this gender opposition marks the apex and the beginning of Kondh divinities. Boora Pennu,[8] the god of light or the sun god and the 'self-existing . . . source of Good and Creator of the Universe' created for himself a consort, Tari Pennu, the earth goddess and source of evil. As known from tribal religions of Southeast Asia, as well as those of the Chhotanagpur tribal complex, the supreme deities thus unite and oppose the sky and the earth, with the latter being included in the former. The sun or the light, as the formula for the good, can only be conceived in contrast to its opposite, created by the supreme deity for this very purpose.

If hierarchy, or the superior including the inferior, is the initial doctrine of the Goomsur Kondh, this structural concept, also read by Dumont[9] into the model of the caste system, is to be reiterated at the subsequent levels. In the Kondh case, the earth had been created, but walking upon it revealed a certain deficiency to the supreme being.

Boora Pennu finds his wife 'wanting in affectionate compliance and attention as a wife' which technically means, as Macpherson does not fail to point out in a footnote, that she 'refused to scratch the back of Boora's neck when requested to do so'. Kondh women – and tribal women in general – are not known to accept the Hindu ideal of subordination, so Tari represents the feminist protagonist. The male, however, wants 'the most assiduous and devoted service' (223).

For this reason Boora resolves to create human beings, a move Tari, of course, tries to sabotage, resulting in genesis being delayed in a dialectical process. He does succeed finally, but she is able to reverse the order of creation by diverting the earthen seed he is throwing. Instead of a human being, vegetation comes first into existence by the combined, if mutually opposed, effort of the divine couple, then fish and all water animals, then the lower animals of the land, wild and tame, and fourthly all creatures which fly. Only when Boora physically prevents Tari from interception, is he – in the fifth attempt – able to fulfil his intention and create the human race out of earthen seed entered into the ground in a straightforward manner. Tari then covers the earth, i.e. herself, with her hand and disallows further acts of creation. Then Boora's exudation of sweat from his body is collected by his hand and thrown around with the words: 'To all that I have created!' (224). As a result, love, sex, and fertility become the human condition.

The above episode of the myth, as is obvious, operates with the usual reversals of mythological constructs, seniority being a major issue. This value has been found to govern most middle Indian tribal systems of ideas in the present Orissa Research Programme. Vegetation rather than humanity achieves the senior rank in the Kondh order of creation because of the intervention of the mundane or female efforts, though the male god had wanted humans to be the first on earth. Perhaps for this reason, Kondh totems, or markers of exogamous clans, all seem to refer to a species of vegetation only,[10] whereas other tribes of the Gond and the Koraput complex apply animal totems and the Chhotanagpur clans combine a variety of plants, animals and planets in a systematic manner.

The sun god creates the various forms of life by throwing earth-seed behind him in the manner of a sower, but the earth goddess catches and diverts these particles to the sides. Thus the normal creative process, involving straight-forward insemination, is diverted by the female. In the end, Tari Pennu 'placed her hands over the earth' (223), i.e. over herself, thus obstructing further creation by closing her body to the sun god. As a consequence, the latter throws his bodily exudations over the beings he has created, thus terminating genesis. Normally bodily exudations of the male initiate the creative process, so again reversal indicates the genesis of the species as a whole in stark contrast to individual love, sex, and fertility that – as in the Bible – begins when the holistic generation has come to an end. Divine creation of the whole is senior to the human generation of individuals.

Within this final and overall message, the initial reversal has already been noticed above. The diverted seed results in non-human forms of life before the straightforward seed leads to humanity. The former four classes are again ordered in two sets of oppositions: Vegetation, or life rooted in the earth, is senior to fish and other species living in the water; similarly land-bound animals, wild and tame, are senior to 'all creatures which fly' (223). Jointly, plants and water animals, creatures of the ground and those of the air, are the seniors of humans, because the female sabotaged the plan of the male. And yet, his divine or overall creative effort could be completed against her inferior designs and as the senior or superior holistic act opposed to the junior or human individual procreation.

Kondh paradise, the subsequent epoch, hardly differed from similar Biblical conditions, as far as general peace and harmony, leisure and abundance are concerned. Humanity as a whole, however, not just Adam and Eve, went unclothed. Moreover, humans had power to move in every environment, earth and sea, land and air, just as all animals were innocuous.

The junior-most form of life included and ruled over the capacities of the four senior forms. Such conditions caused the rebellion of the earth goddess who was now 'sowing the seeds of sin in mankind as in a ploughed field'. While the sun god is initially presented as casting the seed, his female opponent is thus associated with plough cultivation,[11] generally viewed as a later or developed form of agriculture. She brings sin and diseases, deadly poisons and 'every element of disorder'. In this gift, individual moral failure is opposed to physical malfunctioning, lethal physical powers to societal collapse, and all are combined as the contrary to the previous paradisiacal conditions. All Boora can do is to arrest physical evil by antidotes. Man (in the sense of *Mensch*) was left 'perfectly free to receive or to reject moral evil'. The Kondh were thus protected at first, but subsequently burdened with the responsibility of free will power.

Only a few individuals remained without sin, becoming deified in turn, but also responsible for the disobedient rest of humanity. Withdrawing the physical antidotes, Boora then let loose all evils upon these corrupted humans, subjecting them to death. 'All nature became . . . disordered' (224) in very much the manner we can observe today. Moreover 'Boora and Tari contended for superiority in fierce conflict' (225) in all domains. Only at this point, Macpherson registers thc first dissent within the community of the believers.

One 'sect' has Boora triumph and allow Tari's evil interventions only where he desires to punish. For the other 'sect', she remains unconquered in the continued struggle. Boora does represent the good and the supreme divine power which is yet 'insufficient for the effectual protection of men when Tari resolves to inflict . . . destruction' (*ibid.*). The goddess, on her own, is able to 'confer every form of earthly benefit' (*ibid.*). In other words, the tensions between the conflicting opposites remains.

BOORA'S CLASSIFICATION

Macpherson continues with the cosmological order of Boora's people and their positive approach. Humans, by practising virtue, may rise after death. In addition to the first sinless humans, Boora appointed a subordinate category of gods who, if properly worshipped, were to teach and protect humans and regulate the powers of nature. The senior divine couple is thus opposed to junior or inferior divinities who in turn rank as senior sinless humans against junior subordinate divinities. Once again the latter appear in a binary opposition: The senior ones sprang from Boora and Tari and have a general jurisdiction over humans for ever. Ranking below are the tutelary gods of 'tribes and branches of tribes', also immortal and unchangeable, but confined to local rather than tribal jurisdiction (227). In the overall picture then, the Goomsur Kondh oppose the divine couple and the original sinless – thus deified – humans. Junior to this opposition, the general guardian deities are posited as superiors in the opposition with local or segmentary deities. Both of them yet include their descendents, a third class of 'strictly minor and local deities . . . of every spot on earth' (*ibid.*). Thus the general pattern may be presented in the following series of oppositions of:

KONDH CATEGORIES OF DEITIES

1. Boora and Tari, the universal creators, vs.
   inferior deities <u>who include</u>:
2. the deified first humans or 'guardians of man' (226) vs.
   the subordinate functional deities <u>who include</u>
3. deities of general functions vs.
   those with local jurisdiction over tribes and branches of tribes and
4. <u>both</u> categories of No. 3, vs.
   innumerable minor and local 'gods of every spot on earth having power . . . there' (227).

The deities of opposition No. 3 begin with the functional category made up of seven deities. These may, in my view, once again be divided into several mutually inclusive oppositions, the first six being responsible for the fate of the living, while the seventh is *Dinga Pennu*, the judge of the dead. His six colleagues, in my eyes, subdivide into those covering creation and increase while opposing those covering destruction and limitation. Creation and increase obviously unite:

Pidzu Pennu, the god of rain and *Boorbi Pennu*, the goddess of new vegetation and first fruits. These two <u>concrete</u> functions are <u>abstracted</u> in *Pitterri Pennu*, the god of increase and of gain in every possible shape.

Since the Kondh are seen 'tribes subsisting by agriculture and the chase' (227), the second aspect of these modes is given emphasis in the context of destruction and limitation:

Klambo Pennu is the god of hunting, or the killing of animals, while *Loha Pennu* is the god of war, or the killing of humans. Both of these functions refer to the termination of life in a very <u>concrete</u> sense. The more <u>abstract</u> version is *Sundi Pennu*, the god of boundaries in general.

The seventh functional deity is *Dinga Pennu*, the judge of the dead. Onto a very slippery rock he is writing the history of every human's action, during every life passed upon earth. Some 'souls', on reaching him, are, by their past virtue, capable of beatification, and pass on to a rank 'little inferior to minor gods' (230), while others are, by their ambivalent existence on earth, detained in *Grippa Valli* for punishment, before being reborn 'in the same tribe' (229). In Macpherson's terminology, the tribe always stands for the exogamous patrilineal clan of anthropological jargon,[12] thus a soul never leaves the clan. 'Upon the birth of every child, the priest declares, after inquiry, which of the members of the tribe has returned' (228).[13]

The term soul is, of course, a highly insufficient translation for the concepts involved. According to Macpherson, one type of soul is capable of beatification, another one of reincarnation, a third one suffers at *Grippa Valli* and yet another 'dies on the dissolution of the body' (*ibid.*), so it is quite clear that one immaterial aspect of a person continues until the body is dissolved, while another one remains within the patrilineal descent group. One may suffer purgation at *Grippa Valli* while another one may be deified. Macpherson also mentions the role of a priest, perhaps meaning a shaman, whose 'soul always leaves the body for a time' (*ibid.*), but this aspect stands quite apart from the retributive justice administered by the god of death. The basic idea of this system is close to that of Hindu India. Rebirth may – by virtuous action – be avoided in exceptional cases, but is normally experienced along with punishments. The clan (and perhaps the family) however, remains the same from rebirth to the next. No (Hindu) change of status is involved. Like all middle Indian tribal social conceptions, Kondh society as a whole, and Kondh clans in particular, represent a closed recycling system of the living and those who have died. At the same time, every clan 'invokes the souls of the deceased ancestors in endless array at every ceremonial . . . and they especially remember those men renowned for good and great actions' (230).

The greatest possible actions are also enlisted by Macpherson (230), and they seem to reflect the Maussian spirit of the gift,[14] i.e. the taking and giving of life in a secular or, greater still, a sacred context. Reciprocity is the formula of a social existence in the commandments:

1. To kill a foe in public battle.
2. To fall in public battle.
3. To be a priest. And amongst the sacrificing tribes.[15]
4. To be a victim to the Earth Goddess.

TARI'S CLASSIFICATION

Tari's followers, in Macpherson's account, share the above concepts of their tribesmen but, even if Boora remains supreme, they recognize agency on the part of the earth goddess as well. She, not Boora, is supposed to have put an end to disorder, introducing agriculture, hunting, and war. She does demand a price, however. For the sake of their continuation, she requires a regular human sacrifice.

In the origin, at work with vegetables, she cut her finger and each drop oozing out made the earth dry and firm. She therefore encouraged her fellow Kondh to cut up her whole body to complete the task, but the latter would not sacrifice one of their own. Instead they purchased and adopted victims from others, and these human sacrifices were responsible for the introduction of proper family relations and proper agriculture. Furthermore, speaking through a shaman, she classified the animal world into those fit or unfit to hunt. She also taught them to go to war. Of these gifts, complementary oppositions seem to link family and agriculture (generation), hunting and war (destruction). Most remarkably, by introducing the sacrificial ceremony, its efficacy was to embrace all humankind, since 'the responsibility for the well-being of the whole world has rested upon' the sacrificers (232).

Personally I experienced this universalism among the Dangria Kondh. After visiting my student Dagmar Stachowski, a long-term fieldworker,[16] at the Dangria village of Kambesi in summer 1983, her hosts went out of their way to order and send a written invitation requesting me in no uncertain terms to participate in their grand sacrifice of the subsequent spring season. Two decades later, in spring 2002, I tried to attend the same event in the neighbouring village of Hundijalli, when I learnt that several German researchers had, a few months earlier, visited that village for three weeks, distributing considerable sums of money for the cooperation received. Other outsiders had earlier proceeded in a similar manner with the result that I was no longer a welcome guest at the sacrifice. In fact, the initial fee of Rs. 3,000 was demanded at the village entry in advance and, had I paid up and continued to stay, further such demands would certainly have followed. Twenty years ago, communication had worked on the basis of hospitality, the refusal of which, according to Macpherson, would have been a 'chief sin' (229) for the Kondh. But now the status of Europeans visitors[17] has undergone a metamorphosis. They have turned into prey for the hunters. The latter art was also taught by Tari and 'she introduced cruelty . . . into the world'(232). In fact one of the gentlemen demanding money from me[18] had hacked a fellow villager to death a few months earlier, but was not tried by an Indian court, because only informal local gossip, not a proper eye witness, had associated him with the deed. Generally, eye witnesses are lacking in such cases and the police, for good reasons, hesitate to apply the usual third degree methods to the mountain people.

The above anecdote may help to convey that Tari is still 'worshipped, like Boora, at great social festivals held periodically by tribes, branches of tribes, and villages' (232). Boora's people, on the other hand, regard human sacrifice 'with the utmost abhorrence' (233), so that the male god is known to have interfered on behalf of the victim on several occasions, if we are to believe Macpherson's informants. The chapter on 'Doctrines of the sect of Tari' (231) generally lacks the impressive ethnographic details of the earlier sections, however.

FEMALE INFANTICIDE

Even more than the ethnographic account on Tari, Macpherson's final section on 'female infanticide' offers his argument rather than ethnographic data. It has, through McLennan, received wide publicity. Furthermore, within the administrative type of ethnography that monopolized Indian anthropology over many decades, starting with Risley,[19] Macpherson's story of Kondh infanticide continued to be repeated from one author to the next, even though none of the census data ever indicated a significant male majority (if at all one), the revealing evidence in comparative cases of the Punjab and Rajasthan.[20]

The argument primarily associates 'the sect of Boora'(270) with the practice of killing a female infant shortly after her birth, even though it suspects all Kondhs in a general fashion. It does not refer to any substantial case or particular observation in a village but begins with the question of causation, as if the practice as such had been proved beyond doubt. The cause is attributed to the gender issue, and the argument is not without amazing manoeuvres.

Women, Macpherson (rather than an indigenous informant) argues, are privileged among the Kondh in an extraordinary manner. 'Their opinions have great weight in all public and private affairs; and their direct agency is often considered essential in the former' (271). This seems to be the crux of the matter. In battles, sisters of a tribe[21] must be present to aid and encourage the warriors, 'and the intervention of its wives, who are neutral between the tribes of their fathers and those of their husbands, is necessary to make peace' (*ibid.*).

Thus the general affinal rule of 'restricted exchange'[22] is rightly indicated 150 years ago, just as the (later) world-wide observation of belligerent relations between the affinal 'sides' is discovered in the particular case. However, the discovery contains a logical flaw. If, given the observed affinal reciprocity, the sisters of side 1 are the wives of side 2 and vice versa, sisters as such can-not be supporting their brothers while wives take a neutral position, because the sisters of one side will always be the wives of the other. Logically, women as such can only be either supporters of one side, or neutral.

Leaving behind female interference in battle, Macpherson then turns to gender morality, or the 'extraordinary matrimonial privileges' ascribed to Kondh women. His somewhat indirect Victorian phrasing tells us that married women are allowed to have lovers while married men suffer under public sanctions for extramarital affairs. A wife may leave her husband at will and enter the house of the man she desires. The latter is not allowed to prevent her from establishing herself as his mistress (271). For the Victorian writer, such practices, known in milder versions from the works of later and more sensitive ethnographers, must have been as revolting as the two versions of unnatural death in the account.

Scandalous financial dealings are then added to the immorality of the people, since 'a large consideration in cattle and money' (271) were to be paid by the bridegroom to the wife's father who, in turn, redistributed the amount among his agnates.[23] When, however, a wife left her husband, the cumbersome process must be reversed. That means the father must return the bride wealth or he has the chance to reimburse himself at the expense of the new husband or the latter's clan, in case the latter have the necessary means. However, the father of a woman may be forced to return the dower without being able to compensate the loss. At this point, the administrator, rather than the ethnographer, dominates the argument. If, for example, a Kondh woman leaves her husband and enters the house of another man she desires (probably without his consent), and the latter is bound to accept her, the two husbands as well as her father are forced to be involved in a financial mess. Further complications arising out of transfers and transactions could, of course, be imagined. For the Scottish ethnographer, 'three-fourths of the sanguinary quarrels and hereditary feuds which distract the Khond country' (272) must be attributed to women. The obvious consequence is placed into the mouth of an unknown informant: 'By the death of our female infants before they see the light, the lives of men without number are saved, and we live in comparative peace' (*ibid.*).

Along with this pragmatic argument, Macpherson refers to the religious sanction of Boora only in general terms. He then mentions a custom which members of the present Orissa Research Programme found among several central Indian tribes, the habit of naming a newly born child only after several (in this case seven) days and the belief that only with the name would a soul enter the child. In other words, just as death as defined by society does not coincide with what we know as physical death, a new human being comes into existence by the forces of nature grafted by a social sanction, so that no harm is done by killing a girl before this act of naming. The author does not re-enforce this argument (as he did when describing human sacrifice) by a single case study. The only ethnographic evidence is a simple reference to the Kondh prayer for many male children.

CONCLUSION

Macpherson's account offers valuable ethnographic information, as far as the Goomsur Kondh mythology is concerned. Kondh genesis may be related in different versions in other parts of the Kondhmals,[24] but the reported mytho-logic as such is convincing. Similarly, the Kondh classification of divinities, as presented in Macpherson's account, is highly plausible, because of its structural logic – or relational pattern – that could not possibly have been invented or manipulated by commonsensical informants or ethnographers. As far as I know, no other ethnographic source has been able to offer such a convincing pattern among the multitude of Kondh gods and goddesses, linked to Kondh values as such. As ethnographers, we tend to recognize the Kondh quest for a life full of joy, as well as the belligerent tradition. Anyone who has experienced the sacrificial frenzy when the *Meriah* buffalo was hacked into pieces within seconds, or the indifference of a man when his own death was at stake, will be able to accept the reported religious 'doctrines' of the Kondh, just as the sheer hard work of tribal men and women under the 'pestilential' climatic conditions can be understood within this religious tradition.

But I have never heard of a 'sect' confined to either the followers of Boora Pennu or of Tari Pennu, and Macpherson's account does not offer convincing details for their existence. In contemporary society, all informed Kondh accept the fact that their forefathers had formerly conducted human sacrifice and that this ritual was abandoned or altered under the orders of Macpherson and Campbell, two officers of the Raj. No Kondh and no neighbour of Kondh settlers, malevolent or not, has ever been found to report Kondh female infanticide, however, even though this practice was alluded to in innumerable publications such as the District Gazetteers and Settlement Reports. I have no doubt about Macpherson's intentions to offer an honest and meticulous picture of Kondh religion, but the passages on female infanticide are entirely based upon his own reasoning and the moral and financial considerations of the Victorian phase in Scottish culture.

When it came to human sacrifice for the earth goddess, or *Meriah* in the Oriya language, Macpherson could offer many ethnographic details, having intervened and saved many possible victims. But he could not describe the socio-religious system as such, not the complex ritual links between a number of settlements and clans over specified phases of sacred time. Since his account was not improved on by later ethnographers – who took their clues from Macpherson – the sacrifice is generally considered to be a primitive, bloody excess rather than an important and complex aspect of a highly sophisticated tribal religion. Similarly marriage or affinal relations have – for the Kondh – always been described in the tradition of the Victorian prejudices of Macpherson's account. Hardenberg's monograph will correct these two clear manifestations of a cultural bias.

If in the end the admirable aspects of Macpherson's ethnography must be remembered, they are not really given emphasis in his own account. They help to link the divine world or the relational pattern of their divinities with Kondh social structure. Elementary relationships of affinity and descent – differentiated by local and functional specification – are identified in the divine world by the author in a manner that will allow their rediscovery in ritual performance and in socio-religious relations by the ongoing anthropological research.

NOTES

1. See S. Charles Macpherson, 1852, 'An Account of the Religion of the Khonds in Orissa', *The Journal of the Royal Asiatic Society of Great Britain and Ireland,* Vol. 13, p. 221. My other descriptive data refering to Macpherson are taken from this article. This author, like many others, had his own way of spelling the tribal name which is now normally written as in the above title. 'Kondh' or 'Kondho' is the name outsiders apply to the people, whereas they themselves use a variety of terms of their own (Dravidian) languages meaning 'humans' or 'hill people'.
2. Campbell's account in no way matches that of his colleague and arch enemy, since it is substituting egocentric history for ethnographic inquiry. See Campbell, John, 1864, *A Personal Narrative of Thirteen Years Service Amongst the Wild Tribes of Khondistan for the Suppression of Human Sacrifice*, London: Hurst & Blackett. The (Muslim) version of the regional name is the authors invention and has not been used by others.
3. His first direct reference to Macphersons's work is in his article on 'Hill tribes in India', in *The North British Review* 34/1863, as referred to by Peter Rivière in his 'Introduction' to MacLennan's *Primitive Marriage* of 1865. In this latter book, his anthropological argument (1970: 40/41) rightly takes the side of Macpherson against Campbell. This thesis made the author one of the discipline's founding fathers, since it argues out the general social issues of marriage (or 'affinity' in anthropological jargon) on the basis of ethnographic data supplied by Macpherson's account. See McLennan, John Ferguson, 1865, *Primitive Marriage, an inquiry into the origin of the form of capture in marriage ceremonies*. Reprinted and edited with an Introduction by Peter Rivière, Chicago: The University of Chicago Press, 1970.
4. See Frazer, James George, 1922 [1983 Paperback edition quoted], *The Golden Bough. A Study in Magic and Religion*, London: Macmillan, pp. 338, 571, 730.
5. See F. G. Bailey, 1960, *Tribe Caste, and Nation*, Manchester: University of Manchester Press.

6. Hermann Niggemeyer, 1964, *Kuttia Kond: Dschungel-Bauern in Orissa.* München: Renner. This work is based upon an extended excursion to Belghar, where the ethnographer (and Mrs. Niggemeyer) stayed in the Rest House of the Forestry Department. The answers of their Kondh informants where first translated into Oriya and then into English. Being a man of the museum, Niggemeyer's technical descriptions are superb, just as he adds new local versions of Kondh myths.
7. Barbara M. Boal, 1997, *Human Sacrifice and Religious Change: The Kondhs*, New Delhi: Inter-India Publications.
8. I retain Macpherson's original spellings to avoid further complications.
9. Louis Dumont, 1966, *Homo Hierarchicus: Le Système des Castes et Ses Implications,* Paris: Editions Gallimard.
10. R. Hardenberg informed me of this point in November 2002. Twenty years earlier, a knowledgeable Dangria Kondh informant (dead since long) had begun to relate their creation myth to me; it differed totally from Macpherson's version, but made sure that the clan totems (in the order of their respective creation) refered to species of vegetation.
11. All the Kondh I visited hardly bothered about the gender-wise division of labour with the exception of plough cultivation. In fact, females were not even allowed to touch the plough.
12. Perhaps Macpherson did not apply the term 'clan', because the Scottish clans, though name-givers of the anthropological category are never exogamous, whereas 'anthropological' clans always are. See Ian Grimble, 1993, *Scottish Clans and Tartans*, London: Lomond Books.
13. In March 2000, R. Hardenberg and I witnessed such a ritual in the Kuttia Kondh village of Burlabaru.
14. See Marcel Mauss 1969 [French orig. 1925], *The Gift. Forms and Functions of Exchange in Archaic Societies*, London: Routledge & Kegan Paul.
15. The term in this case seems to refer to a particular functional local descent group of a village (*jani*) rather than a clan. I have described the order, but Hardenberg will undoubtedly offer the appropriate ethnographic background. See G. Pfeffer, 1997, 'The Scheduled Tribes of Middle India as a Unit: Problems of Internal and External Comparison', in G. Pfeffer and D. K. Behera (eds.), *Structure and Process, Contemporary Society: Tribal Studies*, Vol. 1, New Delhi: Concept, pp. 3-27.
16. She lived in Kambesi for about 18 months and is remembered there to this day. Children have been named after her.
17. For the sake of development, a road had been built to Kambesi in the 1980s. It could be used by the jeeps of development officers inspecting their achievements, and by commercial tour operators transporting Europeans and Japanese on one-day photo safaris among the tribal people. The tourists are the ones who like to buy what they call authentic culture rather than holiday comforts.

18. Initially asking whether I would take photographs (and pay for each one in the standard manner), he was disappointed and disbelieving when I denied carrying a camera. So he opened my bag, but no camera was found. Again disappointed, he suggested the purchase of drinks which would neither have been the starters, nor the last of the day.
In villages away from such facile touristic access, joyful (and drunken) sacrificial celebrations had never been a problem for me.
19. See Herbert Risley, 1915, *The People of India*, Delhi: Oriental Reprint (1969), p. 173. This work repeats the widely circulated Census Reports of the 1890s.
20. See James Tod, 1920, *Annals and Antiquities of Rajasthan or the Central and Western Rajput States of India*, Vol. II, Oxford: Oxford University Press, pp. 740-6.
21. As always, 'tribe' refers to the exogamous 'clan' of anthropological jargon.
22. See Claude Lévi-Strauss, 1969, [French orig. 1967], *The Elementary Structures of Kinship.* Revised edition, Boston: Beacon Press, pp. 29 f.
23. 'His own branch' (271) in Macpherson's terms.
24. My student Albert Götzelmann took note of a mythological account among the Kuttia Kondh showing the earth goddess to give birth to the different clans thus determining the particular order of seniority.

REFERENCES

Bailey, F. G., 1960, *Tribe, Caste, and Nation*, Manchester: University of Manchester Press.

Boal, Barbara M., 1997, *Human Sacrifice and Religious Change: The Kondhs*, New Delhi: Inter-India Publications.

Campbell, John, 1864, *A Personal Narrative of Thirteen Years Service Amongst the Wild Tribes of Khondistan for the Suppression of Human Sacrifice*, London: Hurst & Blackett.

Dumont, Louis, 1966, *Homo hierarchicus: Le système des castes et ses implications*. Paris: Editions Gallimard.

Grimble, Ian, 1993, *Scottish Clans & Tartans*, London: Lomond Books.

Frazer, James George, 1922 [1983 paperback edition used], *The Golden Bough. A Study in Magic and Religion*, London: Macmillan.

Lévi-Strauss, Claude, 1969 [French orig. 1967; earlier French edition of 1949], *The Elementary Structures of Kinship.* Revised edition, Boston: Beacon Press.

McLennan, John Ferguson, 1865, *Primitive Marriage, an inquiry into the origin of the form of capture in marriage ceremonies*. Reprinted and edited with an introduction by Peter Rivière, Chicago: The University of Chicago Press, 1970.

Macpherson, S. Charles, 1852, 'An Account of the Religion of the Khonds in Orissa', *The Journal of the Royal Asiatic Society of Great Britain and Ireland,* Vol. 13, pp. 216-74.

Mauss, Marcel, 1969 [French orig. 1925], *The Gift: Forms and Functions of Exchange in Archaic Societies*, London: Routledge & Kegan Paul.

Niggemeyer, Hermann, 1964, *Kuttia Kond: Dschungel-Bauern in Orissa*, München: Renner.

Pfeffer, Georg, 1997, 'The Scheduled Tribes of Middle India as a Unit: Problems of Internal and External Comparison', in G. Pfeffer and D. K. Behera (eds.), *Structure and Process, Contemporary Society: Tribal Studies*, Vol. 1, New Delhi: Concept, pp. 3-27.

Risley, Herbert, 1915, *The People of India,* Delhi: Oriental Reprint (1969).

Tod, James, 1920, *Annals and Antiquities of Rajasthan or the Central and Western Rajput States of India*, Vol. II, Oxford: Oxford University Press.

CHAPTER 19

Some Remarks on the Vāmadeva Saṃhitā: *A Śaivite Version of the Pūjā Manuals of Lord Jagannātha*

G. C. TRIPATHI

While I was working (1970-5) on the Pūjā ceiemony of the Jagannātha temple under the auspices of the Orissa Research Project and looking for Sanskrit texts containing the *pūjāpaddhati* or mode of worship followed in this temple, I was told that the library of the Mukti Maṇḍapa Pandit Sabhā in the temple contained some such texts, the most authoritative among them being the '*Vāmadeva Saṃhitā*'. After some personal efforts and thanks to the recommendations of some influential people in Puri, the temple authorities finally agreed to allow us to make a copy of the manuscript through one of our scribes, Pt. J. D. Mishra, who did the job wonderfully well sitting in the temple. When, however, this fact came to the notice of the brahmin priests of the temple they were rather displeased at the foreigners encroaching upon their spiritual heritage. The Sabhā then decided to pre-empt the effort by the Germans to publish the text (though this was never our intention) and to bring out the text by itself, which it did in Oriya characters in 1972. Pt. K. C. Rajguru, the then Paricchā (Superintendant) of the temple who was the head of the team which was assigned the task of editing it, told me later (in 1973) that because the text was very corrupt and full of grammatical mistakes, they had to amend and change it considerably. This was certainly true, because when I compared the printed text with our transcript prepared by Pt. J. D. Mishra, I noticed that the printed version had lost much of its originality and much of its importance due to uncritical scholarship of the editors. Two MSS were perhaps used in preparing the Pandit Sabhā editon. Since I feel that the ORP transcript has more genuinely preserved the original, I shall quote only from that and not from the Sabhā editon.

The *Vāmadeva Saṃhitā* (*VS*) is substantially different from all other *pūjāpaddhatis* of the Jagannātha temple because of its very explicit Śaivite leanings. It also has a setup and structure much different from the others. The basic source of the *Vāmadeva Saṃhitā* is certainly the *Nīlâdrimahôdaya* (*NM*),[1] though it has greatly changed the character of the ritual at many places. Its very title, namely the choice of the word 'Saṃhitā' betrays the effort of the author to name his work after the *Sūta Saṁhitā*, the popular title of *NM* (2.4.4). The *VS* tries to present the extensive material contained in the latter work in a more concise and simple form after giving it an explicit Śaivite imprint. With its twenty-five adhyāyas and some 1350 ślokas it is only a little more than one-fifth of *Nīlâdrimahôdaya*. The extent of each adhyāya is, generally and on an average, of about 50 ślokas, though some exceptionally short ones (e.g. No. 10, containing only 7 ślokas) or exceptionally long ones (No: 6, containing 106 ślokas) aslo figure in it.

Although not in the subject matter itself, yet definitely in the arrangement of the matter and in the general plan of the work, the author shows considerable originality. The following synopsis of the *VS* shall give an idea of its structure:

(1) Adh. 1 to 5: Importance of the *kṣetra*, detailed description of all shrines, legend of the foundation of the temple (Indradyumna-legend).
(2) Adh. 6 to 7: The mode of worship in the temple.
(3) Adh. 8 to 10: General rules for offering the *bhoga*, the way of cooking the divine food in the kitchen and a description of kitchen utensils.
(4) Adh. 11 to 12: Description of qualifications of temple-*sevakas* (Agniśarmā, Dayitā, Svāra and Pūjaka) as well as of *avakāśa* rites (bathing and clothing, etc., of the deities).
(5) Adh. 13: The regular daily, weekly and fortnightly *nītis* (ceremonies)
(6) Adh. 14 to 22: The 12 main *yātrās* (annual festivals) of the deities.
(7) Adh. 23 to 25: The *upayātrās* (the 15 most important sub-festivals) of the deities.

This analysis of the contents of *VS* also reveals, by the way, that the second part of the *Nīlâdrimahôdaya* (Adh. 38-91) containing a detailed description of the daily *pūjā* has hardly been utilized by the author of the *VS*. He has in fact, taken recourse to the *Nīlâdrināthasya-pūjāvidhi* and some traditionally transmitted *dhyāna*-verses for writing the two chapters on *pūjā* (Adh. 6-7). The reason might either be that he was not acquainted with second part of the *NM*[2] or that he found it to be too extensive and elaborate for his purpose.

Nothing is known about the author of the *Vāmadeva Saṃhitā* except for the fact that he must have been a Pūjāpaṇḍā of Jagannātha temple like the author of the *NM*. The following statement of the author glorifying the person of a *pūjaka* unmistakably points towards this:

> *'pūjakasya tu santoṣe tuṣṭo bhavati devatā'* / 7.31 ab
> *'pūjako devarūpaḥ syān nâtra kāryā vicāraṇā'* //7.37cd
> *'jagadīśagṛhe devi pūjakaḥ sarvapūjitaḥ/*
> *tasmai dattva yathākiñcit santuṣṭaḥ puruṣottamaḥ'* // 7.38
> *'sa tu tuṣṭe devatuṣṭir bhavati cārulocane'* / 7.39ab
> *'brahmāṃśāt pūjako jātaḥ . . .'* /11.4ab
> *'trayo'pi pūjakāḥ śreṣṭhā devatānām prapūjakāḥ'* / 11.25ab

If one reads the work carefully and tries to understand the mental framework of the author, it appears that the author was most probably a Pūjāpaṇḍā of Balabhadra.

Let us first take the title of this work. *Vāmadeva* is a well-known epithet of Śiva. There are five chief forms or aspects of Śiva which are known as Aghora, Tatpuruṣa, Vāmadeva, Sadyojāta and Īśāna. The work *Śaivakalpadruma* of Lakṣmīdhara (later seventeenth century, not yet published) gives a detailed description of these aspects of Śiva and their worship. The *VS* is so named because it is in the form of a series of questions and answers between Vāmadeva and Pārvatī. Pārvatī puts questions regarding the worship of Jagannātha and Vāmadeva answers them. One would concede that naming a work on the pūjā of such an important Vaiṣṇava deity as Jagannātha after Śiva is rather unusual. The second point of interest in this connection is the identity established between Śiva and Viṣṇu and the spirit of harmony which is taught to the worshippers of the two. 'Śiva bears

Viṣṇu in the form of Garuḍa, and Viṣṇu, assuming the shape of bull, carries Śiva. Śiva is Viṣṇu and Viṣṇu is Śiva. Those who discriminate between the two fall in formidable hells for the duration of fourteen Indras (= fourteen *kalpas* each amounting to one thousand yugas)':

mama tasya na bhedo 'sti bhedaṃ karoti mūḍhadhīḥ / 7.33cd
ahaṃ ca khagarūpeṇa tasyaiva vāhanam priye/
so 'pi vṛṣabharūpeṇa mamaiva vāhakas tathā // 12.24
mama viṣṇor bhedarūpaṃ ye kurvanti narādhamāḥ /
patanti narake ghore yāvaccandradivākarau //
ahaṃ so 'pi so 'pyahaṃ vai atra bhedaṃ prakurvatām /
teṣām uddharaṇaṃ nāsti yāvad indrāś caturdaśa // 12.18.19

We shall not go astray if we postulate that this reflects an antagonism between the Śaivas and the Vaiṣṇavas at some stage in later medieval Orissa and the passages like the above had the purpose of bringing about a reconciliation and harmony between the two groups having their centres at Bhubaneswar and Puri respectively.

The third point which strikes a reader immediately is the unusual importance attached to the worship of Bhairava as a form of Śiva in this work which is actually written for the glorification of Kṛṣṇa-Jagannātha. The worship of Bhairava is recommended, first of all, in the process of the worship of the Sun god (6.34). Thereafter, in the second instance, a Pūjāpaṇḍa is to meditate upon Bhairava and to invoke him for the protection of the rite of worship even before he undertakes to perform the worship of different door-attendants outside the main temple, since it is he (Bhairava) who is responsible for the safety of the temple (*atra sthale hanta tavâdhikāraḥ*, 6.61). The *dhyāna* of Bhairava here consists of three ślokas (2 Anuṣṭubh and 1 Upajāti) in which Bhairava is depicted riding on a horse, having sharp teeth, and holding a sword and a shield each in his two hands (6.59, 60, 61). Again, when the Pūjāpaṇḍās of Jagannātha enter the sanctum of the deities, they are enjoined to sing a rather long hymn in praise of Bhairava who has his seat on the *siṃhāsana* of Jagannātha, and to offer him *naivedya* before commencing the worship of Jagannātha (6.82-102ab). Two verses of this *stotra* are quoted here as a sample:

Śrībhairam taṃ praṇatârtihāriṇam
mahônnatam dīrghakarālajihvam /

karāladaṃṣṭram dvibhujam sakṛṣṇakam
asidhṛtaṃ saṃyatakeśadhāriṇaṃ //
namāmi côgraṃ bhṛkuṭīkarālam
mahôgradaṃṣṭram ca sudīrgharūpam /
vājisthitam taṃ jagadīśvarasya
śrīkṣetrapālam tv asidhāriṇaṃ ca //

VS (MS) 6.89, 90

If it is not possible to offer him *naivedya* in the very beginning, this should be offered to him during the worship of Jagannātha or, at least, after the worship. If a Pūjāpaṇḍā fails to comply with this, he should be punished by the king (6.102cd-104ab). The reason for worshipping Bhairava, as given by the *VS* itself, is that Śiva as the protector of the *kṣetra* is present here as Bhairava who deserves to be worshipped first; only with his permission can one proceed to perform the worship of Jagannātha (6.85-8; cf. also 12.25ab *ahaṃ bhairavarūpeṇa tvameva bhairavī bhava*; *ahaṃ* = Vāmadeva, *tvaṃ* = Pārvatī). An examination of this rite shall, however, show that the deity who deserves worship at this time is Kṣetrapāla (a form of Śiva, 'the Lord of the religious complex') and not Bhairava. But the latter is identified here with the former.

The fourth time when an obeisance to Bhairava is prescribed is the point when the worshipper has already taken his seat on the jewel-pedestal of the deities and has finished the preliminaries of worship. Before he embarks upon the actual pūjā, he should pay reverence to Bhairava and seek his permission for commencing the act of worship (7.5-8). A long *dhyāna* (in Śārdūlavikrīḍita metre) of Bhairava, which is not found in any of the *pūjāpaddhatis* of Jagannātha occurs here (as 7.6), accompanied by the traditional Anuṣṭubh verse which only is prescribed in the older texts (cf. *Puruṣottama-māhātmya* of *Skandapurāṇa* 30.12) for expressing devotion to Bhairava (the first half) and for seeking permission from him (the second half):

tīkṣṇadaṃṣṭra mahākāya kalpântadahanôpama /
bhairavāya namas tubhyam anujñāṃ dātum arhasi //[3]

Of these four instances, the fourth is the only one when obeisance is done to Bhairava in the traditionally handed down form of worship, all other three instances have been introduced by the author of the *Vāmadeva Saṃhitā suo moto,* which characterizes him clearly as a man of Śaivaite leanings who wanted Śiva to be worshipped in the temple of Jagannātha as Bhairava.

Among the three (or four, if we add the Pūjāpaṇḍa of the Sun god, etc.) Pūjāpaṇḍas of Jagannātha, Balabhadra and Subhadrā it is only the worshipper of Balabhadra who has some Śaivite traits since Balabhadra is very often indentified with Śiva. The following points bear sufficient testimony to this:

(1) The *nyāsa* used in the worship of Balabhadra (i.e. *Śrī-kaṇṭhâdinyāsa*) is used, as a rule, for the worship of Śiva.
(2) The unpublished *'Nīti-* text of the Deula Karaṇa[4] mentions on Folio 9 that at the time of *Anavasara* (when the deities are re-painted following the great bath on Jyeṣṭha-pūrṇimā and hence no one is allowed to see them) the practice till Narasiṃha and Deva of Khurdā (AD 1623-47) was to hang three painted images of the deities on a bamboo-curtain in front of the sanctum as a substitute for the wooden images inside, in which Balabhadra was represented by a the painted figure of Śiva.
(3) The *Gopālârcanapaddhati* of Vāsudeva mentions that Bala-bhadra should be bathed in the morning to the accompaniment of the mantras from Nīlasūkta of the *Rudrâṣṭadhyāyī* of the *Yajurveda* (Adh. 16).
(4) To these may be added the statement of *Vāmadeva Saṃhitā* itself (11.25cd) that the worshipper of Balabhadra should smear his body with ashes (*sīrapāṇeḥ pūjākas tu kuryād bhasmasya dhāraṇam).*

The Śaivaite leanings of the author of *VS*, therefore, I believe, point towards the fact that he was a Pūjāpaṇḍā of Balabhadra and the main purpose of the *paddhati* was to highlight the importance of the Role of Śiva in the Pūjā ritual of the Jagannātha temple. It may be pointed out that not all Pūjāpaddhatis written by or for the Pūjāpaṇḍās of Balabhadra are Śaivite in character. In fact the *paddhati* which is now used for the worship of Balabhadra and which K. C. Rajguru procured for me from the residence of a Pūjāpaṇḍā of Balabhadra, called *Vāsudeva Pūjā*, is totally Vaiṣṇavite in character and there 'Vāsudeva' stands for Baladeva, not for Kṛṣṇa.

THE DATE OF THE *VS*

The date of the *VS* can be fixed within a fair limit of certainty on account of some valuable internal evidence. While dealing with the worship of Bhairava, the author has indirectly mentioned twice that **an image of Bhairava** has its place by the side of Jagannātha:

(1) *tīkṣṇadaṃṣṭra namas te 'stu* ***bhairava viṣṇupārśvaga*** / 7.8ab
(2) (*nṛpaṃ provāca jagatāṃ patiḥ* . . .)
matsthāne mama pūjāyāṃ bhairavadhyānakaṃ kuru /
Matpārśve tiṣṭhati *rudro nāmā bhairavanāmtaḥ //*
mamaiva pārśve sa tiṣṭhed ahaṃ tasyâpi pārśvake/
VS 14.11, 12 cd.

We know that an image of Bhairava did, in fact, exist in the Jagannātha temple by the side of Jagannātha on the jewel pedestal till about 1800. During the reign of Divyasiṃha Deva (1783-95), however, this image was removed from the sanctum on the occasion of repair work of the Ratnavedī by some influential 'Byragees' (Vaiṣṇava mendicants) with the support of a certain 'Brahmachārī', the religious preceptor of the Marathas.[5] They were also successful in removing the images of Śaṅkarâcārya and Padmapādâcārya from the sanctum and ultimately destroying them, as attested by the *Mādalā Pāñjī* (Prācī edn., p. 81).

It is obvious that reference to the Bhairava image by the side of Jagannātha and the emphasis which the *VS* lays on its worship can be relevant only during a time when the image really stood in the temple and was worshipped. Once the image was banished and its worship came to be looked down upon in Vaiṣṇava circles, no Pūjāpaṇḍa could possibly think of propagating it. As the *terminus ante quem* of the composition of *VS*, therefore, we may safely accept the period immediately preceding the year 1790.

The *terminus post quem* of the compositions of the *VS* is provided by its indebtedness to the Sanskrit *Guṇḍīcā Campū* of Cakrapāṇi Paṭṭanāyaka. While describing the ritual and ceremonies of the car festival of Jagannātha, the author of the *VS* goes beyond the scope of his work and describes in a semi-poetical manner the movement of the car on its way to Guṇḍīcā temple, the joyous atmosphere of the main street and the mental disposition as well as the activities of the pilgrims in some 15 verses of Upajāti metre (16.13-37). The most beautiful ideas of this passage have been borrowed by our author from the *Guṇḍīcā Campū* written in chaste Sanskrit (unfortunately not yet published).

I quote from the Palm-leaf MS No. L/124 of this work preserved in the Orissa State Museum, Bhubaneswar. Compare, for example:

1 (a) ***Guṇḍīcā Campū***, śl. 10
(. . .) giriguhântare viśati kiṃ navâbhrâvalī
kiṃ atra yamunā svayaṃ kanakaśailam āliṅgati //
tamistracayatūlikā milati kiṃ nu sandhyā divā
rathe rathapadâyudhe milati jātam ity adbhutam//

(b) ***Vāmadeva Saṃhitā***, 16cd, 17
rathoparisthaṃ mahad adbhutaṃ tat
bhavet tu devi yamunā svayaṃ ca //
meruṃ samāliṅgati parvatasya
guhântraṃ kiṃ viśati hi tv abhram/
sandhyā divā kiṃ ghaṭanaṃ tayoś ca
cakrâyudhe milati tv adbhuto bhūt//

When Jagannātha of dark colour is brought to be seated in the chariot of bright colour, the poet imagines that 'the entrance of the statue of Jagannātha into the chariot looks as if a (dark) cloud would be entering the cave of a mountain, or the river Yamunā would be embracing the mountain of gold (i.e. Sumeru), or the evening would be uniting itself with the day, etc. The *VS* not only repeats these ideas and similes but also the words of *Guṇḍīcā Campū* (cf. *guhântare = guhântaram, viśatti = viśati, navâbhrâvalī =abhram, yamunā svayam = yamunā svayam, āliṅgati = samāliṅgati, sandhyā divā = sandhyā divā, milati = milati, rathapadâyudhe = cakrâyudhe, adbhutam = adbhutaḥ*).

Compare further:

2 (a) ***Guṇḍīcā Campū***, śl. 23
bhagavato rathacaraṇarekhāṃ vilokya . . . uktvā:
iyam amaradhunī sarasvatîyam

iyam iha yamunā ca gomatī ca/
harirathacaraṇaughatīrtharekhā
śiva śiva mām api pāpinaṃ punātu//

(b) ***Vāmadeva Saṃhitā***, 16.24
rathasya rekhām avalokya lokā
vadanti yām atra ca jahnukanyā/
sarasvatī vâpyatha gomatī ca
vayaṃ punantu rathapādarekhāḥ//

The furrows created by the wheels of the car of Jagannātha are compared with the holy Gaṅgā, Yamunā, Sarasvatī and Gomatī unto which the pilgrims utter a request for their own purification. Mark the verbal similarity between the two (e.g. *rathacaraṇarekhāṃ = rathapādarekhāḥ, amaradhunī = jahnukanyā, sarasvatī-gomatī = sarasvatī-gomatī, punātu=punantu, vilokya=avalokya*).

We cannot give more such detailed quotations from both the texts. We can, however, point towards some more similarities in short: cf. ***Guṇḍ. C.***, śl. 25 *grāmyā dvijātimahilāḥ . . . vallabham ābhaṇanti, kālakṛtiḥ kathaya ko yam atīvaśuklaḥ* with *VS* 16.26 *grāmyā mahilā dhavam ābhaṇanti, ko'yam ca kṛṣṇo dhavalaśca ko'yam* or ***Guṇḍ. C.***, śl. 26 *sakhi saphalaya cakṣur bandhuvargair udagraiḥ* with *VS* 16.27 *paripaśya . . . tvadbandhuvargaiḥ sahitā,* etc.

The similarity in these passages is too obvious to be denied. And as to the point who has taken from whom, hardly any doubt can arise. A poetic depiction of the street-scene on the car festival-day is not relevant within the *Vāmadeva Saṃhitā*, whereas it forms the sole subject matter of *Guṇḍīcā Campū*. And even the most sympathetic critic of *VS* would concede that its author is absolutely worthless as a poet, whereas the *Guṇḍīcā Campū* of 'Vakravāk' Cakrapāṇi is full of brilliant imagery. It is the poet who has inspired the Pūjāpaṇḍā and not the other way round.

Cakrapāṇi Paṭṭanayāka had the privilege of having been born in a family of poets. Both his father, Brajasundar Paṭṭānāyāka and grandfather, Balabhadra, happened to be talented poets, as noted by K. N. Mahapatra,[6] Brajasundar Paṭṭanayāka was a court poet of King Puruṣottama Anaṅga-bhīmadeva of Baḍa Khemuṇḍi (1728-76) and Cakrapāṇi seems to have taken the same office after his father under the same king. As far as the date of composition of *Guṇḍīcā Campū* is concerned, Mahapatra quotes the following two ślokas occuring in the end of a Palmleaf MS of this work (No. L/97b) of the Museum) which was collected from the village Kapileśvara near Bhubaneswar:

samāptā guṇḍīcācampūr iyam atyantadurlabhā/
kṛtā kāyasthajenâpi kṛtinā cakrapāṇinā//
virakeśaridevasya rāmabāṇâṅkake site/
kārttikaikādaśī kāvyavāsare likhitā māyā//[7]

Mahapatra takes these lines to be written by the poet Cakrapāṇi himself, and as this date (Friday, the 11th day of the bright fortnight of the month Kārttika in the 53rd Aṅka of Virakeśarī Deva of Khurdhā dynasty) falls on the 16 October 1778, he believes that the *Guṇḍīcā Campū* was composed in 1778.

But a careful examination of these two Anuṣṭubh verses reveals that they occur only in a single MS of *Guṇḍīcā Campū.* In both the other MSS of the Museum L/124, and L/125a) these verses are conspicuous by their absence. This alone renders it most likely that the verses constitute the colophon written at the end of the work by the scribe, an impression which is corroborated by interpreting the ślokas more minutely. Let us try to translate the verses properly:

(Here) ends this *Guṇḍīcā Campū*, extremely difficult to get, composed by the learned (or, virtuous) Cakrapāṇi, although ('api', this particle may as well be superfluous) born in a Kāyastha family. It has been written by me on Friday . . . in the 53rd Aṅka of Vīrakeśarī Deva.

This is a typical example of a colophon as they are usually written towards the end of the MS by the scribes. The root '*likh*' in connection with the MSS hardly ever denotes '*composing a work*' for which the roots '*kṛ*' and '*rac*' are normally reserved. The scribes are called '*lekhakas*'. They start a work with the words *atha . . . likhyate* and end with *iti . . . samāptaḥ* or *likhitam . . . (amukena).* The scribe of this text keeps the roots '*kṛ*' and '*likh*' strictly apart: 'The Campū has been "written" (*kṛtā*) by Cakrapāṇi and copied by me'. He does not identify himself with Cakrapāṇi. And the expression 'which is extremely difficult to get' (*atyantadurlabhā*) can have a relevance only when the scribe is not identical with the author; the scribe has been able to procure this work only with great difficulty because it is not easily and ubiquitously available (*sulabhā)*.

The year AD 1778, therefore, cannot be the year of the composition of the *Guṇḍīcā Campū*. It is the year when this particular copy (MS No. L/97b of the Museum) of *Guṇḍīcā Campū* was prepared. A time-span of some 20 to 30 years at least must be allowed (if not more), for the work to have become popular in Orissa (and to have become rare at the same time). AD 1750 to 1760 is, therefore, the approximate date of the composition of the *campū* and even if we assume that the work became known in Puri earlier than anywhere else, it could not have been before, say, 1770 when a Pūjāpaṇḍa of Puri possessed a copy of this work and utilized it for his own composition on the Pūjā of Jagannātha.

On the basis of the foregoing discussion, therefore, it seems most likely that the *Vāmadeva Saṃhitā* was composed sometime between the period 1770 and 1790.

THE NATURE OF THE *VS*

If we look away from the subject-matter of *VS*, there is hardly anything else in it to impress us. The author is not even mediocre as far as his command of Sanskrit grammar and prosody is concerned. The language, in general, is faulty, sometimes even full of blunders, and the literary expression rather poor. The author is not even capable of differentiating between the long and short syllables in his Sanskrit composition, obviously because no such difference exists in spoken Oriya (except between *a* and *ā*). The following passages shall illustrate this:

(1) *te'**pi** sadā muktipatham labhantyante vasan**ti** nṛhareḥ pade' 'pi* /1.55

(Upajāti metre)

The bold syllables 'pi' and 'ti' must be long

(2) *etat tu pūjānam **api** (to be pronounced apī) jagadīśituś ca paśyanti ye'**pi** ca janāḥ kathayanti nityam* / 6.106

(Vasantatilakā metre)

In one and the same śloka, once the syllable 'pi' in 'api' is long (bold) and once short.

(3) *yato 'pi devasya ca bhojanasya*
*sthānaṃ hi vid**dhi** nṛpa pūjyapūjya* / 8.23
(Upajāti metre)

The bold syllable 'dhi' must be long.

(4) ***ya**di bhaven maṇḍalabāhyam eva*
*tasyô**pari** ballava (?)-bhāṣaṇam* ca/8.28
(Upajāti metre)

both bold syllables must be long.

(5) *yadā daivayogād vipattir bhavet tu*
*tadā tatra kī**dṛ**ga**pi** karma kuryāt* /9.47
(Bhujaṅgaprayāta metre)

Both bold syllables must be long.

(6) *śṛ**ṇu** hi de**vi** kathayāmi tatra / 16.3*
(Upajāti metre)

both bold syllables must be long (for '*śṛṇu*' which must be read as '*śṛṇū*', cf. also 9.49).

The grammatical mistakes are too numerous to be counted. The following examples have been picked up randomly from the first eight adhyāyas:

1. *manmukhe '**dadat*** / 1.17
   (conjugation of *dā* as if it were a verb of Group I (*bhvādi*). cf. also the example No. 11 below).
2. *mahyam **devī** na **kathitā** dakṣayajñam prati gatā* / 1.20
   *prātaḥkāle mayā **gataḥ*** / 1.30
3. *tato '**pyaham agād** yajñam* / 1.21
4. *phalamūlâdikaṃ bhuṅkṣva mitra **mabhāgya āgataḥ*** / 3.23
   (*absence of saṃdhi in a compound; otherwise . . . Bhāgyam āgatam*).
5. *tac chrutvā brāhmaṇo **brūyān** na bhakṣye darśanâvadhi* /3.24
   (an optative form is often used in the case of Imperfect, cf. also *āniya yajñaśālāyam nirodhanagṛhe nyaset* 5.25 which means

that the king **brought** the *dāru* and **kept** it in an enclosure in the *yajñaśālā*. So also the form *brūyāt* in this example stands for *abravīt* 'the brahmin **said**, I would not partake of food till I have the darśana').

6. *. . . stutim cakre sa bhūpatiḥ /*
   menire *muktibhājaṃ ca vidyāpatim* ***abhāṣayat*** // 4.4
   (*mene* & *abhāṣata* would have been the correct forms)
7. *nārado nrpatim babre (!)* / 4.37
   rājānaṃ nārado babre . . . / 5.3
   so 'pi ***babre*** *nrpaśreṣṭha pratimām te karomy aham* / 5.27
   (a III p.s. of the root *brū* in Perfect, a form which does not exist at all!)
8. *muniḥ rājānam* ***pratibodhitaḥ*** / 5.23 *(pratyabodhayat)*
9. *iti* ***kathitvā*** *rājagre . . . / (kathayitvā)*
10. *sa tu* ***tuṣṭe*** *devatuṣṭir bhavati* / 7.42 (*tasmin tuṣṭe*)
11. *evam jñātvā priye tatra caṇḍanaivedyakam* ***dadet*** / 7.42
    (cf. No: 1 above)
12. ***anyaiś*** *ca varṇair yadi tad* ***viśanti*** / 8.29
    (subject of the sentence in instrumental with verb in active voice).
13. Very often the Ātmanepada roots have been conjugated as Paraṣmaipada, cf., e.g. *labhanti* (very often) of example No. 1 of 2.5.11 (*te'pi sadā muktipatham labhanti, VS* I.55).

In the last śloka referred to (1.55) just now, the verb-form *labhanti* which stands at the end of the third *pāda* should be joined with the word 'ante' of the next *pāda*. But it cannot obviously be done since the fourth *pāda* would then be short of one syllable. In fact, the author is not even in a position to compose passable Anuṣṭubh śloka. Very often the verses are lame and lacking in rhythm because the author has failed to comply with the simple rules with regard to the quantity of different syllables. Here are some examples:

(1) *nirguṇo 'haṃ ca gunavān* ***jāto 'smi pṛthi ('thvi) maṇḍale*** /
1.12
(2) *dantakāṣṭhaṃ darśayitvā* ***punar dvādaśagaṇḍūṣam*** / 6.33
(3) *bhaviṣye daivayogācca* ***hyutpāto bhavati yāda*** / 9.29
(4) *etasmin samaye devi* ***na karma bhillijātinām*** / 14.31

The author's lack of command over the language shows itself in stuffing up the framework of a verse with many superfluous words, a feature which is characteristic of an author who has limited choice of words and limited possibilities of expression. Note, for example:

(1) *vimal**ānāmni nāmataḥ*** /1.23; *pārvat**īnāma nāmataḥ*** / 1.24
(2) *te **vai sadā** sukhatamam **pra**labhanti **śīghram***
*ante vasanti bhavane nṛhareḥ sukhe **'pi*** /

A number of ślokas of the author, especially the longer ones, are replete with such 'fillers' as *vai, tu, api, hi, ca* (. . . *na gacchanti hi ke 'pi ca*), *iti, eva, tathā, su* . . . , *bho & c. & c.*

The passages quoted above thus go a long way to prove that the value of the *VS* as a literary work is next to nil. And even though the learned editors of the printed version of the *VS* (of whom one was Pt. K. C. Rajguru) have taken great pains to make it acceptable to Sanskrit scholars by removing the grammatical mistakes and improving upon the expression, etc., they have hardly been able to change the general character of the work and to cover up the incapabilities of the author throughout. This might perhaps be one of the reasons why the popularity of the *VS* has not spread beyond the limits of Puri town. The few known MSS of this work are found only within the Jagannātha temple or with persons closely connected with it.

NOTES

1. The most 'authoritative' and extensive work on the rituals of Jagannātha temples, composed perhaps during the middle of the eighteenth century published twice, once in Oriya characters by the Raja of Sonepur (for free distribution) in 1926 and again in Nāgarī characters by S. Mahapatra Sharma in 1984.
2. The *Nīlâdrimahodaya* is internally divided into two parts. The first part (Chaps. 1-37) contains the rites and ritual of the temple festivals and the second (Chaps. 38-91) deals with the pūjā. The MSS of these two parts are mostly found separately.
3. This śloka occurs in the Pūjā texts of *Gopālârcanavidhi, Nīlâdrināthasya Pūjāvidhi, Gopālârcanapaddhati* and *Nīlâcaleśârcana-candrikā* as well.
4. The South Asia institute (Südasien-Institute) of the University of Heidelberg in Germany. Collection of Orissa Research Project in its library.

5. P. Mukherjee, 'The Missing Bhairava Image of the Jagannātha Temple', in *Jagannāth, Smārika*, Delhi, 1970, pp. 33-4; *History of the Jagannātha Temple in the 19th century,* Calcutta, 1979, pp. 21-3.
6. K. N. Mahāpatra, *Cat. of Sans. Mss. in Orissa*, Vol. II, Bhubaneswar, 1960, Intr, p. CLXXI.
7. The reading *likhitā* has however been tacitly changed by Mahapatra into *racitā* in this portion (cf p. CLXX of the *Catalogue of Manuscripts*, VR. II).

Hermann Kulke: A Bibliography

1962 *Indien: Land zwischen Tempelstadt und Rourkela,* Freiburg.

1969 'Funktionale Erklärung eines südindischen Māhātmyas: die Legende Hiraṇyavarmans und das Leben des Cōḷa-Königs Kulottuṅga I', in: *Saeculum,* 20, pp. 412-22.

1970 *Cidambaramāhātmya: eine Untersuchung der religionsgeschichtlichen und historischen Hintergründe für die Entstehung der Tradition einer südindischen Tempelstadt,* Wiesbaden (Freiburger Beiträge zur Indologie, Vol. 3).

—— 'Der Sturz Sihanouks - Angkors zweiter Tod?' in: *Internationales Asienforum,* 1, pp. 325-40.

1973 'Some Remarks about the Jagannātha Trinity', in: *Indologen-Tagung 1971*, ed. Herbert Härtel and Volker Moeller, Wiesbaden, pp. 126-39.

1974 'Der Devarāja-Kult: Legitimation und Herrscherapotheose im Angkor-Reich', in: *Saeculum,* 25, pp. 24-55.

—— 'Kings Without a Kingdom: the Rajas of Khurda and the Jagannatha Cult', in: *South Asia,* 4, pp. 60-77.
Reprinted in: *Glimpses of Orissa*, ed. Binod S. Das, Calcutta, 1986, pp. 9-50.

—— *Orissa: a Systematic Bibliography of an Indian State (Preliminary draft).* Orissa Research Project, South Asia Interdisciplinary Regional Research Programme, Heidelberg: South Asia Institute, University of Heidelberg.

—— *Hermann Goetz: Studies in the History, Religion and Art of Classical and Medieval India*, ed. Hermann Kulke, Wiesbaden (Schriftenreihe des Südasien-Instituts, Vol. 16).

—— 'Bibliography of the Works of Hermann Goetz', in: *ibid.*, pp. 124-48.

1976 'Ein hinduistischer Tempel unter muslimischer Herrschaft', in: *Saeculum,* 27, pp. 366-75.

—— 'Kshatriyaization and Social Change: a Study in Orissa Setting', in: *Aspects of Changing India: Studies in Honour of Prof. G.S. Ghurye,* ed. S. Devadas Pillai, Bombay, pp. 398-409.
Reprinted as: Kṣatriyaization and Social Change in Post-Medieval

Orissa, in: *German Scholars on India*, ed. the Cultural Department of the Embassy of the Federal Republic of Germany, Vol. 2, Bombay, 1976, pp. 146-59.

1977 'Early State Formation and Royal Legitimation in Late Ancient Orissa', in: *Sidelights on History and Culture of Orissa*, ed. Manmatha Nath Das, Cuttack, pp. 104-21.
Reprinted as: 'Early State Formation and Royal Legitimation in Tribal Areas of Eastern India', in: *Aspects of Tribal Life in South Asia* I: *Strategy and Survival*, ed. Rupert R. Moser and Mohan K. Gautam, Bern, 1978 (Studia Ethnologica Bernensia, Vol. 1), pp. 29-37.

—— 'Indien: Tempelstädte und Ritualpolitik - indische Regionalreiche', in: *Stadt und Ritual: Beiträge eines internationalen Symposions zur Stadtbaugeschichte Süd- und Ostasiens (Urban Space and Ritual: Proceedings of an International Symposion on Urban History of South and East Asia)*, ed. Niels Gutschow. Darmstadt (Beiträge und Studienmaterialien der Fachgruppe Stadt, Technische Hochschule Darmstadt, Fachbereich Architektur, Vol. 11), pp. 68-73.

1978 *The Cult of Jagannath and the Regional Tradition of Orissa*, ed. Anncharlott Eschmann, Hermann Kulke, and Gaya Charan Tripathi, New Delhi (South Asian Studies, Vol. 8).

—— 'Royal Temple Policy and the Structure of Medieval Hindu Kingdoms', in: *ibid.*, pp. 125-38.

—— 'Early Royal Patronage of the Jagannātha Cult', in: *ibid.*, pp. 139-55.

—— 'The Formation of the Jagannātha Triad', by A. Eschmann, H. Kulke and G. C. Tripathi, in: *ibid.*, pp. 169-96.

—— 'Jagannātha as the State Deity under the Gajapatis of Orissa', in: *ibid.*, pp. 199-208.

—— 'The Struggle between the Rājās of Khurda and the Muslim Sūbahdārs of Cuttack for Dominance of the Jagannātha Cult', in: *ibid.*, pp. 321-42.

—— "Juggernaut" under British Supremacy and the Resurgence of the Khurdā Rājās as "Rājās of Puri", in: *ibid.*, pp. 345-57.

—— *The Devarāja Cult*, transl. from the German by I. W. Mabbett with an introd. by the author and notes on the translation of Khmer terms by J. M. Jacob. Ithaca (Data Paper, Southeast Asia Program, Department of Asian Studies, Cornell University, Vol. 108) [transl. of: *Der Devarāja-Kult* (1974)].

—— 'Khurdā rājavaṃśa o Jagannātha dharma', in: *Pauruṣa,* 12, 1, pp. 17-28.

1979 'The Devarāja Cult: a Reassessment of the Evidence', in: *Proceedings, 7th Conference of the Intern. Assoc. of Historians of Asia 22-26.8.1977*, Bangkok, pp. 1371-84.

—— 'Geschichtsschreibung und Geschichtsbild im hinduistischen Mittelalter', in: *Saeculum,* 30, pp. 100-12.

—— *Jagannātha-Kult und Gajapati-Königtum: ein Beitrag zur Geschichte religiöser Legitimation hinduistischer Herrschaft*, Wiesbaden (Schriftenreihe des Südasien-Instituts, Vol. 23).

—— 'The Value of Anthropological Studies in Understanding History', in: *Interdisciplinary Approach to History,* ed. M. N. Das, Bhubaneswar, pp. 26-35.

—— 'Indra', in: *Wörterbuch der Symbolik*, ed. Manfred Lurker, Stuttgart (Kröners Taschenausgabe, Vol. 464), pp. 266-7.

—— 'Jainismus', in: *ibid.*, pp. 276-7.

—— 'Shiva', in: *ibid.*, S. 523-4.

—— 'Vedismus', in: *ibid.*, pp. 606-7.

—— 'Yama', in: *ibid.*, p. 645.

—— 'Rathas and Rajas: the Car Festival at Puri', in: *Mobile Architecture in Asia: Ceremonial Chariots, Floats and Carriages,* ed. D. Jones and G. Michell, London (AARP - Art and Archaeology Research Papers, Vol. 16), pp. 19-26.
Reprinted in:
- *The Journal of Orissan History,* 1 (1980), pp. 28-39.
- *The Cult and Culture of Lord Jagannath*, ed. D. Panda and S. C. Panigrahi, Cuttack, 1984.
- *Puri Sri Jagannath Research Centre*, Puri, 1993.

1980 'Die Geschichte Orissas im Überblick', in: *Orissa: Kunst und Kultur in Nordost-Indien*, ed. Eberhard Fischer, Sitakant Mahapatra and Dinanath Pathy, Zürich, pp. 27-34.

—— 'Legitimation and Town-planning in the Feudatory States of Central Orissa', in: *Ritual Space in India: Studies in Architectural Anthropology*, ed. Jan Pieper, London (AARP, Vol. 17), pp. 30-40.
Reprinted in:
Städte in Südasien: Geschichte, Gesellschaft, Gestalt, ed. Hermann Kulke, Hans Christoph Rieger and Lothar Lutze, Wiesbaden (Beiträge zur Südasien-Forschung, Vol. 60), pp. 17-38.

1981 'King Anaṅgabhīma III, the Veritable Founder of the Gajapati Kingship and of the Jagannātha Trinity at Puri', in: *Journal of the Royal Asiatic Society of Great Britain and Ireland*, pp. 26-39.

—— *Orissa: A Comprehensive and Classified Bibliography*, by Hermann Kulke in collaboration with Gaganendranath Dash, Manmath Nath Das and Karuna Sagar Behera. A joint venture of South Asia

Institute, University of Heidelberg, and Post-Graduate Department of History, Utkal University, Cuttack [also printed as: Beiträge zur Südasien-Forschung, Vol. 72, Wiesbaden, 1982].

1982 *Städte in Südasien: Geschichte, Gesellschaft, Gestalt*, ed. Hermann Kulke, Hans Christoph Rieger and Lothar Lutze, Wiesbaden (Beiträge zur Südasien-Forschung, Vol. 60).

—— 'Einführung', by H. Kulke, Hans Christoph Rieger and Lothar Lutze, in: *ibid.*, pp. XI-XVIII.

—— *Indische Geschichte vom Altertum bis zur Gegenwart: Literaturbericht über neuere Veröffentlichungen*, by Hermann Kulke, Horst-Joachim Leue, Jürgen Lütt and Dietmar Rothermund, München (*Historische Zeitschrift*, Special Vol. 10).

—— *Geschichte Indiens*, by Hermann Kulke and Dietmar Rothermund, Stuttgart.

—— 'Fragmentation and Segmentation versus Integration? Reflections on the Concept of Indian Feudalism and the Segmentary State in Indian History', in: *Studies in History* [Delhi], 4, pp. 237-63.

—— 'State Formation and Legitimation in Early Java', Working Paper of the Third Bielefeld Conference on Southeast Asia 'The Interpretative Study of Java'.

—— 'Gibt es ein indisches Mittelalter? Versuch einer eurasiatischen Geschichtsbetrachtung', in: *Saeculum*, 33, pp. 221-39.

1983 'Jagannath: the State Deity of Orissa', in: *Reflections on Indian Art and Culture*, by S. K. Bhowmik, Baroda (Bulletin, Baroda Museum and Picture Gallery, 33, 1978/9: Special Issue in Honour of Hermann Goetz), pp. 69-89.
Reprinted in:
- *Bulletin of History Seminar* (Utkal University Bhubaneswar), 1 (1983/4), pp. 20-33.
- *Multiverse* (Cuttack: Institute of Oriental and Orissan Studies), 1 (1980), pp. 91-104.
- *Sri Sri Jagannath - the Symbol of Syncretic Indian Culture*, ed. the Sri Jagannath Central Library and Research Institute, Puri (n.d.).

—— 'Life and Work of Hermann Goetz', in: *India and the West*, ed. Joachim Deppert, New Delhi, pp. 13-23.

1984 'Local Networks and Regional Integration in Orissa: Ritual Privileges of the Feudatory Rajas of Eastern India in the Jagannatha Cult of Puri', in: *Changing South Asia: Religion and Society*, ed. Kenneth Ballhatchet and David Taylor, Hong Kong (paper presented to the 7th European Conference on Modern South Asian Studies, Vol. 1), pp. 141-8.

—— 'Jagannatha under Muslim Rule', in: *Unmana: Akhila Bharat Jagannath Consciousness Conference*, Cuttack, 28-31 December 1984, pp. 17-32.

—— 'Orthodoxe Restauration und hinduistische Sektenreligiosität im Werk Max Webers', in: *Max Webers Studie über Hinduismus und Buddhismus: Interpretation und Kritik*, ed. Wolfgang Schluchter, Frankfurt (Suhrkamp-Taschenbuch Wissenschaft, Vol. 473), pp. 293-332.

—— 'Tribal Deities at Princely Courts: the Feudatory Rājās of Central Orissa and their Tutelary Deities (*iṣṭadevatās*)', in: *Folk Ways in Religion: Gods, Spirits and Men*, ed. Sitakant Mahapatra, Cuttack (Folk Culture, Vol. 2), pp. 13-24.
Reprinted in: *The Realm of the Sacred*, ed. Sitakant Mahapatra, Calcutta, 1992, pp. 56-78.

1985 *Regionale Tradition in Südasien*, ed. Hermann Kulke and Dietmar Rothermund, Stuttgart (Beiträge zur Südasien-Forschung, Vol. 104).

—— 'Region, Regionale Tradition und Regionalismus in Südasien: Versuch einer Einführung in die Thematik', by Hermann Kulke and Dietmar Rothermund, in: *ibid.*, pp. IX-XXIV.

—— 'Die frühmittelalterlichen Regionalreiche: ihre Struktur und Rolle im Prozeß Staatlicher Entwicklung Indiens', in: *ibid.*, pp. 77-114.

—— 'Mahārājas, Mahants and Historians: Reflections on the Historiography of Early Vijayanagara and Sringeri', in: *Vijayanagara: City and Empire*, ed. Anna Libera Dallapiccola and Stephanie Zingel-Avé Lallemant, Stuttgart (Beiträge zur Südasien-Forschung, Vol. 100), pp. 120-43.

1986 'The Early and the Imperial Kingdom in Southeast Asian History', in: *Southeast Asia in the 9th to 14th Centuries*, ed. D. Marr and A. Milner, Singapore, pp. 1-22.

—— 'The Historical Background of India's Axial Age', in: *The Origins and Diversity of Axial Age Civilizations*, ed. S. N. Eisenstadt, New York, pp. 374-92.

—— *A History of India*, by Hermann Kulke and Dietmar Rothermund. Beckenham, Kent [translation of *Geschichte Indiens*, 1982]; American edition: Totowa, N. J., 1986.

—— 'Max Weber's Contribution to the Study of "Hinduization" in India and "Indianization" in Southeast Asia', in: *Recent Research on Max Weber's Studies of Hinduism*, ed. D. Kantowsky, München, pp. 97-116.

—— *Kaṭakarājavaṃśāvaliḥ: A Traditional History of Orissa*, ed. and transl. G. C. Tripathi and Hermann Kulke, Allahabad.

1987 'The Chronicles and the Temple Records of the Mādaḷā Pāñji of Puri: a Reassessment of the Evidence', in: *Indian Archives,* 36, pp. 1-24.
Reprinted in: *Kṛṣṇa Pratibhā. Studies in Indology (Prof. Krishna Chandra Panigrahi Commemoration Volume),* ed. H. C. Das, S. Tripathy and B. K. Rath, Delhi, 1994, Vol. II, pp. 395-414.

—— 'Überlegungen zu den Quellen der Tempelchroniken der Mādaḷā Pāñji Puris', in: *Hinduismus und Buddhismus: Festschrift für Ulrich Schneider*, ed. H. Falk, Freiburg, pp. 173-207.

—— 'Die historischen Ursprünge der indischen Achsenzeit', in: *Kulturen der Achsenzeit. Ihre Ursprünge und ihre Vielfalt*, ed. S.N. Eisenstadt. Teil 2: Spätantike, Indien, China, Islam, Frankfurt (Suhrkamp-Taschenbuch Wissenschaft, Vol. 653), pp. 204-33.

1989 *Hinduism Reconsidered*, ed. G.-D. Sontheimer and H. Kulke, New Delhi (South Asian Studies, Vol. 24).

1990 'Überlegungen zur Begegnung Europas und Asiens bis ins 19, Jahrhundert', in: *Oriens Extremus,* 33, pp. 5-18.

—— *A History of India*, by Hermann Kulke and Dietmar Rothermund, 2nd rev. edn., London/New York.

—— 'Indian Colonies, Indianization or Cultural Convergence? Reflections on the Changing Image of India's Role in South East Asia', in: *Onderzoek in Zuidoost-Azie: Agenda's voor de jaren negentig*, ed. H. Schulte-Nordholt, Leiden (*Semaian*, 3), pp. 8-32.

1991 'Grāmakāma - "das Verlangen nach einem Dorf", Überlegungen zum Beginn frühstaatlicher Entwicklung im vedischen Indien', in: *Saeculum,* 41, pp. 111-28.

—— 'Some Considerations on the Significance of Buddha's Date for the History of North India', in: *The Dating of the Historical Buddha. Die Datierung des historischen Buddha,* ed. H. Bechert, Göttingen, Vol. 1 (Abh. d. Akademie d. Wiss. zu Göttingen. Philol.-Hist. Klasse, 3. Folge, Vol. 189), pp. 100-7.
Reprinted in: *When Did the Buddha Live? The Controversy on the Dating of the Historical Buddha,* ed. H. Bechert, Delhi, 1995, pp. 161-7.

—— 'Der asiatische Seehandel im 11, Jahrhundert, Überlegungen zur Frage "Gibt es eine asiatische Geschichte?"', in: *Periplus: Jahrbuch für außereuropäische Geschichte*, 1, pp. 7-24.

—— *Storia dell' India*, by Hermann Kulke and Dietmar Rothermund, Traduzione dall' inglese di Mario Cristiani [translation of: *A History of India,* 1986], Garzanti.

—— *A History of India*, by Hermann Kulke and Dietmar Rothermund, Indian edition, New Delhi; paperback edition, Calcutta, 1991.

—— 'Ansprache des Geschäftsführenden Direktors des Historischen Seminars', in: *In Memoriam Karl Dietrich Erdmann*, ed. Rektorat der Universität Kiel, Kiel, pp. 13-16.

—— 'Epigraphical References to the "City" and the "State" in Early Indonesia', in: *Indonesia*, 52, pp. 3-22.

—— 'Die indische Debatte über asiatische Produktionsweise und indischen Feudalismus', in: *Nachdenken über Geschichte: Beiträge aus der Ökumene der Historiker,* in *Memoriam K. D. Erdmann,* ed. H. Boockmann and K. Jürgensen, Neumünster, pp. 305-20.

1992 'Kṣatra and Kṣetra: The Cult of Jagannātha of Puri and the "Royal Letters" (*chāmu ciṭāu*) of the Rājās of Khurda', in: *The Sacred Centre as the Focus of Political Interest,* ed. H.T. Bakker, Groningen (Groningen Oriental Studies, Vol. VI), pp. 131-42.

—— 'Präkoloniale Staatenbildung in Südostasien', in: *Staatenbildung in Übersee*, ed. J. Elvert and M. Salewski, Wiesbaden (*Historische Mitteilungen,* Supplementary Issue 2), pp. 61-70.

—— 'The Rājasūya - a Paradigm of Early State Formation in India?' in: *Ritual, State and History in South Asia: Essays in Honour of J.C. Heesterman,* ed. A. W. van den Hoek, D. H. A. Kolff, and M. S. Oort, Leiden, pp. 188-98.

—— 'Ausgrenzung, Rezeption und kulturelles Selbstbewußtsein. Formen indischer Reaktion auf fremde Eroberungen in der frühen Geschichte', in: *Kulturen der Achsenzeit II. Ihre institutionelle und kulturelle Dynamik,* ed. S. N. Eisenstadt. Teil 2: Indien. Frankfurt/ M. (Suhrkamp-Taschenbuch Wissenschaft, Vol. 930), pp. 17-37.

1993 *Kings and Cults: State Formation and Legitimation in India and Southeast Asia,* New Delhi; paperback edition 2001.

—— 'Regionen und Regionalkulturen in der indischen Geschichte', in: *Die anderen Götter: Volks- und Stammesbronzen aus Indien*, ed. C. Mallebrein, Köln (*Ethnologica*, N.S., Vol. 17), pp. 15-20.

—— '"A Passage to India": Temples, Merchants and the Ocean', Contributions to Indian Studies in JESHO with Particular Reference to Economic History, in: *Journal of the Economic and Social History of the Orient,* 35, pp. 154-80.

—— 'Indonesien: VI. Kultur, Religion, Bildung', in: *Staatslexikon,* ed. the Görres-Gesellschaft, Vol. 7: Die Staaten der Welt, II, Freiburg, pp. 802-4.

—— 'Malaysia: VI. Kultur, Religion, Bildung', in: *ibid.*, p. 811.

—— 'Thailand: VI. Kultur, Religion', Bildung, in: *ibid.*, pp. 822-5.

—— 'Kadātuan Śrīvijaya: Empire or Kraton of Śrīvijaya?' in: *Bulletin de l'Ecole française d'Extrême-Orient,* 80, 1, pp. 159-80.

1994 *Religion and Society in Eastern India: Anncharlott Eschmann*

Memorial Lectures 1978-1987, ed. G. C. Tripathi and H. Kulke, New Delhi.

—— 'Ethnisch-nationalistische Konflikte und Fundamentalismus in Südasien', in: *Bericht der 7. Sitzung des Gesprächkreises 'Kultur und Entwicklung', 12.11.1993*, Sankt Augustin, 1994, pp. 19-28.

—— 'Der Babri-Masjid-Ramajanmabhumi-Konflikt: Eine ausgewählte Dokumentation', in: *Internationales Asienforum*, 25, pp. 345-74.

1995 *The State in India 1000-1700*, ed. H. Kulke, New Delhi; paperback edition 1997.

—— 'The Study of the State in Premodern India', in: *ibid.*, pp. 1-47.

—— 'The Early and the Imperial Kingdom: A Processural Model of Integrative State Formation in Early Medieval India', in: *ibid.*, pp. 233-62.

—— 'Srivijaya - Ein Großreich oder die Hanse des Ostens?', in: *Versunkene Königreiche Indonesiens*, ed. Arne and Eva Eggebrecht, Mainz, pp. 46-76.

Reprinted in: *Der indische Ozean*, ed. S. Conermann, Hamburg, pp. 57-88.

1996 'Der militante Hindunationalismus und die Zerstörung der Babri-Moschee in Ayodhya', in: *Religionen - Fundamentalismus - Politik*, ed. D. Lange, Frankfurt, pp. 177-208.

—— 'Periodization of Pre-modern Historical Processes in India and Europe: Some Reflections', in: *Indian Historical Review*, 19, pp. 21-36.

1997 *Hinduism Reconsidered*, ed. G.-D. Sontheimer and H. Kulke, 2nd rev. and enlarged edn., New Delhi; paperback edition 2001.

—— 'Some Observations on the Political Functions of Copper-Plate Grants in Early Medieval India', in: *Recht, Staat und Gesellschaft im klassischen Indien (The State, the Law, and Administration in Classical India)*, ed. B. Kölver, München, pp. 237-43.

—— 'Mongolen in Asien *und* Europa? Einleitende Überlegungen zur Ringvorlesung', in: *Die Mongolen in Asien und Europa*, ed. S. Conermann and J. Kusber, Frankfurt, pp. 9-26.

1998 *A History of India*, Hermann Kulke and Dietmar Rothermund, 3rd edn., London/New York; also paperback edition.

—— *Geschichte Indiens. Von der Induskultur bis heute*, Hermann Kulke and Dietmar Rothermund, 2nd rev. and enlarged edn., München.

—— 'Die Geschichte maritimer Beziehungen im Indischen Ozean. Einführung in das Thema', in: *Der Indische Ozean*, ed. S. Conermann, Hamburg, pp. 1-8.

—— 'Geschichtsschreibung als Heilung eines Traditionsbruches?

Überlegungen zu spätmittelalterlichen Chroniken Südasiens', in: *Die Vielfalt der Kulturen: Erinnerung, Geschichte, Identität*, ed. M. Gottlob, A. Mittag, and J. Rüsen, Frankfurt (Suhrkamp-Taschenbuch Wissenschaft, Vol. 1405), pp. 422-40.

1999 'Die frühen Reiche vom 5. bis 15. Jahrhundert', in: *Südostasien-Handbuch*, ed. B. Dahm and R. Ptak, München, pp. 98-111.

—— 'Südostasien und Indien', in: *ibid.*, pp. 349-56.

—— 'Rivalry and Competition in the Bay of Bengal: A View from the Eleventh Century and its Bearing on Indian Ocean Studies', in: *Commerce and Culture in the Bay of Bengal, 1500 - 1800*, ed. Om Prakash and Denys Lombard, New Delhi, pp. 17-36.
Reprinted as: 'Trade and Politics in Eleventh Century Bay of Bengal', in: *Maritime Heritage of India,* ed. K.S. Behera, New Delhi, pp. 214-25.

—— 'Zur älteren Geschichte Indiens', in: *Dokumentation. Revision des Indienbildes im Schulunterricht.* Fachtagung der Landeszentrale für politische Bildung Baden-Württemberg in Zusammenarbeit mit der Deutsch-Indischen Gesellschaft vom 5. bis 7.6.1998, Bad Urach, Stuttgart, pp. 66-71.

—— 'Sectarian Politics and Historiography in Early Sri Lanka: Wilhelm Geiger's Studies on the Chronicles of Sri Lanka in the Light of Recent Research', in: *Wilhelm Geiger and the Study of the History and Culture of Sri Lanka*, ed. U. Everding and A. Tilakaratne, Colombo, pp. 112-36.

2000 'Asien im Jahr 1000. Einige einleitende Gedanken', in: *Periplus. Jahrbuch für außereuropäische Geschichte,* 10, pp. 1-12.

2001 *Explorations in South Asian History. Essays in Honour of Dietmar Rothermund,* ed. G. Berkemer, T. Frasch, H. Kulke and J. Lütt, New Delhi (South Asian Studies, Vol. 36).

—— 'Historiography in Early Medieval India', in: *ibid.*, pp. 71-84.

—— *Jagannath Revisited: Studying Society, Religion and the State in Orissa*, ed. H. Kulke and B. Schnepel, New Delhi (Studies in Orissan Society, Culture and History).

—— 'Jagannath and Orissan Studies', by H. Kulke and B. Schnepel, in: *ibid.*, pp. 1-25.

—— 'Historiography and Regional Identity: The Case of the Temple Chronicles of Puri', in: *ibid.*, pp. 211-26.

—— 'Die Seidenstraße in der eurasiatischen Geschichte', in: *Die Seidenstraße: Handel und Kulturaustausch in einem eurasiatischen Wegenetz*, ed. U. Hübner, J. Kamlah and L. Reinfandt, Hamburg, pp. 1-16.

—— *Hindustan Tahiri*, by Hermann Kulke und Dietmar Rothermund [Turkish translation of *Geschichte Indiens*, 1998], transl. by Mufit Gunay, Ankara.

2002 'Mythen und Mythos der Zeitenwenden in den mittelalterlichen Chroniken Südasiens', in: *Zeitenwenden: Historische Brüche in asiatischen und afrikanischen Gesellschaften*, ed. S. Sellmer und H. Brinkhaus, Hamburg, pp. 257-72.

2004 'The Making of a Local Genealogy: The Ranpur Rājavaṃśa Itihāsa', in: *Text and Context in Orissa*, ed. J. Beltz, H. Frese and C. Mallebrein, New Delhi, pp. 43-66.

—— 'Some Thoughts on State and State Formation under the Eastern Vākāṭakas', in: *The Vakataka Heritage. Indian Culture at Cross-roads*, ed. H. T. Bakker, Groningen Egbert Forsten, pp. 1-10.

2005 *Südasien. Von den ältesten Reichen bis zur Untergang des Mogul-Reiches*, München (= Oldenbourg Grundriß der Geschichte, Vol. 34).

in print 'Maritimer Kulturtransfer im Indischen Ozean: Die "Indisierung" Südostasiens', im 1. Jahrtausend n. Chr., in *Saeculum*.

—— 'The *Vana* in the *Kṣetra*? Some Remarks on Günther Sontheimer's Concept of the *Vana* and the *Kṣetra*', in: *Günther Sontheimer Memorial Volume*.

—— 'The Construction of the Past: Ramachandra of Khurda and Puri's Yayati Kesari Legend', in: *Rethinking Orissa Society, Culture and History*, ed. P. K. Nayak, Bhubaneswar.

—— 'The Integrative Model of State Formation in Early Medieval India: An Exercise in Historiography', in: *The State in India. Past and Present*, ed. M. Kimura and A. Tanabe, Kyoto.

—— 'Trade and Politics in Eleventh Century Bay of Bengal', in: *Water and State in Europe and Asia*, ed. M. Krieger and P. Borschberg, New Delhi.

Contributors

MARTIN BRANDTNER: Senior Research Fellow, Chair of Asian History, Kiel University.

SHISHIR KUMAR PANDA: Professor, Department of History, Berhampur University.

KISHOR K. BASA: Director, Indira Gandhi Rashtriya Manav Sangrahalaya, Bhopal.

BHAIRABI PRASAD SAHU: Professor, Department of History, University of Delhi.

DIETMAR ROTHERMUND: Professor Emeritus of South Asian History, South Asia Institute of Heidelberg University.

SNIGDHA TRIPATHY: Former Epigraphist, Orissa State Museum, who has authored 3 volumes on the Inscriptions of Orissa and Coins and Currency System of Early and Mediaeval Orissa.

HARRY FALK: Professor at the Department of Indian Languages and Literature, Freie Universtitat Berlin.

ALOKA PARASHER-SEN: Professor, Department of History, University of Hyderabad.

RANABIR CHAKRAVARTI: Professor, Department of History, Jawaharlal Nehru University, New Delhi.

HANS BAKKER: Gonda Professor of Hinduism in the Sanskrit Tradition & Indian Philosophy at the University of Groningen.

UPINDER SINGH: Reader, Department of History, University of Delhi.

SWAPNA BHATTACHARYA: Department of South and Southeast Asian Studies, Calcutta University.

NIVEDITA MOHANTY: Historian; the revised edition of her book *Oriya Nationalism: Quest for a United Orissa, 1866-1956* has been published in 2005. Presently she is working on the socio-cultural history of Jharkhand.

ISHITA BANERJEE-DUBE: Associate Professor, Centre for Asian and African Studies at EI Colegio de Mexico, Mexico City. She is the author of *Divine Affairs* (2001), *Entangled Histories* (forthcoming) and in Spanish, *Fronteras del Hinduismo* (forthcoming).

YAAMINEY MUBAYI: Author of *Altar of Power: The Temple and the State in the Land of Jagannatha*. She is presently working with NGOs on issues of urban governance.

CHANDI PRASAD NANDA: Department of History, Sambalpur University.

BISWAMOY PATI: Department of History, University of Delhi.

JOANNA WILLIAMS: Professor for History of Art and South and Southeast Asian Studies, Department of South and Southeast Asian Studies, University of California, Berkeley.

GEORG PFEFFER: Professor at the Department of Social Anthropology, Freie Universitat Berlin.

G. C. TRIPATHI: Head of 'Kala Kosha' (Publication Series), Indira Gandhi Centre for Arts, New Dehli.